AF731531

Challenges to Central Banking in the Context of Financial Crisis

Challenges to Central Banking in the Context of Financial Crisis

The International Research Experience

Editor

SUBIR GOKARN

ACADEMIC FOUNDATION
NEW DELHI
www.academicfoundation.com

भारतीय रिज़र्व बैंक
RESERVE BANK OF INDIA
www.rbi.org.in

First published in 2011
by

ACADEMIC FOUNDATION
4772-73 / 23 Bharat Ram Road, (23 Ansari Road),
Darya Ganj, New Delhi - 110 002 (India).
Phones : 23245001 / 02 / 03 / 04.
Fax : +91-11-23245005.
E-mail : books@academicfoundation.com
www. academicfoundation.com

in association with:

Reserve Bank of India
Central Office Building,
Shahid Bhagat Singh Marg, Mumbai - 400 001.
Tel: 022 - 2260 1000
Fax: 022 - 2266 0358
E-mail: helpdoc@rbi.org.in
www.rbi.org.in

Disclaimer:
The views expressed in these papers are solely those of the authors and should not be interpreted as reflecting the views of their organisation. The papers in this volume reflect developments up to the date of the Conference and do not take account of subsequent events.

Copyright:
© Reserve Bank of India 2011

ALL RIGHTS RESERVED.
No part of this book shall be reproduced, stored in a retrieval system, or transmitted by any means, electronic, mechanical, photocopying, recording, or otherwise, without the prior written permission of the copyright holder(s) and/or the publishers.

Cataloging in Publication Data--DK
Courtesy: D.K. Agencies (P) Ltd. <docinfo@dkagencies.com>

Challenges to central banking in the context of financial crisis
: the international research experience / editor, Subir Gokarn.
p. cm.
ISBN 13: 9788171888733
ISBN 10: 8171888739

1. Financial crises--Congresses. 2. Financial crises--India--Congresses. 3. Banks and banking, Central--Congresses. 4. Banks and banking, Central--India--Congresses. 5. Monetary policy--Congresses. 6. Monetary policy--India--Congresses. I. Gokarn, Subir. II. Reserve Bank of India.

DDC 332.042 22

Typeset by Italics India, New Delhi.
Printed and bound in India.

Contents

Preface 9

1. Challenges to Central Banking in the Context of the Financial Crisis
   DEEPAK MOHANTY 11

2. Challenges for Central Banks in the Context of the Crisis
   DUVVURI SUBBARAO 15

3. Heralding a 'New Normal': The Perfect Growth Model Still Eludes Us
   ANDREW MICHAEL SPENCE 27

Section I

Challenges and Response to Conduct Monetary Policy during the Financial Crisis

4. Monetary Policy Flexibility: Solution or Problem?
   WILLIAM POOLE 45

   Discussion:

   4.1 Solutions: Global Checks on Capital Markets
   JOHN LIPSKY 54

   4.2 No Right Answers, Only Tough Trade-offs
   WILLIAM R. WHITE 58

5. Learning from the Crisis: What can Central Banks do?
   BENJAMIN M. FRIEDMAN 65

   Discussion:

   5.1 Some Problems of Feasible Policies
   JØRGEN ELMESKOV 91

6. Unconventional Monetary Policy:
Experience and Possible Exit Strategies
JØRGEN ELMESKOV and MAKOTO MINEGISHI 95

7. Inflation Targeting after the Financial Crisis
LARS E.O. SVENSSON 141

Discussion:

7.1 Inflation Targeting after the Crisis
WILLIAM POOLE 155

8. Summing-up: Should Monetary Policy Chase Other Hares?
CHARLES R. BEAN 159

9. Summing-up: Is Central Bank Indeed the
Best Regulator of the Banking System?
SUBIR GOKARN 163

Section II

Globalisation, Market Failures and Challenges Posed to Central Banks

10. The Impossible Trinity and Constraints on Policy Options
IRMA ROSENBERG 167

Discussion:

10.1 What if the Globally Traded Asset is not Debt,
but Equity?
BENJAMIN M. FRIEDMAN 180

11. The Future of Public Debt: Prospects and Implications
STEPHEN G. CECCHETTI, M.S. MOHANTY
and FABRIZIO ZAMPOLLI 183

Discussion:

11.1 Where is the Hero Who Saves the Day?
ESWAR PRASAD 218

12. The Great Recession and International Policy Coordination
CARLOS A. PRIMO BRAGA 223

13. Summing-up
LARS E.O. SVENSSON 239

14. Summing-up
SHYAMALA GOPINATH 241

Section III

Disruptions in Financial Systems and Challenges to Regulation and Supervision

15. The Post-Crisis Fix: Regulatory or Monetary Policy Remedies?
STEPHEN S. ROACH 245

Discussion:

15.1 Time for a New Analytical Framework
WILLIAM R. WHITE 264

16. Why All Central Banks are not the Same
WILLIAM R. WHITE 267

17. Managing Financial Innovation in Emerging Markets
JOHN LIPSKY 291

Discussion:

17.1 Regulate the Subatomic Fragments of Finance
STEPHEN G. CECCHETTI 302

18. Systemic Risk: How to Deal with it?
JAIME CARUANA 309

19. Summing-up
JAIME CARUANA 327

20. Summing-up
USHA THORAT 329

Section IV

Financial Stability as an Objective of Monetary Policy

21. Two Cheers for Bagehot
JOHN C. WILLIAMS 333

Discussion:

21.1 New Research Agenda of the Central Banks
STEPHEN S. ROACH 348

22. Crisis and Implications for Central Bank Balance Sheets: Policies, Effectiveness and Designing an Exit
KRISHNA SRINIVASAN 351

Discussion:

22.1 Central Banks need to Find a Mid-Path
ESWAR PRASAD 401

23. Monetary Policy Challenges for Emerging Market Economies
GILL HAMMOND, RAVI KANBUR and ESWAR PRASAD 405

24. Summing-up
MICHAEL FOOT 431

25. Summing-up
K.C. CHAKRABARTY 435

Section V

Governors Speak

26. Governors Speak—Panel I: Domestic Monetary Policy 439

27. Governors Speak—Panel II: International Monetary System 459

Summing-up of the Proceedings

K.U.B. RAO 479

List of Contributors 489

Preface

The Reserve Bank was established on April 1, 1935 and celebrated its Platinum Jubilee year during 2009-10. In celebration of the Bank's Platinum Jubilee year, this International Research Conference was organised. This volume brings together the papers and proceedings of the Conference.

The recent global recession, a fall-out of the unprecedented financial crisis, is the most serious economic crisis that the world has faced since the Great Depression of the 1930s. While recovery is underway and may well strengthen in due course, the role of central banks in managing the crisis and minimising the pains of adjustment has been remarkable.

The crisis posed multifaceted challenges to central banks. The first set of the issues relates to conduct of monetary policy. The discussion on this subject examines the implications of financial disruptions and manoeuvrability of the monetary policy in the backdrop of credit freeze, dysfunctional markets and uncertainty of transmission processes. The second set of the challenges arises from the systemic disruptions and the consequent implications for regulation and supervision. This brings to fore the need to revisit regulation and supervision from time to time. Further, there are other challenges too. Can ensuring financial stability be a key purpose of monetary policy? In what manner the central banks' liquidity operations should be handled to ease credit conditions and bring in financial stability? What are the implications of relevant measures for central bank balance sheet? What are the constraints posed by 'Impossible Trinity' on policy options? Despite the prevalence of a well-established regulatory structure, financial institutions found it relatively easy to move substantial activities outside the regulatory perimeter. This has opened a host of new challenges relating to better understanding of the build-up of systemic risks and reining in of financial disruptions without repressing the innovation. Another important issue before the central banks is to lay down the modalities of a timely exit from the expansionary monetary policy adopted in the post-crisis scenario. A continuing but pertinent question relates to how to secure a reasonable balance between the development of real sector and financial sector and the role of central banks in this context. While the current crisis saw remarkable cohesive actions and governance—should these be formalised to bring about policy co-ordination amongst central banks? Finally, do we need a global framework for international governance for the prevention and management of financial crises?

Against this backdrop, the theme of the Conference 'Challenges to Central Banking in the Context of Financial Crisis', is of contemporary relevance, which sketches a broad canvas of issues relevant to resolve the crisis and redefine the role of global central banks. Through this Conference, the Reserve Bank brought together veteran central bankers, academicians, policymakers, financial regulators and supervisors and market-players on a common platform to share their thoughts and to evolve solutions pertaining to the above questions through two special talks, four technical sessions and two Governors' panel discussions. The discussions and analyses in this volume are relevant for the events currently playing out in the global financial arena and would need to be heeded by all policymakers—present and future.

The task of bringing out this comprehensive Volume was completed under the overall guidance of Mr. Deepak Mohanty, Executive Director. The Division of Reports and Knowledge Dissemination, Department of Economic and Policy Research was associated with the preparation of the Volume at various stages and its contribution is gratefully acknowledged. In particular, I would like to record my sincere appreciation of the painstaking work by Dr. Mohua Roy, Director and her team under the able supervision of Mr. K.U.B. Rao, Officer-in-Charge, Department of Economic and Policy Research. I do hope that the readers will find this Volume informative and useful for reference.

— Subir Gokarn

1 Challenges to Central Banking in the Context of the Financial Crisis*

DEEPAK MOHANTY

Mumbai, a fishing hamlet was gifted in dowry by Portugal to England, and later leased to the East India Company for £10. Today you cannot get even a square inch of land in Mumbai for that price. Mumbai has moved on and gained in value and stature. Mumbai is the gateway to modern India and India's commercial capital. Home to the world's largest film industry, this 'city of dreams' has been popularised by Danny Boyle's 'Slumdog Millionnaire' and in A.R. Rahman's tunes 'Jai Ho'. Mumbai is a city that never sleeps. This you may have experienced by now, as most international flights land in the middle of the night. I hope you had some rest and are ready for the day. The city has weathered many adversities only to spring back to life with greater vigour—that is the spirit of Mumbai. I hope during your stay you will get to experience Mumbai's vibrancy.

Let me say a few words about our First International Research Conference. As you know, the Reserve Bank of India (RBI) is celebrating its Platinum Jubilee year—an important milestone in the history of this ever-evolving institution. The Bank was established on April 1, 1935. It transitioned from being a privately-owned institution to a government-owned institution in 1949. In these 75 years, the Bank has witnessed momentous changes securing its pre-eminent position in the economic policy space of the country.

The Reserve Bank of India in many ways is a full service central bank. It has a broad spectrum mandate extending beyond monetary policy, such

* Based on the Welcome Remarks at the First International Research Conference on 'Challenges to Central Banking in the Context of Financial Crisis', Reserve Bank of India, Mumbai.

as currency management, regulation of banks and non-bank financial institutions, regulation of money, foreign exchange and government securities markets and public debt management. Our research focus too therefore has a wider canvas than that of most central banks.

To mark and celebrate the Bank's Platinum Jubilee year, we have taken a series of initiatives and organised a number of events. The celebrations have run parallel in three directions. First is a series of learning events to build support for the Reserve Bank's agenda and to showcase the Bank as a knowledge institution. Second is a set of internal events involving current and former Reserve Bank staff to reinforce a sense of belonging and inclusiveness among members of the Reserve Bank family. Third is the outreach programme of financial inclusion and financial literacy with an overall objective of connecting with the common person of this country. In this Platinum Jubilee year, we are thus trying to cover a vast expanse by reaching out from the remotest village to the global intellectual opinion as yours.

The global reach of the financial crisis reminds us that irrespective of the degree of globalisation of a country and the soundness of its domestic policies, no economy can insulate itself from the financial turmoil. The crisis has challenged many of our fundamental beliefs and could well turn out to be the defining moment for a paradigm shift in macrofinancial policy framework. In this context, the theme of the Conference 'Challenges to Central Banking in the Context of Financial Crisis' is perhaps apt.

With the benefit of hindsight, the crisis has been a great learning experience for all. Although the jury is still out on many issues, some broad lessons can still be drawn from the crisis. First, there is increasing support for the view that policy objectives of central banks would have to be broader than price stability as conventionally defined. Second, the crisis has reminded us of the virtues of fiscal consolidation in good times to generate the fiscal space to deal with crisis conditions. Third, and perhaps the most widely agreed lesson, is that financial institutions would have to be less leveraged and better regulated. This does not imply more regulation but sharper regulation. Finally, preventing and dealing with a crisis in an increasingly globalised world need far-reaching reforms in the international financial architecture.

Against this backdrop, let me now turn to the format of the Conference. We will cover the Conference theme in two special talks and four technical sessions. We begin with the inaugural address by our Governor Dr. D. Subbarao followed by the keynote speech by Prof. Andrew Michael Spence. Then we move on to the presentation of papers and discussions. The first technical session will deal with the experience and lessons from the conduct of monetary policy in the wake of the crisis. The second session will explore how globalisation of financial markets, on the one hand, and financial innovation, on the other, impinge on the conduct of monetary policy. The third session will deal with the challenges to regulation and supervision in the context of developments in the financial sector. The fourth and final session of the day will discuss the design of appropriate exit policy from the current expansionary monetary and fiscal stance.

We resume tomorrow with two sessions of panel discussion of Governors. Both the panels will be moderated by noted economist and columnist Mr. Martin Wolf.

The first panel will focus on the areas of monetary policy. It will cover issues such as the implications of the crisis for inflation targeting; the role of asset prices in monetary policy; the changing role of central banks from managing the crisis to managing the recovery.

The second panel will focus on the global financial architecture. It will cover issues such as the reform of the International Monetary Fund (IMF); regional monetary arrangements; the future of global reserve currency system; and capital flows and exchange rate policies.

I think this is an opportune time, as the world is finding its feet after the storm, to introspect and think out of the box to make the financial world a safer place. I am sure that this high-level Conference, benefiting from your vast experience and wisdom, would contribute immensely to our understanding of the challenges to central banking in the coming times.

2 Challenges for Central Banks in the Context of the Crisis*

DUVVURI SUBBARAO

Central banks and central bankers have been at the heart of the global financial crisis. We have been blamed for policies and actions that got the world into the crisis; we are also being praised for leading from the front in getting the world out of the crisis. I believe this is fair critique—central banks have been a part of the problem and a part of the solution.

As we emerge out of the crisis, central banks have their task cut out for them: to distil the lessons of the crisis, translate them into concrete reform measures and get cracking on implementing them. I believe this involves central banks changing in important ways both in terms of what they do and how they do it. It is against this backdrop that the Reserve Bank of India (RBI) thought it fit to organise this Conference on the challenges for central banks in the context of the crisis as a flagship event of our Platinum Jubilee celebrations. I have great pleasure in welcoming all our invitees—colleague governors of central banks, leading international and domestic policymakers and experts—to this Conference, the First International Research Conference being organised by the Reserve Bank. I want to specially acknowledge noted economist and Nobel Laureate Prof. Andrew Michael Spence who will be delivering the keynote address.

I struggled quite a lot in defining what I should say in this opening address. Given the breadth and depth of expertise that you all collectively bring to this forum, it would be presumptuous on my part to lay out the agenda of deliberations over the next two days. I will attempt something much less ambitious—just by way of a curtain raiser, I will set out the

---

* Based on the Inaugural Address at the First International Research Conference on 'Challenges to Central Banking in the Context of Financial Crisis', Reserve Bank of India, Mumbai.

major challenges to central banks in the wake of the crisis. In particular, I will put forward five challenges. My effort, as you will notice, will be to flag the issues rather than argue them out extensively.

First challenge: Managing monetary policy in a globalising environment

The crisis has clearly demonstrated the challenges of macroeconomic management in a globalising world. Even as governments and central banks acted with unusual show of policy force, they found that they were not able to get the situation under control because of the interconnectedness of the financial system and the positive and negative cross-border externalities to domestic policy actions. Most importantly, they found that sentiment and confidence were remarkably correlated across countries around the world. When the history of this crisis is written, the London G-20 summit in April 2009 will be marked as a clear turning point, showing that in the age of globalisation, a financial crisis cannot be managed without global cooperation and global response.

The question is, with the benefit of that hindsight, how are central banks going to manage the challenges from globalisation to their macroeconomic policies. Experience shows that external developments interact with domestic macro-variables in complex, uncertain and even capricious ways, and central banks need to deepen their understanding of these interactions. Some of the channels through which cross-border transmission occurs are quite familiar—global prices including commodity price movements, synchronisation of business cycles, capital flows, strong co-movement of asset prices, not necessarily correlated with the degree of a country's financial integration, exchange rates of key international currencies and interest rate policies of major central banks. Some of the transmission channels are not so familiar. For example, we now know that even differences in regulatory regimes can trigger arbitrage-based action and dilute the efficiency of domestic policies.

Is the challenge posed by globalisation similar for all central banks? Obviously, the more open the economy, the greater the impact of globalisation on domestic policies. Beyond that, it seems logical to conjecture that the broader the mandate of a central bank, the larger the influence of globalisation on the effectiveness of its policies. There is a view that open economies can retain strong control over the medium and long-term inflation trends even in the face of globalisation. This is a debatable proposition, and at best true only in the case of pure inflation targeting central banks. Central banks with wider mandates need necessarily to factor in external developments into their domestic policy calculus.

Let me illustrate the challenge of globalisation with the issue of managing capital flows. Emerging market economies (EMEs) saw 'sudden stop' capital outflows during the crisis as a result of global deleveraging. Now the trend has reversed once again and many EMEs are seeing net inflows—a consequence of a global system awash with liquidity, the assurance of a low interest rate regime in advanced countries over an 'extended period' and the promise of growth in EMEs.

One little known aspect of capital flows, what could perhaps be called the law of capital flows, is that they never come in at the precise time or in the exact quantity you want them. Managing these flows, especially if they are volatile, is going to test the effectiveness of central bank policies of semi-open EMEs. If central banks do not intervene in the foreign exchange market, they incur the cost of currency appreciation unrelated to fundamentals. If they intervene in the forex market to prevent appreciation, they will have additional systemic liquidity and potential inflationary pressures to contend with. If they sterilise the resultant liquidity, they will run the risk of pushing up interest rates which will hurt the growth prospects. Capital flows can also potentially impair financial stability. How EMEs manage the Impossible Trinity—the impossibility of having an open capital account, a fixed exchange rate and independent monetary policy—is going to have an impact on their prospects for growth, price stability and financial stability.

Globalisation is not new; its risks and rewards are also not new. What is new, and what the crisis has revealed, is the ferocity with which the forces of globalisation can strike and the diversity of channels through which they can transmit across borders. The challenge for central banks is to better understand the interplay of global factors and domestic variables, and factor that into their policy calculus.

Second challenge: Redefining the mandate of central banks

Let me now move on to the second issue which is the challenge of redefining the mandate of central banks. The crisis has triggered a vigorous and wide-ranging debate on the role and responsibilities of central banks. Let me focus on three main, and largely interrelated, issues:

i. Should central banks persist with pure inflation targeting?

ii. What is the role of central banks in preventing asset price bubbles?

iii. Should central banks also be doing regulation and supervision of banks?

Let me take them up one by one.

(i) Should central banks persist with pure inflation targeting?

The first question is, should central banks persist with inflation targeting. The years before the crisis saw a powerful intellectual consensus building around inflation targeting. A growing number of central banks, starting with New Zealand in the late 1980s and currently numbering over 20, geared monetary policy almost exclusively to stabilising inflation. Even where central banks did not target a precise inflation rate, their policy objectives were informed, if not dominated, by price stability. This approach seemed successful. There was an extended period of price stability accompanied by stable growth and low unemployment. In the world that existed before the crisis, central bankers were a triumphant lot. They had discovered the Holy Grail.

The unravelling of the Great Moderation during the crisis has diluted, if not dissolved, the consensus around the minimalist formula of inflation targeting. The mainstream view before the crisis was that price stability and financial stability reinforce each other. The crisis has proved that wrong. We have seen that price stability does not necessarily ensure financial stability. Indeed there is an even stronger assertion that there is a trade-off between price stability and financial stability and that the more successful a central bank is with price stability, the more likely it is to imperil financial stability.

All in all, the crisis has given fresh impetus to the 'new environment hypothesis' that pure inflation targeting is inadvisable and that the mandate of central banks should extend beyond just price stability. Let me, therefore, turn to what the mandate should extend to.

(ii) What is the role of central banks in preventing asset price bubbles?

A dominant issue in the wake of the crisis has been the role of central banks in preventing asset price bubbles. The monetary stance of studied indifference to asset price inflation stemmed from the famous 'Greenspan orthodoxy' which can be summarised as follows. First, asset price bubbles are hard to identify on a real-time basis, and the fundamental factors that drive asset prices are not directly observable. A central bank should not, therefore, second-guess the market. Second, monetary policy is too blunt an instrument to counteract asset price booms. And third, central banks can 'clean up the mess' after the bubble bursts. The surmise, therefore, was that the cost-benefit calculus of a more activist monetary stance of 'leaning against the wind' was clearly negative. In other words, it is not the job of central bankers to remove the punch bowl no matter that the party is getting wild.

The crisis has dented the credibility of the 'Greenspan orthodoxy'. The emerging view post-crisis is that preventing an asset price build-up should be within the remit of a central bank. Opinion is divided, however, on whether central banks should prevent asset bubbles through monetary policy action or through regulatory action. On one side, there is a purist view that the case for monetary tightening to check speculative bubbles is questionable. Opposed to this is the argument that a necessary condition for speculative excesses is abundant liquidity, and that controlling liquidity should be the first line of defence against 'irrational exuberance'.

Some economists take a more granular position on this, and the argument goes as follows. It is important to differentiate between speculative excesses fuelled by bank lending and those that are not, such as, the IT bubble. Central banks have a role in preventing 'bank-centred' bubbles, but the instrument for this is not monetary policy but regulatory intervention.

No matter how this debate settles, if it will at all, what is beyond debate is that central banks' efforts to check asset price bubbles demand not just analytical capability but mature judgement of the nature of the risk.

(iii) Should central banks also be doing bank regulation and supervision?

The third issue that I want to address in regard to the mandate of central banks is the question of whether central banks should also be doing bank regulation and supervision.

This is yet another issue on which the crisis has triggered a vigorous debate. There is a variety of regulatory models around including those where the central bank is a pure monetary authority with bank regulation and supervision vested with another agency. Post-crisis, the emerging view is that the crisis was caused, at least in part, by the lack of coordination and communication between the separate bodies and that it is optimal, in the interest of financial stability, to entrust the function of regulation and supervision of banks also to central banks.

The case for this is made mainly on two arguments. The first argument is that regardless of the regulatory architecture, there is no dispute that the central bank has to remain the lender-of-last-resort (LOLR) for the financial system. A central bank can discharge its LOLR function more efficiently if its mandate extends beyond merely monitoring financial institutions to taking preventive action. This becomes possible if the central bank also has responsibility for bank supervision.

The second and broader argument is that there is a natural synergy between monetary policy which is macroprudential and bank supervision which is microprudential. The micro-level information coming from supervision of individual institutions can be a valuable input for shaping the macro perspective. Vice versa, a broad macro-level understanding of trends can be effective in instituting prudential safeguards at the micro-institutional level.

Admittedly, there are strong arguments to the contrary, in support of keeping bank regulation and supervision away from central banks. By far the most persuasive argument stems from the moral hazard perspective.

There is a risk that a central bank may extend regulatory forbearance to a weak bank instead of allowing it to fail since a failed bank could aggravate instability. Such action becomes more likely if the overall macroeconomic situation is weak. In an extreme case, it is possible that the monetary stance of the central bank may be dominated by concerns about protecting weak banks since central banks may view a 'failed bank' as a blot on their reputation.

Whether central banks should also be regulating and supervising banks is an issue that has frowned on moderation. Evidently, there is no one-size-fits-all answer as indeed evidenced by the variety of regulatory models around. Going forward, every country and every central bank has to confront and resolve this issue in light of their specific circumstances.

Third challenge: Responsibility of central banks towards financial stability

Let me move on to the third challenge on my list concerning what responsibility, if any, should central banks have towards financial stability. Although this question belongs to the mandate of central banks that I have just spoken about, I have decided to address financial stability as a separate and distinct challenge because post-crisis, financial stability has become the elephant in the room.

While there is broad agreement that financial stability is neither automatic nor inevitable, there is less agreement on whether it should be explicitly included in the mandate of central banks. There is an argument that explicit inclusion would be redundant since financial stability is a necessary, although not sufficient, condition for achieving the conventional central bank objectives relating to inflation, output and employment. On the other hand, post-crisis, there is a growing view that unless financial stability is explicitly included in the mandate of central banks, it is likely to fall through the cracks.

But how does one define financial stability in a precise, comprehensive and measurable manner? This is something that is proving to be quite intractable. Be that as it may, we now know that two attributes of financial instability are: (i) excessive volatility of macro-variables such as interest rates and exchange rates which have a direct impact on the real economy;

and (ii) financial institutions and markets threatened by illiquidity to the extent of jeopardising systemic stability.

One clear instrument available to central banks for preserving financial stability is the LOLR function. Over the years, we have come to believe that LOLR is a fairly robust instrument for combating threats of illiquidity. Note that one of the important ways in which this crisis has been different from past financial crises is that this one arose from the asset side of banks' balance sheets whereas past crises had all arisen from the liability side. This crisis, hence, has shown that the LOLR instrument loses much of its potency in a 'bank run' from the asset side.

Let me explain. During the crisis, central banks pumped in enormous amounts of liquidity to defreeze the system through the LOLR window. While this made individual institutions liquid, the market still remained illiquid, thereby showing up the limitation of the LOLR instrument in combating illiquidity. Much like taking a horse to water, a central bank can infuse liquidity, but how can it ensure that the cheap and abundant money thus available is used to purchase assets whose value is rapidly eroding? The only option then is for the central bank itself to buy the assets. This means that in addition to being the LOLR, a central bank also has to be the market-maker-of-last-resort (MMLR).

To sum up, the main issues surrounding the role of central banks in financial stability are the following:

- How does one define financial stability?
- Should central bank mandates include financial stability as an explicit objective?
- Should this be an exclusive or shared responsibility?
- Do central banks have the instruments to address the mandate of financial stability?
- In what ways does responsibility for financial stability encroach on the independence of central banks?

All of these issues are yet to be clearly defined, let alone resolved. Given that the lessons of the crisis relating to financial stability have been forceful, it is important that governments and central banks resolve these questions soon.

Fourth challenge: Managing the costs and benefits of regulation

Nearly everyone now has her or his own list of causes for the crisis; and almost every list includes the failure of regulation as a leading cause. Quite unsurprisingly, the post-crisis reform agenda is dominated by regulatory reforms at macro and micro levels. Admittedly, these reforms are being thought through carefully through international consultative processes. Even so, there is a risk of going overboard on the rebound and getting the balance between costs and benefits wrong.

In order to safeguard financial stability, in the Reserve Bank, we have traditionally used a variety of prudential measures such as specifying exposure norms and pre-emptive tightening of risk weights and provisioning requirements. But these measures are not always costless. For instance, tightening of risk weights arguably tempers the flow of credit to certain sectors, but excessive, premature or unnecessary tightening could blunt growth. Similarly, exposure norms offer protection against concentration risks; however, such limits could restrict the availability of credit for important growth sectors. Thus, as in the case of price stability, central banks face the challenge of managing the trade-off between financial stability and growth.

It needs to be recognised that after a crisis, with the benefit of hindsight, all conservative policies appear safe. But is there a risk of throwing away the baby with the bathwater? Excessive conservatism in order to be prepared to ride out a potential crisis could thwart growth and stifle innovation. The question is what price are we willing to pay, or put another way, what potential benefits are we willing to give up, in order to cope with a black swan event? Experience shows that managing this challenge, that is balancing the costs and benefits of regulation, is more a question of good judgement rather than analytical skill. This judgement skill is the one that central banks, especially those of developing countries such as India, need to hone as they simultaneously pursue the objectives of growth and financial stability.

Fifth challenge: Managing the balance between the autonomy and accountability of central banks

Finally, let me turn to the fifth challenge, as I see, which is to do with managing the balance between the autonomy and accountability of central banks. This is a broad spectrum topic that draws from several issues that I have touched upon earlier.

The 70-odd years since the Great Depression saw a famous rivalry between fiscal and monetary policies for influence. Historically, central banks suffered from fiscal dominance since they had to acquiesce in governments 'borrowing as much as required at as low a cost as possible'. This state of affairs started changing in the 1980s with a wave of support for central bank independence. The support was largely in response to the damage inflicted by the stagflation of the 1970s and the clear lesson that high inflation is detrimental to sustainable growth. So, fiscal dominance gradually yielded to independent central banks targeting largely, and in some cases exclusively, price stability, free of short-term political imperatives. Empirical work shows that in the two decades during which central bank independence gained ascendancy, there was a negative correlation between inflation and the degree of independence of the central bank across both developed and developing economies. In some cases, though, reverse causality—low inflation performance leading to central bank independence—cannot be ruled out.

Notwithstanding their record on price stability, the crisis has dented the credibility of central banks. The blame on central banks is wide-ranging—loose monetary policies coupled with neglect of asset price developments, exclusive focus on inflation to the detriment of financial stability and lax and inept regulation that failed to keep pace with innovation. There is resentment, if not outrage, against the famed independence of central banks; and there is an outcry for clipping their mandates and tightening the accountability mechanisms.

Beyond the short-term, the threat to the independence of central banks emanates from factors apart from public anger. Notably, the crisis saw unprecedented expansionary fiscal and monetary policies launched by governments and central banks in coordination. As countries contemplate exit from these expansionary policies, the familiar tensions between monetary and fiscal policies are showing up again. Many believe that these tensions are temporary, and will melt away once recovery takes root.

That may not well be the case. There is widespread apprehension that many advanced country governments will not be able to wind down borrowing because of demographic factors and consequent growing social security payments. IMF studies estimate that even if the governments in the advanced economies reverse the crisis-induced fiscal stimulus, these economies will still end up with a structural primary deficit of 2 per cent of GDP. Government debt in the advanced economies is projected to jump from the pre-crisis level of 78 per cent of GDP in 2007 to 118 per cent by 2014 assuming some discretionary tightening beginning this year. In such a scenario, what are now seen as cyclical fiscal deficits may, in fact, morph into structural fiscal deficits. We may then see the return of fiscal dominance and undermining of the independence of central banks.

I spoke earlier about the role of central banks in preserving financial stability and, in particular, about how the responsibility for financial stability may be delineated. By its very nature, the responsibility for financial stability has to be shared by the government, the central bank and other regulators. In and of itself, that sharing is no problem. But there are two related concerns. The first is that rescuing financial institutions is an inherently political act and getting involved in such decisions may compromise the technocratic credentials of central banks. The second concern is the risk that coordination with governments in the area of financial stability may spill over into other areas within central bank purview, thereby undermining their independence.

All in all, the case for central bank independence is coming under increasing assault as a result of crisis-led developments. The challenge for central banks is to make the case for independence not through weighty arguments but through more vigorous and voluntary efforts to be transparent, responsive and accountable.

Conclusion

I have raised, what are in my view, five challenges that central banks will have to address. They are the following:

i. Managing monetary policy in a globalising environment.

ii. Redefining the mandate of central banks.

iii. Responsibility of central banks towards financial stability.

iv. Managing the costs and benefits of regulation; and

v. Managing the balance between the autonomy and accountability of central banks.

This listing of challenges is by no means exhaustive. And many different nuances are possible. I hope that our deliberations over the next two days will give us greater clarity on the challenges that we face collectively and individually, and a better understanding of how to begin addressing them.

A final thought. In his recent best seller, *The Ascent of Money* (2008), Niall Ferguson says that, 'sometimes the most important historical events are the non-events: the things that did not occur.' The spectacular non-event of this crisis is that the Great Recession did not turn into the second Great Depression as we had feared. For this, central banks should get a part of the credit. But they cannot rest on their laurels—they have big challenges ahead as the crisis winds down. Their biggest challenge by far is to regain their credibility.

3 Heralding a 'New Normal'

*The Perfect Growth Model Still Eludes Us**

ANDREW MICHAEL SPENCE

I congratulate the Reserve Bank of India (RBI) on its long history of many jobs well done, particularly in the context of the financial crisis that began in 2007. I thoroughly endorse several times RBI Governor D. Subbarao's view that this central bank and other central banks had a major role in preventing another Great Depression. Just 10 months out of the depths of the crisis, it was quite clear that India and China had weathered the storm better than any other country in the world. This is noteworthy and impressive.

I am not a central banker and I am not going to pretend to have either the insight or the experience of one. So, I will simply try to interpret the experience of growth in the post-war period, which has been really quite remarkable in the developing world by historical standards. I will comment on what the lessons of the crisis are and then turn to some pressing questions relating to central banks, globalisation and taking monetary policy forward.

I am relying on the work of the Commission on Growth and Development, which has been functioning since 2006 and has issued two reports. This is a Commission populated mainly by political and policy leaders from the developing world. I had the privilege of chairing it and learning from my colleagues. So, this is a perspective from the developing world.

---

* Keynote Address at the First International Research Conference on 'Challenges to Central Banking in the Context of Financial Crisis', Reserve Bank of India, Mumbai.

Sustained high growth in the developing world

In the post-war period, 13 countries have managed to grow at the rate of seven per cent or more on an average, for over 25 years. Most of us are quite sure that two other countries will join that group. India is one (it is just a matter of time) and Vietnam is probably the other.

Moreover, a pattern was evident before the crisis of expanding real growth in the developing world on quite a broad front, but it remains to be seen whether that broad pattern of growth will return and be sustained in the post-crisis period.

This is really quite a small number of countries compared with the whole developing world and I will talk a little bit about what the basis of this kind of growth is and how it relates to the crisis and the environment that we are going to face in the future.

The Group of 20 countries (G20) accounts for about 85 per cent of global gross domestic product (GDP) at this point and about two-thirds of the world's population. It is clearly the main event in the global economy. It is also the place where incomes are either high or the rates of growth are predictably high. It is clearly going to be the dominant influence in international policy coordination in the future.

Now, let me talk about this pattern of high growth. The strategies and policies employed by these 13 countries were designed to take advantage of the growing integration and resources available in the global economy. The global economy provided two essential ingredients. One was knowledge, technology, management skills and know-how, which was transferred via various channels. That increased the productive potential of these economies much faster than would have been possible on a stand-alone basis.

The second ingredient was a vast global market, in which they could grow quickly without dramatically increasing market share and without turning the terms of trade against themsleves in almost all cases, with the possible exception of China recently. So, the strategies leveraged the global economy into rapid growth.

On the domestic front, what were the key ingredients in the recipe? One was the maintenance of a stable macroeconomic environment that was conducive to investment. This growth is driven by private sector investment, both domestic and multinational, by the way of foreign direct investment (FDI).

A second key ingredient of this kind of growth was very high levels of investment, including public sector investment. As a kind of benchmark, the Commission felt that to sustain growth at that rate, you needed public sector investment of the order of 5 per cent to 7 per cent of GDP and overall investment at or above 25 per cent of GDP. It is very difficult to be very precise about that, but many, many countries in the slow growth category fall short of that standard.

We were not able to find a case in which most of that investment was not funded primarily from domestic savings. In other words, it seems that empirically that funding that kind of investment in relatively poor countries entirely or largely from foreign capital and foreign savings is a risky proposition. There are lots of examples of that.

To sustain that kind of growth, the primary assets you really need are people. So, a key component of high growth in developing countries was very heavy investment in human capital. Where investment is efficient in education and human capital, the output is the development of cognitive and non-cognitive skills.

My fellow commissioners, I know, would say that the other key ingredient at this level of generality is, what Indians have taught us to call, 'inclusiveness'. We cannot find an example of sustained high growth that does not have both the intent and to some extent, the accomplishment, over time, of including everybody in the process.

There are two reasons for this inclusiveness. The economic reason is to sustain high growth. It is necessary to take advantage of the people in the economy and their potential increased productivity to sustain a high growth level. The second reason is that if you leave a whole lot of people out of the process of development, then you will develop political economy problems.

Why are large Latin American economies called middle income economies? The reason is that the average income is a middle income level of $5,000 to $10,000, which in most cases is an average of very high incomes at one end and very low incomes at the other. The high income part has growth potential of the same order as in advanced countries and the low income part has been left out of the economy. It is a dual economy structure and so, growth simply cannot go up and stay up at those 7 per cent to 9 per cent levels. As an aside, the accelerating growth in several Latin American countries, prominently Brazil, is running in parallel with a rising pattern of inclusion and a declining Gini coefficient.

At the microeconomic level, the dynamics require a willingness to sustain and support and promote, what I would call, the chaotic micro-economic dynamics of the competitive process. This involves competition, entry, exit, continuous diversification and structural change in the economy. It is uncomfortable. There are all kinds of pressures to resist it. Perhaps, the most obvious one that you can see in a number of middle income countries is the attempt to keep the labour-intensive export sectors alive, even as incomes rise and point to their decline. You cannot run labour-intensive goods and services and industries and sell them to the global economy and have income levels of, say, $8,000. The effect of this resistance is a decline in productivity and income growth and a slowing of the rate of structural change in the economy.

On the political economy side, I would note two things. Governments of developing countries have essential roles to play and these roles are somewhat different from those in an advanced economy. It is an investor in hard and soft infrastructure that supports the growth process. Leadership is important too. Growth is a very difficult process that people have to, in some sense, buy into. It involves a long-term perspective and a willingness to sacrifice consumption now for investment in the future. It also requires a great deal of pragmatism, a willingness to use judgement, a willingness to make mistakes and a willingness to experiment. This is a world in which the models are incomplete. We do not know the necessary and sufficient conditions for growth and development and poverty reduction. The models are still incomplete. Successful governments are ones that take that in stride and act accordingly.

John Williamson wrote down a list of guidelines for growth and development in 1989, that came to be called the Washington Consensus. These guidelines had a somewhat macroeconomic focus, but they were very intelligent and I think they have stood the test of time rather well. The problem with the Washington Consensus was not in its formulation but rather in its application. People interpreted it as a formula for success, assuming the guidelines to be necessary and sufficient conditions. The Washington Consensus was also interpreted in parts of the world as a prescription for limited government, on the ground that governments make mistakes, crowd out the private sector and waste resources. All of which is true in many cases, but writing governments out of the script is not the solution. More effective governments, with recognition of their critical complementary role, is closer to the growth experiences of the successful cases.

A number of areas of the Washington Consensus prescriptions involve benefits and risks and judgements. Industrial policy and the promotion of export diversification is one such area and exchange rate management is another. The pace and sequencing of the opening up of the capital account is the third and finally, the pace of opening up of the real economy to maintain a reasonable balance of job creation and the job destruction process in the course of growth, is yet another area.

These areas remain controversial in academic literature. Successful high growth countries managed to find a balance between them in various ways. One of those ways involved respect for market forces on the one hand and a recognition that in a developing economy, market forces and signals alone are insufficient and sometimes lead to suboptimal results.

What about forms of governance? Well, if you look at these 13 or 15 high growth countries, what you find is that they are all over the map in terms of forms of government. Some are democracies, some are quite autocratic. Some started out quite autocratic and evolved into multi-party democracies, with dominant political parties.

If you look at the failures, the countries that did not grow, you see a similar pattern of extreme variability in the form of governments. Perhaps, the sensible conclusion to draw is that the form of governance is not the correct explanatory variable, at least with respect to economic performance.

Economic performance seems to have more to do with the intent and conduct of government. It has to do with whether the government intends to grow and reduce poverty and proceed in a fairly inclusive way and so on. The growing field of research in political economy in developing countries is trying to fathom these conundrums.

What explains the shortcomings in the performance of the fairly large collection of countries that, at least, for an extended period of time, did not seem to grow and take advantage of the global economy?

Well, you see fiscal and monetary instability quite frequently—and that I think most agree—is destructive. Hyperinflation, unsustainable fiscal positions, defaults, crises of various kinds are fatal to the investment process and to growth. You also see low public sector investment to a surprising extent. Most now agree that the government and the private sector are complementary inputs to a dynamic process, where public sector policies and investments create an environment in which both public and private sector dynamics can work. An important part of that is public sector investment in hard and soft infrastructure.

A third explanation for countries that have failed to attain high growth levels are major failures of inclusiveness. If the Gini coefficient serves as a measure of effective inclusiveness, then the parts of the world where the Gini coefficient is as high as 0.5 or more, are Latin America and Africa. A fourth explanation for failed growth is excessive reliance of developing countries on foreign savings, expecially when borrowing is in a foreign currency. Internal shocks lead to distress and defaults and external shocks like the current crisis lead to vulnerability.

Central banks' role in encouraging growth

Central banks have played a key role in this spreading pattern of growth. They became increasingly competent at controlling inflation—and that was an important contribution. They also became increasingly expert in managing shocks, both those generated internally and externally. The current financial crisis is an excellent illustration of that trait, but certainly not the only one.

They managed volatility with skill and judgement and that is critical for the investment environment to drive the growth process. They achieved a level of autonomy that allowed them to make politically unpopular choices and acquire the kind of credibility, that is an important and tangible asset.

There is, however, a balance to be struck between autonomy and independence on the one hand and what is sometimes called 'accountability' on the other. One of my fellow Commissioners, in a fit of frustration, privately described the central bank in his country as an independent republic. This is actually a fairly hard problem.

Central banks do need independence. They do need to be able to act autonomously both in and out of crisis. Yet, the components of a successful growth strategy have to fit together in a coherent fashion, if it is going to work. One of those pieces is open economy monetary and exchange rate policy. As in other areas, balance and judgment is required.

The crisis and its impact

Let me turn to the crisis. I think there was an implicit assumption that the global economy was a relatively stable place. Admittedly, there were local and regional episodes of instability of which, some were quite serious like the crisis in 1997-98. The core of the global economy, though—the advanced countries—were assumed to be financially and economically stable.

That assumption did not turn out to be true. What we had, instead, in the advanced countries, particularly the United States, was a dangerous asset inflation, fuelled by largely unregulated excess leverage accumulation. The epicentre of this was the United States economy and to some extent, Europe, although the pattern of leverage in magnitude and location by sector does differ across countries in ways that are important.

When the crisis hit, asset prices declined and credit nearly froze. The balance sheet damage spread to the real economy reducing consumption, investment and employment, which, in turn, fed back negatively onto balance sheets.

The crisis spread to the developing world via two channels. The financial one was a rapid withdrawal of capital from developing economies, because of domestic balance sheet damage in the advanced countries and a sudden severe tightening of credit. The second channel was a fall in aggregate demand, that turned into a very sharp drop in trade. All high-growth developing economies are trade-exposed. The effect was a sharp drop in real growth rates.

The response by the countries that had the resources and capacity has been impressive. Using a combination of quantitative easing and policy rate reduction, major developing countries restored credit conditions. On the trade side, to varying extents, they were able to deploy fiscal stimulus to cushion the shocks. Not surprisingly perhaps, resilience has turned out to be highest in China and India.

Smaller, poorer countries did not have the capacity to respond to the outflow of captial and the drop in external demand. These countries have fared less well. One of the lessons of the crisis is that the International Monetary Fund (IMF) is important to these countries for interim financing. Its capitalisation is, therefore, important. Also, important is getting its governance structure right so that it can function effectively as a trusted lender-of-last-resort, an important step in creating greater resilience in the global economy in the future.

Central banks were the key policy actors that prevented a much worse Depression-like scenario. They used their autonomy to act aggressively, quickly and unconventionally. Speed was of importance in a panic situation. The political system simply cannot act that quickly. It does not matter how it is configured. It has to debate and discuss things and you just do not have time.

As the normal channels for credit intermediation froze, central banks became lenders-of-last-resort. The Federal Reserve was buying commercial paper and a whole range of risk assets through agents and expanding its balance sheet to over $2 trillion. I am sure that this was uncomfortable territory for the central bankers and something that they would rather not do. I think it is the majority view that the central bankers had the lead role in saving us from a very serious Depression-like scenario.

Post-crisis challenges and lessons from the crisis

The immediate challenge is the timing and implementation of the exit from the crisis and response mechanisms. I think the central banks, if allowed to, can do this reasonably well in a measured way. There is a delicate balancing act on the monetary policy side. On the one hand, rising interest rates risk further damage to still-fragile balance sheets with a negative impact on the real economy. On the other, there is the global risk of excess liquidity, asset bubbles, distortions of prices and exchange rates that require policy responses in developing countries.

An additional concern is the fiscal situation in advanced countries. At some point, accumulated deficits become so large that inflation becomes the only feasible exit. Markets may anticipate that and accelerate the process through rising long-term bond rates. The other concern, however, is that the central banks that resist inflationary pressures, will have their independence undercut in the course of trying to do the exit.

Developing countries in the post-crisis environment

We, at the Growth Commission, met after the crisis to ask ourselves whether everything that we had said just four months back was wrong or in need of substantial modification. We had had the good sense of timing the publication of our main report, called the Growth Report in May 2008, just before the full force of the crisis hit in the fall of that year. We met again in April of 2009, just as the crisis dynamics were stabilising. Asset prices bottomed out in March 2009.

Our focus was on lessons from the crisis and adaptation of growth strategies in developing countries. What modifications are required in developing countries in terms of growth strategies and what lessons have we learnt that are important for economic progress? I will try to dwell on these questions.

I think the developing countries, on balance, withstood the crisis remarkably well and beyond anybody's expectations, with India and China in the lead. There are a number of reasons for that and I think they hold lessons for at least medium-term growth. First, financial institutions and other entities in developing countries did not hold, what are now called, 'toxic assets'. They were mostly free of excess leverage, especially in the household sector. The balance sheets of their major financial institutions were not badly damaged. That was an important factor in being able to respond quickly to the credit challenge.

Second, the dominant presence in the developing country's financial systems is still largely banks and they are substantially domestically owned. This turns out to be crucial. The reason is the central bank needs working partners in responding to a credit crisis. The simple truth is that in a crisis of this magnitude in the advanced countries, the government and the central banks change their roles from referee and regulator to referee, regulator and major player.

The multinational entities, who are based in advanced countries, are then marching to a drum that is being beaten by its own government and that is the domestic agenda. The bottom line is that substantial domestic ownership of banks is prudent and the opposite leaves one very vulnerable. An important corollary is that in this and other dimensions, there are limits to globalisation of markets, in the absence of parallel globalisation of governance and regulatory institutions. The crisis makes the vulnerabilities more visible. The limits are imposed as a matter of national policy.

Another contributor to resilience in developing countries was the absence of financial institutions with major liabilities to foreigners. The limited cross-border balance sheet activity meant that the 'too big to save' problem that appeared prominently in Europe, was mostly not an issue in developing countries.

In most developing countries, the shadow banking system is small. Banks dominate in the provision of credit. That turned out to be an asset. That is not to say that securitisation should be avoided. It has clear benefits in terms of spreading risk and reducing capital costs. It does, however, require legal and regulatory infrastructure.

The benefits of securitisation of credit can be achieved with relatively plain vanilla forms of it. The more complex derivative securities, sometimes highly leveraged, turned out to be dangerous and should be restricted as a matter of regulatory policy. Finally, and somewhat more controversial, some version of the utility banking model, in which there is a restraint on what the banking sector can do in other parts of the financial system, seems prudent.

The Commission did not take a position on where to draw the line between banking and other activities. The Volcker Rule, which would separate proprietary trading, is one possibility. But the goal is to have a system in which all the channels of credit intermediation are unlikely to fail at the same time.

Montek Singh Ahluwalia, who is the member of this Commission and Deputy Chairman of the Planning Commission in India told me, 'if you want to say something, say something that somebody disagrees with, or it is not worth saying.' So, let me take a shot at it. By the way, he attributed that view to the US President, Barack Obama's chief economic advisor, Larry Summers, and I think that sounds right in the given history.

One of the lessons of the crisis is that singular focus on inflation targeting or price stability, narrowly defined, is not a wise course of action for central banks. In the global economy, there are lots of reasons why inflation can be under control. In the pre-crisis decade, China was becoming a major force in the manufacturing area. It is fairly easy to demonstrate that they drove down the relative price of manufactured goods in the global economy. As a result, one element of potential inflationary pressure was removed from the system. Excess consumption in the United States was accommodated by surpluses in other countries and so, that source of inflationary pressure was removed for a period of time.

The question really is: what is the default and where does the burden of proof lie? If there is no inflationary pressure, do you relax and leave interest rates low? The risk, of course, we know with the benefit of hindsight, is the creation of asset bubbles fuelled in part by leverage. If the central bank or the regulator suspects that there are elements of unsustainability in the system, but cannot prove it, is the default no action, or pre-emptive action with the risk of misjudgment?

It seems clear that the macroeconomic and financial management of the economy is going to have to include attention to the balance sheets and to the stability and sustainability of the system. A narrow focus on prices or even flow variables like growth, will not suffice. How one does that and which entities are assigned various parts of the regulatory oversight, is the challenge we now face in re-designing regulatory architectures. Of central importance is the monitoring and responding to systemic risk. Considering the state of our knowledge about stability in the financial system, this function is going to require judgment, at least for a while. That will not appeal to everyone. The central bank will surely continue to use monetary policy to tackle inflation, interest rates and in some cases, growth and employment, as a primary mandate. For that, it needs to continue to have autonomy.

The RBI Governor, D. Subbarao, has hinted that the central bank may have a comparative advantage in the area of macroprudential supervision, which means assessing whether the system is becoming unstable, at least on its terms. It certainly has an informational advantage because of the work it does. It frequently also has a human capital advantage, much as an entity like the IMF has—and that is superb analytical talent.

When I went around the developing world in the course of my work with the Growth Commission, I was very much struck by the concentration of analytical talent that is located in central banks. So, I think for all kinds of reasons it makes sense to have the central bank at least as an important player in the management of an oversight of the stability of the system, which means paying attention to balance sheets, asset prices, leverage and other things that may seem to be relevant.

That, however, raises two issues. What policy instruments, facilities and authorisations does the central bank need to discharge the expanded responsibility for systemic stability? It surely cannot be true that monetary policy variables will be sufficient? Perhaps, more fundamentally, will governments delegate that much power to a single entity? A central bank that is relatively autonomous, carries out conventional monetary policy, has the power to respond unconventionally in a crisis and is the systemic stability regulator, is a powerful entity. Perhaps, too powerful in a democratic setting.

I do not know what to do about that. I rather like Andy Lo's[1] proposal to create a financial version of National Transport Security Board (NTSB). The NTSB is an entity in the United States that investigates airline accidents or near accidents. The advantage of that system, as described by Andy Lo, is that, it is its only function and because it is its only function, it does not have conflicts of interest. It does not regulate and, hence, cannot be responsible for accidents that it is investigating. In the financial setting, an analogous entity would investigate the causes of crises and would issue

1. Andrew Lo is MIT professor of finance.

warnings about systemic risk. The regulators and lawmakers could ignore it, but not without political cost.

The Commission spent some time thinking about what constitutes resilience on the real economy side of a developing country. If we are going to rewrite the first report, I think we would have increased the priority attached to things that fall under the heading of resilience. Where does resilience with respect to external shocks come from? Reserves turned out to be fairly important in restoring credit and maintaining control of the currency.

Second, current account deficits are a vulnerability, as they imply a dependence on foreign finance that may not be there in a crisis. While a persistent current account deficit is a vulnerability, a persistent current account surplus is a waste. There is no strategic reason connected to sustained growth for running a current account surplus. High investment and savings rates are important, but not excess savings. China currently faces the structural challenges of raising household income and lowering a deeply structurally embedded tendency toward excess savings.

Low government deficits and public debt seem clearly important and, therefore, provide the capacity for fiscal stimulus. There is a widespread challenge of deeply embedding counter-cyclical policies and attitudes and cultures. It is not confined to macroeconomic management. It is also a challenge in the investment world, where it takes the form of chasing returns and ignoring or hiding risk.

The global economy emerging from the crisis

The largely self-regulatory model of the financial system has been rejected. We now have to replace it with something without doing excessive damage to the systems' capacity to allocate capital, spread risk, and innovate. There are externalities that run from the financial sector to the real economy. Those externalities are never fully internalised by the financial institutions alone. They have to be controlled by regulation.

There is a growing fiscal problem in the US and in a number of European countries. According to a recent IMF study, much of the fiscal deterioration is because of the non-discretionary component of stimulus, reduced tax revenues, increased unemployment insurance payments and so on. That is worrying. It means that eliminating the discretionary part of the stimulus may not be enough to restore stability and that structural changes on the revenue and benefit side may be needed.

Rebalancing and restoring global aggregate demand, with the attendant benefit of reducing the rather strong and worrisome protectionist pressures, is an important global policy coordination challenge. China, Germany, Japan and other surplus countries will need to get rid of their surpluses if the problem is to be addressed effectively. It is hard to know whether we are progressing on this. John Lipsky has been centrally involved and will have an informed view.

I know the Chinese side pretty well. They do understand that it is in their own as well as the global interest to get rid of the current account surplus in a way that does not damage growth. They, however, understand and, I think the rest of the world does not completely understand, that it is not mainly an exchange rate issue. It involves a rather complex set of internal structural transformations, that involve increasing household income and reducing household savings. It will take time.

The openness of the global economy is the single-most important asset available to the developing world. Its continuation will determine whether the spreading pattern of growth and prosperity that we saw for much of the post-war period resumes. China or India may do relatively well by gaining market share, as a result of their competitive strength. But the combined growth aspirations of the developing countries are not achievable in an environment with deficient aggregate demand and rising protectionism.

In my view, advanced country growth is likely to be relatively low for an extended period of time coming out of the crisis for structural reasons. Deleveraging takes time. Leveraging up on the public sector side has its limits. Savings in the US is likely to remain above the depressed pre-crisis levels, barring another asset bubble. Unemployment is stubbornly high. This is what has come to be called the 'New Normal'. There is a growing awareness that the current deep recession is not a mean-reverting event and that a return to the old pre-crisis 'normal' is neither likely nor desirable.

The 'New Normal' is not just something that can be forecast. It is a work in progress. How it comes out will depend partly on effective management of the exits, on financial sector re-regulation and on the pursuit of growth-oriented policies and investments in advanced and devleoping countries. It is also going to depend on the success (or lack of it), with which we tackle the major global issues—a coordinated restoration of aggregate demand and avoidance of expanded protectionist measures.

It is easy to be pessimistic about this, but one can always hope that one's pessimism is excessive. But one point is clear. The architects of the 'New Normal' will include the major developing countries. That is new and challenging but, on balance, an important positive step in the evolution of the global economy and its governance.

Section I

Challenges and Response to Conduct Monetary Policy during the Financial Crisis

Section I

Challenges and Response to Conduct Monetary Policy during the Financial Crisis

This section corresponds to Session I of the First International Research Conference on 'Challenges to Central Banking in the Context of Financial Crisis', Reserve Bank of India, Mumbai.

Chairman: Charles R. Bean

Co-Chair: Subir Gokarn

4 Monetary Policy Flexibility

Solution or Problem?

WILLIAM POOLE

My remarks today will focus on the US experience, which I know far better than that of other economies elsewhere. I will concentrate on policies to avoid a crisis rather than those for managing one.[1] Without doubt, during a crisis a degree of flexibility is essential, because the particulars of every crisis are inevitably different. That said, a consistent approach to handling a crisis is essential to help shape market expectations in a constructive way. Without dwelling on the matter, note that permitting Lehman Brothers to fail after bailing out Bear Stearns and the uncertain handling of the Troubled Asset Relief Program (TARP) exacerbated the crisis in the United States.[2] In thinking about what happened, consider this question: How could we all have missed the coming of the financial crisis that rocked the United States and shook the world around 2007 and 2008? I do not recall warnings from any senior policymaker, either publicly or internally in the United States, that the entire financial system was vulnerable to extreme crisis. I was a senior policymaker in the United States Federal Reserve until some months after the crisis had broken. I attended every meeting of the Federal Open Market Committee (FOMC) from March 1998 to January 2008 and read the steady stream of staff briefings and papers. At the St. Louis Fed, I had an excellent research department to provide analysis and insight. My colleagues around the Federal Reserve System (FRS) frequently sent me interesting papers to read. The fact is that we all missed the coming of the crisis.

1. My views on the crisis are stated in detail in Poole (2010).
2. Taylor (2009) argues that the Government's uncertain handling of the TARP rather than the Lehman failure was responsible for most of the financial disruption starting in mid-September 2008.

Of course, 'we all missed' is somewhat an exaggeration, but the fact remains that the analysis that seems so obvious today was simply not discussed before the crisis. There were abstract discussions of crises, but that is not what I have in mind. A convincing analysis of the risk of a crisis would have required detailed discussion of house prices, data on the nature of mortgage holdings (direct and securitised) by major financial firms, probable losses on these mortgages should house prices fall and the extent of the equity cushion in major firms to withstand the losses. The data required for this analysis were available before the crisis, but were not exploited to explain the US economy's vulnerability to the crisis.

Here is my sketch of what happened. By early 2006, house prices had been bid for, to excessive levels. Yet, we believed that the probability of a significant decline in housing prices on a national average basis was remote. This was the view within the FRS, among most private economists and among most portfolio managers. We did not understand how leveraged a large number of households were, or at least the significance of that leverage for a potential financial crisis. We did not understand the extent to which household defaults would lead to widespread foreclosures.

We did not understand how leveraged many financial institutions holding mortgage-related assets were. Moreover, as unemployment rose, so did defaults on auto and credit card loans. The business contraction damaged cash flow on many commercial real estate projects, creating further losses on bank balance sheets. We did not understand how many of the portfolios of mortgage assets, which have long maturities, were financed by short-maturity liabilities and minimal capital. We did not understand that these risky portfolios were not just scattered throughout the US economy but were widespread across the US and many parts of the world. These were not isolated weak portfolios. They were everywhere.

The vulnerabilities within the financial systems seem so obvious today that I still wonder how I and everyone else, missed the impending peril. This is where the housing bubble differs from the dot-com stock market bubble of the late 1990s. Alan Greenspan had warned of 'irrational exuberance' in the stock markets then and his warning had been repeated endlessly, although not by him. After his initial attempt, he did not believe that the warning would be effective. Indeed, that warning did not prevent the stock market from inflating unreasonably, but it does show that policymakers were aware of the risk then.

In the decade that followed, monetary policymakers in the United States were not completely oblivious to the risk of a financial crisis either. I gave many speeches from August 2002, warning of the danger posed by Fannie Mae and Freddie Mac.[3] What was more important, Alan Greenspan worked, both behind the scenes and publicly, to get the US Congress to reform Fannie and Freddie. In my speeches, I argued that Fannie and Freddie had portfolios that were riskier than they appeared, especially given their very thin capital positions. If one of them were to stumble, the consequence would be a worldwide financial crisis of immense proportions. Ultimately the US government placed the two firms into conservatorship and full Federal control in September 2008, before their failure could cause a financial crisis.

The crisis has been extraordinarily costly. What should be done to avoid a repeat in the future? Tougher regulation? A monetary policy that pricks asset price bubbles? Policies to alter the incentive for leverage? I will discuss these in turn.

Tougher regulation

Few specifics typically accompany calls for regulatory reform. One common approach is to require more capital. The form additional capital would take matters enormously. The only form that provides deep market discipline is subordinated debt. This idea has been discussed for many years. My version of the plan can be found in a recent article in the *Financial Analysts Journal*.[4]

Here is a brief sketch of the plan. Every firm with a bank charter would be required to maintain subordinated debt outstanding equal to 10 per cent of its total liabilities. The debt would consist of bonds with original maturity of 10 years. When an issue of subordinated debt matures, the bank could, at its option, convert the debt to equity at a conversion rate

3. Poole (2002). A number of additional speeches of mine are available at *http://fraser.stlouisfed.org/historicaldocs/952/*

4. Poole (2009).

set in the bond indenture. This provision permits the bank to conserve capital rather than pay out cash when a bond matures. However, the bank would have to sell a new issue of sub debt to replace the maturing issue, or would have to shrink so that the remaining sub debt outstanding was 10 per cent of liabilities.

This sub debt requirement would be a tough regulation. It has the advantage of being market-based, as a bank unable to roll over maturing sub debt would have to manage its own restructuring. This provision has a major advantage over that of having regulators decide how to restructure a bank in trouble. Unfortunately, calls for tougher regulation do not usually go this far. Those advocating tougher regulation do not want regulation this tough.

Why not? For one thing, regulators, regulated firms and the US Congress prefer discretion. Discretion provides great latitude for bargaining and for members of Congress to harvest campaign contributions from financial firms. Financial firms want to shape the outcome and, within limits, will do so. They will be at least partially successful in getting obscure special provisions written into law that will soften regulation and perhaps even provide competitive advantage. That is the way democracy works when it emphasises administrative discretion.

Another regulatory approach is to restrict bank activities. Much has been said of proprietary trading operations. This approach is not satisfactory. Trying to enforce a list of permissible activities is a recipe for endless regulatory avoidance as lawyers, accountants and consultants create structures that fall within, or are arguably within the boundaries of permissible activities. Regulatory flexibility is part of the problem that created the financial crisis. Tougher standards in the law and less regulatory discretion are the need of the day.

With regard to recent regulatory discretion, note that the Securities and Exchange Commission (SEC) lowered minimum capital requirements on investment banks in 2004.[5] Note also that regulators in many countries

5. The issue is complicated because the SEC capital requirement never applied to the holding company of a broker-dealer. The point here is simply that the 2004 change illustrates a possible outcome of regulatory discretion.

joined together to set new standards in the Basel II Accord. That negotiation lasted many years, and worked in the direction of reducing capital standards. It certainly made the standards much more complex. The negotiators had almost unlimited discretion. They had the authority, if they wanted to use it, to completely gut capital standards.

The way to think about regulation is the way we think about a sound portfolio-management policy. In the case of portfolio management, for instance, there should be a policy on asset allocation that has been found to be appropriate across a wide range of market situations. The portfolio manager can then stick with the policy whatever be the current state of the markets, till a new policy is substituted, which too will be followed across all market conditions. That is how we ought to think about regulatory policy. The rules should provide discipline and consistency. They should not change based on regulators' gut feelings or hunches about the current business environment.

Another problem is that certain regulatory practices, such as a list of permissible activities, may require international coordination to be effective. Tight international coordination will prove unattainable in the long run. Countries have different views and different market situations. Governments will naturally want to gain competitive advantage for firms based in their countries. If country X thinks it can gain an advantage over New York and London, then X will certainly try to bend its regulations to the advantage of its firms. Competition tends to undercut regulation, especially in financial services businesses.

This argument holds with equal force for capital regulation, such as a subordinated debt requirement. However, the competitive disadvantage of sub debt should not be large. Indeed, to the extent that sub debt is a substitute, as it should be, for the heavy hand of discretionary regulation, the costs to banks of dealing with the regulatory environment should be lower rather than higher. In any event, whatever other countries do, the United States must end the moral hazard created by the bailouts. If other countries want to prop up weak banks, so be it. That is not something the US government should do.

Pricking asset price bubbles

Many believe that a central bank ought to be prepared to change monetary policy to affect asset prices. Although the difficulties of such a monetary policy have been widely discussed, advocates argue that the costs of the housing price bubble have been so large that an imperfect policy is preferable to no policy. That is a dangerous view. It has been a standard practice in macroeconomics research for several decades to embed a policy rule in a macro model. There is, for example, no way to evaluate Taylor-type rules with different coefficients without embedding the rule in a macro model. Equations describing private sector behaviour depend on the policy rule, and the rule cannot be evaluated without specifying how private behaviour is affected by different rules.

To evaluate the likely effects of an asset-price intervention policy (APIP), there is no substitute for an approach that embeds the policy in a macro model. There are many possible variants of an APIP. One possibility would be to add a term to the typical Taylor rule. An approach like this seems to be what some advocates have in mind. The central bank might set the interbank interest rate higher than would otherwise be the case if some asset price were deemed 'too' high.

The APIP term in a Taylor-type monetary policy rule might be the gap between an actual asset price, like an index of equity prices, and an assumed equilibrium asset price. The gap would be multiplied by a coefficient, as with the GDP gap term in a Taylor rule. To be operational, the model would have to specify the equilibrium equity price index and the macro model would have to integrate asset prices in, for example, business fixed investment decisions.

To my knowledge, no one has attempted to specify an asset price term in a monetary policy reaction function and then embed that function in a macro model. The fact is that we just do not know what the effects of an APIP would be, even in a simple illustrative 'toy' macro model. To me, it is simply foolish to argue that monetary policy should nevertheless be adjusted to 'take account of' asset prices. There is indeed extensive experience with interventions in one asset market—the market for foreign exchange. The intent of this APIP is to move the exchange rate to an 'appropriate' level, or to lean against prevailing speculative winds. Foreign exchange intervention among major high-income countries has fortunately fallen into disuse. The record is a sorry one, with intervention creating additional uncertainty and, sometimes, massive losses for the governments involved.

In a democracy, every important policy has a political component. Did the US architects of the TARP to recapitalise banks anticipate that the programme would morph into a programme to control executive compensation in banks? I fear that those who want the central bank to intervene to influence asset prices do not understand the forces they are unleashing and the unintended consequences, political and economic, that would flow from the effort.

When a policy cannot be defended by careful economic reasoning and modelling, then it is especially ripe for political capture. Policymakers should not respond to 'do something' pressures. That is how the United States got wage-price controls in 1971, and there are many other examples. As with regulatory flexibility, monetary policy flexibility, which I interpret as an absence of standards for conducting monetary policy, will be a recipe for increased economic instability and increased risk of financial crises.

Limiting leverage

The financial crisis broke out in August 2007, after house prices in the United States declined at a relatively modest rate. True, expectations of further house price declines were widespread, but even there, the extent of the actual and anticipated house price declines was small relative to the stock market declines earlier in the decade. Why did the house price decline create a crisis whereas the stock price decline did not?

The difference was leverage. Mortgages were widely held in highly leveraged accounts. Moreover, many of these portfolios had a large duration imbalance between assets and liabilities. The mortgage assets were long term. In many portfolios, a major share of the liabilities was due within one year and the portfolios had relatively little equity capital. In contrast, common stock was held largely in unleveraged portfolios, such as mutual funds and household investment portfolios.

Without question, leverage makes the economy more vulnerable to financial crisis. Why, then, does the US tax code subsidise leverage? The reasons are in part historical and in part a function of the political strength of financial and real estate interests that traditionally finance their activities heavily through debt. Instead of simply exhorting households and firms to rely less on debt, Congress should phase out the deductibility of interest on all personal and business tax returns.

A quick calculation on US corporate returns indicates that a revenue-neutral reform would be to reduce the statutory corporate tax rate from 35 per cent to 15 per cent while phasing out the deductibility of interest. That reform would certainly reduce the incentive for high leverage. I see no good argument against that reform.

Concluding comment

The financial crisis offers an immense word of caution on the potential that discretionary policy has to control the economy. There are two issues. One is that unless we find a way to put smarter and more effective policymakers in office than we have in the past, we can expect that policymakers will miss some important developments as they, and I, did with the growing risk of a financial crisis during the 2002-2007 period. It is often said that this was a period of regulatory failure. In fact, the problem was more serious. The failure was a consequence of economists not figuring out the risks in housing markets and in housing finance.

The second key issue is that even if policymakers identify a risk, getting the political system to respond appropriately is a huge problem. The problem is not a new one. We have known since the late 1970s, for example, that changing demographics would require major revisions in the US social security and medicare systems. Year after year, social security actuaries' reports have confirmed this bleak outlook. Yet, nothing has been done. It is my conviction that had regulators warned the US Congress and banks in 2001-2005 that mortgage products were creating a grave risk of financial instability—such warnings would have made no difference.

I conclude that we need to search for structural reforms, in the tax code, for instance, so that it increases economic and financial stability. We should not be dependent on the expertise of policymakers and the timeliness of legislative action to stabilise the economy. A useful analogy is that US political stability is dependent primarily on the Constitution and a body of law, custom and experience that condition what individual Presidents and Congresses can do. We need to look to ways to embed that sort of institutional strength in our financial system to create deep and lasting financial stability.

References

Poole, William (2002). "Financial Stability". Remarks before the Council of State Governments. Southern Legislative Conference Annual Meeting. New Orleans, Louisiana. August 4. [*http://fraser.stlouisfed.org/historicaldocs/1098/download/41143/20020804.pdf*]

———. (2009). "Moral Hazard: The Long-Lasting Legacy of Bailouts", *Financial Analysts Journal* 65: 17-23, (November-December).

———. (2010). "Causes and Consequences of the Financial Crisis of 2007-2009", *Harvard Journal of Law and Public Policy* 33 (2010) (forthcoming).

Taylor, John (2009). *Getting Off Track: How Government Actions and Interventions Caused, Prolonged, and Worsened the Financial Crisis*. US: Hoover Institution Press.

4.1 DISCUSSION

Solutions: Global Checks on Capital Markets

JOHN LIPSKY

Bill Poole began by asking why the crisis was missed. He told us that we did not see the amount of leverage in the system. We underestimated the maturity mismatches. Among other things, we did not see in the United States, the insidious effects of the incoherence in the mandates of the large government-sponsered enterprises (GSEs), Fannie Mae and Freddie Mac. We also did not see the global reach of the toxic assets that were being created in the United States and the implications, that held for the crisis. He asks if there was a regulatory failure and the answer is certainly, yes.

He also ascribes part of the problem to the failure of economists and other analysts to understand what was happening. But I would hasten to add, and I suspect he would agree, that first and foremost, this crisis was the failure of market participants themselves. It was a failure of risk management; it was a failure of corporate governance; it was a failure of discipline and a failure of due diligence. Clearly, regulators failed to rectify these errors, but the errors primarily were those of market participants.

It is worth asking, as Prof. Poole does, whether regulatory reforms could be helpful? One of the first potential reforms he lights upon is more capital and I think there is a very broad agreement that this is certainly one result, or should be one result, of fixing the problems in a post-crisis environment. He suggests a programme of subordinated debt for banks. If we examine his argument closely, he even accepts the very tough implications of that suggestion.

He acknowledges that if in a crisis, should specific banks find it extremely costly to roll over debt as prescribed under his plan, they would

---

Comments by John Lipsky on the paper presented by William Poole 'Monetary Policy Flexibility: Solution or Problem?'.

be forced to shrink their balance sheets. In other words, the remedy here neither obviates the possibility of bank runs nor that of procyclical shrinkage of credit in a crisis. So, to cut a long story short, Prof. Poole's recommendation may prove helpful in one sense, but it would not necessarily prevent a crisis.

In general, Prof. Poole thinks there should be less discretion in regulation but at the same time, he is sceptical of potential measures. Let us call these concrete measures—such as specific prohibitions on activities by individual agents or types of agents. One of the aspects of discretion that Prof. Poole sees as troublesome is the implication that there needs to be international coordination and he cites the difficulty of that occurring. But it strikes me that the need for international coordination is not a function of discretion but inevitably a function of modern capital markets and their relative openness. Any measure taken in one market will have international implications and, to be effective, will have to be considered in that environment.

One of the signals, or rather, admonitions of Prof. Poole, is a need to stop the bail-outs. I think that is something on which we can all agree. It should not be forgotten, however, that in the United States, shareholders of financial institutions did suffer grievous losses despite the bail-outs and, hopefully, will have learnt some lessons. I reiterate a point I have made earlier—that in the creation of the global financial crisis of 2007-08, the basic failure was the failure of the comportment of financial market participants.

Turning to the potential remedies, Prof. Poole questions whether it makes sense for monetary policy to explicitly take into account asset prices and points out that there is no clear theoretical or model-based foundation for undertaking specific actions. That is certainly true, although I think it is a little stark to say that if you do not have an iron-clad theory, you should not do anything at all. That would be a rather high bar for any policy action under any circumstances.

In general, my colleagues at the International Monetary Fund (IMF) and I agree that monetary policy understood as policy rates, interest rates, etc. is a very blunt tool for dealing with asset markets. And we think that regulatory measures are likely to be much more productive in avoiding future booms and busts. Prof. Poole also suggests that it would be useful and important to end tax subsidies that tend to increase leverage and that is another measure on which, I think, there is broad agreement. But, of course, individual tax subsidies that increase leverage are going to be difficult to remove, even though that seems a good idea in most cases.

Prof. Poole expresses a somewhat sceptical view of the potential efficacy of regulatory cooperation and the desire to limit discretion. I would like to suggest that there is, in fact, very broad consensus internationally on taking actions that would limit the potential risks of 'too big to fail' institutions. I would say the current drive towards regulatory and other reforms—let us call it broad financial sector reforms—really reflects a clear consensus around four broad principles.

First, the perimeter of regulation needs to be redrawn so that systemically important institutions in all markets fall within the regulatory perimeter. It sounds simple, but in fact, would imply substantial changes in the structure of regulation. It would also imply broad agreement on the need for greater capital, limits on leverage and aligning compensation more accurately with the interests of the market.

To my mind the second principle should be a broad agreement on the need for macroprudential as well as microprudential aspects of regulation—a difficult recipe but on which there is agreement. Third, there should be agreement on the need for resolution mechanisms, including ways to resolve institutions that operate across borders. Finally, and this is a point that is often underemphasised, not only should regulation be strengthened, but so should supervision, to make regulation work. Supervision is of critical importance—and there has been a significant problem on this score before.

There is a forum of cooperation internationally in this arena and that is the Financial Stability Board (FSB). It was founded less than a year ago (April 2009) and is, I think, making good progress. I would hesitate before making too dire a judgement on prospects for successful international cooperation. A final word—there is obviously an important need for better macroeconomic policy management globally. The crisis showed this in an extreme form. But there has been response.

The Pittsburgh Group of 20 Leaders' Summit (2009) created a new framework for strong, sustainable and balanced growth that involves a Mutual Assessment Process that is currently getting underway. It is novel, innovative and holds out the prospect for effective engagement in making macroeconomic policies consistent across the major economies of the world. It is a tall order but then, it is just getting started. It is an important task, but one that should not be overlooked.

4.2
DISCUSSION

No Right Answers, Only Tough Trade-offs

WILLIAM R. WHITE

The title, 'Monetary Policy Flexibility: Solution or Problem' implies a focus on crisis management. William Poole has made a number of comments on crisis prevention. I, too, will indulge myself in doing so.

Crisis management

Identifying some shortcomings in public sector responses

Central banks, particularly those from the largest financial centres, have been rightly proud that their interventions prevented the 'cardiac arrest' in the financial markets from becoming terminal. Yet, as Bill Poole notes, the possibility of such a crisis was never acknowledged by the authorities in advance. Thus, they were almost completely unprepared for the crisis when it did hit. This had two unfortunate implications for crisis management.

First, many of the preparations for a possible crisis, that ought to have been made in advance, had not, in fact, been made. In many countries, deposit insurance schemes were woefully inadequate. In Europe, this first implication resulted in guarantees being given by the Irish government to essentially all of the liabilities of Irish banks. Within days, amid fears of cross-border flows, this led to similar guarantees being offered in a number of other (and far larger) countries.

Insolvency laws, to allow banks to be wound down in a rapid and orderly way, also proved inadequate as did Memoranda of Understanding (MoU) between different government bodies on 'who would do what' in rapidly changing circumstances. At the international level, previous efforts

---

Comments by William R. White on the paper presented by William Poole 'Monetary Policy Flexibility: Solution or Problem?'.

to deal with winding down of large complex financial institutions (LCFI) had also come to nothing, as had efforts to work out 'burden sharing' arrangements across countries.

The second disadvantage of not having anticipated the crisis, and of not discerning its true nature, was that its magnitude, scope and duration were beyond everyone's expectations. For a long time 'denial' was the order of the day, and in some respects it still is. Recall, for example, that when the financial crisis first began, it was said by the US authorities that the bad loans would amount to only $50 billion and that they would be confined to the subprime sector of the mortgage market. When it became impossible to deny that the crisis was spreading far beyond that sector, it was said that the underlying problem was a shortage of liquidity.

The idea that there might in fact be widespread insolvencies and systemic threats to the financial system was denied. When this possibility also had to be confronted, what was denied was that there might be significant effects on the real economy. Evidently, this contention also had to be withdrawn when the global economy turned down sharply in the second half of 2008. Not only did demand dry up in big debtor countries (like the US), but it had massive and unexpected effects on creditor countries as well (like Germany and Japan) through trade and other links.

Today, this denial continues since many people persist in underestimating the effects yet to be seen on the supply side of the real economy. Many sectors, where production capacity got too large during the global boom, will now have to shrink. Perhaps, the impact of the crisis will prove even worse for many Asian countries, which are all geared up to export to countries that can no longer afford to buy. During the long period that such adjustments will take, it is inevitable that structural unemployment will be higher than it would otherwise have been.

Why was the crisis unanticipated?

Evidently, the next question is why the crisis was unanticipated? As a matter of record, I must note that a number of people at the Bank for International Settlements (BIS) did see it coming. Moreover, they warned repeatedly both privately and publically of the dangers that were building up. The fact that Bill Poole says that he attended every meeting of the

Federal Open Market Committee (FOMC) for many years, and that neither the chairman nor the president of the Federal Reserve Bank of New York (FRBNY) ever passed on the concerns being expressed in Basel, 'speaks volumes' for the impact international influences have on policy-making in the United States.

Perhaps, the most fundamental reason why neither senior central bankers nor their staff anticipated the crisis was that their models (in effect, their analytical frameworks) had no room for crises of this (or indeed any) sort. The Keynesian models favoured by central bankers are essentially one-period models in which stocks, or 'imbalances' play essentially no role. The new classical, new Keynesian and dynamic stochastic general equilibrium (DSGE) models favoured by academics assume that the economy is self-equilibrating and expectations are 'rational'. Thus, there can be no such problems by assumption.

In effect, all these analytical frameworks missed the build-up of a number of 'imbalances' that are at the core of the current crisis. Asset prices rose to levels that could not be justified by normal criteria. Financial institutions became ever more exposed to a wide variety of risks. Spending patterns changed in bizarre ways so that US spending became almost entirely dependent on households. Chinese investment (as a proportion of GDP) rose to a level never seen in other large countries. And, finally, trade imbalances rose to unprecedented heights. The analytical models in wide use gave no indication that this would lead to a highly non-linear and convulsive crisis. Many policymakers felt a faint disquiet, but that was it.

The second reason why the crisis was unanticipated has to do with something in human nature. We seem inclined to say 'never look a gift horse in the mouth.' Over the last decade or so, the private sector could not see beyond the extraordinary profits they were making. This did not make it easy for those with a risk control function in financial institutions. Similarly, central bankers could not look beyond the fact that they were achieving their objective of price stability. Indeed, what is truly astonishing is how price stability was ultimately deemed to be 'sufficient' to avoid macroeconomic problems, when the original thought was only that it was 'necessary'.

Implications for managing the downturn

The failure to understand the character of the crisis led to a long period of denial. One important implication of this was that insolvency problems in the financial sector were not addressed as quickly or comprehensively as they might have been. Indeed, in the light of the continuing uncertainty about the magnitude of the losses still to be taken on 'toxic assets' in many jurisdictions, and potential future losses associated with the economic downturn, it might even be felt that the insolvency problem has still not been dealt with comprehensively.

Another implication of not really understanding the nature of the crisis has been an almost wholesale recourse to Keynesian solutions, not least the sharp easing of monetary and fiscal policy almost everywhere. As necessary as these macroeconomic policies might have been to stabilise the situation, two other considerations are important. First, macroeconomic policies might prove inadequate to re-establish robust real growth. Second, to the extent they do work to stimulate the real economy in the short-term, they could do so in ways that would worsen economic prospects over the medium-term.

I have recently written a paper[1] which evaluates the arguments for 'cleaning up' after a crisis as opposed to 'leaning against' the wind of the credit excesses in the first place. I have come to the conclusion that cleaning up might become increasingly difficult and could, in the end, prove impossible as the transmission mechanism turns increasingly ineffective.

The 'headwinds' of debt increasingly constrain both the willingness to borrow and to spend. Moreover, for financial institutions, the 'headwinds' of capital inadequacy increasingly constrain the willingness to lend. Recall that Chairman Greenspan first used the word 'headwinds' in the early 1990s to describe this process. We have now had 20 more years to allow those headwinds to gain further force.

Even if easy money policies do succeed in stimulating real growth in the near- term, they might also have unwanted medium-term implications.

1. See White (2009).

One possibility is that such easing would work through creating yet another asset price bubble. What has gone on in financial markets since the March of 2009, especially in a number of emerging market economies, supports the view that this might indeed be happening.

A second possibility is that very easy monetary conditions, sustained for a long time, might have negative supply-side effects. In such an environment, 'zombie' companies are encouraged to drag down the healthy ones, and the same situation prevails in the banks that finance them. In addition, saving is further discouraged by such policies with potentially serious implications for countries that suffer from a chronic lack of saving and investment.

Finally, there is a low but still significant probability that very easy monetary conditions will eventually cause inflationary expectations to come unstuck in spite of stagnant output. We know this is possible since we have seen such processes at work in Latin America for decades. Evidently, countries with large external deficits and a vulnerable exchange rate would be most exposed to such a stagflationary outcome.

Recognising all of these potential shortcomings of easy money implies that we should be thinking beyond demand-side remedies for the crisis. Supply-side responses also have a role to play, not least better procedures for writing off debt, structural reforms to increase economic potential, and policies to support (rather than interfere with) needed adjustments out of declining industries. If this is what Bill Poole means, when he talks of 'structural reforms... to increase economic and financial stability', then I am with him all the way.

Regardless of what many academics assume, it is evident that our economic and financial system is not inherently stable and self-equilibrating. Thus, we need reforms to make it more stable. Moreover, we need measures to prevent the economy from being pushed beyond the 'corridor of stability' where instability becomes much more likely.[2] This brings me to the second issue of crisis prevention.

2. See Leijonhufvud (2009).

Crisis prevention

William Poole makes suggestions concerning regulation, monetary policy and measures to limit leverage. Let me briefly address each in turn.

Tougher regulation

Bill Poole's proposal on subordinated debt seems to me to be fundamentally sound. Nevertheless, I still wonder how it relates to other proposals that would turn such debt into equity using some form of a 'capital trigger'.

On rules *versus* discretion, I am also sympathetic to his preference for the use of rules, though perhaps for somewhat different reasons. In particular, using discretion to lean against the upswing of the credit cycle, with either regulatory or monetary policy, might prove too difficult. Both popular opinion and the political establishment would be against it. In contrast, it is not too hard to think of rules that would gross up capital requirements (set under Pillar 1 of Basel II) to resist procyclicality in the system as a whole. In effect, we would have 'automatic' financial stabilisers to complement the generally accepted use of 'automatic' fiscal stabilisers.

Finally, Bill Poole is opposed to the 'Volcker rule' to prevent banks from doing proprietary trading. He is certainly right that this will be technically difficult. I would also add that this solution also fails to address the still more fundamental issue of 'ignorance' on the part of both bankers and rating agencies, which led to the huge losses associated with structured products. Super-senior tranches of structured products were rated AAA and kept on the books of the banks because they were thought riskless. What only became clear after the event was the extent to which some of the highly technical assumptions behind these judgments really mattered.

Monetary policy

I am certainly in agreement with William Poole that 'targeting' asset prices as an objective of policy is not a good idea. Rather, we need to think of using such variables as 'indicators' in Taylor-type reaction functions to condition monetary policy to lean against imbalances of various sorts. What I do not agree with, however, is his notion that, without an adequate formal modelling of the implications of such a policy for the real economy, nothing should be ventured. In a nutshell, my response would be that, 'the best is often the enemy of the good'. History, in fact, provides us with plenty of guidance on what policymakers should be worried about and how they might react in consequence.

Finally, he raises the issue of novel policies and the law of unintended consequences. I agree in principle that this is always a problem. However, I also feel that a credible commitment on the part of policymakers to resist credit bubbles (and such symptoms as generalised asset price increases) might well change people's behaviour in a more stabilising way. Indeed, do central bankers not believe that their commitment to keep inflation under control led to a similar and stabilising change in wage-setting behaviour?

Limiting leverage

I agree with Bill Poole that leverage has been an important contributor to the current crisis. Yet, leverage is also the essence of a fractional reserve banking system and there are not too many people supportive of the 100 per cent reserve alternative. In my judgment, we have to balance off the advantages of leverage, speculation and risk taking (the process of 'creative destruction') against the disadvantage of occasional crises. How much repression is enough? Do his conclusions go too far? These are questions for which there are no right answers, only difficult tradeoffs.

References

White, William R. (2009). "Should the Monetary Authorities 'Lean or Clean'?," *Working Paper* 34. Federal Reserve Bank of Dallas: Globalization and Monetary Policy Institute.

Leijonhufvud, Axel (2009). "Out of the Corridor: Keynes and the Crisis", *Cambridge Journal of Economics* 33: 741-757.

5 Learning from the Crisis

What can Central Banks do?

BENJAMIN M. FRIEDMAN

Unusual events, when of an immense magnitude, usually lead to introspection and learning, especially when they bring unwanted consequences. Even if no one is at fault for causing the event in the first place (an earthquake, for example), it is only natural to seek ways to mitigate the consequences, should a similar catastrophe recur. When what went wrong was itself the result of human action, the issue at stake is not merely containment but prevention.

The broader question is, to what extent are the lessons from such unusual events applicable in more normal times? No one expects the typical massive traffic jams when residents evacuate a coastal city before a hurricane, to occur at other times. Learning to manage such evacuations is helpful for occasions when they occur, but the knowledge has limited relevance for controlling ordinary traffic patterns.

As economists and policymakers now begin to sort out the wreckage of the financial crisis and economic downturn that began in 2007, these distinctions will inevitably be central to any normative lines of inquiry. What can central bankers, regulators, and others in positions of responsibility, do to constrain this kind of disruption?

If such a crisis does recur, what steps should policymakers take to contain its extent within the financial system and to limit its contractionary impact on non-financial economic activity? Does what policymakers did (or failed to do) during the crisis, shed light on how they should conduct monetary policy, or regulate banks and other financial institutions, in more normal times?

The crisis and downturn that began in 2007 constituted one of the most significant economic events since World War II. In some countries, the real economic costs—costs in terms of reduced production, lost jobs, shrunken investment and foregone incomes and profits—exceeded that of any prior post-war decline. In the United States, for example, the peak-to-trough decline in real output was 3.8 per cent, slightly greater than in 1957-1958. Even though unemployment has not reached the level that followed the 1981-82 recession, it seems likely to remain abnormally high for much longer than it did then.

To a greater extent than usual, the decline affected countries in all parts of the world, though it affected some more than others. With the overall volume of world trade down by 12 per cent in 2009 (by International Monetary Fund estimates), it is hardly surprising that so many export-oriented economies were affected. The sector most impacted by this latest episode, however, was the financial sector.

The collapse of major financial firms, the decline in asset values and consequent destruction of paper wealth, the interruption of credit flows, the loss of confidence both in firms and in credit market instruments, the fear of default by counter-parties and, above all, the intervention by central banks and other governmental institutions—both in scale and in form—were extraordinary. Whether this episode constitutes the worst real economic downturn since World War II, is for many countries, a close call. But there is no question that for the world's financial system, what happened was the greatest crisis since the 1930s.

This contrast—between a financial crisis exceeding anything in the prior two-thirds of a century and an economic downturn much more in line with prior post-war experience—immediately suggests where the most useful opportunities for learning may lie. What did policymakers do that so contained the crisis within the financial markets? What aspects of what they did offer lessons that may be applicable to more ordinary times? What changes are needed to lessen the likelihood of future crises, or to render them more readily containable should they occur?

I now spell out some of my principle conclusions. In determining how monetary policy influences non-financial economic activity, what principally matters is not money, but credit—its volume, its price and its availability. In setting interest rates, central banks now do not have just one policy instrument, but two. Over time horizons long enough to matter for monetary policy, the quantity of central bank liabilities can be varied more or less independently.

The composition of central bank assets also matters. Central bank securities holdings, when in large volumes, affect market interest rate relationships. In contrast, policymakers have not yet figured out what instruments are effective for restoring the vitality of bank lending markets, once lenders have become severely impaired.

What is now necessary is additional financial regulation, implemented by public policy. Neither self-regulation nor regulation by capital market creditors is effective for complex institutions in today's markets. One element of that regulation should be a separation between the deposit and credit aspects of banking and inherently risk-oriented trading activities (but not activities including trading and underwriting, in which risk is incidental to the provision of banking services).

In some countries, most obviously the United States, governments need expanded authority to resolve the failure of bank holding companies, independent broker-dealers and insurance companies. The classical rule for lender-of-last-resort policy—rescue illiquid firms but not insolvent ones—is no longer useful. In a financial crisis, the distinction between illiquidity and insolvency has become largely non-operational. A lender-of-last-resort policy, as well as regulation, would do well to distinguish between financial losses that reflect genuine loss of wealth to the economy and those that are merely one side of a zero-sum bet.

The crisis and the policy response

The broad story of the financial crisis that began in 2007 is by now well-known.[1] Beginning in the late 1990s, but especially once the relatively mild

1. There are numerous useful accounts that provide helpful narrative and detailed supporting statistical information. Some of the most recent examples include the IMF's October 2009 *Global Financial Stability Report* and Ch. 3-4 of the October 2009 *World Economic Outlook*; Part I of the OECD's December 2009 *Financial Market Trends*; and Ch. 2 of the BIS's December 2009 *Quarterly Review*; also see previous issues of the same publications. Central banks have also issued numerous useful accounts.

2001 recession had ended, house prices in the United States began to rise rapidly. Increasingly lax underwriting standards—high loan-to-value ratios, back-loaded payment schemes and little, if any, documentation—were both a cause and a consequence of the rise in prices. Less onerous lending conditions spurred demand for houses, while the rising value of the underlying collateral lessened concerns for the creditworthiness of borrowers.

Securitisation of a large fraction of the newly issued mortgages further lessened the originators' interest in their integrity. Investors in the created securities, or in derivatives based on them, either misled themselves (for example, similarly counting on rising house prices to nullify the implications of borrowers' lack of creditworthiness) or were misled by rating agencies that carried out inadequate analysis and also faced serious conflicts of interest. Significantly, many of these investors were non-US entities.

At the same time, two more general developments, one concerning financial institutions and the other concerning financial instruments, rendered the US financial system, and those who participated in it, more vulnerable. First, the distinction between banking and trading mostly disappeared—and not simply as a consequence of the formal repeal in 1999 of what remained of the Depression-era Glass-Steagall separation, which had largely eroded long before.

Most of the large commercial banks, facing the need to raise their own capital in competitive securities markets, relied increasingly on trading profits, in effect turning themselves into hedge funds. (Otherwise they would have had little reason to retain shares of the mortgage-backed securities that they earned fee income from, by packaging and selling.) Meanwhile, most of the large investment banks, which already had significant trading operations, increasingly used the repurchase-agreement market to fund themselves with what, in effect, amounted to short-term deposits.

Second, the continuing development of the market for financial derivatives moved beyond the role of enabling investors (including financial institutions) to hedge risks that they already bore and instead increasingly provided vehicles for taking on new, unrelated risks. This permitted participants to either speculate on changes in the market price of those risks, or to simply generate a new form of fee income. As a result, many of the risks to which investors became exposed bore little or no connection to fluctuations in any component of the economy's actual wealth. The risks borne, increasingly, were merely bets on one side or the other of a zero-sum game.

Given the vulnerability created by these two more fundamental developments, it is not surprising in retrospect that a sufficient catalyst would trigger a widespread crisis. The turnaround in US house prices, that began in late 2006, provided such a catalyst. By late 2007, house prices on a nation-wide basis were falling at a double-digit annual rate. By late 2008, the rate of decline was nearly 20 per cent nation-wide.

In some states, and in many local residential markets, the declines were significantly greater. (Because what matters for any individual mortgage is the specific house collateralising that loan, and the dispersion of price changes around a given average rate of decline worsens the probability of default.) Delinquencies and defaults increased especially in the market for 'subprime' mortgages. In time, so did foreclosures. In some areas, spreading foreclosures helped drive house prices down still further.

The resulting loss of value on mortgage-related securities accrued not only to investors, but also to many of the banks and other firms that had sponsored and distributed these securities (again, because they were acting as traders in addition to their role as originators and distributors). With only thin capitalisation—leverage ratios of 12-15 for a typical large commercial bank and 25-30 for a typical investment bank—the institutions taking the largest paper losses also lost the confidence of both equity investors and creditors.

Rolling over their short-term funding, therefore, became problematic. In effect, institutions that were not banks, sustained 'bank runs' on liabilities that were not deposits. (In the UK, where deposit insurance had long been inadequate, there were actual deposit runs on banks.) Interbank lending markets became subject to unprecedentedly wide spreads, and in many cases largely ceased to function. Moreover, once financial institutions lost the market's confidence, they became unable to participate in a wide variety of auxiliary transactions from which they ordinarily earned fee income. The counter-party risk that they presented was too great.

With so many banks and other lending institutions impaired in any or all these ways, credit for non-financial borrowers became increasingly scarce—and not just for housing finance. In August 2008, the month before the Lehman Brothers' failure, outstanding commercial and industrial loans of US banks totalled $1,558 billion.[2] By December 2009, these outstandings were only $1,343 billion. Over the same period consumer loans, from banks as well as other lenders, declined from $2,578 billion to $2,483 billion (latest data for October 2009).

The contraction of credit was much sharper in capital markets. The volume of asset-backed commercial paper outstanding dropped from $1,208 billion in July 2007 to only $489 billion in December 2009. Unsecured commercial paper issued by non-financial firms continued to increase irregularly through December 2008, reaching $206 billion, before falling to just $108 billion in December 2009. The total volume of new bond issues sold in the United States on behalf of US corporations, fell from $2.3 trillion in 2006 to only $749 billion in all of 2008.

In addition, declining asset values imposed a sizeable loss of real wealth on both households and firms. The value of corporate equities outstanding in US markets dropped from $26.4 trillion in the summer of 2007 to $13.9 trillion in early 2009. The value of residential real estate owned by households declined from $22.9 trillion at year end 2006 to $15.7 trillion in early 2009. Both the unavailability of credit and the loss of wealth presumably played a part in the drop in spending that ensued. Similar patterns, in greater or lesser degree, appeared in many other countries as well.

The sequence of actions that many of the world's central banks took in response to these events has been extraordinary and in the financial realm, is in many ways comparable to the broader burst of economic experimentation undertaken by the Roosevelt administration during the 'New Deal' period in the mid-1930s. As was the case then, some of the steps implemented seem to have enjoyed success while others have not. Relatively few have proved outright counter-productive (at least within the limited time to date).

---

2. Data, here and below, are from the Federal Reserve System (FRS).

In the United States, the initial indication of extraordinary action came in December 2007, when the Federal Reserve System (FRS) implemented the first of what would become a series of new credit facilities, the term auction facility (TAF), to channel additional central bank credit to commercial banks needing reserves. In March 2008, the Federal Reserve established two further credit facilities, the term securities lending facility (TSLF) and the primary dealer credit facility (PDCF) to extend central bank credit against a broader class of collateral, and also to non-banks.

In the same month, the Federal Reserve also provided an emergency loan to J.P. Morgan to facilitate the bank's takeover of Bear Stearns. In May 2008, the Federal Reserve expanded the TSLF to accept high-rated asset-backed securities as collateral. In July 2008, the Federal Deposit Insurance Corporation (FDIC) took over mortgage lender IndyMac. In September 2008, the US government placed the mortgage agencies Fannie Mae and Freddie Mac in receivership. Following the Lehman failure that month, the Federal Reserve approved the applications of Goldman Sachs and Morgan Stanley to become bank holding companies.

The Office of Thrift Supervision (OTS) closed mortgage lender Washington Mutual and the Securities and Exchange Commission (SEC) banned short-selling of financial stocks. In October 2008, the US Congress raised the limit on FDIC insurance to $250,000 per account. The Federal Reserve introduced a commercial paper funding facility (CPFF) and a money market investor funding facility (MMIFF). It also expanded several of its existing new Facilities. The US Treasury announced a plan to inject up to $250 billion of capital directly into key financial institutions (and the definition of Tier I capital was changed to include stock purchased by the Treasury).

The FDIC guaranteed the senior indebtedness of all regulated US financial institutions. In November 2008, the Federal Reserve and the Treasury jointly extended an emergency loan to insurance company AIG (American International Group Inc.). Both of them plus the FDIC extended special aid to Citigroup (including a non-recourse loan from the Federal Reserve), and the Federal Reserve began direct purchases of obligations issued by Fannie Mae and Freddie Mac.

In January 2009, the Federal Reserve, the FDIC and the Treasury jointly extended aid to Bank of America, on similar terms to what Citigroup received (including the non-recourse loan from the Federal Reserve). In February 2009, the Federal Reserve expanded its recently created term asset-backed securities loan facility (TALF) to $1 trillion and further widened the range of eligible collateral. As in the year before, so in 2009 too, the list of actions taken did not end here.

Outside the United States, extraordinary actions to arrest the crisis began even earlier. In September 2007, the Bank of England extended an emergency loan to Northern Rock. In February 2008, Britain nationalised Northern Rock outright. In October 2008, the Government of Ireland guaranteed the liabilities of the country's six largest banks. Several other European governments, most notably Iceland, either rescued outright major banks that were impaired or guaranteed their domestically domiciled banks' liabilities.

In January 2009, the UK government announced its comprehensive bank rescue plan. Beginning at the end of September 2008, the European Central Bank (ECB) undertook a special term-refinancing operation (in the amount of €20 billion), changed the tender procedure in its regular monetary policy operations to provide additional liquidity to the banking system, narrowed and then re-widened the 'corridor' between the interest rates on its two standing facilities (see the discussion below on the operation of 'corridor' systems for central bank setting of interest rates), lengthened the average maturity of its operations, expanded its list of eligible collateral, and introduced several special facilities allowing the bank to transact with new counter-parties or to undertake new kinds of transactions.

In Japan, which had been employing extraordinary policy measures since the early 1990s (so that by the time this crisis occurred, they no longer seemed so extraordinary in the Japanese context), the Bank of Japan expanded its securities lending facility. It increased both its outright purchases of Japanese government securities and its purchases via repurchase agreements. It expanded the range of private securities eligible for repurchase. The Bank of Japan also introduced outright purchases of commercial paper and corporate bonds and undertook special operations to provide funding for Japanese corporations.

At the same time, central banks carried out conventional monetary policies as well, though often in unconventional ways. In September 2007, the US Federal funds rate was 5.25 per cent. By January 2008, the Federal Reserve had lowered it to 3 per cent. In October 2008—after the Lehman collapse—it lowered the funds rate to just 1 per cent, and in December 2008, it went to 0.

The ECB, with its near-exclusive statutory focus on price stability, waited until October 2008 to lower its fixed rate, from 4.25 per cent to 3.75 per cent. By December 2008, the rate was down to 2 per cent. In March 2009, the ECB lowered it to 1.5 per cent, and in May 2009 to 1 per cent. The Bank of Japan, likewise, waited until October 2008 to ease monetary policy, cutting the uncollateralised call loan rate from 0.5 per cent to 0.3 per cent. In December 2008, it reduced the rate further, to 0.1 per cent.

International coordination among central banks was also a part of this story. To cite just one instance—in October 2008 or three weeks after the Lehman failure, the Federal Reserve, the ECB, the Bank of England, the Swiss National Bank, the People's Bank of China, the Bank of Canada and the Sveriges Riksbank, all cut their policy interest rates simultaneously. Most of the major central banks also took pre-emptive measures to enable themselves to act in support of stability in the foreign exchange markets. In December 2007, the Federal Reserve established new swap lines with the ECB and the Swiss National Bank, although for only $20 billion and $4 billion, respectively.

Over successive months, both lines were increased several times. In addition, Federal Reserve swap lines were opened with other central banks, including the Reserve Bank of Australia, the Sveriges Riksbank, Norges Bank, and Danmarks Nationalbank. By September 2008, the Federal Reserve's swap lines with these and other central banks totalled $620 billion. In October 2008, the Federal Reserve established new swap lines with the central banks of Brazil, Korea, Mexico and Singapore, in each case for $30 billion.

Although fiscal policy is beyond the scope of this paper, it is important to note that once the downturn began, many countries also enacted fiscal measures directed at stimulating economic activity. In the United States, for example, in January 2008, Congress passed a $150 billion stimulus package providing for cheques to be sent directly to households. In February 2009, Congress passed a $787 billion stimulus package combining a variety of spending increases (spread out over several years) and tax reductions.

Among other countries, the most notable fiscal action taken was the RMB 4 trillion ($586 billion) stimulus package announced by the Chinese government in November 2008. In the backdrop of decades of resistance to using discretionary fiscal policy to deliberate counter-cyclical stabilisation, these actions also stand out as among the extraordinary policy responses to the crisis and downturn that began in 2007.

Let us remember that this resistance to using fiscal policy for such purposes has prevailed among both professional economists and many policymakers for a variety of reasons. The grounds for resistance include the difficulty of knowing when such measures would be helpful, the difficulty in agreeing on what to do, the time required for implementation, and concerns that such measures would be an opportunity for politically motivated and unproductive spending.

Implications for monetary policy

In the context of monetary policy, the strongest single lesson of the crisis and the response to it, is that what matters is not money but credit.[3] Indeed, the economics profession's half-century-long fixation with money—how to measure it, how to control it, why households and firms hold it—appears, in retrospect, as mostly a distraction. Much of this was amply evident well before 2007. Most central banks had long given up their monetary targeting regimes. But the events of the crisis since 2007, and ensuing downturn, dramatised the point more sharply.

In most countries, money stock (however measured) had not fallen. The central bank had not allowed the monetary base to decline. There was no cause to believe that the reason households and firms were not spending,

3. In sufficiently simple textbook models—for example, when banks' assets consist only of loans and reserves, all bank liabilities are monetary deposits, banks' capital and reserves are fixed, and there are no non-bank lenders—money and credit move amorphically so that there is no point in drawing the distinction. But such models bear little relation to the modern world of banking and finance where banks have non-monetary sources of funding, their capital is not fixed, capital rather than reserves is often the binding constraint on their credit creation, and many credit-creating institutions are not banks and do not hold reserves with the central bank.

was that their holdings of money balances were too low. There was also no evidence that central bank restrictiveness in providing reserves was a cause of high interest rates. Soon into the crisis, risk-free interest rates in most countries were at historic lows. The obligations of private borrowers bore high rates because of perceived risk and the unavailability of credit and not because of insufficient reserves. The causes of the downturn lay elsewhere—specifically in restricted credit flows and depressed asset prices.

A second lesson, less widely recognised, is that nowadays most central banks do not normally set interest rates by increasing or decreasing the volume of reserves that they provide to their banking systems.[4] The traditional understanding of how a central bank sets a (presumably, short-term) interest rate involves its varying the supply of bank reserves, or some other subset of its own liabilities, in the context of an interest-elastic demand for those liabilities on the part of the private banking system.

The central bank may perhaps perceive this demand for its liabilities among other holders as well, including the non-bank public, if the measure of central bank liabilities taken to be relevant includes currency in circulation. It is clear that the central bank has monopoly control over the supply of its own liabilities.

Familiar reasons for banks holding central bank reserves include the need for balances with which to execute interbank transfers, as part of the ordinary payments mechanism. Banks also hold central bank reserves for a further need for currency to satisfy everyday demands of customers, specifically in systems in which vault cash is a part of banks' reserves. In some countries (for example, the United States) outright reserve requirements are imposed by the central bank.

The negative interest elasticity on the demand side follows as long as banks have, at least, some discretion in the amount that they hold for any or all of these purposes. It also depends on whether the interest that they earn on their reserve holdings differs from the appropriately risk-adjusted rates of return associated with alternative assets to which they have access.

Long before the crisis that began in 2007, however, this standard textbook account had ceased to bear a visible relationship to the way

4. The discussion of this point here follows that in Friedman and Kenneth (2009).

monetary policy was actually conducted by most of the world's major central banks. In the United States, though, central banking institutions still prevailed, particularly, reserve requirements and until 2008, the fact that no interest was paid on reserve balances. In the US, therefore, at least in principle, the standard story ought to have applied most naturally.

Yet, evidence indicated that before 2000, the amount by which the FRS increased or decreased bank reserves, to move the prevailing Federal funds rate, was not only extremely small, compared to the size of the markets in which US banks operate, but was becoming smaller over time. On many occasions moving the rate required no, or almost no, central bank transactions at all.

Since 2000, the amount by which reserves have changed on days of policy-induced changes in the Federal funds rate, has become noticeably larger on an average. But in a significant fraction of cases—one-third to one-fourth of all policy-induced rate changes—the movement in reserves has been in the wrong direction—a decrease in reserves accompanying a reduction in the interest rate, or vice versa.

In many systems outside the United States, where the central bank normally relies on a 'corridor' system to fix its policy interest rate, the absence of any relationship between the volume of reserves supplied and the movement in the rate follows more directly, at least at a daily frequency of observation. The implications of this absence of any relationship between reserves and interest rate movements have not received widespread attention, however.

ECB, for example, maintains standing facilities both for banks' deposits of reserves and for marginal lending of reserves by the Eurosystem central banks. The rate for banks' borrowing from the central bank is normally 200 basis points above the rate at which their deposits of excess reserve balances are remunerated. Other central banks maintain similar systems[5] and so may the United States, once the current period of near-zero short-term interest rates is over.

5. For a useful early analysis of the working of corridor systems for central bank interest rate setting, see Guthrie and Wright (2000).

As of 2008, the Federal Reserve now pays interest on excess reserves, at least in principle. As a result, it has to maintain a constant degree of supply-demand pressure in the market for reserves, at the margin, regardless of the total quantity supplied. Therefore, by varying the upper and lower boundaries of the corridor together (which is the usual practice in many such systems effected automatically by the structure of the two standing facilities), the cental bank can change its policy interest rate without necessarily making any change in its own balance sheet. The movement of the corridor, instead, changes banks' demand for reserves at a given interest rate.

This separation between the central bank's balance sheet and the influence it is exerting on short-term interest rates, either directly in a system like the ECB's, or more opaquely in the Federal Reserve's case, bears two significant implications. At a fundamental level, it represents a departure from the role of central bank liabilities that has underpinned much of monetary economics for more than a century. According to Wicksell's classic analysis, what was necessary to expand economic activity by maintaining the market interest rate above the 'natural' rate, was not just a one-time injection of additional reserves but a continual increase in the supply of reserves.

The 'accelerationist' view of inflation, by which real economic activity maintained at greater than the natural rate would lead, not to a one-time increase in prices but to a perpetual increase (in some renderings, a perpetual increase in the rate of increase), was therefore, consistent with the classical notion of a fixed relationship between prices and money—in this case, central bank money.[6]

In contrast, if a corridor system for interest rate setting enables the central bank to hold interest rates at a 'subnatural' level without any

6. 'If, other things remaining the same, the leading banks of the world were to lower their rate of interest, say 1 per cent, below its ordinary level, and keep it so for some years, then the prices of all commodities would rise and rise and rise without any limit whatever... the upward movement of prices, whether great or small in the first instance, can never cease so long as the rate of interest is kept lower than its normal rate, i.e., the rate consistent with the then existing marginal productivity of real capital.' Knut Wicksell (1907). "The Influence of the Rate of Interest on Prices", *Economic Journal* 17: 213-220; emphasis in the original.

increase in the supply of its liabilities, then at least one relationship in the chain running from interest rates, to real activity, to prices, to money, must break down. (Alternatively, over time the interest rate that the central bank sets in this manner would become 'decoupled' from the rest of economic activity—in particular, from anything bearing a connection to the marginal product of real capital.)[7]

The crisis and the policy response to it, however, have highlighted a further, more practical implication. At least over some period of time, potentially sufficient to matter for macroeconomic purposes, central banks have not one instrument of conventional monetary policy as is usually assumed, but two—not just the short-term interest rate or the quantity of central bank liabilities, but both the short-term interest rate and the quantity of central bank liabilities.

A reductionist form of this proposition had already become evident from the 'quantitative easing' programme undertaken by the Bank of Japan in the 1990s. But in that case, the central bank did not actually have two effective policy instruments. The occasion for the quantitative easing in the first place was that the Japanese short-term risk-free interest rate had reached the zero lower bound, so that the quantity instrument was a replacement for the interest rate instrument. In a narrow sense, the same is true in the United States today, where too the Federal funds rate is at the zero lower bound.

This focus, however, places too narrow a construction on the point at issue. For more than a decade, when US short-term interest rates were mostly far from zero, the quantity of reserves that US commercial banks held with the Federal Reserve, fluctuated narrowly around $40 billion. Reserves were approximately $40 billion when interest rates were high, and they were approximately $40 billion when interest rates were low.

Movements of the Federal funds rate implemented by the Federal Reserve had little or nothing to do with the quantity of reserves. But this absence of a relationship in turn implies that the Federal Reserve did not have to maintain the reserve quantity at $40 billion through all of this time. Presumably, it could have varied that quantity. And, especially if it

7. See Friedman (2000) for an analysis of what such a 'decoupling' would mean.

had implemented a corridor system (which it now has, at least in principle, since 2008), it could have varied the quantity of reserves with little or no implication for its ability to impose the interest rate level it chose.

In fact, the Federal Reserve did not avail itself of this opportunity. But once the crisis hit in 2007, the central bank significantly expanded its balance sheet. In December 2007, total reserves were (as usual) \$43 billion. By December 2008, they were \$820 billion. By December 2009, they were \$1,153 billion. (In contrast, the outstanding currency increased at a more normal pace, from \$758 billion in December 2007 to \$812 billion in December 2008 and \$858 billion in December 2009.)

Even considering the size of the US securities markets, these were very large increases in reserves and, therefore, in the total quantity of central bank liabilities. Other central banks implemented similar balance sheet expansions. The Bank of England's total assets are normally somewhat below 5 per cent of UK's gross domestic product (GDP). By mid-2009, they were nearly 16 per cent. The comparable increase for the ECB was from 10 per cent to almost 18 per cent of Euro-area GDP.

Moreover, once the central bank has a second, quantity-based instrument with which to affect the financial markets, the composition of the assets that it holds represents a further degree of freedom. Here the Federal Reserve presents the most striking case. As of year-end 2009, the Federal Reserve held \$2,220 billion of assets (against bank reserves, currency outstanding and all other liabilities). Nearly half of this total—\$910 billion—consisted of direct holdings of mortgage-backed securities (MBS) guaranteed by Fannie Mae, Freddie Mac or Ginnie Mae.

In ordinary times, the US central bank would have held none of these securities. Much of the rest of the year-end 2009 balance sheet likewise consisted of assets that the Federal Reserve ordinarily would not hold, or credit extended against securities that the Federal Reserve ordinarily would not accept as collateral. Only \$777 billion, out of the \$2,220 billion total, consisted of US Treasury obligations.

Presumably, these capital market interventions were intended not merely to affect the overall level of interest rates, but also to influence the structure of market interest rates—in other words, spreads. Were they effective? The Federal Reserve's objective in buying nearly \$1 trillion of mortgage-backed securities (MBS) was to restore liquidity to the market for these securities and reduce mortgage interest rates, thereby increasing the demand for houses and, hence, supporting house prices and stimulating residential construction.

Although, so far, there is little formal evidence bearing on the success of this large MBS purchase programme, conventional home mortgage rates in the United States have fallen from nearly six per cent in the summer of 2008 to below five per cent in the latter months of 2009, while Treasury rates remained roughly unchanged. More formal evidence for some of the Federal Reserve's other targeted lending facilities indicates an effect that is both statistically and economically significant.

After controlling for influences, such as the Federal funds rate, the Treasury bill rate, the Baa-Aaa bond spread, and the ratio of financial to non-financial firms' stock prices, regression-based evidence suggests that each $1 billion of purchases of commercial paper by the CPFF narrowed the spread between commercial paper rates and OIS (overnight indexed swap) rates by 2-4 basis points. In analogous regressions, the estimated per-dollar impact of use of the TAF is roughly twice as large.[8]

The remaining question, however, is what policy measures can restore the market for bank lending. Small businesses seeking to expand or finance inventories, and households seeking to buy automobiles or undertake other ordinary consumer expenditures, do not have access to the capital markets. As Japan discovered more than a decade ago, reviving bank lending in the wake of a financial crisis is highly problematic. As of December 2009, the US banks' portfolios of commercial and industrial loans, consumer loans, credit card loans, and interbank loans were all still shrinking.

Policy measures taken by agencies other than the Federal Reserve—emergency loans and direct injections of capital to the large banks, relaxation of rules for marking bank assets to market, and the likes may

8. Colin Motley, 'The Commercial Paper Funding Facility' (thesis in progress, Harvard University). The equation also includes the Aaa bond rate, the five-year credit default swap index for financial firms, the assets of money market funds and money market mutual funds, the volume of Federal Reserve term auction credit, and a dummy variable for the initial establishment of the CPFF. The dependent variable is the spread between the rate on three-month AA-rated financial company paper and the three-month OIS rate.

The notion of corporate governance exercised by a board of directors (with the board in turn responsible to the shareholders), has long been something of a fiction for most large publicly held companies. But many fictions are useful. What the crisis has helped demonstrate, is the extent to which this fiction has ceased to be useful. With an ever greater fraction of most corporations' stock held by passive entities, and shareholders not allowed even a non-binding advisory 'say' on compensation, it is not surprising that management incentives are often at odds with those of the firm's ultimate owners.

Yet another and also related lesson of the crisis is that vigilance by creditors is no effective substitute for regulation. Whether because they too face faulty governance and perverse incentives (reliance on what Louis David Brandeis a century ago, famously labelled 'Other People's Money' in 1914), or because they have become convinced that governments will issue blanket guarantees of insolvent firms' obligations, the idea of restraint exercised by lenders is no longer credible. Nor are the judgments of firms, like credit rating agencies, that supposedly serve as sources of information for lenders.

The implication is that, regulation is necessary and that, it is the responsibility of public policy to provide it. At least in the US context, the leading example of regulation that is needed but still missing, is a separation between trading functions—in which risk-taking is not an incidental consequence of providing some banking-related service (like underwriting or credit provision), but rather the central definition of the activity—and ordinary banking. In recent years, the tendency has been toward an ever greater fraction of banks, of any significant size, taking on proprietary trading activities that, in effect, amount to sole ownership of a hedge fund.

There is, however, no evidence of meaningful synergy between such risk-taking and either the deposit or the lending business. One possible explanation is that, margins in both deposit-taking and lending have been so competed away that ordinary banking business is no longer viable without a subsidy. Profits from an affiliated hedge fund operation are then, the most convenient way of providing that subsidy. Such a model is clearly not sustainable, however. (Why would hedge fund owners want to divert their profits to subsidise banking activity, or anything else for that matter?).

have prevented these declines from being still larger.[9] But at least so f have not yet stimulated any increase in lending. Perhaps, the best solı not to allow the banks to become so impaired in the first place—iı words, to rely on regulatory policy before the fact, not either monetar or lender-of-last resort policy once the crisis has occurred.

Implications for financial regulation

One inescapable principle that the events surrounding the crisi commenced in 2007 in the United States highlighted, is that, a dem gets the regulation it chooses. If voters elect public officials who c believe in regulation, and those office-holders appoint people who a not believe in regulation to lead the key agencies within the na regulatory apparatus, then there will not be effective regulation, no r what the prevailing statutes say.

Another lesson from the crisis, which makes this basic princi democratic governance all the more important, is that self-regulati 'for-profit private firms' is insufficient to meet the challenges present today's complex financial markets. One reason, to repeat, is that fina firms must raise their own capital in competitive securities marke second is that, a variety of features of today's financial firms, begir with limited liability but hardly limited to that one feature of the mc corporate structure, provide sharply distorted incentives compared to effective self-regulation would require.

When reading the classic texts on banking, like Thornton Bagehot, it is worth recalling that in Henry Thornton's time all Lor banks, except the Bank of England, had to be in partnerships wi maximum of six partners.[10] No other limited-liability 'joint stock ba were allowed. A third reason is that, the governance structure of l modern corporations in general, not just financial firms, is inadequate effectively guarding even the interests of these firms' stockholders.

9. Notwithstanding the widespread discussion of market-to-market accounting—and numerous complaints from bank officials—US commercial banks are required to v only a relatively small fraction of their assets in this way; see Pozen (2009). In 2(only 22 per cent of banks' assets were subject to market-to-market accounting purposes of either regulatory capital or income statements.

10. See Dunbar (1922). I am grateful to Kevin Hoover for the reference to Dunbar's t

Moreover, as the financial crisis that began in 2007 has shown, it is not clear whether this kind of trading is always profitable. When the losses accrue to banks in particular, the outcome involves externalities that impose potential costs or, more broadly, costs, that in the end, the taxpayer has to bear. If it were true that ordinary lending and deposit-taking were not viable businesses without a subsidy, the more plausible remedy would be some kind of pubic utility model. The need for a subsidy in the first place is, however, far from demonstrated.

The more apt lesson to draw from the crisis is that the regulatory structure should impose (in the United States, reimpose!) a separation between inherently risk-taking trading and banking. Banking in this context includes not only lending and deposit-taking, but also related activities, like trading, where risk-taking is not inherent, but rather ancillary to the provision of banking services. Whether such a separation need take the form of an outright prohibition, or merely incentives provided through tax and accounting mechanisms, is an open question that merits serious analysis.

In numerous other settings, for example, accounting rules distinguish between gains and losses on positions taken to hedge other positions and those taken 'naked.' To cite the most obvious application, it would be relatively straightforward to distinguish between credit default swaps (CDS) used by banks to hedge the risk associated with extending credit to a corporate borrower (where a CDS position would be no greater than the amount of the bank's credit exposure) and the use of CDS simply as a speculative vehicle.

Since the outstanding market of CDS volume today is normally large compared to the indebtedness of the firms against which these swaps are written, it is likely that many participants in this market are using them for the latter purpose. Either barring banks outright from doing so, or providing tax and accounting incentives to prevent them from doing so, would be one useful element of a regulatory separation between banking and inherently risk-oriented trading.

Another question of some immediate significance in a number of countries (the US included), is what role central banks should play in the regulation of banks and, perhaps, of other financial firms as well. This issue lies well beyond the scope of this paper. It is useful to note, however, that evidence for the United States indicates significant cross-relationships between the kind of macroeconomic information that central banks ordinarily create and use in the course of monetary policymaking and the information that is usually at the heart of most bank supervision activity.

Specifically, information contained in US banks' CAMEL ratings turns out to have significant marginal predictive value for key macroeconomic variables of interest to monetary policy (output growth, for example, or unemployment), and information contained in the Federal Reserve's internal macroeconomic forecasts (the 'Greenbook') likewise, has significant marginal predictive value for aggregate bank ratings and outcomes.[11]

Implications for lender-of-last-resort policy

Lender-of-last-resort policy is different now than it was when Henry Thornton and Walter Bagehot wrote about it.[12] Banks are no longer the simple partnerships that they were in Thornton's day, and Bagehot's assumption that the overwhelming majority of banks were soundly managed and 'solvent' would sound hopelessly naive today. (What remains unchanged, however, is the potential fall-out from the failure of a large bank. As Bagehot wrote, 'no cause is more capable of producing a panic, perhaps none is so capable, as the failure of a first-rate joint stock bank in London.') More importantly, the difficulty of assessing a proper value for illiquid assets has rendered Bagehot's famous rule—'lend freely at a penalty rate against good security'—impossible to implement. In situations like the crisis that commenced in 2007, in which banks held large volumes of securities (compared to their capital) that were not trading, and for which prospects for future cash flows were highly uncertain, distinguishing what was or was not a 'good security' was precisely the sticking point.

For just the same reason, the frequently stated corollary of Bagehot's rule—'come to the rescue of illiquid firms but not insolvent ones'—has become equally impossible to implement in such a crisis. For practical

11. See Peek *et al.* (1999).

12. See Thornton (1802) and Bagehot (1873).

purposes, the distinction between illiquidity and insolvency has disappeared. Depending on the hypothetical value attached to these illiquid securities with uncertain future cash flows, any given bank was either solvent or not.

To be sure, fair-value accounting does not require holders to price illiquid assets at 'fire sale' prices. But for many of the securities at the heart of the crisis that originated in 2007, the gap between the price that a forced liquidation would fetch and the present discounted value of all of the promised cash flows if paid as scheduled, was vast—and for many securities remains vast. What arbitrary valuation to place on them, somewhere between those respective lower and upper bounds, was (and for many banks remains) the difference between solvency and insolvency.

The more obvious lesson of the crisis in the United States, is the need for enhanced resolution authority for cases in which the central bank (or other elements of the government) chooses not to effect a rescue. Under prevailing US law, the Office of Comptroller of the Currency (OCC) and the FDIC are empowered to take over a bank, but there is no such authority for a bank holding company.

If policymakers had wanted to temporarily nationalise one or another of the most impaired commercial banks, rather than buy shares in them and guarantee their liabilities, they would have had to leave both the holding companies and all of their other constituent parts in private hands (but without the prospect of support from the bank). There is similarly no such authority for the government to take over an insurance company, or an independent broker-dealer. Bankruptcy remains a possibility, of course, but without the expedited resolution that the OCC/FDIC procedure provides.

As a result, the choice policymakers face is often between supporting impaired and perhaps, insolvent firms on terms unfavourable to taxpayers and risking the market disorder consequent to a protracted bankruptcy procedure—like what occurred after the Lehman failure. Moreover, because impaired firms' owners and managers understand that this is the choice policymakers face, they are able to use the threat of bankruptcy—'playing the bankruptcy card'—to extort terms in a voluntary takeover that are more favourable to themselves and even more unfavourable to the taxpayer. This is what happened in the takeover of Bear Stearns by J.P. Morgan.

Legislation to provide expanded resolution authority is now pending before the US Congress. Enacting it would fill a significant gap in US policy authority. Another helpful measure, for use in cases in which either the central bank acts as lender-of-last-resort or the relevant authority nationalises an impaired firm, would be to distinguish (along the lines suggested above) between losses that are reflections of genuine losses to the economy and losses that represent merely one side or the other of a zero-sum bet.

When the value of a house falls, for example, that is a loss of wealth to the economy as a whole. If the homeowner continues to service the mortgage, he bears the loss himself. His net worth is diminished by the amount of the price decline. If the homeowner defaults on the loan, then someone else—either the bank that originally lent the money or some investor to whom the bank sold the loan—also bears part of the loss. If the government steps in and reimburses the bank, or the investor, then taxpayers will bear part of it too.

This loss is divided, however. What is inescapable is that someone, somewhere, will bear it. What much of the debate surrounding the crisis of 2007 and after, was (and still is!) about how these losses should be divided among homeowners, banks, loan-purchasing investors and the taxpayers. But the losses that occurred must be borne by someone and the US economy is poorer because of them.

In comparison, if two firms have bet on, say, whether the peak temperature in Mumbai on some designated day would exceed 90°F, one will turn out to be right, the other wrong. One will win, the other will lose and the amount the winner wins will be identical to what the loser loses. There is no loss of wealth to the economy involved, merely a transfer of wealth from the loser to the winner. Many of the huge losses that financial institutions around the world sustained in the recent crisis were of this second kind.

For each of these positions, on the other side of the bank or insurance company (the obvious US example was AIG) that posted losses and turned to the taxpayers for assistance, there was also somewhere, a winner. The most transparent example of this phenomenon, and the most important in the crisis that began in 2007, is again credit default swaps. In the case of many, if not most of these contracts, the volume of swaps outstanding far exceeded the amount of debt that the specified company, whose credit was being insured, owed.

Most of these swaps, therefore, had nothing to do with allocating genuine losses of wealth. Instead, they simply created losses for the firms that bet incorrectly, exactly matched by gains for the corresponding winners. This fundamental distinction, between shares in losses to the economy and what are instead, merely the losing side of zero-sum bets, has potentially important implications for lender-of-last-resort policy.

It should matter, in deciding which insolvent institutions to rescue and which to let fail, whether the losses incurred represent a share of a genuine loss to the economy or the losing side of a zero-sum bet. Moreover, (as the discussion above has already indicated), this distinction also has implications for regulation. There is a clear case for discouraging, or possibly even barring, institutions that might be eligible for government bailouts from making these zero-sum bets.

A more fundamental question

Right at the start, I have summarised my principal specific conclusions for monetary policy, for financial regulation and for lender-of-last-resort policy, so there is no need to restate them. Instead, it seems appropriate in conclusion, to pose a more fundamental question. How well is the world's financial system, or the financial system of any specific country, performing the economic function it is supposed to be serving? And at what cost?

For the past two years, at least in the United States, attention has mostly been focused on investors' losses from buying mortgage-backed assets at inflated prices. There has not been much focus on the implied consequence, that if the bond prices were too high then mortgage interest rates were too low and hence, the economy built, and Americans bought, too many houses.

In just the same way, when the 1990s stock market boom crashed, what most people talked about was investors' losses on their telecom stocks, not the fact that if the stock prices were too high, then the cost of capital to the firms that issued them was too low and so, the communications industry world-wide laid millions of miles of fibre optic cable that nobody ended up using. In both instances, the cost was not just financial losses, but wasted real resources.

The crucial role of the financial system in a free-enterprise economy is to allocate capital investment towards the most productive applications. (As noted above, the financial system also provides payment services, along with safe and convenient saving vehicles for individuals, but these are more straightforward tasks that a public utility arrangement could just as well handle.)

The energetic growth and impressive technological advance of the Western economies, over what is now a long period of time, suggest that their banks and their stock and bond markets steer investment capital reasonably well to firms that will use them productively. In the United States, and in some other economies too, start-up firms trying out a wholly new idea (for example, Microsoft, or Google, or Apple) enjoy access to bank loans, venture capital investments, and other forms of funding. The financial crisis and economic downturn that began in 2007 blemishes this record of accomplishment, but certainly does not wipe it away.

But the issue is important enough to warrant questioning and even serious empirical investigation, not just simple faith. Moreover, framing the question in terms of just how efficient a financial system is in allocating capital provides a natural point of entry for also asking at what price that efficiency comes.

If a new fertiliser offers a farmer the prospect of a higher crop yield, but the price of the fertiliser and the cost of transporting and spreading it exceeds what the additional produce will fetch at the market, the investment is a bad deal for the farmer despite the greater technical efficiency. Most investments in mechanisms that make things happen are subject to the same principle. A financial system, which allocates scarce investment capital, is no different.

What does the Western world's way of allocating an economy's capital cost to run? In the United States in recent years, the financial industry has accounted for an unusually large share of all profits earned. The 'finance' sector's share of total corporate profits rose from 10 per cent on an average, from the 1950s through the 1980s to 22 per cent in the 1990s and 34 per cent in the first half of this decade.[13]

In a fundamental sense, these profits accruing to the financial sector are part of what the economy pays for the mechanism that allocates its investment capital (and also provides other services, like checking accounts and savings deposits). Even a bare-bones notion of the cost of running the financial system, however, includes not just the profits financial firms earn, but also the salaries, the office rents, the travel budgets, the advertising fees and all of the other expenses they incur. The finance industry's share of US wages and salaries has likewise been rising, from three per cent in the early 1950s to seven per cent in the current decade.[14]

The counterpart to this rising fraction of wages and salaries paid is the financial system's absorption of an ever greater share of the economy's human resources. This pattern has been especially evident among the most highly skilled. For years now, much of the best young talent in the Western world has gone into private financial firms. At Harvard University, for example, more than one-fourth of recent graduating classes have gone to work at hedge funds, private equity firms, investment banks and the like.

The same is true elsewhere as well and more so over time. The extent to which employees in the US economy's financial sector are more likely to have college educations than employees working elsewhere in the economy, has more than tripled over the last three decades. At the individual level, no one can blame these new graduates.

At the aggregate level, however, the question is whether the economy is making the best use of one of its most precious resources. While some part of what these people do helps to allocate our investment capital more effectively, much of their activity adds no apparent economic value.

Finally, to return to the lessons of the experience beginning 2007, this latest episode is a sharp reminder that the simple operating expense of running the financial system (including both the profits accruing to

---

13. Data are from the US Department of Commerce. 'Finance' here excludes both insurance and real estate; with those additional firms included, the share of total profits in 2001-2005 was 37 per cent.

14. See Philippon and Reshef (2007).

financial firms and the wages and salaries they pay) is not the only cost if this system also exposes the economy at large to occasional losses in the form of foregone production and incomes, and to the need for taxpayer assistance.

To recall the example of what makes a new fertiliser a good deal for the farmer, it is not just that it delivers greater production per acre, but that the added production is sufficient to pay the manufacturer and leave an excess to increase the farmer's own return. What makes a more efficient financial system economically worthwhile, is not just that it facilitates greater production and economic growth, but that the rest of the economy benefits. The more the financial system costs to run—including costs like those incurred in the crisis beginning 2007 and the ensuing downturn—the higher is the hurdle for satisfying that criterion.

References

Bagehot, Walter (1873). *Lombard Street: A Description of the Money Market*. London: Henry S. King and Co.

Dunbar, Charles F. (1992). *The Theory and History of Banking*. G.P. Putnam's Sons.

Friedman, Benjamin M. (2000). "Decoupling at the Margin: The Threat to Monetary Policy from the Electronic Revolution in Banking", *International Finance* 3(2): 261-272.

Friedman, Benjamin M. and Kenneth N. Kuttner (2009). "Implementation of Monetary Policy: How Do Central Banks Set Interest Rates?". *Handbook of Monetary Economics* 3. October 29-30, (forthcoming). Elsevier.

Graeme, Guthrie and Julian Wright (2000). "Open Mouth Operations", *Journal of Monetary Economics* 46(2): 489-516. October. Elsevier.

Joe, Peek, Eric S. Rosengren and Geoffrey M.B. Tootell (1999). "Is Bank Supervision Central to Central Banking?", *Quarterly Journal of Economics* 114: 629-653. May.

———. (forthcoming). "Is Financial Stability Central to Central Banking?", *After the Fall: Re-evaluating Supervisory, Regulatory and Monetary Policy*. Federal Reserve Bank of Boston.

Philippon, Thomas and Ariell Reshef (2007). "Skill Biased Financial Development: Education, Wages and Occupations in the U.S. Financial Sector", *NBER Working Paper* No. 13437.

Pozen, Robert C. (2009) "Is It Fair to Blame Fair Value Accounting for the Financial Crisis?", *Harvard Business Review* 87(11). November.

Thornton, Henry (1802). *An Enquiry into the Nature and Effects of the Paper Credit of Great Britain.* Hatchard.

5.1
DISCUSSION

Some Problems of Feasible Policies

JØRGEN ELMESKOV

I will mainly focus on two observations Prof. Friedman makes on monetary policy and both relate to feasibility. The first, is that the crisis response has revealed that it is feasible for central banks to divorce interest rate setting from liquidity supply. The second observation is that it is feasible for central banks to affect asset prices and market interest rates through the composition of the asset side of their balance sheet.

That something is feasible does not, of course, mean that it is without problems and limits. Some of the problems and issues with these feasible policies come out clearly whenever these crises-driven policies are relinquished. So, I will focus on some of the issues that have arisen when central banks have exited from such policies, but will dwell on them in more detail in the chapter that Makoto Minegishi and I have authored together. I will also make a few remarks on points Prof. Friedman raises on a central bank's lender-of-last-resort policies.

So, I begin with the point on the decoupling of interest rate and liquidity policy. This will be relevant in the context of central banks wanting to exit from policies dictated by the crisis and when they want to raise interest rates, while banks still have huge excess reserves. When excess reserves are ample, it is hard for central banks to raise the overnight rate unless the rate on deposits, which acts as a floor under overnight rates, is raised as well. This is feasible now that most central banks pay interest on deposits.

There are a number of downsides to this approach, though, which essentially makes the deposit rate the central bank's main instrument for

---

Comments by Jørgen Elmeskov on the paper presented by Benjamin M. Friedman 'Learning from the Crisis: What can Central Banks do?'.

macro-stabilisation. One of the downsides is that continuing with ample liquidity and using the deposit rate as the main instrument could effectively kill the money market. Another downside is that very large reserves in the banking system may at some point spill over into money and/or credit.

A bit of that would, of course, be nice in current circumstances. But a risk is that rapid money or credit growth could destabilise inflation expectations. There is also a risk that the liquidity could spill over into asset price movements out of line with fundamentals. So, a policy that is feasible, is not without problems. Because of the problems I mentioned, as well as others, central banks may prefer to mop up liquidity as conditions in the financial sector improve and aim to get back to something resembling a more normal situation on excess reserves.

The mopping up should occur more or less automatically as far as the various extensions of traditional liquidity instruments are concerned, assuming that they are reversed. I am thinking of extensions of the duration and amounts of liquidity operations, the range of collateral, and the range of counter-parties. In some countries, however, liquidity has also been boosted by the purchase of long-dated assets. In these cases, mopping up the corresponding liquidity will require action by the central bank which, apart from selling the assets back, could include using the long-dated assets to perform reverse repos, offering long-term deposits, or issuing central bank bills.

This brings me to Prof. Friedman's observation on the role central bank asset purchases play. A number of central banks have engaged in the outright purchase of long-dated assets. In particular, both the US Federal Reserve and the Bank of England have intervened heavily in the government bond market. The Federal Reserve has, however, also intervened heavily in markets for mortgage-backed securities. These long-dated interventions have probably helped boost activity, but they expose the central bank balance sheet to interest rate risk and in the case of private assets, to credit risk, at least when the assets are not underwritten by the government.

Continued holding of these assets is also likely to continue to affect the relevant prices, with the risk of inducing economic distortions. That may be a particular concern for housing markets that are very susceptible to mortgage interest rates. Getting out, though, is not so simple. Selling the long-dated assets could generate volatility in the respective markets and can be expected to be politically unpopular. It will probably have to be a slow process.

It would most probably also lead to the realisation of losses on bonds bought while prices were high. These losses could be potentially large. That again could pose political and credibility problems for the central bank. This political risk is less of a concern if, like the Bank of England, the central bank has an explicit *ex ante* agreement with the government to be indemnified for any losses. In any case, my point is again that a policy which is feasible is not without problems.

Let me conclude with two brief remarks on Prof. Friedman's observations concerning the lender-of-last-resort function of central banks. First, it is, of course, true that it has become more difficult to distinguish illiquidity from insolvency with the increased role of financial products that are not traded on exchanges and whose markets tend to become very illiquid in a crisis. Before resigning in the face of this development, though, it should be noted that some of the financial reforms currently being discussed relate exactly to OTC (over-the-counter) products and the scope for moving these onto exchanges.

Second, the distinction between genuine losses of wealth to the economy and losses that occur as a result of a zero-sum game is analytically attractive. As an example of the latter, Prof. Friedman suggests bets on today's temperature in Mumbai. But I wonder about the relevance of this distinction for resolution of lender-of-last-resort policies. The institutions that bet wrongly on the temperature in Mumbai could still be systemic ones, unless institutions are functionally separated so that those engaging in zero-sum games are not covered by the lender-of-last-resort function and vice versa. Undertaking such a separation may not be easy.

So, let me end by repeating that I mostly agree with Prof. Friedman. But he talks of drawing lessons for policy in normal times. And I guess I would want to reserve the monetary policies that I have discussed, and which are indeed feasible, for extraordinary circumstances.

6 Unconventional Monetary Policy

Experience and Possible Exit Strategies

JØRGEN ELMESKOV
MAKOTO MINEGISHI

Central banks in the Organisation for Economic Cooperation and Development (OECD) countries have responded vigorously to the challenges posed by the crisis. They have used their traditional monetary policy instruments to the extent possible, taking policy rates to very low levels. Going beyond conventional instruments, they have expanded the scope of liquidity management beyond traditional counter-parties, term length and sources of collateral to provide ample liquidity to the banking system.

Moreover, some central banks have engaged in open market operations covering a range of assets to stimulate aggregate demand and safeguard financial stability. These unconventional monetary policy measures have, along with traditional interest rate policy and government fiscal and financial market policies, helped contain the economic downturn and strengthen confidence in the financial markets.

We document these unconventional measures, assess their impact and discuss possible exit strategies in the cases of the five major OECD central banks.[1] We first summarise measures taken in response to the crisis, focus on how they have led to changes in both size and composition of the monetary base and assess their impacts on financial market developments.

1. Minegishi and Cournède (2010) provide evidence also pertaining to Sveriges Riksbank (Riksbank) and the Swiss National Bank (SNB).

We then discuss the potential implications of the exit strategies for financial market functioning and inflationary concerns and finally, highlight the importance of formulating, communicating and ultimately executing appropriate exit strategies. We conclude with some open questions on how the overall framework for monetary policy implementation may have to be reassessed after central banks exit from the measures taken to combat the financial crisis.

Monetary policy measures taken in response to the crisis

Monetary policy responses of major advanced economies

As the financial crisis intensified, the reactions of central banks were unprecedented in both speed and scope (Table 6.1). Apart from exhausting the use of the traditional tool of short-term interest rates, major central banks took on more risk than usual and occasionally become *de facto* market-makers in a number of important areas. Monetary policy measures taken so far can be largely categorised into the following five elements:[2] (i) lowering policy rates to very low levels, (ii) increasing the liquidity provision for financial institutions,[3] (iii) intervening directly in wider segments of the financial market, (iv) purchasing long-term government bonds, and (v) supporting specific institutions.

While these actions are similar in some aspects (for example, the provision for ample liquidity), they nevertheless differ considerably across central banks in both scope and magnitude. Discrepancies are particularly large on the extent to which central banks have intervened in wider market segments and taken on long-dated assets (see below). These differences are highlighted by a significant divergence in the stated focus. Each central bank has communicated a set of policy actions using its own terminology, such as 'credit easing' for the US Federal Reserve, 'enhanced credit support'

2. Many of these measures were aimed at restoring stability in the financial markets and were not necessarily directly linked to the macroeconomic goal of price stability. Indeed, one could narrowly focus on unconventional measures that solely target stimulating aggregate demand, as was done by Meier (2009). However, in the current crisis, financial stability and macroeconomic stability objectives have been intertwined: measures to restore financial stability have been taken so as to prevent a negative feedback loop whereby financial weakness induces economic sluggishness.

3. As by-products, liquidity-absorbing measures have also been extended.

for the European Central Bank (ECB) and 'quantitative easing' for the Bank of England (BoE).[4] The difference appears to reflect dissimilarities in central banks' pre-existing operational and institutional setups, in the structures of their economies, as well as in the judgements made on the functioning of monetary transmission.

Table 6.1

Central bank measures in response to the crisis

	Fed	*ECB*	*BoJ*	*BoE*	*BoC*
Lowering policy rates to very low levels	x	*De facto*	x	x	x
Increasing liquidity provision to financial institutions	x	x	x	x	x
Intervening directly in wider segments of the financial market	x	x	x	x	
Purchasing long-term government bonds	x		x	x	
Support for specific institutions	x		x	x	

Lowering policy rates to very low levels

In response to the crisis, central banks have aggressively cut policy rates in most cases to levels where the zero lower bound is effectively binding (Figure 6.1). Moreover, with the aim of influencing expectations so that bond yields fall beyond the shortest horizon, some central banks have explicitly indicated that exceptionally low interest rates are to be maintained for some time. They have done this either through verbal guidance without date specification (as has the Fed), conditional commitment until a specific date (as in the case of the Bank of Canada) or publication of a future policy rate path (like the Sveriges Riksbank).

Increasing the provision for liquidity for financial institutions

The crisis had immediate effects on the money market. As market participants faced exceptional uncertainty about their own liquidity needs,

4. We do not use these terms to avoid confusion. The wording 'quantitative easing' appears particularly problematic, as it is also used in a broader sense to imply any policy that involves an active use of the balance sheet of central banks. Borio and Disyatat (2009) argue that the discussion of unconventional measures has been complicated by the use of different definitions and propose a systematic framework to categorise them, focusing on the differing use of balance sheets.

while becoming extremely wary of counter-party risk, money market interest rates rose relative to risk-free rates. With many banks simply hoarding liquidity, the transaction volume in the market reportedly diminished considerably. In response, central banks greatly eased the conditions under which they lend liquidity to banks.

The new focus on the available amount rather than simply the price of liquidity has been dictated to some extent by effectively reaching the zero lower bound. But many central banks started to increase the liquidity provision significantly, while the policy rate was still clearly in positive territory. The objective was to meet the significantly increased demand for liquidity, caused by higher liquidity preference, prompted by stronger precautionary demand and lower opportunity costs of holding reserves.

Enhanced liquidity measures taken by central banks exhibit a number of common characteristics, despite a wide variety in actual schemes. For instance, amounts of liquidity offers have been significantly expanded (through the introduction of the term auction facility (TAF) for the Fed, for instance) or in some cases made limitless (as in the case of full allotment of the ECB's refinancing operations).

This contrasts sharply with the pre-crisis norm, in which central banks provided only a limited amount of liquidity to the money market, just enough to align the effective market rate with the policy rate. The duration of liquidity operations has been significantly lengthened in contrast to much shorter pre-crisis norms (typically overnight or one week).

In addition, relying on mutual currency swap agreements across major central banks, liquidity in foreign currency was also provided to financial institutions directly from the respective central banks. Moreover, particularly where the traditional lists of acceptable collateral and monetary policy counter-parties were restrictive, requirements for collateral eligibility were relaxed and eligible counter-parties to central bank operations expanded.

Central banks have also introduced new liability management tools to drain excess liquidity. For instance, short-term central bank bills have been introduced by the Bank of England (and the Swiss National Bank), and been used more actively by the Riksbank, but this instrument does not exist for the Fed. Government deposits have sometimes played a role in effectively draining liquidity from the banking system (for example, the Fed). In addition, many central banks (Fed, Bank of Japan, Bank of England and Bank of Canada) now remunerate excess reserves at the policy target rates.[5] On the other hand, the deposit rate in the Euro area has been kept significantly below the main policy rate.[6] In an environment of ample liquidity provision, effective market rates have tended to fall to below the main policy rate to levels much closer to the deposit rate (Figure 6.1).[7] This implies that the main refinancing rate can no longer be considered as the main indicator of the monetary policy stance (ECB, 2010).

Intervening directly in wider segments of the financial market

Central banks have also moved beyond traditional activity in money markets to intervene directly in other market segments, to boost market sentiment, increase market liquidity and uphold prices. Reflecting differences in financial market structures across economies, these types of central bank interventions differ more than in the case of liquidity provision (Table 6.2). Given the importance of capital market funding to the US economy, the Fed has been the most active in this regard.

Many other central banks have also decided to purchase outright various categories of private sector assets, although the magnitude of interventions has generally been far smaller in comparison with the Fed. Some central banks have intervened in an even more unusual way. The Bank of Japan (BoJ) has decided to resume its purchases of corporate equities with the aim of reducing banks' risk exposure to fluctuations in share prices.[8] Outside the major OECD central banks, the SNB has

---

5. This may have the effect of discouraging lending activity in the interbank market, as banks are reluctant to lend to each other, relying instead on central bank facilities.

6. The Riksbank has also maintained a relatively wide corridor and the standing deposit facility now yields negative interest rate. In practice, however, it has been seldom used as the Bank conducts large liquidity absorbing fine-tuning operations at a significantly higher positive rate.

7. The effective overnight rate for euro (EONIA) was about 30 bps at the beginning of March 2010, much closer to the rate in the deposit facility (25 bps) than to the main refinancing rate (100 bps).

8. As a legacy of traditional cross-holding of stocks, the equity holdings of Japanese banks have typically been important.

Figure 6.1

Policy-determined and money market interest rates

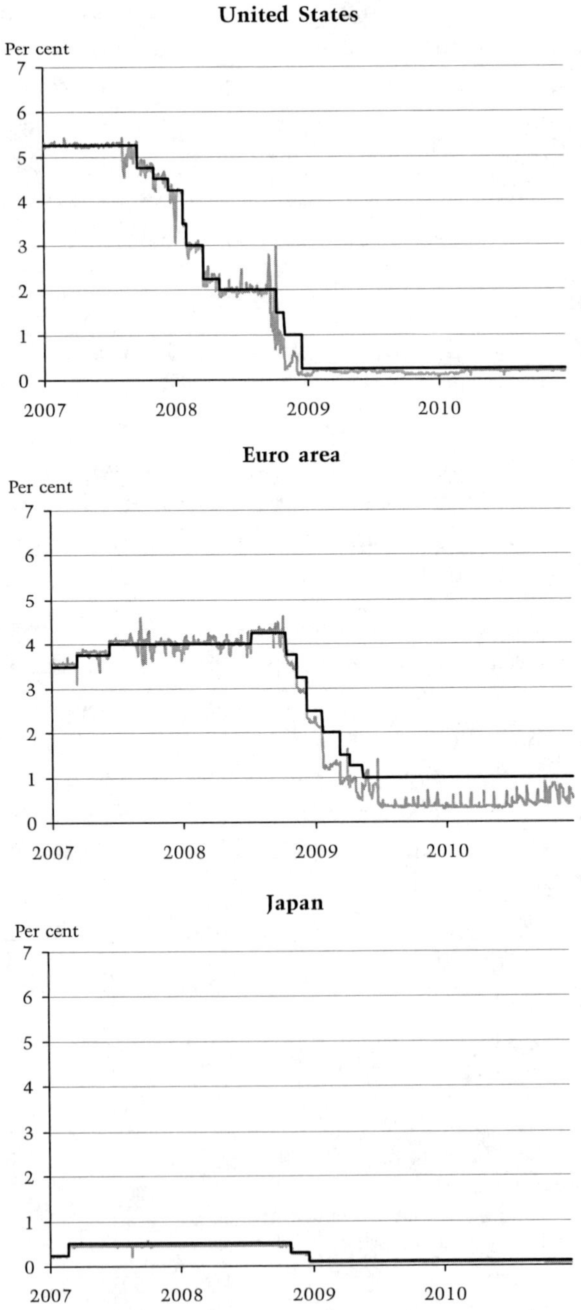

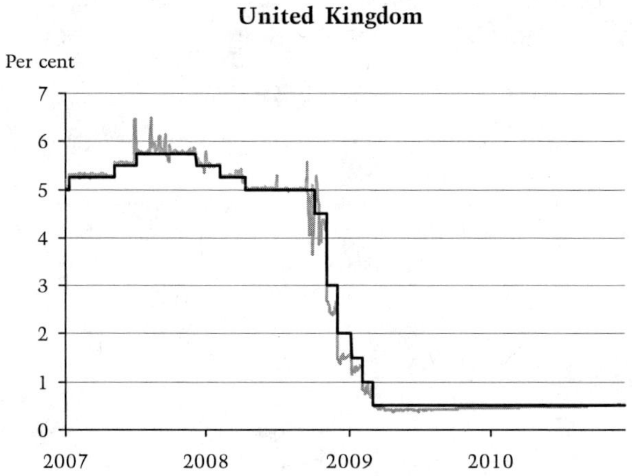

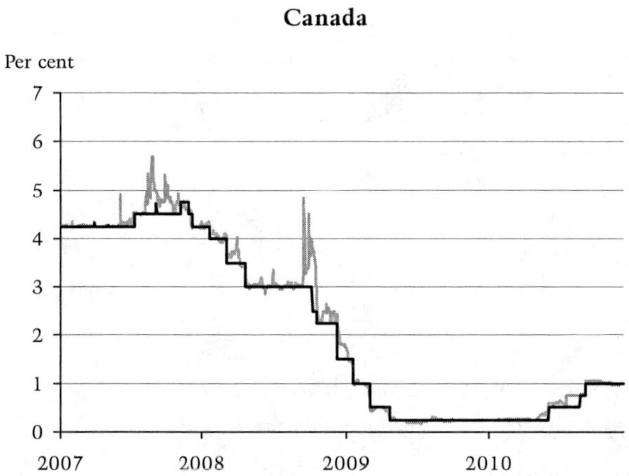

Note: The solid line represents the policy rate of the central banks. United States: federal funds target rate; Euro area: main refinancing operations, minimum bid rate; Japan: overnight uncollateralised call rate; United Kingdom: repo rate; Canada: Bank of Canada's target for the overnight financing rate.

The grey lines show actual money market rates. Money market interest rates; United States: effective federal funds rate; Euro area: EONIA (Euro overnight index average); Japan: collateralised unconditional overnight call rate; United Kingdom: SONIA (Sterling overnight index average rate); Canada: call loans overnight rate.

Sources: Bloomberg, Bank of Japan, Datastream and ECB.

conducted unsterilised interventions in the foreign exchange market to prevent further appreciation of the Swiss franc against the Euro.

Table 6.2

Direct intervention and purchase of long-term government bonds by central banks

	Fed	*ECB*	*BoJ*	*BoE*	*BoC*
Commercial paper	x[1]		x[2]	x[5]	
Corporate debt			x[2]	x[5]	
Mortgage-backed securities	x[2]				
Agency bonds	x[2]				
Securitised products	x[3]				
Covered bonds		x[2]			
Equity			x[4]		
Long-term government bonds	x[2]		x[6]	x[5]	

Notes: 1. Asset-backed commercial paper money market fund liquidity facility (AMLF), Commercial paper funding facility (CPFF) and Money market investor funding facility (MMIFF).
2. Direct purchase programme.
3. Term asset-backed securities loan facility (TALF).
4. Direct purchase of equity held by banks.
5. Asset purchase facility (APF).
6. Increased monthly pace of outright purchases.

Purchasing long-term government bonds

In addition, some major central banks have introduced or increased outright purchase of long-term government bonds (Table 6.2). They have purchased government bonds to either facilitate the liquidity provision over longer-term horizons (like the BoJ), to lower the risk-free rate over medium to long-term horizons (thereby easing credit conditions across a wide spectrum as in the case of the Fed) or to expand the monetary base (like the BoE). Central banks have, however, refrained from purchasing government bonds in the primary market, to avoid fuelling fears that they might monetise fiscal deficits.

Support for specific institutions

Both the Fed and the BoE (as well as the Riksbank and the SNB) have engaged in emergency liquidity provisions to individual financial institutions.[9] Although these measures may be considered to be a part of the traditional lender-of-last-resort function of central banks, the counterparty sometimes included institutions that have been normally considered to be beyond the scope of the lender-of-last-resort function. Central banks also seem to have gone beyond the usual criteria for the quality of the collateral they have accepted in some of these operations.

Response from monetary authorities in emerging economies

Reflecting the truly global nature of the crisis, monetary authorities in emerging economies have also significantly eased monetary policy (Ishi *et al.*, 2009 and Yehoue, 2009) in ways that in some respects resemble actions by central banks in major advanced economies. A number of central banks in emerging countries have substantially reduced policy interest rates, among them—Brazil, Chile, China, India, Israel and South Africa. Liquidity injection in domestic currency has been substantially increased, either by setting new liquidity lines from central banks (as in India) or easing compulsory reserve or liquidity requirement (as in Brazil, China, India and Indonesia).

However, reflecting economic and institutional differences, measures in emerging market economies have also shown notable differences with those of major advanced economies, especially in the forms of the policy measures. Provision of US dollar liquidity has been much more important and has been provided through central bank swap lines as well as by using foreign reserves.

Unlike in advanced economies where the foreign currency liquidity provisions have been targeted to financial institutions, beneficiaries in emerging economies have often been non-financial corporations with large dollar-denominated obligations. On the other hand, measures involving large-scale purchase of assets appear to have been quite limited, even though examples do exist such as Israel, where the central bank bought government bonds.

9. The supported institutions were Bear Sterns and American International Group (AIG) in the United States, Kaupthing Bank and Carnegie Investment Bank in Sweden, and UBS in Switzerland. In the United Kingdom, in addition to the previously announced support for Northern Rock, it was revealed with a significant time lag that massive liquidity support was extended at the height of the crisis to Royal Bank of Scotland and HBOS. In addition, the BoJ decided to provide subordinated loans to banks, although the actual provision of loans has been extremely limited.

Changes in the monetary base: A summary indicator of the various policy instruments

The overall changes in policy stance resulting from the various initiatives taken by central banks cannot be easily summarised in a single number.[10] All measures have resulted in significant changes on both sides of central banks' balance sheets and their size and composition provide an indication of shifts in the policy stance. Hence, since changes on either side of the balance sheets are ultimately reflected in the monetary base, it may serve as a rough proxy of the policy stance, even where this aggregate is not a direct policy target.

The increase in the monetary base during the crisis differs markedly across key monetary authorities (Figure 6.2(a)).[11] Particularly large changes

Figure 6.2(a)

Increases in the monetary base over the pre-crisis norms (Percentage change to end-February 2010 vis-à-vis the January-July 2007 averages)

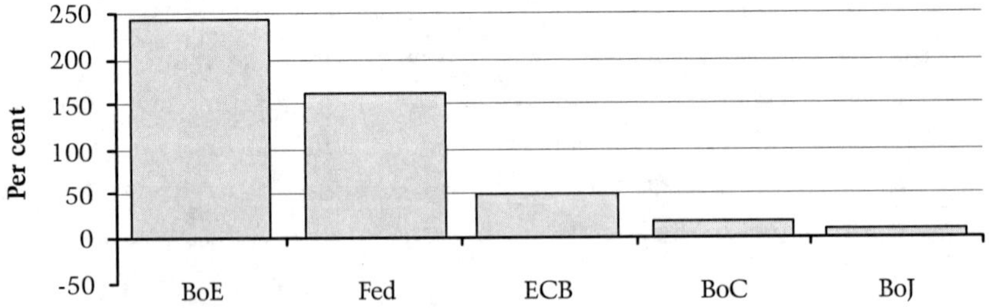

Note: For details on all countries, please see footnotes at the end of Figure 6.2(b).

Sources: For source see Figure 6.2(b).

10. This is in contrast to the case for the BoJ under its 2001-2006 quantitative easing policy where the outstanding amount of reserve balances was given a clear role to indicate the stance of monetary policy.

11. Data on the monetary base have been calculated from balance sheet information using a narrow definition of currency in circulation plus reserves to ensure comparability across central banks to the extent possible. The standing deposit facility has been included in the monetary base, because such deposits are very liquid and its economic effect is likely to be the same as excess reserves. Monetary base developments thus computed are largely consistent with the official data. The size and composition of the monetary base at each point in time have been compared with the pre-crisis levels, for which the January-July 2007 averages have been used as the base. Where international comparison is made, the size of monetary base is normalised using the 2007 GDP.

have been observed for BoE and the Fed, with the monetary base increasing by 100 per cent or more. At the other side of the spectrum are the BoJ and the BoC, with an increase of less than 20 per cent.

These differences obviously reflect the different policy measures implemented during the crisis. For all major central banks, the increases in the monetary base were initially driven by liquidity support to the banking sector (Figure 6.2(b)). This component has in most cases tended to shrink over time, as financial market conditions have improved.

More recently, central banks have decided accordingly to scale down several programmes (see Box 6.1). For the Fed and the BoE, subsequent large increases in the monetary base were largely due to the substantial

Figure 6.2(b)

Increases in the monetary base over the pre-crisis norms (Percentage change vis-à-vis the January-July 2007 average)

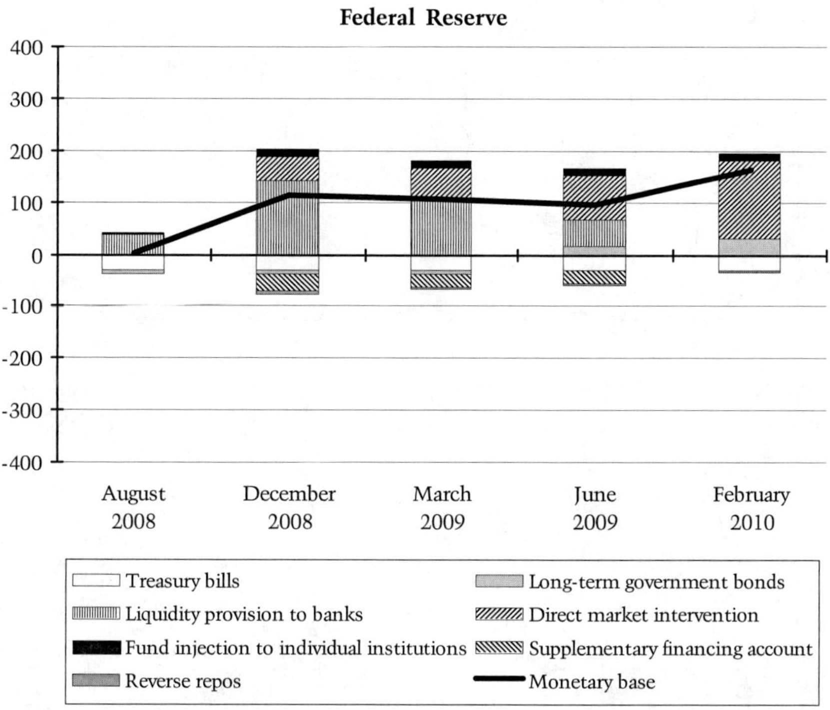

European Central Bank

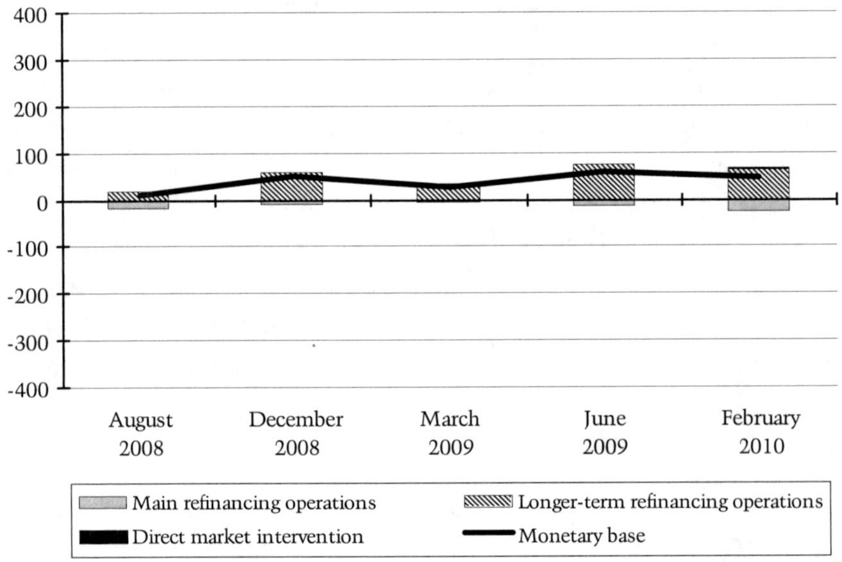

Bank of Japan

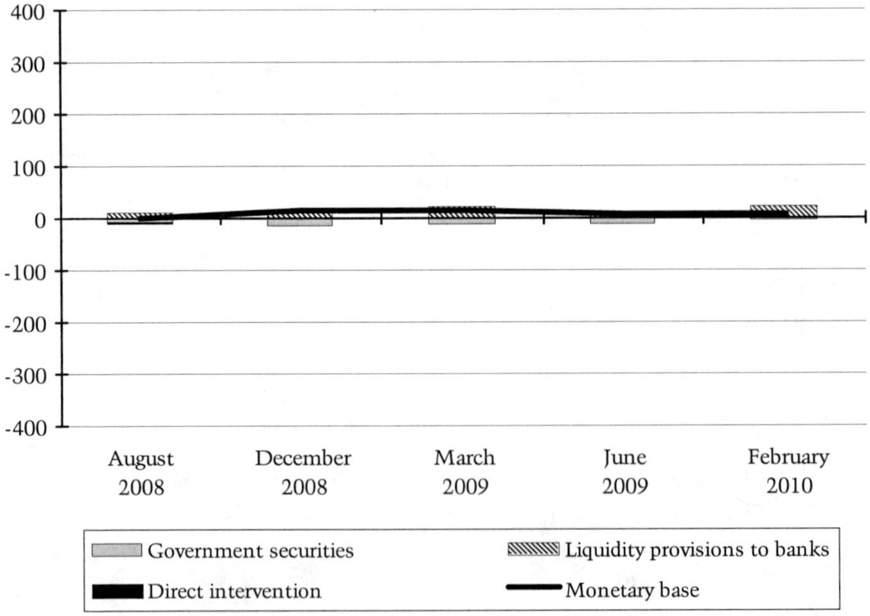

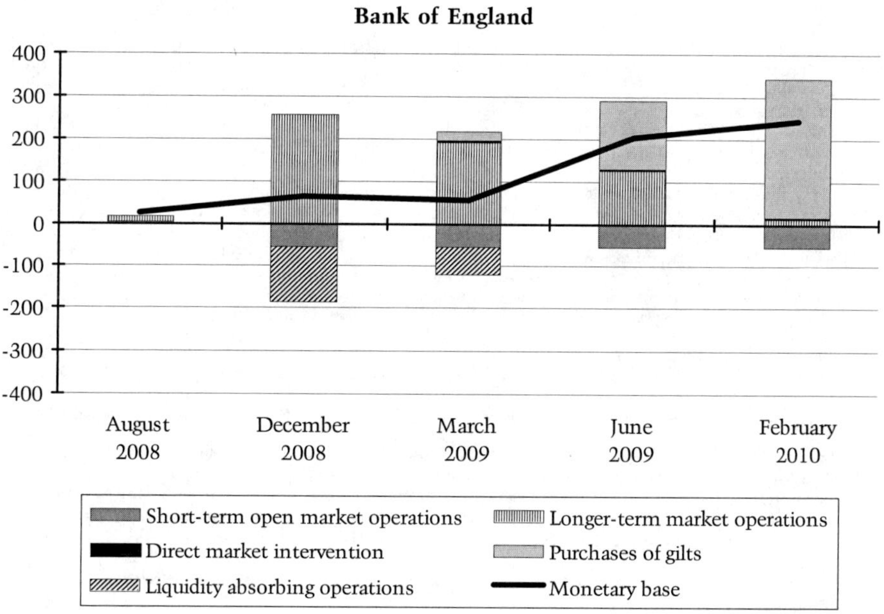
Bank of England
400
300
200
100
0
-100
-200
-300
-400
August 2008
December 2008
March 2009
June 2009
February 2010
Short-term open market operations
Longer-term market operations
Direct market intervention
Purchases of gilts
Liquidity absorbing operations
Monetary base

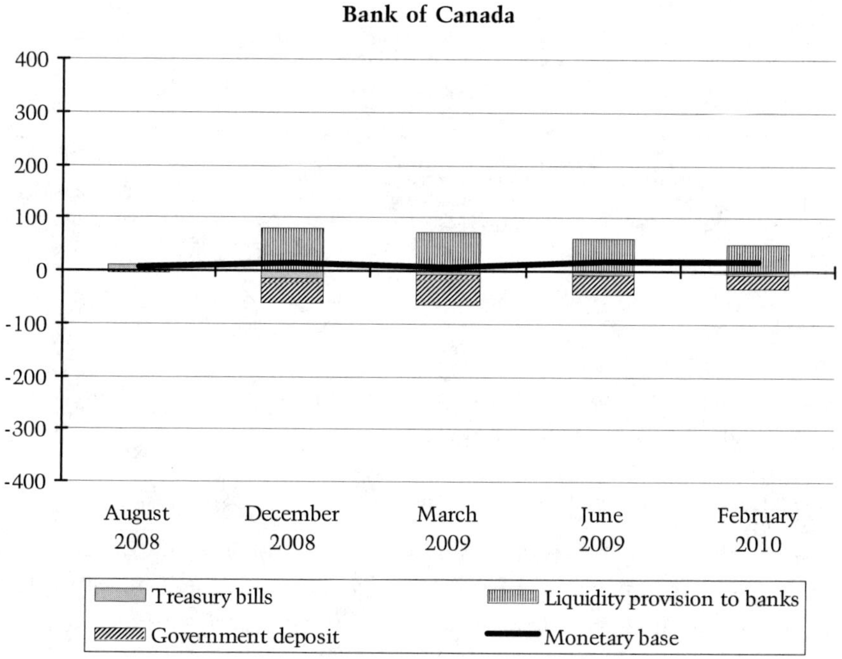
Bank of Canada
400
300
200
100
0
-100
-200
-300
-400
August 2008
December 2008
March 2009
June 2009
February 2010
Treasury bills
Liquidity provision to banks
Government deposit
Monetary base

Note:

1. The data for the Fed are based on 'Factors Affecting Reserve Balances'.
   Monetary base = currency in circulation + reserve balances + service-related deposits.
   Liquidity provision to banks = repurchase agreements + term auction credit + primary credit + secondary credit + seasonal credit+ primary dealer and other broker-dealer credit + central bank liquidity swaps.
   Direct market intervention = federal agency debt securities + mortgage-backed securities + term asset-backed securities loan facility + asset-backed commercial paper money market mutual fund liquidity facility + net portfolio holdings of commercial paper funding facility, limited liability company (LLC) + net portfolio holdings of LLCs funded through the money market investor funding facility.
   Fund injected to individual institutions = credit extended to American International Group, Inc., net + net portfolio holdings of Maiden Lane LLC + Net portfolio holdings of Maiden Lane II LLC + net portfolio holdings of Maiden Lane III LLC.
2. The data for the ECB are taken from 'Weekly Financial Statement'.
   Monetary base = banknotes in circulation + current accounts (covering the minimum reserve system) + deposit facility.
   Direct market intervention = securities held for monetary policy purposes (i.e., covered bonds).
3. The data for the BoJ are based on 'Monetary Base and the Bank of Japan's Transactions'.
   Monetary base = banknotes and coins in circulation + current account balances.
   Liquidity provision to banks = purchases of JGSs under repurchase agreements + funds-supplying operations against pooled collateral + purchases of CP under repurchase agreements + special funds-supplying operations to facilitate corporate financing + loans pursuant to Article 33 of the Bank of Japan Law.
   Direct market intervention = outright purchases of CP + outright purchases of corporate bonds + stocks held as trust property.
4. The data for the BoE are taken from 'the Bank returns' supplemented by detailed information about the asset purchase facility.
   Monetary base = notes in circulation + reserve balances + cash ratio deposits.
   Direct market intervention = commercial paper and corporate debts held by the asset purchase facility.
   Purchase of gilts = gilts held by the asset purchase facility.
5. The data for the BoC are taken from 'Weekly Financial Statistics, Table B2, Bank of Canada: Assets and Liabilities'.
   Monetary base = notes in circulation + Canadian dollar deposits of chartered banks, other and other members of the Canadian payments association (for the calculation of the pre-crisis averages) + Canadian dollar deposits, members of the Canadian payments association.
   Liquidity provision to banks = securities purchased under resale agreements + advances (including the term loan facility) and all other assets (that included securities purchased under resale agreements prior to October 3, 2007).

asset purchase programmes. For the other central banks, the increases in the monetary base remained much smaller and were driven mainly by liquidity support to the banking sector.

The impact on market developments

Assessing the isolated impact of liquidity and credit intervention measures initiated by central banks is difficult, not least because these measures have also been matched by forceful government emergency financial policy measures.[12] Although the impact of each policy measure cannot be assessed in isolation, as a whole, the responses from central banks and governments seem to have contributed to improvements in market functioning, now that the stress in many financial markets seem to have largely receded.

It is, perhaps, premature to arrive at a decisive conclusion about the exact contribution of unconventional monetary policies at this stage, but empirical studies have found some positive effects of these measures on market developments. For instance, Aït-Sahalia *et al.* (2009) find that macroeconomic and financial sector policy announcements have had positive impacts on inter-bank credit and liquidity risk premia in the United States, the Euro area, Japan and the United Kingdom.

More narrowly focusing on the liquidity facilities, Christensen *et al.* (2009) also conclude that they helped to lower liquidity premiums embedded in money market rates in the United States, and Meier (2009) tentatively finds positive effects for the United Kingdom. Special liquidity measures may have had wider positive effects. Yehoue (2009) has, for instance, found some positive effects in emerging market countries. Evidence on experience with unconventional monetary policy in Japan, reviewed in Minegishi and Cournède (2010), is also suggestive of similar positive effects.

Turning to specific market developments, stress in the money market has largely receded (Figure 6.3). Indeed, spreads between unsecured three-month inter-bank rates and average expected overnight rates have fallen to levels that are close to their pre-August 2007 averages, with bouts of improvement tending to follow announcements of major unconventional initiatives. Significant improvement in the functioning of money markets allows earlier aggressive policy rate cuts to be transmitted more fully to the economy, as it enables banks to access short-term funds at a very low price (Figure 6.4).

12. In a number of countries, governments have recapitalised banks. A series of temporary guarantee schemes at various levels have also been implemented. Since October 2008, temporary schemes have been introduced in some countries where governments guarantee newly-issued bank debt or money market transactions. At the retail level, deposit insurance has been extended, whereas a temporary blanket guarantee has also been granted in few countries.

Figure 6.3

Money market conditions
Three-month spreads, last observation: March 10, 2010

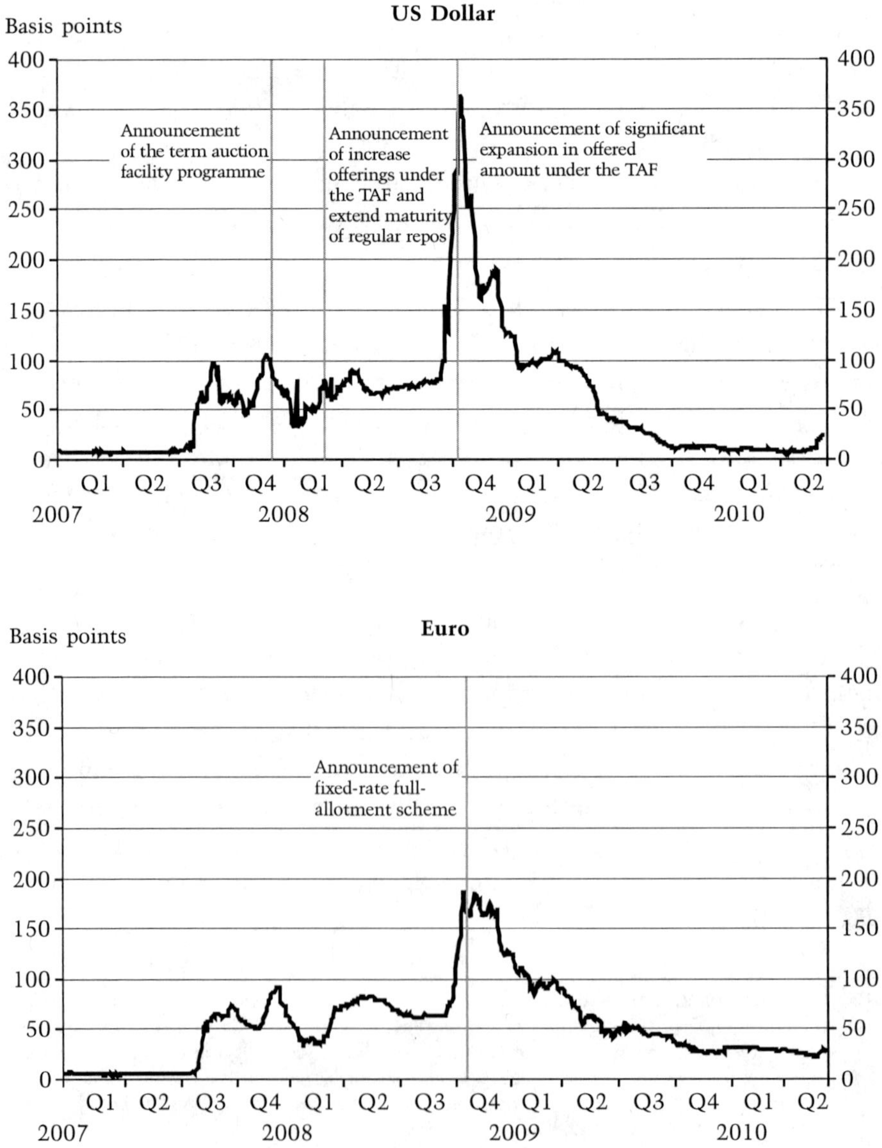

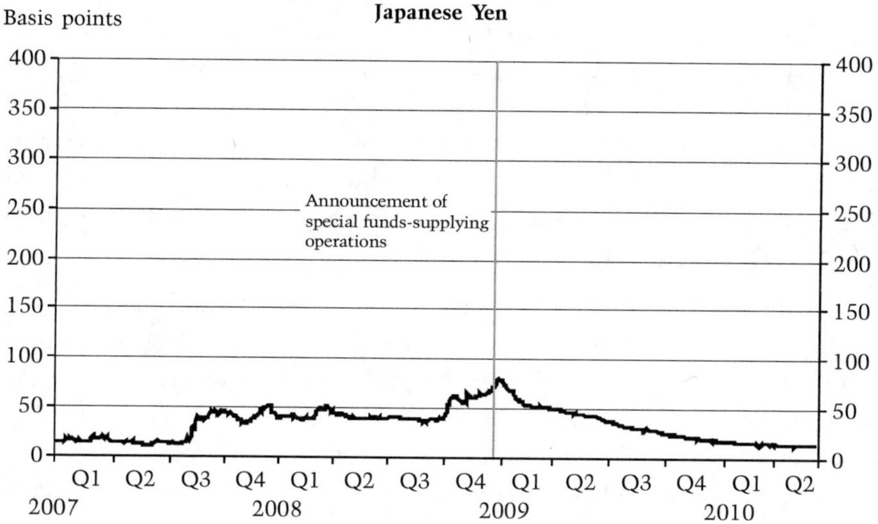

Note: Spread between three-month EURIBOR and EONIA swap index for euro area; spread between three-month LIBOR and overnight indexed swap for the United States and Japan.
Sources: Datastream and Bloomberg.

Figure 6.4

Inter-bank lending rates
Last observation: March 10, 2010

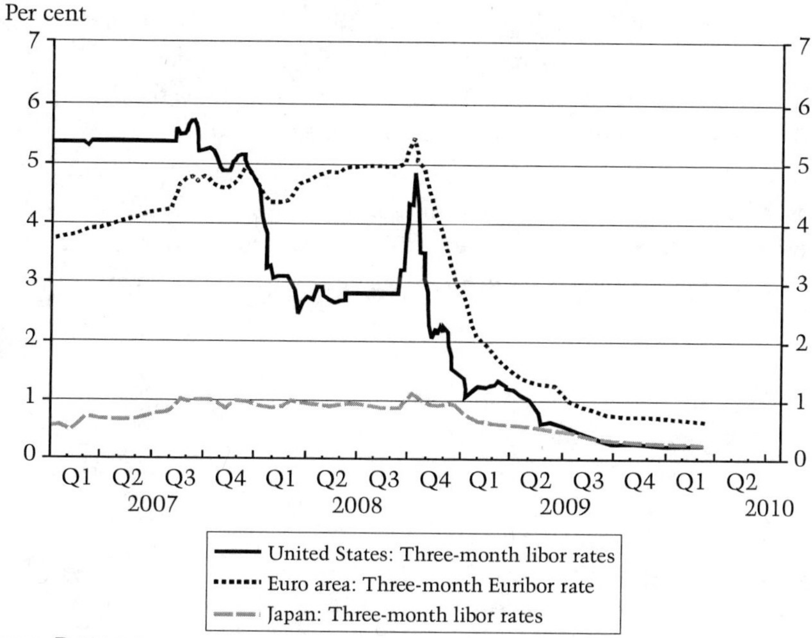

Source: Datastream.

Other market segments have also shown marked improvements, particularly where central bank interventions have been important (Figure 6.5). In the United States, owing in some measure to Fed purchases of mortgage-backed securities, the spread of conventional mortgage rates over government bond yields has come down from the peak of around 250 basis points (bps) in December 2008 to about 50 bps at the beginning of 2010. This trend has helped stabilise the housing market.

Although quantifying the effects of asset purchases by central banks remains challenging, the New York Fed has estimated that large scale asset purchase programmes conducted by the Fed taken together (totalling $1.8 trillion) have reduced the 10-year government bond yield by as much as 50 bps (Sack, 2009). Based on the fall in yields immediately after purchases, Gagnon (2009) concludes that the impact is larger. Each $1 trillion purchase of longer term assets would lower the 10-year government bond yield by 54 bps. In the Euro area, although the magnitude of the central bank intervention has been much smaller relative to the size of the market, the ECB's decision to purchase covered bonds preceded a significant narrowing of spreads, possibly reflecting confidence effects (ECB, 2009).

In Japan, the decision by the BoJ to purchase commercial paper outright was followed by an immediate reduction in the spread. In the United Kingdom, the widening of the spread of swap rates over government bond yields has been taken as an indication that BoE purchases of gilts have reduced yields (Bean, 2009).[13] All in all, these measures seem to have contributed to alleviating stress in financial markets and to restoring appetite for risk, as has been evident in the reduced corporate bond spread and CDS rates for banks, and more generally, in the increase in equity prices.

13. By late November, however, the swap spread had returned to its pre-purchase level.

Figure 6.5

Selected market developments where central bank interventions have been important

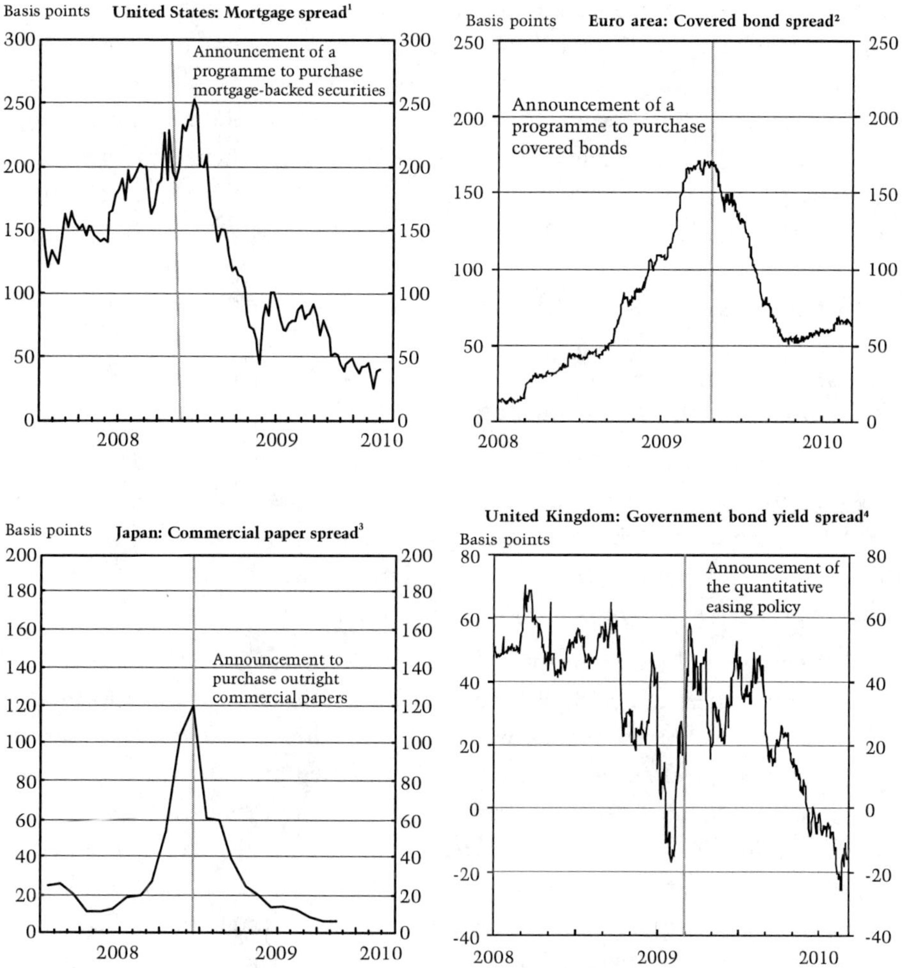

Note: 1. Conventional mortgage rate (30 years)—Treasury benchmark bond yield (30 years).

2. IBOXX Euro covered bond yield-swap rates.

3. Average issuance rate of CP (rated A-1 or higher)—short-term government security yield (three months).

4. 10-year swap rate—10-year government bond yield.

Sources: Central bank data, Datastream.

These improvements should, however, be seen in the perspective of the massive central bank and government intervention. Indeed, central banks have become dominant market players in important areas. In the mortgage-backed securities market in the United States, for instance, the Fed has been the predominant buyer since the introduction of the direct purchase scheme. In January 2010, the Fed's acquisition of mortgage-backed securities exceeded 50 per cent of the total volume of new issuance in the corresponding period. In the United Kingdom, the net increase in gilt holdings by the BoE has exceeded new issuance of public debt by a large margin. As of January 2010, more than 20 per cent of the total amount outstanding of gilts was held by the central bank.

Potential risks associated with unconventional measures

The implications for asset prices and the functioning of financial markets

The benefit of unconventional monetary policy measures should outweigh the potential risk of significantly distorting market signals, as long as the market malfunctions that warranted their introduction are still present.[14] These measures could have undesirable consequences if maintained for too long, however, as market conditions further improve.

If exceptional monetary policy measures are kept in place beyond the period when their targeted markets are dysfunctional, their distortionary effects on asset prices may weaken economic performance. Large interventions to purchase securities backed by lending to specific sectors, such as housing, can result in artificially low costs of mortgage borrowing, for example, which could in turn contribute unduly to house price appreciation and attract excessive investment in residential construction.[15] Previous OECD work suggests that an overly easy stance of conventional monetary policy, as reflected in interest rates well below 'Taylor rates' for

14. There may be sporadic incidents where central bank intervention has shown some signs of negative influence. For instance, in Japan, firms have occasionally issued commercial paper at lower yields than government bills of the same maturity.

15. Even where intervention is judged to be necessary to attain public policy objectives (*e.g.* to encourage home ownership in the United States), this role should normally be reserved for fiscal authorities (Goodfriend, 2009).

an extended period of time, is frequently followed by the build-up of financial imbalances in housing markets (Ahrend *et al.*, 2008). If such effects can arise when monetary easing is not specifically targeted toward housing, they can be expected to be more likely when ultra-low rates are coupled with very large purchases of assets backed by mortgages.

As segmentation across markets recedes, however, sector-specific effects should become less acute, as the effect from exceptional monetary operations spills over to classes of assets that are substitutes for the targeted categories. In the same way, the effect of large purchases of agency mortgage-backed securities can spread to government bonds, artificially reducing their yield. Hence, cross-sectoral distortions may diminish, but concern about economy-wide effects may increase.

A sign of excess liquidity inflating asset prices, for instance, would be asset classes (which in normal times show no or negative correlations) beginning to appreciate jointly. In this context, it may be useful to watch whether the positive correlations observed in the course of 2009 between shares and bonds, and between gold and bonds, persist into 2010 (Figure 6.6).

Figure 6.6

Developments in share, bond and gold prices (March 9, 2009 = 100)

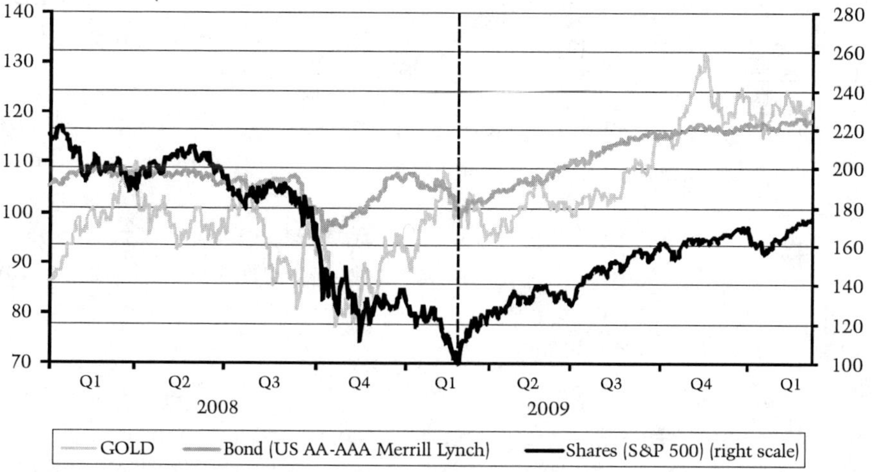

Source: Datastream.

Another possible risk associated with the continuation of special liquidity programmes over the medium-term is that they can result in an inefficient allocation of money across the financial sector. An advantage of the decentralised money market is that participants monitor each other and incorporate their assessment of the credit risk of counter-parties in the price of inter-bank loans. As such, a decentralised money market incorporates a built-in feedback mechanism that should put a price on counter-party risk.

These functions are lost in a regime of full allotment, where all participants can borrow unlimited liquidity from the central bank at a fixed rate. These considerations would call for restoring normal liquidity operations as soon as the money market can function on its own. Even so, at least part of the market discipline may be lost permanently because most participants will conclude from this and previous crises that the monetary authorities will always intervene whenever money markets are in turmoil. (Rochet and Tirole, 1996; Rochet, 2009).

The implications for inflation expectations and inflation

From the viewpoint of macroeconomic stability, unconventional measures, if maintained for too long, could destabilise inflation expectations and induce inflationary pressures. In a more normal environment, where financial intermediation is functioning smoothly and the precautionary demand for liquidity is reduced, the huge accumulation of reserve balances could result in a rapid increase in the aggregate money stock, which in turn could eventually boost aggregate demand and inflationary pressures.

The risk of future inflationary pressures of this nature can be incorporated in inflationary expectations at present, thereby prompting changes in prices and wages that raise inflation in the near-term. In general, while some increases in inflation expectations are not problematic in a situation where actual inflation is low and the risk of deflation is not fully eliminated, increases beyond central banks' implicit and explicit targets would be destabilising.

Amid weak developments in bank lending, increases in monetary aggregate such as M_1 and M_2 so far appear to reflect a preference for liquidity among the household and corporate sectors and lower the opportunity cost of holding money (Figure 6.7). With uncertainty still prevailing in the economy and the stress in the banking sector still elevated, most of the extra liquidity obtained from central banks has been simply hoarded, as is evident in the plunging money multipliers in countries, where the monetary base increased the most (Figure 6.8).

As long as this remains the case, massive injection *per se* is unlikely to lead to inflationary pressures (Keister and McAndrews, 2009). The previous Japanese experience suggests that, as long as weakness in the banking sector persists and the credit channel remains impaired, a massive increase in monetary base *per se* is unlikely to lead to inflation. Besides, a significant expansion in the monetary base in itself may not be a good leading indicator for inflation, particularly where major changes in monetary policy implementation (the remuneration of excess reserves for example) have most probably altered the relationship between base and broad money.

As market stress continues to subside, however, banks could start to rely on a continued abundance of liquidity as a basis for stronger credit and monetary expansion. While such a development should be welcome to a certain extent, its potential implication for inflationary pressure cannot be ignored.

Figure 6.7

Recent changes in aggregate money stock
(Year-on-year percentage changes, January 2010)

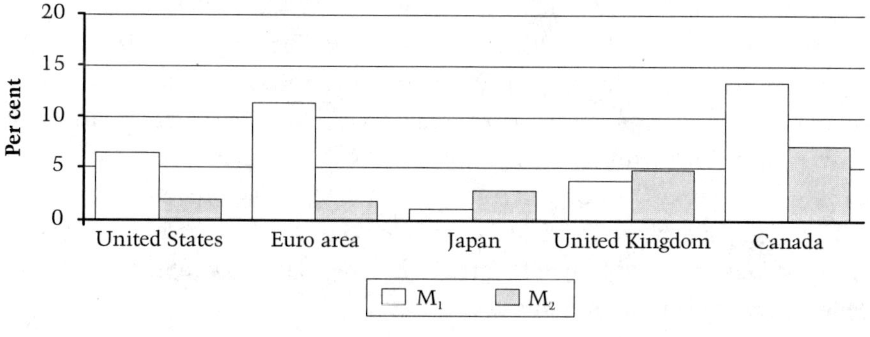

Note: All data are for January 2010, except for M_2+ in Canada (December 2009 data).
Source: OECD Main Economic Indicators.

Another important channel by which unconventional monetary policy actions could influence inflation expectations is through credibility and perceived independence of the central bank. Inflation expectations may drift upwards if economic agents perceive a greater risk of central bank actions being constrained by their expanded balance sheets, preventing them from adjusting interest rates in a timely manner.

Figure 6.8

Changes in money multipliers and the monetary base

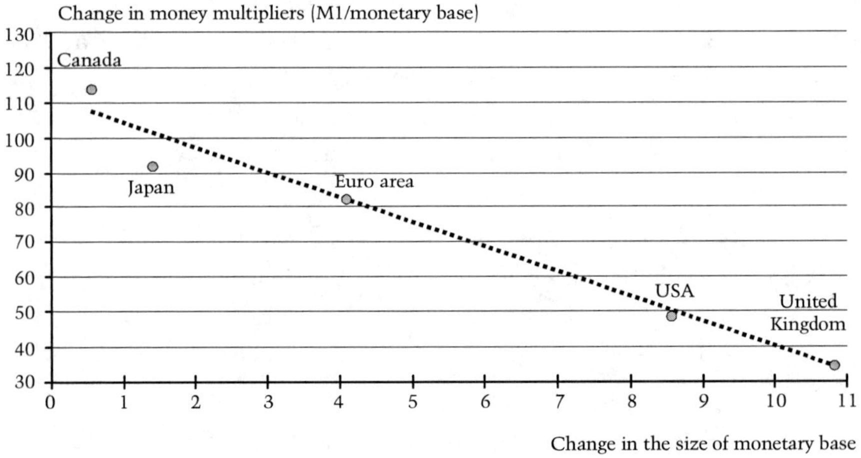

Notes: All data are for January. The vertical axis measures the size of money multipliers (M1/monetary base) with pre-crisis averages (January–July 2007) set to 100. The horizontal axis refers to changes in the size of monetary base measured as per cent of 2007 GDP).

Sources: OECD Main Economic Indicators; individual central bank data.

Moreover, central banks' balance sheets have become exposed to much larger risk than would normally be the case. Taking riskier assets as collateral, intervening directly in credit markets and injecting funds to individual institutions all imply credit risk. The risk is likely to be manageable in the case of extending normal liquidity provision to banks against collateral, because credit is extended only for a short period of time and losses are incurred only when the collateral market collapses and banks pledging that collateral fail simultaneously.

However, the risk may be more pronounced for measures involving outright purchases of private sector instruments. This is particularly the case for lending against or purchasing assets whose value is hard to determine, such as securitised products bought under the Fed's TALF programme. The value of such assets may have been distorted significantly by central bank intervention. Moreover, funds injected into individual institutions are also risky, if they end up as *de facto* solvency rather than liquidity support.[16]

At the same time, holding longer term assets imply that central banks are being exposed to interest rate risk, as central banks have bought these assets at relatively high prices in an environment of low interest rates. The degree of interest rate risk incurred by central banks may have important implications for the exit which are discussed below. If losses occur, or the public perceives that to be the case, the associated burden for tax-payers may raise the issue of credibility. If losses have to be compensated *ex post* by the government, the reliance on finance ministries may undermine the perception of independence.

Preserving the perception of central bank independence could as well be more challenging in an environment where central banks have taken measures to directly affect long-term government bond yields in times of ballooning budget deficits. Putting these concerns in perspective, however, survey data on inflation expectations show no major sign of drifting up so far, suggesting that economic agents largely expect the exit from various unconventional measures to be achieved in a smooth fashion.

Possible exit strategies

Central banks need exit strategies from current settings of both unconventional and conventional policy instruments, which involve two inter-related but conceptually different goals. On the one hand, central banks will need to scale back their intervention in financial markets and reduce excess liquidity. On the other hand, central banks must at some point start adjusting interest rates in view of their macroeconomic objective of price stability. The large scale of the needed liquidity withdrawal and the uncertainty concerning the effectiveness of the various tools (to be

16. This indicates that central banks' exposures should promptly be transferred to the government. Funds injected to individual institutions by the BoE and the Riksbank have already been transferred to the government.

discussed later) taken separately, necessitate that central banks rely on a combination of different tools to achieve the exit.

Ideally, the exit strategy should ensure that these two goals be pursued separately, as the optimal timing and sequence for achieving them are likely to be different. An appropriate exit strategy would ideally 'decouple' changes in balance sheets, either in terms of their size or composition from the level of interest rate (Borio and Disyatat, 2009). Central banks are already well-positioned to achieve this. The fact that a number of unconventional measures, such as the TAF in the United States, were initiated well before the room for conventional interest rate cut was exhausted, attests to decoupling in the early stage of the crisis.

Tools for the exit

In discussing the exit, it is useful to rely on a stylised diagram following Keister *et al.* (2008), Ennis and Keister (2008) and Goodfriend (2002), depicting how the overnight money market interest rate is determined (Figure 6.9). The interest rate on reserves (i.e., the overnight money market rate) is determined by the interaction of demand and supply. As central banks can always adjust the volume of supply by way of market operations, the supply curve is vertical at any level desired by the monetary authorities.[17]

Under the most common monetary policy implementation scheme, central banks project demand for reserves and adjust the amount of liquidity supplied through open market operations, so that the total amount of lendable reserves in the money market is consistent with a desired level of short-term interest rates. The demand curve is downward sloping, with the rates on standing facilities providing the cap and the floor. Banks generally should have no incentive to pay an interest rate in the money market which is higher than the rate on standing loan facility available from the central bank.[18] Likewise, no bank would lend at a rate lower than the deposit rate, which provides a risk-free alternative.

---

17. In the case of full allotment, the central bank loses the ability to position the supply curve. However, the crisis measure of full allotment can be interpreted as having the same effect as shifting the supply curve to the far right of the diagram.

18. The 'cap' may be less binding if there is stigma associated with borrowing from the standing loan facilities.

The movement in the vertical direction (i.e., the level of interest rates) corresponds to the central bank's concern for the macroeconomic objective of price stability. Under normal circumstances, this is the predominant concern for monetary authorities that sets the supply of reserves to attain the desired level of the interest rate. The movement of the supply curve in the horizontal direction in the region where the lower bound of interest rate has already been reached can be considered as quantifying concern for financial market issues. Central banks supply reserves in excess of what would be required to keep the interest rate at the desired level because they want to support financial stability.[19]

An outward shift of the demand curve reflects an increase in liquidity preference on the part of market participants, as was seen during the crisis. At the current conjuncture, most major OECD central banks operate in the region of Point A, where abundant liquidity is provided and where the lower bound of the interest rate is effectively binding (the ECB being in the situation of having overnight rates well below the main refinancing rate, but still somewhat above the deposit rate).

Figure 6.9

Determination of money market interest rate: A stylised illustration

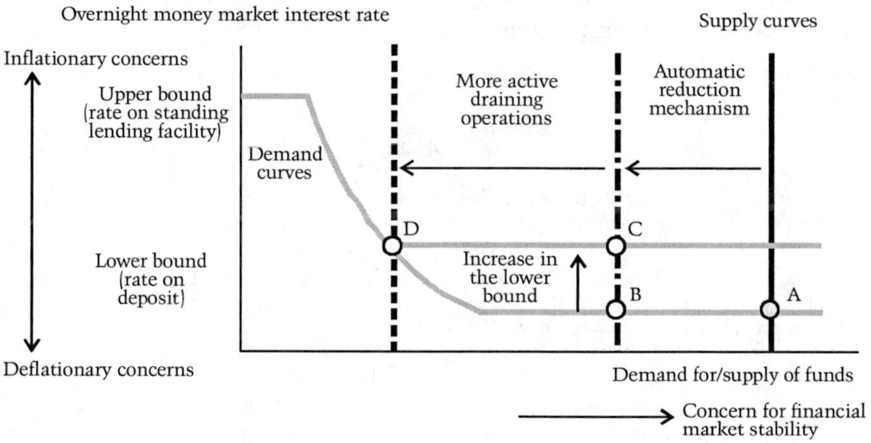

19. The current unconventional measures are the most conspicuous example, but central banks have temporarily increased liquidity provision to ensure market stability in the past, such as after the 9/11 attack.

Automatic reduction by relying on market mechanisms has already been initiated

Many central bank programmes embody incentives whereby an improvement in market functioning more or less automatically discourages financial market participants from using these facilities. The clearest example is where the facility involves upfront fees (e.g. the commercial paper funding facility (CPFF) operated by the Fed). To a lesser extent, this is also generally true when the required collateral is subject to stringent trimming (a 'haircut'). If pledging collateral is costly, banks should find it cheaper to borrow on an unsecured basis from the money market once it has recovered sufficiently.

In practice, and in line with the improvement in financial markets, the demand for some central bank facilities has already been on a downward trend (see Figure 6.2 (b)). In the case of the Fed, the amount outstanding in its CPFF peaked in January 2009 and has more or less been steadily decreasing thereafter. As for the ECB's one-year refinancing operations based on full allotment procedure, demand for the second operation in September and the last operation in December 2009 turned out to be significantly lower than that for the first operation in June.

More generally, for many central banks, some of the programmes have become heavily undersubscribed. In the light of these developments, exit steps have already been taken as outlined in Box 6.1.

Box 6.1

First steps toward the exit

Although conditions in financial markets have far from returned to normal, the exit from a series of unconventional measures has nonetheless proceeded in line with significant improvement in the functioning of markets.

First, some temporary liquidity measures adopted at the height of the crisis have become less used, as improved market conditions have greatly reduced the need for market participants to rely on central bank facilities. To the extent that this is the case, central banks have decided to let crisis measures expire at the pre-announced date.

- The Fed let expire most of its special facilities (such as the asset-backed commercial paper money market mutual fund liquidity facility (AMLF) and the commercial paper funding facility (CPFF)) at the pre-announced date of February 1, 2010. All dollar-liquidity swap positions were also closed by the same date.

contd...

...contd...

- For the BoJ, the programmes to purchase commercial paper and corporate bonds (remaining maturity up to one year only) expired in December 2009.
- The BoC has terminated two of its three emergency measures (the private sector term purchase and resale agreement programme, and the term loan facility).
- The SNB and the ECB terminated the Swiss franc swap arrangements at the end of January 2009.

Second, even for liquidity measures that have continued to be used by market participants, some central banks have judged that market improvements have rendered the case for the special facilities less compelling and that it is warranted to discontinue those programmes. To avoid abrupt absorption of liquidity, however, central banks that have decided to terminate the special programmes have pre-announced these decisions well in advance of the expiry date and have often stressed the intention to nonetheless provide sufficient liquidity.

- The Fed terminated the term auction facility with its last auction in early March 2010. The use of discount window programmes is now subject to tighter conditions, as the required interest rate has been increased somewhat (yet the spread over the Federal funds target rate is still lower than in the pre-crisis period) and the maturity has returned to the pre-crisis norm of overnight.
- The ECB conducted the last one-year refinancing operation in December 2009 and the last six-month operation is to be conducted in March. For both these operations, the full allotment procedure remains in place, but the rate payable is made variable as the average minimum bid rate of the main refinancing operations over its life. From April onward, regular three-month longer term refinancing operations will be subject to the traditional variable rate tender procedure. On the other hand, the main refinancing operations (one week maturity) as well as special-term refinancing operation (up to one month) will continue to be carried out as fixed rate tender procedures with full allotment as long as needed and at least until mid-October.
- The BoJ has also decided to discontinue the special funds-supplying operations to facilitate corporate financing at the end of March 2010. The Bank has also indicated, however, its intention to continue providing ample liquidity from April 2010 onward, relying on the traditional scheme.

Even in cases where the purchase of longer-dated assets is involved, the exit is gradually taking place.

- The Fed completed its purchases of Treasury securities at the end of October 2009. It has also indicated that the pace of purchases of mortgage-backed securities and agency bonds will gradually slow and the programme is expected to be completed by the end of the first quarter of 2010.
- The BoE has already completed the £200 billion programme of asset purchases.

Although these measures are likely to prevent further expansion of central bank balance sheets, some central banks will continue to hold large stocks of long-dated assets on their balance sheets and the exit from the corresponding liquidity impact has not started. Partly reflecting a relatively restrictive pre-crisis implementation scheme for monetary policy, the Fed, however, is now in the process of preparing technical steps required for the exit, as mentioned by the US Federal Reserve chief Ben Bernanke (2010), while emphasising that it does not imply any imminent initiation of the exit in this regard.

A scheme is now available, for instance, in which the Fed carries out reverse repurchasing operations with primary dealers against collateral of Treasury and agency securities. The Fed intends to further expand the capacity of reverse repos by extending counter-parties and allowing collateral use of mortgage-backed securities. At the same time, it has also made public a proposal to establish a term-deposit facility (again as a means to drain reserves), and it expects to conduct test transactions soon.

Exit will also require discretionary actions

The magnitude of the reduction in the supply of reserves that can be achieved through this type of automatic exit is unlikely to be sufficient for all central banks to be able to adjust interest rates. In the context of Figure 6.9, it will merely shift the position from A to B, where the deposit rate is most likely to remain binding. A primary reason for exit for both the Fed and the BoE is that they have accumulated massive amounts of long-term assets on their balance sheets (Figure 6.10). These central banks cannot rely on the repayment of the securities to absorb liquidity. As of early-March 2010, for instance, none of the mortgage-backed securities held by the Fed will mature within a year and only one-tenth of its holdings

Figure 6.10

Short-dated versus long-dated measures
(Differences from the January-July 2007 average to end-February 2010, per cent of 2007 GDP)

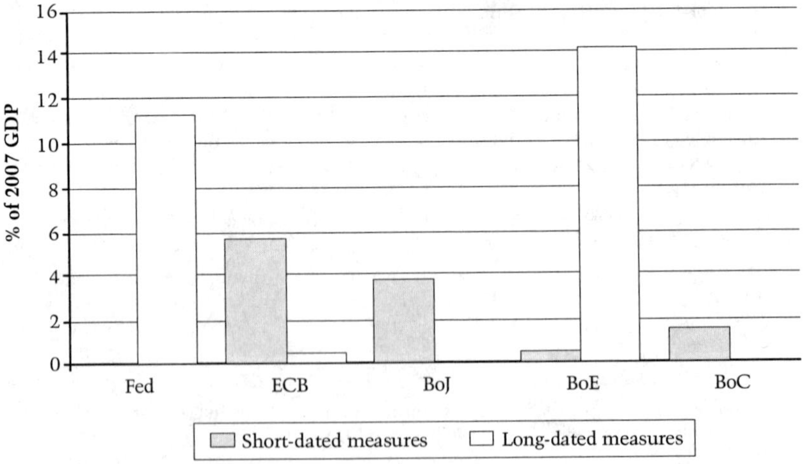

Note:	The classification of short-dated and long-dated measures is based on data used for Figure 2. Items showing negative deviation from the pre-crisis averages have been excluded in calculation.
Fed	Short-dated measures= liquidity provision to banks. Long-dated measures=direct market intervention+long-term government bonds+fund injection to individual institutions.
ECB	Short-dated measures= Longer-term refinancing operations. Long-dated measures=direct market intervention.
BoJ	Short-dated measures= liquidity provisions to banks.
BoE	Short-dated measures= Longer-term market operations. Long-dated measures=direct market intervention+purchase of gilts.
BoC	Short-dated measures= liquidity provision to banks. Long-dated measures= none.

of US Treasury securities will do so (Table 6.3).[20] Consequently, for these central banks, the overall size of the monetary base has remained quite elevated, even though their provision for shorter term liquidity has come down significantly from its peak.

Table 6.3

Assets held by the Fed: Positions maturing within one year

	Total		*Maturing within one year*
	Amount in billion (US$)		*Per cent of the total*
Term auction credit	15	15	100%
US Treasury securities	777	85	11%
Federal agency debt securities	168	27	16%
Mortgage-backed securities	1,027	0	0%
Commercial paper	3	3	100%

Note: The data are as of March 3, 2010.
Source: Federal Reserve.

Central banks, that have not purchased large amounts of long-dated securities, face a risk. A simple termination of temporary programmes might result in liquidity supply being cut off too abruptly, which may have adverse consequences for financial stability. Thus, the termination of the programmes may have to be smoothed so that a certain portion of maturing positions get rolled over under more stringent conditions like fewer amounts, higher rates or shorter maturities.

The previously mentioned BoJ decision to terminate some of the temporary programmes, for instance, came with a continued commitment to provide ample liquidity to the market using the existing operations. This need for intermediate steps is particularly clear where 'humps' exist in the pattern of liquidity provisions.

The first one-year refinancing operation by the ECB resulted in a massive liquidity provision equal to about 40 per cent of the monetary base, for instance, which will be taken out of the system on July 1, 2010. To smooth out its liquidity impact, the ECB has decided on a special fine-

20. The problem is less acute in the BoJ programme to purchase corporate bonds as the Bank has purchased a limited amount of issues that mature in less than a year.

tuning operation with fixed rate and full allotment procedure, so that the maturing one-year operations can be bridged subsequently to liquidity provision under regular main refinancing operations.[21]

Exit tools involving more active actions on the part of central banks

For the reasons discussed above, the exit will not be purely automatic. Even if some facilities unwind on their own, central banks will have to also take specific actions. In the terminology of Figure 6.9, central banks can take two approaches, either shift the demand or shift the supply curves. Even though these two approaches are often interlinked, we will discuss each separately in the light of their distinctive characteristics.

Let us first consider measures to increase the demand for reserves. The first option is to shift the bottom part of the demand curve upward, so that the existing supply of reserves is consistent with a higher level of interest rates, and the market equilibrium shifts from Point B to Point C. This is possible to the extent to which central banks are able to raise interest rates payable on excess reserves.

One of the benefits of relying on the deposit rate is that, it enables central banks to start adjusting interest rates, regardless of the level of excess liquidity remaining in the banking system. Thus, this is an attractive option for central banks that have engaged in long-dated measures. Other central banks can use this option to maintain their liquidity support measures longer. Another important merit of this option is its relative simplicity at the operational level, as the application and the enforcement of the decision can be simply left to the market, rather than having to rely on an array of separate liquidity-absorbing operations (to be discussed below).

There are a number of caveats to this approach, however. First, obviously, central banks must be able to remunerate excess reserves so that the deposit interest rate can be controlled. Most central banks can now do

21. The maturity of this fine-tuning operation is set to fall on the date of the next main refinancing operations, both of which are to be conducted under the fixed rate and full allotment procedure. Thus, banks will be able to roll over any maturing portions, if they wish, first through the fine-tuning operation and then with the main refinancing operations. However, it entails a significant shortening of the maturity.

so.[22] Second, the mechanism will be more effective if excess reserves are remunerated under similar conditions for all major participants in the market for central bank money. If big market players are left outside the remuneration scheme, such as the government sponsored enterprises (GSEs) currently in the United States, they may continue to have an incentive to lend below the rate on the deposit facility, which complicates the process and makes the lower bound less binding.[23]

Third, the relative pace of increase in the deposit rate *vis-à-vis* the pace of increase in the main target rate has implications for the functioning of financial markets. Central banks usually operate with a corridor between the main target rate and the deposit rate, so that banks have an incentive to lend money out in the market rather than simply deposit money at the central bank facility. In the current environment where the main target rate has come down to very low levels, however, the corridor has often either completely disappeared or narrowed to a very small margin.

To the extent that this is the case, the increase in the deposit rate would have to come with a nearly equal increase in the main target rate or the deposit rate would have to increase less than the main target rate. As long as there is excess liquidity in the system, however, the deposit rate will be the effective money market rate, which will continue to discourage activities in the money market.

Fourth, the deposit rate has never been a prominent indicator of policy stance in the past, so its new role as a main signalling device of the policy stance would have to be clearly communicated to the market. This would be particularly important for central banks that have maintained a relatively wide corridor, as in the Euro area. In the Euro area, where an environment of unlimited liquidity provision prevails, the deposit rate has gained traction in determining the level of interest rate prevailing in the money market, so that an increase in the deposit rate would imply a tightening of monetary policy.

22. The BoJ initially introduced this measure as a temporary facility, which it has recently decided to maintain for the time being.

23. Currently in the United States, the effective Federal funds rates are lower than the deposit rate. The exemption of the GSEs from the remuneration scheme appears to be one reason for this, another reason being general reluctance on the part of banks to arbitrage this situation (Kohn, 2009).

Lastly, even though the reserve remuneration allows interest rates to be increased, the large amount of reserves in the banking system would increase the risk of expansion in money aggregates with consequent inflationary pressure. All in all, even though arguments can be advanced in favour of using the deposit rate, a monetary policy framework that heavily depends on the deposit rate would breach traditional practice. These caveats highlight the need to take measures to withdraw liquidity at the same time, as discussed below.[24]

Let us now dwell on measures to reduce supply of reserves. The second option for central banks is to reduce the supply of reserves, so that the supply curve shifts inward to the left. In the context of Figure 6.9, this corresponds to the move from Point B to Point D. In this regard, central banks can use a number of tools.

Central banks holding large amounts of long-dated assets always have an option to engage in outright sales. Asset sales also have the benefit of removing credit risk from their balance sheets. Unwinding central bank positions would also help to reduce potential distortions across market segments. This is particularly important if market developments, such as increases in transactions and opportunities for arbitrage, are judged to be insufficient to correct distortion in a spontaneous way.

In view of these considerations, outright sales are more compelling for private securities, which expose central banks to higher credit risk and whose distortive impacts on markets are likely to be greater than in the case of government bond holdings. However, central banks may have little scope to sell assets in the immediate future unless the economic recovery and the underlying normalisation of financial markets turn out to be proceeding at a much faster pace than expected. In a weaker environment, large-scale sales could be destabilising for financial markets and long-term rates, possibly jeopardising the economic recovery.

In normal times, decisions to divest long-dated assets should be motivated solely by monetary policy considerations, with any profits and losses resulting from interest rate movements simply incidental to the

24. The potential case for central banks to continue supplying ample liquidity and operate conventional monetary policy solely with the deposit rate is discussed in the final section of the paper.

decision. In a similar vein, where assets are purchased specifically for monetary policy purposes, changes in their valuation should not have policy implications as they neither add to nor withdraw liquidity. In current circumstances, however, the strategy concerning asset sales may also be coloured by the potentially large losses from interest rate movements for the central banks that have actively acquired long-term assets.

The average remaining maturity of long-dated assets held by the Fed (Treasury securities, agency bonds and mortgage-backed securities) for instance, appears to be on the whole in the vicinity of 10 years. If the market interest rate moves up from the current level of 3.5 per cent to 5.2 per cent, a level more or less in line with the long-term equilibrium as assumed in OECD (2009), the loss could exceed by a wide margin from the normal level of annual profits of the Fed or its capital buffer.

For the BoE, whose gilts holdings have, on an average, a remaining maturity of nearly 14 years, an increase in the interest rate from the current level to the long-run neutral rate assumed in OECD (2009) could also result in a massive loss.[25] Reflecting the special nature of monetary policy, long-term assets held by central banks are not necessarily subject to marked-to-market valuation. The Fed, for instance, keeps them at historical value (Federal Reserve, 2008). This would imply that losses would have to be recognised only when the assets are sold in an environment where interest rates have risen, while, if kept to maturity, losses can be smoothed over the remaining life of the security, as the premium paid over par values can be amortised. The concern would be that substantial losses could affect central bank credibility:

> In the event of large sales and realised losses, the central bank may be indemnified by the government or receive a capital injection from the fiscal authorities, threatening actual or perceived independence. If assets are kept to maturity, the losses will be spread over time, reducing transfers from the central bank to the fiscal authorities over an extended period. This could also possibly compromise independence, although the smoother profile of the impact may imply a weaker risk. Recognising this concern the BoE, before engaging in massive purchases of long-term assets, obtained an agreement with the government that any losses arising out of or in connection with its quantitative easing policy would be indemnified by the Treasury (Minegishi and Cournède, 2010).

---

25. On the other hand, for the ECB, the potential interest rate risk is likely to be smaller, both because the purchased amount remains smaller and typical maturity of covered bonds is shorter than mortgage-backed securities or gilts.

If central banks choose to keep the assets on their balance sheets until maturity—or at least for some time—they can offset their impact on liquidity via other operations. This effectively amounts to absorbing liquidity from reserve positions while maintaining the size of the balance sheet by way of liability management. Unlike outright sales of long-dated assets, money is not entirely drained from the banking system but less is made available for the inter-bank market, which allows central banks to raise interest rates.[26]

For example, provided that macroprudential considerations also justify this, central banks can introduce or increase the reserve requirement that would shift some portion of the 'excess' reserves into 'required' reserves. Although the level of the monetary base is unaffected by this measure, there will be less lendable funds in the overnight money market, thus effectively reducing supply and leading to upward pressure on interest rates in the market. In most OECD countries, the required reserve ratio has ceased to be used as a monetary policy instrument, since developments in inter-bank markets have made open market operations much more efficient and effective tools.

In the current circumstances, however, the exceptionally high level of reserves may justify measures directly targeted at reducing excess reserves, at least temporarily during the exit phase. The measure could be particularly effective, if a 'faster-than-expected' pace of credit increases were to generate inflationary concerns. The required part of reserves can be remunerated at the prevailing market rate, so as to avoid the problems associated with imposing an implicit tax on reserve holdings.[27] Nonetheless, the combination of the high levels of reserves and relatively low reserve ratios now applied implies that for this measure to have a major impact, the increase in the required reserve ratio would have to be large.[28]

---

26. Some central banks, notably the Fed, appear to have already exhausted the options of selling short-term government securities, because of the massive sales at the early stage of the crisis.

27. As banks are 'forced' to set aside a certain portion of money as required reserves, they are deprived of an opportunity to lend this amount out in the money market. Thus, the associated opportunity cost, which is the prevailing money market rate, can be considered as implicit tax on reserve holding.

28. A universally applicable large increase in the reserve ratio may lead to a distributional problem, given the difficulty of correctly forecasting precautionary demand for reserves that varies from one bank to another.

Central banks can also resort to more explicit liquidity-absorbing operations. First, central banks can conduct reverse repurchasing operations, in which long-dated assets acquired by central banks are sold with a promise to buy them back at a pre-specified date in the future. Second, central banks can offer longer term deposits, in addition to the use of the standing overnight deposit facility. Third, central banks can issue their own bills. The benefit of relying on these operations is flexibility.

Unlike the outright sales of assets, which are costly to reverse, the effect of liquidity absorption can be reset and adjusted according to market developments.[29] And unlike increases in reserve requirements, which are universally applicable, financial market participants retain an option not to participate in such operations, so that they can continue to hold liquidity if judged necessary. Another advantage is that central banks do not incur interest-rate-related losses in such operations.

For these measures to be effectively conducted, a number of points need to be carefully considered. First, just as substantial increases in liquidity provision have been made possible by having a large pool of eligible counter-parties, these liquidity-absorbing operations may have to be carried out against a large number of financial market participants. Where the traditional list of counter-parties for open market operations is short (such as the Fed with primary dealers), it may have to be broadened, so that relatively large scale operations can be conducted without the risk of under-subscription to offers from central banks.

Issuance of bills can be potentially the more convenient tools, as it enables central banks to go easily beyond the traditional list of counter-parties. This issue, however, may be less of a problem in a situation where market functions have completely normalised so that the distribution of liquidity among financial market participants can be left to the market and the arbitrage mechanisms are working efficiently.

Second, in a similar vein to the discussion on the use of the deposit rate, the interest rate at which liquidity is absorbed should be carefully

29. Should markets destabilise, central banks can always 'undo' the impact of asset sales by engaging in liquidity-providing operation or buying long-dated assets again. However, it could have a negative impact on the confidence and credibility.

considered. For financial market participants to have a clear incentive to participate in these operations, the interest rate will have to exceed the standing deposit rate. When the interest rate is endogeneously determined, such as in the case of bill issuance, this is likely to be a less important issue.

Third, the maturity of these operations also matters. Short maturities, such as one week, may be impractical because positions have to be repeatedly rolled over. Thus, longer term liquidity-absorption measures may be desirable. However, from the viewpoint of financial market participants, this can directly compete with other risk-free instruments, such as Treasury bills, thereby exerting upward pressures on the interest rates in the corresponding maturity segment.

In some cases, particularly where central banks do not have the legal authority to issue their own bills (the Fed, for example), the active use of government deposit may be an option. Central banks can cooperate with the government to set up a scheme where the government issues short-term securities to the market and deposits the proceeds with the central bank, as the Fed and the US Treasury have already done through the Supplementary Financing Account. It may not be appropriate, however, to rely on this measure in the process of the exit, as it implies that central banks do not have control over the timing and the pace of the exit, which may compromise the perception of independence.[30]

The timing and the sequence of the exit

The timing and pace of withdrawal of non-interest rate measures should be primarily determined by the progress in financial market normalisation. As financial markets have not been fully repaired, there is a case for central banks to be cautious about the pace at which they withdraw from their exceptional presence in financial markets. First, to the extent that improvements in the functioning of the financial system depend on the presence of exceptional measures, premature withdrawal could destabilise the market again.

30. The use of the Fed's Supplementary Financing Account has diminished in February 2010, causing an additional pressure on its balance sheet. The US Treasury has, however, recently decided to scale up this programme once again.

Second, premature exit could necessitate the reintroduction of once-terminated measures in case of renewed turbulence, which could weaken market confidence and threaten the credibility of central banks. Third, improvement in overall financial conditions may be masking the significant difference in the health of individual banks. In itself, concern for weak banks should not be a reason to hold back on measures to normalise liquidity—such concerns should be addressed by microprudential policy—not least given the risk that, if expectations emerge that abundant liquidity will continue to be available (and at very low interest rates), necessary adjustment in the banking sector would get delayed as economically unviable banks remain in business. Still, to the extent that heterogeneity among banks is judged to be important for the functioning of the market as a whole, because of the remaining fragility in the financial system, it would be warranted to keep system-wide emergency measures in place as a safety back-up line, especially where the stigma problem tends to make the reliance on the standing lending facility less effective.

In withdrawing non-interest measures, the role of endogeneous market-based incentives can be strengthened by increasing the cost of central bank provision of liquidity by increasing fees and 'haircuts' on eligible collateral. Discouraging the use of special liquidity schemes through such market-type mechanisms may be seen as a first step towards termination of such facilities and proceeding in such a gradual manner may imply less risk than abrupt cancellation. Some of the liquidity-management measures taken during the crisis, such as the extension of counter-parties and the introduction of new liability management tools should probably be made permanent.

Given their potentially adverse effects on asset prices and inflation expectations, it would be desirable, in principle, to withdraw direct market interventions and purchases of long-term government bonds as soon as financial markets return to normal. However, selling such assets can be disruptive and, as discussed above, an alternative may be to keep such assets to maturity on central bank balance sheets, with their impact on liquidity offset by other means.

This is particularly the case for holding of government bonds, which pose less credit risk and have less distortive impacts on resource allocation than is the case with holding private securities. Where the purchase of longer term securities is primarily aimed at providing stimulus to the economy, the timing of the withdrawal (or neutralisation) of such measures should depend on the same factors that determine the pace of interest rate increases.

The articulation between the two components of the exit is relatively straightforward if improving financial conditions generate inflationary concerns, as a withdrawal of the volume of liquidity can come hand in hand with increases in its price. Although it would be more complicated if upside risk to price stability emerges while financial markets have not yet fully recovered, the use of various previously-discussed tools should help to address such an eventuality.

Particular complications may arise should asset prices start to move up significantly when financial institutions have yet to regain health and economic recovery remains muted. If, in response, central banks lean against the wind by raising interest rates, this could destabilise the market and slow the healing of the financial system, and might call for slowing the exit from unconventional measures.

Unconventional monetary policy exit and spillovers

The exit strategy for unconventional monetary policy must be gauged in a wider environment where most other crisis-driven measures taken by governments will also need to be reversed or removed at some point. Central bank independence implies that central bank actions should not be conditioned on the pace of withdrawal of government measures. Nonetheless, government actions have spillover effects on financial markets and the overall economy, which, in turn, can have important implications for monetary policy decisions.

At the same time, withdrawing the crisis-driven monetary policy measures can also have repercussions beyond money markets, both domestically and internationally. Thus, the timing, pace and communication of the exit must carefully take these issues into consideration. First, the withdrawal of government emergency financial policy measures, especially liability guarantees, can expose remaining vulnerabilities in the financial system. As a precaution, exceptional liquidity programmes could be kept in reserve until after the financial system has proved resilient to withdrawal of such emergency financial policy measures.

Second, although many unconventional monetary policy measures have been introduced with the primary aim of securing the provision of ample liquidity through the financial system, the fact that these measures have been conducted in an environment of extremely low interest rates has had the side-effect of generating large margins for many banks and other intermediaries. As such, they might have helped banks and other intermediaries in their efforts to rebuild their capital bases. To the extent that these margins are dependent on special liquidity measures, the exit from unconventional measures could affect the process of balance sheet adjustments of banks, with implications for the growth of the wider economy.

Third, and on the other hand, there may be cases where the new regulatory environment actually facilitates the exit process of monetary policy measures. For instance, new regulations requiring financial institutions to hold more liquid assets can make it easier for central banks to sell bonds issued or backed by governments.

Fourth, even when the short-term policy rate remains unchanged, the exit from unconventional measures, such as termination of longer term liquidity provision and asset purchase programmes will probably exert upward pressure on medium to longer term segments of the yield curve, effectively leading to tighter financial conditions. This would also have implications for fiscal authorities, as the cost of servicing government debt would probably increase.

Besides, if a situation arises where some public sector instruments accepted as collateral under a loosened eligibility criteria can no longer be accepted as such, it could further increase the financial cost for the issuer. While these factors should not delay the exit, it may be useful to communicate these risks to the fiscal authorities.

While the timing of the exit must be ultimately determined by national, economic and financial conditions, the exit process will probably have spillover effects internationally. For instance, earlier a faster pace of exit in one country could lead to currency appreciation, which would further add to the tightening of monetary conditions. Reduction in liquidity supply of major currencies (the US dollar, for instance) may have important implications internationally, as was the case in the run-up to the crisis (McGuire and Peter, 2009).

The case for formally coordinating monetary policy actions is less compelling than in the case of emergency financial policy measures, especially government guarantees that directly involve competition issues. In particular, the differences in cyclical positions and financial fragilities across countries (see, for instance, OECD, 2009) will necessarily call for different exit pathways. Nevertheless, the risk of unwarranted exchange rate movement might be reduced by well-coordinated communication.

Given the unprecedented nature of the exit, both in its scope and its scale, a clear communication strategy is essential. Indeed, the communication can be quite challenging for central banks, especially at the start of the exit process. Even a small technical change in monetary policy implementation can easily be taken by market participants as an indication that central banks are tightening policy.

Thus, even in cases where the previously adopted measures are allowed to run off, simply because the expiry date has arrived, central banks may wish to clearly state their intentions of not extending the measures in advance. Announcement of changes of a technical nature, such as fewer liquidity offers made from central banks or changes in collateral eligibility, should be accompanied by a clear explanation in order to clarify the intention of the monetary authorities, so that markets do not misinterpret the nature and scope of the technical steps that will be taken in the process of normalising monetary policy. The importance of this challenge is illustrated by the strong attention that markets paid to recent technical reverse repo transactions by the Fed and changes in collateral rules by the ECB.

Beyond the exit

Over a longer horizon, as financial market conditions normalise, the framework for monetary policy implementation may have to be reassessed against lessons to be learned from the crisis experience. Some of the measures introduced on an emergency basis may be made permanent, as they enhance central banks' operational capacity in normal times.[31] These measures potentially include extension of counter-parties, where the traditional counter-parties to monetary policy operations were quite limited, and interest was paid on reserves. This also holds for other liability management tools, such as the ability to issue central bank bills.

Whether other measures—such as relaxation of standards for eligible collateral and extended maturity of liquidity operations—should be maintained largely depends on how generous central banks should be in providing liquidity to the banking sector in normal times. Restricting the provision of central bank liquidity may help restore some market discipline. The fact that central banks have once significantly extended liquidity provision in response to the crisis may have added an element of moral hazard, though, as market participants now have reasons to expect them to offer more liquidity at low cost whenever liquidity dries up in the market. Dealing with this concern calls for a more stringent regulatory framework.

Finally, the question arises of whether the amount of liquidity provision in itself may in future become a regular instrument of monetary policy implementation even in normal times. This could be the case to the extent where greater weight is put on the objective of financial market stability in addition to the traditional objective of price stability. In the pre-crisis norm of monetary policy implementation, the price and quantity of liquidity were clearly linked, as the deposit rates that formed the lower bound of the money market interest rate were much lower than the main rate, even zero for some central banks.

Central banks, however, cannot be expected to achieve these two different objectives simultaneously at all times if only the single instrument of the interest rate is available. Separating the price of liquidity from its quantity might in principle facilitate the pursuit of price stability simultaneously with a goal of financial stability. Central banks could assign the traditional interest rate tool, which determines the price of liquidity, exclusively to the macroeconomic objective of price stability, while the

31. For instance, Cheun *et al.* (2009) compares a relatively flexible collateral framework in the Euro area with more restricted schemes in the United States and in the United Kingdom and concluded that the inherent flexibility in the Euro area system has served well during the crisis.

financial stability objective would be met by adjusting the quantity of liquidity available in the market and other stability-oriented tools.

This would be possible, for example, if in the previously discussed figure, the supply curve always interacts with the demand curve at a point where the latter is horizontal at the deposit rate. Then, by always setting the interest rate on the standing deposit facility equal to the prevailing market interest rate, central banks would be able to determine the quantity of reserves independently of the price stability consideration (Keister *et al.*, 2009; Goodfriend, 2009; Woodford, 2001).

A clear drawback of such an approach is that it would probably suppress the money market permanently because it would make the opportunity cost of holding reserves essentially zero.

References

Ahrend, R., B. Cournède and R. Price (2008). "Monetary Policy, Market Excesses and Financial Turmoil", *OECD Economics Department Working Paper* No. 597.

Aït-Sahalia, Y., J. Andritzky, A. Jobst, S. Nowak and N. Tamirisa (2009). "How to Stop a Herd of Running Bears? Market Response to Policy Initiatives during the Global Financial Crisis", *IMF Working Paper* WP/09/204.

Bean, C. (2009). *Quantitative Easing: An Interim Report*. Speech to the London Society of Charted Accountants. 13 October. London.

Bernanke, B.S. (2010). *Federal Reserve's Exit Strategy.* Statement prepared for the Committee on Financial Services US House of Representatives. 10 February.

Board of Governors of the Federal Reserve System (2008). *95th Annual Report*.

Borio, C. and P. Disyatat (2009). "Unconventional Monetary Policy: An Appraisal", *BIS Working Paper* No. 292.

Cheun, S., I. von Köppen-Mertes and B. Weller (2009). "The Collateral Frameworks of the Eurosystem, the Federal Reserve System and the Bank of England and the Financial Market Turmoil", *ECB Occasional Paper Series* No. 107.

Christensen, J.H.E., J.A. Lopez and G.D. Rudebusch (2009). "Do Central Bank Liquidity Facilities Affect Interbank Lending Rates?", *Federal Reserve Bank of San Francisco Working Paper* No. 2009-13.

Ennis, H.M. and T. Keister (2008). "Understanding Monetary Policy Implementation", *Economic Quarterly* 94(3), Summer.

European Central Bank (ECB) (2009). *Monthly Report on the Eurosystem's Covered Bond Purchase Programme* (various issues).

———. (2010). "The ECB's Monetary Policy Stance During the Financial Crisis", in *Monthly Bulletin*, January.

Gagnon, J.E. (2009). *The World Needs Further Monetary Ease, Not an Early Exit.* Washington DC: Peterson Institute for International Economics.

Goodfriend, M. (2002). "Interest on Reserves and Monetary Policy", *FRBNY Economic Policy Review* 8(1), May.

———. (2009). "Central Banking in the Credit Turmoil: An Assessment of Federal Reserve Practice", Prepared for a presentation at the Bank of Japan 2009 International Conference: *Financial System and Monetary Policy Implementation*. 27-28 May.

Ishi, K., M. Stone, and E. Yehoue (2009). "Unconventional Central Bank Measures for Emerging Economies", *IMF Working Paper* WP/09/226.

Keister, T., A. Martin and J. McAndrews (2008). "Divorcing Money from Monetary Policy", *FRBNY Economic Policy Review* 14(2). September.

Keister, T. and J. McAndrews (2009). "Why Are Banks Holding So Many Excess Reserves?" *Federal Reserve Bank of New York Staff Reports* No. 380.

Kohn, D.L. (2009). *Central Bank Exit Policies*. Speech at the Cato Institute's Shadow Open Market Committee Meeting. Washington, DC. September.

McGuire, P. and G. von Peter (2009). "The US Dollar Shortage in Global Banking and the International Policy Response", *BIS Working Paper* No. 291, October.

Meier, A. (2009). "Panacea, Curse, or Nonevent? Unconventional Monetary Policy in the United Kingdom", *IMF Working Paper* WP/09/163.

Minegishi, M. and B. Cournède (2010). "Monetary Policy Responses to the Crisis and Exit Strategies", *OECD Economics Department Working Paper* No. 752.

OECD (2009). *Economic Outlook*. No. 86. Paris.

Rochet, J.C. (2009). "An Industrial Organisation Approach to the Too-Big-To-Fail Problem," Paper prepared for the Federal Reserve Bank of Boston *54th Economic Conference*. 21-23 October.

Rochet, J.C. and J. Tirole (1996). "Interbank Lending and Systemic Risk," *Journal of Money, Credit and Banking* 28(4).

Sack, B.P. (2009). *The Fed's Expanded Balance Sheet*. Remarks at the Money Marketeers of New York University. New York City. December.

Woodford, M. (2001). "Monetary Policy in the Information Economy", *NBER Working Paper* No. 8674.

Yehoue, E.B. (2009). "Emerging Economy Responses to the Global Financial Crisis of 2007-09: An Empirical Analysis of the Liquidity Easing Measures", *IMF Working Paper* WP/09/265.

7 Inflation Targeting after the Financial Crisis

LARS E.O. SVENSSON*

As the world economy begins to recover from the financial crisis and the resulting deep recession, there is a lively debate on what caused the crisis and how the risks of future crises can be reduced. Some blame loose monetary policy for laying the foundation for the crisis and there is a lively debate on the future of monetary policy and its relation with financial stability. I will focus on the lessons for inflation targeting after the crisis.

My view is that the crisis was not caused by monetary policy, but mainly by regulatory and supervisory failures in combination with some special circumstances. My main surmise from the crisis so far is that flexible inflation targeting, applied in the right way and using all the information about financial factors relevant for forecasting inflation and resource utilisation in any horizon, remains the best-practice monetary policy before, during, and after the financial crisis.

A better theoretical, empirical and operational understanding of the role of financial factors in the transmission mechanism is urgently required, however, and needs a lot of work—work that is already underway in academia and in central banks. So, I will focus on two particular issues: whether monetary policy caused the crisis and what are the possible lessons for future monetary policy.[1]

---

* I thank Charles Bean, Claes Berg, Alan Blinder, Stephen Cecchetti, Chuck Freedman, Charles Goodhart, Lars Nyberg, Irma Rosenberg, Hyun Shin, Frank Smets and Staffan Viotti for discussions on these issues. The views expressed here are my own and not necessarily those of other members of the Riksbank's executive board or of the Riksbank's staff. Hanna Armelius and Hans Dellmo of the Riksbank's staff contributed to this chapter.

1. I have previously discussed these issues in Svensson (2009b).

Best practice before the crisis: Flexible inflation targeting

It is probably not surprising that I consider flexible inflation targeting the best-practice monetary policy. The Riksbank and all the other inflation-targeting central banks conduct flexible inflation targeting, instead of strict inflation targeting. Flexible inflation targeting implies a monetary policy that aims to stabilise both inflation around the inflation target and the real economy.

Strict inflation targeting, on the other hand, aims at stabilising inflation only, without regard to the stability of the real economy. It is what Mervyn King (1997) has described as being an 'inflation nutter'. By stabilising the real economy I mean stabilising resource utilisation around a normal level, keeping in mind that monetary policy cannot affect the long-term level of resource utilisation.[2] Because of the time lags between monetary policy actions and their effect on inflation and the real economy, flexible inflation targeting is more effective if it relies on forecasts for inflation and the real economy. Therefore, flexible inflation targeting can be described as 'forecast targeting'.

The central bank chooses a policy-rate path so that the forecast for inflation and resource utilisation 'looks good'. When I say a forecast that looks good, I mean a forecast for inflation and resource utilisation that effectively stabilises both inflation around the inflation target and resource utilisation around a normal level.

In the event of conflicting objectives, it achieves a reasonable compromise between stabilising inflation and stabilising resource utilisation. Different central banks express this strategy in slightly different words. The Riksbank has often used the term 'well-balanced' monetary policy.[3] The forecasts for inflation and the real economy are then

2. The term 'inflation nutter', for a central bank that is only concerned about stabilising inflation was introduced in a paper by Mervyn King at a conference in Gerzensee, Switzerland, in 1995 and later published as King (1997). The terms 'strict' and 'flexible' inflation targeting were to my knowledge first introduced in a paper of mine presented at a conference at the Bank of Portugal in 1996, later published as Svensson (1999).

3. The idea that inflation targeting implies that the inflation forecast can be seen as an intermediate target was introduced in King (1994). The term 'inflation-forecast targeting' was introduced in Svensson (1997), and the term 'forecast targeting' in Svensson (2005). See Woodford (2007a, b) for more discussion and analysis of forecast targeting.

conditional to the central bank's view of the transmission mechanism, an estimate of the current state of the economy and a forecast for important exogeneous variables.

The central bank uses all relevant information that has an impact on forecasting inflation and the real economy. In this framework, the central bank takes into account financial conditions such as credit growth, asset prices, imbalances, potential asset price bubbles and so on only to the extent that they have an impact on the forecast for inflation and resource utilisation.

Inflation and resource utilisation are target variables, that is, variables that the central bank tries to stabilise. Financial conditions are not target variables. They are only indicators, as they provide information to the central bank about the state of the economy, the transmission mechanism and exogeneous shocks. Financial conditions then affect policy rates only to the extent they impact the forecast for inflation and resource utilisation.[4]

Now, is there any reason to modify this view of monetary policy in the light of the experience of the financial crisis so far? Let me approach this question by first asking what were the causes of the financial crisis. Did monetary policy contribute to the crisis, and was a different monetary policy warranted that could have prevented or reduced the size of the crisis?

The financial crisis was not caused by monetary policy

Many have claimed that excessively easy monetary policy by the Federal Reserve after 2001 helped cause a bubble in house prices in the US, a bubble whose inevitable bursting proved to be a major source of the financial crisis.[5] However, as I see it, the crisis was mainly caused by factors that had very little to do with monetary policy and were mostly because of background macro conditions.

It was caused by distorted incentives in financial markets, regulatory and supervisory failures (including those when central banks were responsible for regulation and supervision), information problems and

4. Several central banks that do not call themselves inflation targeters effectively do conduct flexible inflation targeting, although they may not be quite as transparent about their inflation target, the role of stability of the real economy, etc.

5. See, for instance, Taylor (2007).

some specific circumstances, including the US housing policy to support home ownership for low income households.[6]

The macro conditions preceding the crisis included low real interest rates worldwide. This condition was associated with global imbalances, as well as the Great Moderation, which entailed a long period of very stable growth and stable low inflation that led to a systematic underestimation of risk and very low risk premia in financial markets. There were distorted incentives for commercial and investment banks to increase leverage that were made possible by lax regulation and supervision and the lack of an appropriate bank resolution regime.

There were also distorted incentives to exercise less due diligence in loan origination because of securitisation and to conduct regulatory arbitrage by setting up off-balance-sheet entities, which for various specific reasons still ended up effectively on the balance sheet. There were also distorted incentives for traders and fund managers to take excessive risks because of myopic and asymmetric remuneration contracts.

There were eventually enormous information problems in assessing the risks of extremely complex asset-backed securities, and there was a huge underestimation of the potential for correlated systemic risks. None of these causes had anything to do with monetary policy, except that monetary policy may have contributed to the Great Moderation.

On the role of Federal Reserve monetary policy in the crisis, there are two relevant questions. First, was the low interest rate reasonable considering the information available at the time? Second, could a different monetary policy with higher interest rates have prevented the crisis? The first question is the relevant one when evaluating monetary policy. It is more relevant to evaluate policy, taking into account the information available *ex ante* to the policymaker rather than information *ex post* that

6. See Bean (2009) for an extensive and excellent discussion of the crisis, including the credit expansion and housing boom, the macroeconomic antecedents, the distorted incentives, the information problems, the amplification and propagation of the crisis into the real economy, the policy responses and the lessons for monetary policy and economics generally. The Bank for International Settlements (2009) provides a more detailed account of the possible macro- and microeconomic causes of the crisis.

was unknown to the policymaker at the time (see Svensson, 2009a, on evaluating monetary policy *ex ante* and *ex post*).[7]

During the period in question, given the information available, there was a genuine and well-motivated fear of the US falling into a Japanese-style deflationary liquidity trap, and the optimal policy in such a situation is a very expansionary monetary policy.[8] Perhaps, in retrospect, the risk of deflation was exaggerated, but there was no way to know this *ex ante*. Hence, I consider the expansionary policy very appropriate. Adding some *ex post* evaluation, one can note that it did not lead *ex post* to very high inflation or an overheated economy.

The second question, whether a different monetary policy could have prevented the crisis, is relevant when assessing to what extent monetary policy can be blamed for causing the crisis, notwithstanding if it was reasonable from an *ex ante* perspective. The credit growth and the housing boom in the US and elsewhere were very powerful. Real interest rates were low to a large extent because of global imbalances, the global saving glut and investment shortage. I believe that somewhat higher interest[9] and a small portion of house-price increases can be attributed to monetary policy.[10]

Bernanke (2010) shows that the recent phenomenon of a higher share of adjustable-rate mortgages was unlikely to have significantly increased the sensitivity of house prices to monetary policy. The availability of new, more exotic mortgage types mattered much more for initial mortgage payments than the level of short-term interest rates.

In my view, interest rates would probably have had to be raised very high so as to cause considerable damage to the real economy to stop the

7. I remember this period very vividly, because I was fortunate to have the opportunity to discuss and debate the problems of current monetary policy, deflation and liquidity traps in a group of great economists at Princeton University that included Ben Bernanke (before he left to be the Governor on the Federal Reserve Board), Alan Blinder, Paul Krugman, Chris Sims and Michael Woodford.

8. See Svensson (2003) for a discussion of policy options before and in a liquidity trap.

9. Bernanke (2010) shows that Fed policy rates do not seem excessively low given real-time FOMC forecasts.

10. See Del Negro and Otrok (2007), Jarocinski and Smets (2008), Edge *et al.* (2008), and Iacoviello and Neri (2008).

credit growth and housing boom.[11] That could have thrown the US right into Japanese-style deflation and eventually a liquidity trap. Certainly, higher interest rates would have had no impact on the regulatory problems, distorted incentives and information problems mentioned above (although they could have ended the Great Moderation with a deep recession and deflation).[12]

However, going beyond the Fed's actual monetary policy, perhaps it is possible that the Fed's emphasis on its readiness to relax monetary policy aggressively in the wake of a sharp fall in asset prices, as expressed by Greenspan (2002) for example, may have induced expectations of a floor under future asset prices and contributed to the asset-price boom, the so called Greenspan Put (Miller *et al.*, 2002). Arguably, this is more of a communication issue than one of actual policy, and less emphasis on the readiness to clean up after a sharp fall in asset prices might have been a preferable alternative.

The International Monetary Fund (2009, Chapter 3) has investigated the role of monetary policy in causing financial crises. A large number of countries and financial crises were included in the sample. Its conclusion is that, 'the stance of monetary policy has not generally been a good leading indicator of future house price busts... There is some association between loose monetary policy and house price rises in the years leading up to the current crisis in some countries, but loose monetary policy was not the main, systematic cause of the boom and consequent bust.'

Moreover, the overall relationship between the stance of monetary policy and house price appreciation across countries in the years before the current crisis is statistically insignificant and economically weak. Monetary policy differences explain only about five per cent of the variability in house-price appreciation across countries.[13]

---

11. See Nyberg (2010) for similar arguments.
12. Kohn (2008), after extensive discussion, concludes that there is insufficient evidence that low interest rates would have contributed much to the house-price boom and that higher interest rates would have had much dampening effect on it.
13. The relationship for the Euro area countries is less weak, but for reasons explained by Bernanke (2010) it is potentially overstated.

Lessons for flexible inflation targeting

What conclusions can we now draw from the financial crisis about the conduct of monetary policy and need to modify the framework of flexible inflation targeting? One obvious conclusion is that price stability is not enough to achieve financial stability (Carney, 2009; White, 2006). Good flexible inflation targeting by itself does not achieve financial stability, if anyone ever believed that. Specific policies and instruments are needed to ensure financial stability.

Another conclusion is that interest rate policy is not enough to achieve financial stability. Other instruments like supervision and regulation, including appropriate bank resolution regimes, should be the first choice for financial stability. In many countries, the responsibility for these instruments rests on authorities other than the central bank. Generally, to the extent financial instability depends on specific distortions, good regulation should aim to attack these distortions as close to the source as possible.

To counter the observed procyclicality of existing regulation, macroprudential regulation that is contingent on the business cycle and financial indicators may need to be introduced to induce better financial stability. Possible macroprudential regulation includes variable capital, margin, and equity/loan requirements. As expressed by Bean (2009), 'the best approach is likely to involve a portfolio of instruments.'[14]

More generally, what is the relation between financial stability and monetary policy? Financial stability is an important objective of economic policy. A possible definition of financial stability is a situation where the financial system can fulfill its main functions (of submitting payments, channelling savings into investment and providing risk sharing) without disturbances that have significant social costs.

I find it helpful to conceptually distinguish financial stability policy from monetary policy. Different economic policies and policy areas, such as fiscal policy, labour market policy, structural policies to improve competition, etc., can be distinguished according to their objectives, the

14. Nyberg (2010) provides more discussion of macroprudential regulation and regulation reform.

policy instruments that are suitable for achieving the objectives, and the authority or authorities controlling the instruments and responsible for achieving the objectives.

Monetary policy aimed at flexible inflation targeting has the objective of stabilising both inflation around the inflation target and resource utilisation around a normal level. The suitable instruments are, under normal circumstances, the policy rate and communication, including possibly a published policy rate path and a forecast for inflation and the real economy.

In times of crisis, as we have seen during the current crisis, other more unconventional instruments can be used, such as fixed-rate lending at longer maturities, asset purchases and foreign exchange intervention to prevent currency appreciation. The authority responsible for monetary policy is typically the central bank.

Financial stability policy has the objective of maintaining or promoting financial stability. The available instruments are under normal circumstances—supervision, regulation and financial stability reports with analyses and leading indicators that may provide early warnings of stability threats. In times of crisis, there are instruments such as lending-of-last-resort, variable rate lending at longer maturities, special resolution regimes for financial firms in trouble, government capital injections and so forth.

The responsible authority or authorities vary across countries. In some countries it is the central bank, in other countries there is a separate financial supervisory authority. Sometimes, the responsibility is shared between different institutions. In Sweden, the Financial Supervisory Authority is responsible for supervision and regulation, the Riksbank is responsible for lending-of-last-resort to solvent banks and for promoting a safe and efficient payment system, while the National Debt Office is responsible for the resolution of failed banks.

During times of crisis, these authorities cooperate closely with the Ministry of Finance. My point here is that financial stability policy and monetary policy are quite different, with different objectives, instruments and responsible authorities, the latter with considerable differences across countries. This does not mean that there is no interaction between them.

Financial stability directly affects the financial markets, and financial conditions affect the transmission mechanism of monetary policy. Problems in financial markets may have a drastic effect on the real economy, as the current financial crisis has shown. Monetary policy affects asset prices and balance sheets and can, thereby, affect financial stability.

The fact that financial stability policy and monetary policy are conceptually distinct, with distinct objectives and distinct suitable instruments, has to be taken into account, however, when considering the lessons of the financial crisis for monetary policy. It makes little sense to extend the mandate of monetary policy to include financial stability.[15]

What are the specific conclusions for flexible inflation targeting? One important lesson from the financial crisis is that financial factors may have a very strong and deteriorating effect on the transmission mechanism, making standard interest rate policy much less effective.

This motivates more research on how to incorporate financial factors into the standard models of the transmission mechanism used by central banks. A rapidly increasing volume of such research is now being produced by academic and central bank researchers and being presented at an increasing number of conferences on financial factors and monetary policy.

Important and challenging questions include how potential output and neutral real interest rates are affected by financial factors and financial distortions (Curdia and Woodford, 2009; Walsh, 2009), and what impact financial factors have on the general equilibrium effects of alternative policy rate paths on inflation and resource utilisation forecasts.[16] Even with much

---

15. However, conceptually distinguishing the two policy areas does not rule out that there might be advantages of keeping a large part of the responsibility for financial stability policy within the central bank, as argued by, for instance, Blinder (2010) and Nyberg (2010).

16. Walsh (2009) points out that when financial factors cause distortions, these distortions will, in general, introduce corresponding terms in a loss function for monetary policy that is a second-order approximation to household welfare. Curdia and Woodford (2009) present a model where the second-order welfare approximation is a standard quadratic loss function of inflation and the output gap between output and potential output, but where potential output is affected by financial factors. Then inflation and the output gap remain the target variables, with and without financial factors. The neutral rate in the model, that is, the real rate consistent with output equal to potential output, is then also affected by financial factors.

better analytical foundations concerning the role of financial factors in the transmission mechanism, there will of course, as always, be considerable scope for the application of good judgment in monetary policy.

Another conclusion, which is not new, is that consideration of the impact of financial factors in forecasting inflation and resource utilisation may require longer forecast horizons. Several inflation-targeting central banks (including the Bank of England, Norges Bank and the Riksbank) have for other reasons, already extended their forecast horizon from the previously common two years to three years.

There is nothing that, in principle, prevents an inflation targeter from considering forecasts beyond a three-year horizon. In practice, however, there is usually little information about anything at longer horizons, except the tendency to revert to the long-term average. What about 'leaning against the wind' (as advocated by, for instance, Borio and White, 2003, and Cecchetti *et al.*, 2002)? The idea advocates that central banks should raise interest rates more than what appears to be warranted by inflation and resource utilisation to counter rapid credit growth and rising asset prices?

It is sometimes not quite clear whether advocates of 'leaning against the wind' feel that credit growth and asset prices should be considered targets and enter the explicit or implicit loss functions alongside inflation and resource utilisation. Or do they perhaps mean that credit growth and asset prices should still be considered just indicators and are emphasised only because credit growth and asset prices may have potential negative effects on inflation and resource utilisation on a longer horizon. In the latter case, 'leaning against the wind' is a way to improve the stability of inflation and resource utilisation in the longer run. Then it is completely consistent with flexible inflation targeting.[17]

---

17. Adrian and Shin (2007, 2009) argue, in a model with a risk-taking channel as in Borio and Zhu (2008), that short-interest rate movements may have considerable effects on the leverage of securities broker-dealers in the market-based financial sector outside the commercial banking sector. However, new regulation may affect the magnitude of these affects, and the size of the market-based financial sector may end up being smaller after the crisis. In Europe, the commercial banks dominate the financial sector.

In line with the previous discussion, however, instruments other than interest rates are likely to be much more effective in avoiding excessive credit growth and asset-price booms, and should thus be used as a first-best alternative. Interest rates that are high enough to have a noticeable effect on credit growth and asset prices may have strong negative effects on inflation and resource utilisation. A central bank will probably rarely have sufficient information about the probable beneficial longer horizon effects on inflation and resource utilisation for the trade-off to be worthwhile and motivated. [18]

If there is evidence of rapidly rising house prices and mortgage loans, and these developments are deemed to be unsustainable and a possible bubble, policy rates are not the most effective instruments for tackling them. Restrictions on loan-to-value ratios and minimum mortgages and requirements of realistic cash-flow calculations for house buyers with realistic interest rates, are much more effective in putting a brake on possible unsustainable developments than a rise in the policy rates.

More transparency about future policy rates, in the form of a policy rate path published by the central bank, may help provide realistic information about future interest rates. Ultimately, my main conclusion from the crisis so far is that flexible inflation targeting, applied in the right way and using all the information about financial factors that is relevant for forecasting inflation and resource utilisation in any horizon, remains the best-practice monetary policy before, during, and after the financial crisis.

As I have said before, a better theoretical, empirical and operational understanding of the role of financial factors in the transmission mechanism is urgently required and needs much work—work that is already underway in academia and in central banks. The outcome might

18. Kohn (2006, 2008) specifies three conditions that should be fulfilled for central banks to take 'extra action' to deal with a possible asset-price bubble: 'First, policymakers must be able to identify bubbles in a timely fashion with reasonable confidence. Second, a somewhat tighter monetary policy must have a high probability that it will help to check at least some of the speculative activity. And third, the expected improvement in future economic performance that would result from the curtailment of the bubble must be sufficiently great.' He concludes, also in 2008 and after thorough considerations, that those conditions would rarely be met. See also Kohn (2009).

very well be that financial factors are considered to have a larger role in affecting the transmission mechanism and as indicators of future inflation and resource utilisation. If so, central banks would end up responding more to financial indicators, in the sense of adjusting the policy rate and policy rate path more to a given change in a financial indicator.

This would, however, not mean that financial factors and indicators have become independent targets besides inflation and resource utilisation in the explicit or implicit central bank loss function. Instead, it would be a matter of responding appropriately to financial indicators to achieve the best possible way to stabilise inflation around the inflation target and resource utilisation around a normal level over time.

References

Adrian, Tobias and Hyun Song Shin (2007). "Liquidity and Leverage", *Journal of Financial Intermediation* (forthcoming). Available as *Federal Reserve Bank of New York Staff* Reports 328.

———. (2009). "Financial Intermediaries and Monetary Economics", in Friedman, Benjamin M. and Michael Woodford, (eds.), *Handbook of Monetary Economics* 3(a-b) (forthcoming).

Bank for International Settlements (2009). *79th Annual Report. www.bis.org*

Bean, Charles R. (2009). "The Great Moderation, the Great Panic and the Great Contraction", *Schumpeter Lecture*. Annual Congress of the European Economic Association. *www.bankofengland.co.uk*

Bernanke, Ben S. (2010). *Monetary Policy and the Housing Bubble*. Speech on January 3. *www.federal.reserve.gov*

Blinder, Alan S. (2010). "How Central Should the Central Bank Be?", *CEPS Working Paper* No. 198.

Borio, Claudio and Haibin Zhu (2008). "Capital Regulation, Risk-taking and Monetary Policy: A Missing Link in the Transmission Mechanism?", *Bank for International Settlements Working Paper* 268.

Borio, Claudio and White, William R. (2003). "Whither Monetary and Financial Stability? The Implications of Evolving Policy Regimes", in *Monetary Policy and Uncertainty: Adapting to a Changing Economy: Jackson Hole Symposium*. pp.131-212. Federal Reserve Bank of Kansas City.

Carney, Mark (2009). "Some Considerations on Using Monetary Policy to Stabilize Economic Activity", in *Financial Stability and Macroeconomic Policy: Jackson Hole Symposium*. Federal Reserve Bank of Kansas City.

Cecchetti, Stephen, Hans Genberg and Sushil Wadhwani (2002). "Asset Prices in a Flexible Inflation Targeting Framework", in W. Hunter, G. Kaufman and M. Pomerleano (eds.), *Asset Price Bubbles: The Implications for Monetary, Regulatory and International Policies*. Cambridge. pp.427-444.

Curdia, Vasco and Michael Woodford (2009). "Credit Frictions and Optimal Monetary Policy", *BIS Working Paper 278*.

Del Negro, Marco, and Christopher Otrok (2007). "99 Luftballons: Monetary Policy and the House Price Boom across US States", *Journal of Monetary Economics* 54: 1962-1985.

Edge, Rochelle M., Michael T. Kiley, and Jean-Philippe Laforte (2008). "The Sources of Fluctuations in Residential Investment: A View from a Policy-Oriented DSGE Model of the US Economy", Paper presented at the *2009 American Economic Association Annual Meeting*. January 3-5.

Greenspan, Alan (2002). "Opening Remarks", in *Rethinking Stabilization Policy: Jackson Hole Symposium*. Federal Reserve Bank of Kansas City.

Iacoviello, Matteo, and Stefano Neri (2008). "Housing Market Spillovers: Evidence from an Estimated DSGE Model", Working Paper 723. Boston College: Department of Economics.

International Monetary Fund (2009). *World Economic Outlook*. October.

Jarocinski, Marek and Frank R. Smets (2008). "House Prices and the Stance of Monetary Policy", *St. Louis Review* 90: 339-365. Federal Reserve Bank.

King, Mervyn (1994). "Monetary Policy in the UK", *Fiscal Studies* 15(3): 109-128.

———. (1997). "Changes in UK Monetary Policy: Rules and Discretion in Practice", *Journal of Monetary Economics* 39: 81–97.

Kohn, Donald L. (2006). *Monetary Policy and Asset Prices*. Speech on March 16. *www.federalreserve.gov*

———. (2008). *Monetary Policy and Asset Prices Revisited*. Speech on November 19. *www.federalreserve.gov*

———. (2009). *Policy Challenges for the Federal Reserve*. Speech on November 16. *www.federalreserve.gov*

Miller, Marcus H., Paul A. Weller, and Lei Zhang (2002). "Moral Hazard and the US Stock Market: Analysing the Greenspan Put", *Economic Journal* 112: C171-C186.

Nyberg, Lars (2010). *After the Crisis*. Speech on February 5. *www.riksbank.se*

Svensson, Lars E.O. (1997). "Inflation Forecast Targeting: Implementing and Monitoring Inflation Targets", *European Economic Review* 41: 1111-1146.

———. (1999). "Inflation Targeting: Some Extensions", *Scandinavian Journal of Economics* 101: 337-361.

———. (2003). "Escaping from a Liquidity Trap and Deflation: The Foolproof Way and Others", *Journal of Economic Perspectives* 17(4): 145-166.

———. (2005). "Monetary Policy with Judgment: Forecast Targeting", *International Journal of Central Banking* 1(1): 1-54.

———. (2009a). "Evaluating Monetary Policy", in Koenig, Evan, and Robert Leeson, (eds.), *From the Great Moderation to the Great Deviation: A Round-Trip Journey Based on the Work of John B. Taylor* (forthcoming). *www.larseosvensson.net*

———. (2009b). *Flexible Inflation Targeting: Lessons from the Financial Crisis*. Speech on September 21. *www.riksbank.se*

Taylor, John B. (2007). "Housing and Monetary Policy", in *Housing, Housing Finance, and Monetary Policy*, Jackson Hole Symposium, 463-476. Federal Reserve Bank of Kansas City.

Walsh, Carl E. (2009). "Using Monetary Policy to Stabilize Economic Activity", in *Financial Stability and Macroeconomic Policy: Jackson Hole Symposium*. Federal Reserve Bank of Kansas City.

White, William R. (2006). "Is Price Stability Enough?", *BIS Working Paper* No. 205. *www.bis.org*

Woodford, Michael (2007a). "The Case for Forecast Targeting as a Monetary Policy Strategy", *Journal of Economic Perspectives*, Fall.

———. (2007b). "Forecast Targeting as a Monetary Policy Strategy: Policy Rules in Practice", in Evan Koenig, and Robert Leeson (eds.), *From the Great Moderation to the Great Deviation: A Round-Trip Journey Based on the Work of John B. Taylor.* (forthcoming).

7.1
DISCUSSION

Inflation Targeting after the Crisis

WILLIAM POOLE

Change structure of incentives for firms

I agree with almost everything Lars Svensson says. Rather than nitpick over minor areas of disagreement, I will emphasise theoretical propositions that underlie Svensson's argument.

The housing and mortgage markets in the United States during 2002-2006 and several other countries are best described as a mania. As with the dot-com mania of the late 1990s, prices were not subject to common sense and continued to rise till they were far above equilibrium. The US Congress and the Bush administration were part of the housing mania, pushing for ever higher home ownership rates and easy credit conditions in the mortgage market. An effort by the Federal Reserve to apply regulatory constraints might well have been met by a public rebuke that it was the policy of the US government to support housing and readily available mortgage finance for all.

In this environment, it is hard to imagine that a Federal funds rate one percentage point higher than actually observed would have made much difference. An even higher Fed funds rate would surely have changed many other things. The economic recovery from the 2001 recession would have been slower—perhaps much slower. It is important to remember that US employment was still falling in the spring of 2003, following the recession trough in November 2001. A policy of flexible inflation targeting implies that the central bank does put considerable weight on the full employment objective. It can do so when inflation expectations are firmly anchored. A

Comments by William Poole on the paper presented by Lars E.O. Svensson 'Inflation Targeting after the Financial Crisis'.

central bank with high inflation-fighting credibility can pursue the employment objective precisely because with anchored inflation expectations, the central bank can push real interest rates down to encourage a growth in employment.

Since inflation credibility is critical to the central bank's success in contributing to more stable employment, the inflation objective must be the prime objective of the central bank and the employment objective secondary. That does not mean that low inflation is more important than high employment. On the contrary, the structure of the economy is such that the central bank can only contribute to high employment, if it is successful in tackling inflation.

One of the lessons from the control theory understood for 50 years or more is that multiple objectives require multiple instruments. To the extent that price level stability and financial stability are separate goals, as Svensson argues and I agree, the central bank needs instruments beyond the inter-bank rate. However, Svensson does not specify what these other policy instruments might be, other than a casual reference to 'variable capital, margin, and equity/loan requirements.'

There is reason to be skeptical about the effectiveness of these other instruments. Margin requirements in the US refer to the percentage that may be lent against stock exchange collateral for buying stock. To get around this regulation, all the borrower needs to do is tell the lender that he is borrowing to finance the down payment on his house, or pay his taxes, or some other valid reason.

In other words, the borrower could use cash that he would otherwise use to pay taxes to buy stock and then use the stock as collateral to borrow from the bank or broker to pay taxes. Other sorts of credit regulations are equally easy to evade. It is simply very hard to stop a mania in a market economy without serious side- effects, including long-run negative effects on financial innovation and competition.

As we think of how to improve financial stability, it is instructive to keep in mind the importance of improvements in economic theory and empirical understanding over the decades. The operation of fractional reserve banking was not understood until the 1920s. The concept of rational expectations was developed in the 1960s and 1970s. The fact that the long-run Phillips curve is vertical was not generally understood until the 1970s. These advances in understanding have been essential to improved monetary policy.

I believe that eventually the economics profession will gravitate to the view that discretionary changes in monetary and regulatory policies are not effective in providing financial stability. Changes in the underlying structure of incentives under which households and financial firms operate are required to create a more stable economic environment. That has been the gist of my argument.

8 Summing-up

Should Monetary Policy Chase Other Hares?

CHARLES R. BEAN

Bill Poole raised the question why (most) policymakers, market participants and academics alike missed the advent of the crisis? I believe that the reason was that the crisis was not caused by a single factor, but rather the joint influence of multiple factors that individually may not have been that significant, but together represented a potent cocktail. Some of these factors, we—or at least some of us—diagnosed ahead of time. But we failed to see the others. Above all, we failed to see the interconnections between them.

I see the crisis as having had both macroeconomic and microeconomic causes. On the macroeconomic front, a number of factors created fertile ground for a credit/asset-price boom. First, the relatively high savings rates in China and other current account surplus countries, along with a shortage of high-quality assets in those regions, led to capital inflows into advanced economies such as the United States, which then led to low real returns on safe assets there.

Second, excessively loose US monetary policy during 2001-2005 resulted in extremely low short-term interest rates and a low cost of short-term debt finance. Finally, the period of stable growth and low inflation that we know as the Great Moderation resulted in an over-optimistic assessment of prospective risks. Together, these conditions encouraged a leveraged 'search for yield', as investors used debt to finance positions in risky assets, particularly those associated with the US subprime housing market.

Summing-up by Charles R. Bean, Chairman, Session I: Challenges and Response to Conduct Monetary Policy during the Financial Crisis.

With hindsight, we can also see that there were a number of distortions on the microeconomic front. A non-exhaustive list would include the moral hazard associated with having financial institutions that are too big or too systemically important to fail, coupled with inadequate regulation and supervision of these institutions.

Other distortions include the incentive to shift financial intermediation off balance sheet to avoid capital requirements and reward packages that encouraged the pursuit of short-term returns and the acquisition of positions of a deeply out-of-the-money option. The reduced incentive for care in the origination of loans when those loans are securitised and the distorted incentives of the ratings agencies, also skewed the microeconomic horizon.

On top of that, the crisis exposed a number of informational problems. These included the difficulty of assessing the value of securities backed by complex asset structures, especially those with complex pay-off structures (like CDOs) or containing embedded options, as in the case of subprime mortgages. Moreover, the high degree of links between financial intermediaries meant that investors needed to know, not only their own exposure to a failing counter-party, but also about the exposure of their other counter-parties to that failing counter-party, a factor that was especially important after the collapse of Lehman Brothers.

Monetary policymakers in the advanced economies have generally acted aggressively during the crisis, but the monetary transmission mechanism has been impaired by financial intermediaries deleveraging. As interest rates approached their zero lower bound, we were forced to adopt unconventional measures. Ben Friedman talked about some of the programmes adopted by the US Federal Reserve, while Jorgen Elmeskov referred to experience elsewhere.

The Bank of England has probably been the most conventional in its application of unconventional policies. It undertook extensive open market purchases of government debt to drive down longer term yields and bypass a crippled banking system. It also swapped illiquid mortgage-backed securities for liquid government debt temporarily.

The Federal Reserve has been more surgical in approach. It introduced a wide range of lending facilities to support particular non-bank financial intermediaries and bought Agency and US Treasury debt. Finally, the European Central Bank has concentrated on providing long-term liquidity support backed by a broad range of collateral. These different approaches reflect both different capital market structures in the various jurisdictions, as well as different perceived problems and constraints.

How effective have these policies been? It is hard to be sure what would have happened in their absence. But the improved climate in financial markets, since the early part of 2009, surely must reflect this aggressive policy stance to some degree.

In passing, it is worth noting that central banks stray onto tricky territory when they buy private sector assets and thus take credit risk onto the bank's (and implicitly also the public sector's) balance sheet. In many ways, this is better thought of as a fiscal action. In the United Kingdom, we have, as Jorgen Elmeskov noted, an explicit indemnity against any losses and thus have, in effect, undertaken such purchases on behalf of the Treasury.

Let me now turn to what the crisis has taught us about the appropriate conduct of monetary policy. In the run-in to the crisis, there was a substantial debate within central banking circles on how to deal with credit/asset-price booms. On the one hand, Bill White and colleagues at the BIS argued that monetary policymakers should 'lean against the wind' (LATW) by holding interest rates somewhat higher during the upswing, to mitigate the risk of a nasty subsequent correction.

On the other hand, Alan Greenspan and Ben Bernanke argued that 'bubble popping' during the upswing was dangerous and that the best policy was simply to clear up in the aftermath of an asset-price crash ('benign neglect').

Before the crisis, I was in the same league as Lars Svensson, namely that an inflation-targeting central bank should take on board credit and asset-price developments to the extent they affect output and inflation prospects down the line. In principle, that justified LATW, but in practice it was difficult to see that it led to substantially different policies, as one was trading off the certain near-term costs associated with higher interest rates against the rather uncertain longer term gains.

Moreover, large rate hikes would probably be necessary to cool excess credit growth, and it is an open question whether that would be politically sustainable. If the Bank's Monetary Policy Committee had held interest rates 2 to 3 percentage points higher in the years preceding the crisis, then I am sure that our independence would have been brought into question.

The crisis has certainly shifted the weight of the argument towards taking pre-emptive action by LATW. But it has not really changed the fundamental analysis above. It has, however, demonstrated that inflation targeting is clearly not sufficient to guarantee financial stability. Indeed, to the extent that inflation targeting is part of the explanation for the Great Moderation, the associated increase in stability may have actually contributed to the decline in the perceived risk that encouraged the leveraged search for yield.

But low and stable inflation was a valuable achievement of the Great Moderation. So, as Lars Svensson argues, the right response to the crisis is surely not to set monetary policy off chasing other hares, but rather to look for other instruments that can be used to curb nascent financial market excesses. That is where macroprudential regulation comes in, though there are still many questions of design and implementation that have yet to be worked through.

Finally, we should recognise that even with a well-designed macro-prudential regulatory toolkit, financial accidents will still happen. So, we should also be looking for other actions that make the system more robust. A number of initiatives play into this, including the work being undertaken by the Financial Stability Board to raise the capital and leverage requirements on banks.

Contingent capital is another initiative, of which Bill Poole's sub-debt proposal is a particular version. Systemic changes that introduce firebreaks within or between institutions, such as the 'Volcker rule' is another way to protect the system (I have a bit more time for initiatives such as this than Bill), along with better resolution mechanisms for failing financial intermediaries—an issue which both Ben Friedman and John Lipsky picked up on.

9 Summing-up

Is Central Bank Indeed the Best Regulator of the Banking System?

SUBIR GOKARN

Since Dr. Bean has summarised the discussion, I will not attempt the same. I would like to make two points which I think are the key messages. One is what appeared to be the divide between Dr. Poole and Prof. Svensson on modification of the Taylor Rule. Both are obviously advocates of rules. But Dr. Poole suggests that the rule can be expanded by bringing in an asset price intervention variable. I think this is an interesting illustration of the trade-off between control and scope. As you expand the rule, you will be giving up some amount of control while attempting to address a larger set of needs. It does fit into the notion of accountability, because, very clearly, the fewer the targets, the more control over them you have and more effective the accountability mechanism is. As you begin to spread across the spectrum, it will be that much more difficult to hold an institution accountable for achieving a whole range of targets. I think this did come up in the opening session on how central banks should make themselves more accountable. Where they place themselves on the spectrum is really going to be the challenge for different central banks in different contexts.

The second point, picks up on Prof. Friedman's issue about what I would call re-writing of the prudential contract. The idea is that the lender-of-last-resort facility is available to different kinds of institutions on different kinds of conditionalities and, particularly in the context of the

---

Summing-up by Subir Gokran, Co-Chair, Session I: Challenges and Response to Conduct Monetary Policy during the Financial Crisis.

crisis, the lobbying role was highlighted in his remarks. This takes us back to two things: first, the line between monetary policy and regulation which, I see now, is rather fuzzy because the integrity of the banking system and its viability and so on are actually critical elements of how effective the monetary policy itself is. Second, to the extent that you need to maintain certain conditions within the system, perhaps the nature of the prudential contract actually becomes a significant input into the effectiveness of the monetary policy. So, we then get back to the issue of whether a central bank is indeed the best regulator of the banking system in order to make monetary policy that much more effective.

Section II

Globalisation, Market Failures and Challenges Posed to Central Banks

Section II

Globalisation, Market Failures and Challenges Posed to Central Banks

This section corresponds to Session II of the First International Research Conference on 'Challenges to Central Banking in the Context of Financial Crisis', Reserve Bank of India, Mumbai.

Chairman: Lars E.O. Svensson

Co-Chair: Shyamala Gopinath

10 The Impossible Trinity and Constraints on Policy Options

IRMA ROSENBERG

After the collapse of Lehman Brothers in September 2008, the financial crisis swept across the world like a tidal wave. Central banks, governments and other authorities were forced to take a range of massive and unconventional measures to prevent a complete breakdown of the international financial system and to try to ward off a deep recession. Even though there are signs of a turnaround, a lot of hard work remains before we are through the financial crisis. Globalisation is at the heart of the problem and intensive international cooperation and coordination will be needed to find new tools to manage risks and prepare for a better-balanced development. The challenges for economic policymakers are huge.

We are grappling now with an 'Impossible Trinity' and the constraints it imposes on policy options. In the choice of monetary policy and exchange rate regime, the trinity concept offers policymakers a choice of only two objectives out of three, namely, free capital mobility, monetary policy independence and exchange rate stability. In an economy that has an open capital account, monetary policy can be oriented towards either an external objective, like the exchange rate, or an internal objective such as the price level, but not both at the same time.

In practice, many emerging market economies have intermediate solutions. The choice between the three objectives is vital, as policy alternatives for managing the consequences of the financial crisis. The trade-offs between these objectives also have consequences for the world economy. The policy response to the surge in foreign currency inflows in emerging market economies in Asia, is one topical example that I would like to comment on. I will also dwell on the choices these countries have made in terms of the Impossible Trinity. I am going to concentrate on policy choices in emerging Asia, but I also cannot help but draw some conclusions from our Swedish experience, where we have different exchange rate and monetary policy frameworks, which may be of interest to other countries.

The 'Impossible Trinity'

The Impossible Trinity or the incompatible trinity, is a concept that goes back to the contributions made by Robert Mundell in the 1960s. It is one of the fundamental conclusions of his analysis about the conditions for success of monetary policy in an open economy.[1] Research in this area is vast. Theoretically, this trilemma is more or less self-evident for academic economists and is a standard part of economic textbooks. In practice, the trilemma has also had a fundamental influence on policy considerations in many countries.

Over the last two decades, there has been a movement from intermediate exchange rate systems of different kinds towards either hard pegs or floats (including independent as well as managed floats) among advanced and emerging market economies, as demonstrated by Fisher (2008). Today, all advanced European countries but one (namely Denmark), have a hard peg or a float and the Danish krone shadows the euro. In Fisher's words, among advanced countries, bipolarity is almost complete. In the classification used by Fisher, the European Monetary Union (EMU) countries are in the hard peg group.[2] Since the euro is floating independently, an alternative way of describing the choice of exchange rate systems in advanced countries is that all but two (Hong Kong and Denmark) have floats and most of them have chosen flexible inflation targeting regimes. Among emerging market economies, many countries still have intermediate solutions, with capital controls and pegs of different kinds or bands.

---

1. This is one of the contributions for which Robert Mundell was awarded the Riksbank Prize in Economic Sciences in Memory of Alfred Nobel in 1999.
2. The classification of exchange rate systems is that of the staff of the IMF, based on their evaluation of the *de facto* exchange rate arrangement in place at the time. According to Fisher, a new classification is being prepared at the IMF where currency unions like the EMU will be classified as independently floating. See Fisher (2008): 370.

The choice of monetary policy and exchange rate regime

In practice, the choice of monetary policy and exchange rate regime is neither simple nor clear-cut and research on the optimal system is vast. Over the past decade, the International Monetary Fund (IMF) has produced three major analytical studies on the choices of exchange rate regimes in different countries in 1999, 2003 and 2009, of which the last one has not yet been published.[3] These reviews are part of the IMF's surveillance mandate and aim at informing member countries of how their choice of exchange rate regime might affect their own macroeconomic performance and contribute to the stability of the international monetary system.

In a brief presentation of the forthcoming 2009 review, Ghosh and Ostry (2009) describe how the preferred exchange rate regime, particularly for developing and emerging market economies, has evolved over time. In the early 1990s, pegging the exchange rate to a strong anchor currency was the popular view. But during that decade, currency crises occurred one after another, and the conclusion was that soft pegs or tightly managed floats cannot be sustainable for extended periods.

When the 1999 IMF review was produced, the regime prescription was the bipolar view, that countries should adopt either a hard peg or a free float without government intervention. In 2002, the collapse of the currency board in Argentina cast shadows over the hard end of the scale. The 2003 IMF review concluded that pegged exchange rates were scarcely beneficial for emerging market economies and that they should adopt freely-floating exchange rates. The same prescription should apply to developing countries as they become more financially integrated.

The 2009 IMF review is based on a broader dataset of IMF member countries for the period 1980–2006, and examines the impact of the exchange rate regime on a wider range of variables. The classification of exchange rate regimes for different countries differs from earlier studies and is based on *de jure* as well as *de facto* exchange rate regimes, i.e., it takes account of both what countries promise to do and what they actually do.

The conclusions in the new study are more varied than in the earlier studies. The message for developing and emerging market economies is

3. See Ghosh and Ostry (2009).

that pegged exchange rate regimes show the best inflation performance, benefitting from the credibility of a formal commitment by the central bank to maintain parity. On the other hand, intermediate regimes with a relatively rigid but not pegged exchange rates, have the best growth performance.

The review also points at three major downsides of the more rigid regimes.[4] First, they 'severely constrain the use of macroeconomic policies'. In other words, the 'Impossible Trinity holds' and according to the authors, it seems to hold good even for countries with less open capital accounts or those that heavily sterilise reserve flows under pegs. It is also striking, according to the authors, that there seems to be less scope even for counter-cyclical fiscal policy in countries with pegs.

Second, the 2009 review also confirms the result from the earlier IMF reviews that the risk for currency and financial crises is higher for pegged and intermediate regimes. On the other hand, the risk for credit booms and sharp falls in growth are about as likely in floating regimes as in more rigid ones, which, according to the authors, the current global crisis has demonstrated.

A third downside is that pegged and intermediate exchange rate regimes 'impede timely external adjustment' both on the deficit side, when deficits grow larger and unwind more abruptly and on the surplus side. On the surplus side, more rigid regimes are associated with large and highly persistent surpluses that can affect the stability of the overall international system.

The trilemma in Asia

Before the onset of the financial crisis, the growth in the gross domestic product (GDP) of emerging Asia was strong, led by a surge in exports. Gross savings increased in relation to investment and many countries, with the exception of India, had substantial surpluses on the current account. On top of that, these countries attracted large capital inflows. They prevented their exchange rates from appreciating correspondingly and accumulated massive foreign exchange reserves.

4. Ibid.: 40.

The magnitude of the capital flows to the emerging market economies in Asia mirrors the trilemma trade-offs made by policymakers in the region. This has triggered a discussion on the choice of monetary policy and exchange rate framework, the balance between exchange rate stability and price stability and the consequences not only for the domestic economies in the region, but also for the world economy.

In recent years, judging from the objectives stated by the central banks, there has been an increasing focus on price stability in Asia.[5] Four countries have moved towards inflation targeting frameworks—Korea in 1998, Indonesia in 1999, Thailand in 2000 and the Philippines in 2002. Singapore, India and Malaysia declare price stability as the monetary policy objective, along with adequate credit supply in the Indian case, and exchange rate stability in the case of Malaysia.

Another underlying trend in these countries is the gradual easing of restrictions on cross-border capital flows. The exchange rate systems in all these countries are managed floats according to the IMF classification.[6] In China, the professed central bank policy objective is stability of the value of the currency. In all these countries, interventions are used but several countries have allowed more exchange rate flexibility in recent years.

One interesting question is whether the inflation performance differs between the inflation targeters and the other countries. Filardo and Genberg (2009) have examined the monetary policy institutional changes in Asia and the Pacific to assess whether these can be traced to subsequent inflation performance. They study 12 countries, of which six are inflation-targeters. In addition to the countries mentioned above, Australia, Hong Kong, Japan and New Zealand belong to this group. Their conclusion is that inflation performance has been 'admirable'. The greater focus on inflation control has translated into a lower and more stable inflation environment.

Comparing the two groups, they find it difficult to document big differences in the inflation performance between explicit inflation targeters and non-inflation targeters. With increased financial integration, the

---

5. See Filardo and Genberg (2009).
6. See Fisher (2008).

trilemma is forcing countries to accept less exchange rate stability or less domestic monetary stabilisation, or a little bit of both. Hannoun (2007) has looked into the policy framework and the policy responses to the surge in capital inflows in the region to study the balance between exchange rate stability and price stability.

He reviewed the development of five key indicators to study the trade-offs—foreign exchange reserves, real exchange rates, interest rate differentials with the United States, real interest rates and balance of payments. The review was made before the onset of the financial crisis and his conclusion was that these indicators pointed 'to a resistance to exchange rate appreciation which might be seen as excessive'.

On the other hand, Hannoun also pointed out that inflation had so far been broadly well-contained and so, it might not be appropriate to say that monetary policy in the region was dominated by exchange rate considerations. An important consideration is also the consequences the choice of monetary policy regimes by different countries has for the world economy. The bigger the economy and the more integrated it is in the global economy, the more its choice of monetary policy and exchange rate system and the policy response to economic developments matters.

The gigantic capital flow to emerging market economies is one important element in the analyses of the onset of the financial crisis. The foreign exchange reserves in emerging market economies were largely invested in government bonds and other assets in advanced countries. This trend contributed to driving down the risk-free real interest rates to historically low levels and in triggering a huge international credit expansion.[7]

Credit terms were eased and search for yield gave a stimulus to the development of new complex structured financial instruments. One interpretation could be that the trade-off between the policy objectives in emerging Asia was fairly well-balanced from the domestic perspective in the region, but contributed to the building up of imbalances in the world economy.

7. See Subbarao (2009).

The financial crisis and the challenges ahead

The Asian economies were not much affected by the financial crisis to begin with, as their direct exposure to the problematic financial instruments was negligible.[8] The favourable economic development in the region continued till mid-2008. After the collapse of Lehman Brothers, however, the economies were hit hard. Dramatically falling export demand and paralysed international financial markets took its toll.

Confidence fell, the financial conditions tightened, domestic demand was dampened, and labour markets weakened. The GDP growth of the Asian economies fell considerably and only China, Indonesia and India escaped a severe recession, because of large policy stimuli and in India, as a result of less dependence on exports. There was a sharp reversal in capital flows and inflows turned into large outflows. Such immense fluctuations in capital flows put enormous strain on economic policy and exchange rates depreciated.

The world economy has started to recover again, with emerging market economies, especially in Asia, in the lead.[9] The economic outlook for Asia has improved markedly already during the first half of 2009. One of the factors behind the rebound is the very expansionary fiscal and monetary policy. The comparably robust fiscal positions in the emerging Asian economies before the onset of the crisis have left room for manoeuvre for a very expansionary economic policy in the region. Another factor behind the rebound is the upturn in financial markets in the spring of 2009, which eased financing constraints in the economies.

The overall health of the banking sector in the region has also limited the impact of the financial crisis. More favourable growth prospects in emerging Asia, along with the prospect of 'an extended period' of low interest rates in the advanced countries, as expressed by the US Federal Reserve, is again driving significant capital flows into emerging markets, particularly in Asia and the Pacific.

There are also indications of increasing carry trades funded in US dollars and other low interest rate currencies.[10] These inflows put pressure

8. For the Indian case see Mohanty (2009).
9. See IMF (2009a).
10. See Gyntelberg and Hördahl (2009).

on exchange rates and monetary policy in the recipient countries. If exchange rates are prevented from appreciating through interventions, this may have consequences for the liquidity of the domestic financial system and lead to increasing inflation pressure, asset price volatility and financial instability.

The larger the inflows, the more difficult it will be to effectively sterilise the interventions and interventions can also be costly.[11] Imbalances may build up with increasing risks of more dramatic corrections further on. In the autumn of 2009, policymakers in a number of countries, India, Korea and Chinese Taipei, have hinted that they would consider measures to limit capital flows.[12]

In its *World Economic Outlook* in October 2009, the IMF points to the need to rebalance global demand. The recovery in the US and in Europe is expected to be sluggish. The argument is that emerging market economies, which have previously relied on export growth, will now have to rely more on domestic demand. Since the upturn is expected to be stronger in emerging market economies, it is probable that they will have to start to unwind the expansionary policy measures earlier than the advanced economies. Greater exchange rate flexibility may be necessary in economies growing at a fast pace to enable them to tighten monetary policy.

If greater exchange rate flexibility is allowed, competitiveness of these economies will be affected by the capital flows. It is not possible to permanently prevent a currency from moving towards its long-run equilibrium value, however. But massive speculative capital inflows and outflows can lead to exchange rate overshooting and undershooting. Carry trades might, for extended periods, drive a currency away from its fair value. This may be a good reason to try to dampen exchange rate volatility. On the other hand, greater exchange rate volatility may make carry trades more risky and dampen the attractiveness of this kind of activities.

As has been touched upon before, increasing financial integration will also bring new risks. Exchange rate volatility will increase costs for

11. See CGFS (2009).

12. See Gyntelberg and Hördahl (2009).

individuals and companies that are engaged in cross-border trade and financial transactions. It is important to have an infrastructure in place for managing these risks effectively. One consideration which was put forth by Hannoun (2007) is that intermediate policy frameworks, where the policy choices are not clear, may make it necessary for the private sector to insure against a wider set of risk with the consequence of higher hedging costs. The incentives for development of markets and products for the purpose may also be diluted.

The conclusion is that lack of products and markets for hedging risks may be a reason for preventing full exchange rate flexibility. But on the other hand, there are no good excuses for not working hard to develop such markets.

The Swedish experience

Talking about the trinity choices, I cannot refrain from drawing on the Swedish experience with different policy frameworks during the last four decades. After the breakdown of the Bretton Woods system in the early 1970s, Sweden tried different exchange rate pegs. The intention was, of course, to 'borrow credibility' from low-inflation countries. But the fixed exchange rate failed to act as a nominal anchor.

Inflation expectations were too high, and there was a succession of cost crises. Economic policy was unable to prevent wages and prices from rising too fast to be compatible with the commitment to maintain a fixed exchange rate. To safeguard employment, the government accommodated wage increases and between 1976 and 1982, the Swedish krona was devalued five times. During the 1980s, the government made various attempts to stabilise wage increases but without success, and Swedish competitiveness eroded.

The country's credit market was successively deregulated and foreign exchange regulation dismantled. Towards the end of the 1980s, Sweden's capital account was wide open. A change of course in stabilisation policy was tried at the beginning of the new decade, with an increased weight on price stabilisation, while the exchange rate remained fixed. But, to cut a long story short, the Swedish fixed exchange rate system was one of those that collapsed in 1992 after dramatic speculative attacks. The krona was allowed to float and a flexible inflation targeting regime was introduced.

Initially, credibility of the new inflation target was low. One reason, of course, was the unfavourable inflation record. At that time Sweden was also in the middle of a severe homemade bank crisis. Another reason was the unsuccessful fiscal policy of the previous decades. The economy was out of balance, with big deficits in both public finances and in the current balance.

A shift in the fiscal policy regime was also needed. In the first half of the 1990s, extensive measures were taken to consolidate government finances. A distinct division of roles in the Swedish economic policy framework was introduced. Fiscal policy would target achieving long-term sustainability in public finances, while monetary policy was given the task of keeping inflation low.

The flexible inflation targeting regime has served the Swedish economy well over the last two decades. Since 1992, inflation has fallen remarkably from an average of more than 8 per cent per year to close to the inflation target of 2 per cent. Inflation expectations have come down and are well-anchored, close to the inflation target. The GDP growth has averaged close to 3 per cent, one percentage point higher a year than in the 1970s and 1980s. Real wages have developed much more favourably.

For a small open economy like Sweden, with a big share in world exports, it is impossible to escape volatility altogether. The difference between the old regime, with a fixed exchange rate and the new regime with a floating krona and an inflation target can be illustrated in different ways. Exchange rate volatility has increased, but the flexible exchange rate has an important stabilising role, which means lower volatility in the domestic economy.

Exchange rate volatility generates higher costs for sectors exposed to international trade and finance and the presence of instruments to manage exchange rate risk is vital. The Riksbank's policy rate is changed much less frequently than it was during the fixed exchange rate regime and the average policy rate is lower. Market interest rates are lower than in the 1970s and 1980s and an important part of the explanation is lower risk premia for Swedish interest rates.

In the early phases of the financial crisis, it seemed as though Sweden, like the emerging market economies in Asia, would be relatively spared from the effects of the turmoil. After the collapse of Lehman brothers, however, the Swedish economy was strongly affected by the paralysed international credit markets, a sharp fall in exports and deteriorating confidence in the economy. With the change in the monetary and fiscal policy frameworks at the beginning of the 1990s, Sweden is now much better equipped to counteract these effects of the global crisis.

There has been scope to stimulate the economy by means of expansionary monetary and fiscal policy. The Swedish krona weakened substantially after the collapse of Lehman Brothers. The lowest point was noted in March 2009 and since then the krona has appreciated somewhat. The weak krona has helped to some extent to counteract the downturn in the economy. It has also had a positive effect on inflation, which fell considerably in the fall of 2008 and is still well below the target.

Conclusion

In addition to my recent term on the executive board of the Riksbank, I was also employed at the bank for a decade during the fixed exchange rate regime. Back then, economists in Sweden, almost without exception, believed that a floating exchange rate would be inappropriate or even dangerous for a small open economy. Nothing could have been more wrong. But there was at least one key factor missing in the Swedish system—credibility.

The Swedish authorities were committed to defending a narrow range of exchange rates. However, time after time, when imbalances built up, the target was abandoned. When Sweden's capital account was deregulated, speculation finally ended the regime. The odds were too high for devaluation. Credibility is built upon openness and transparency and it is necessary to make people understand the measures taken.

Another prerequisite is to be in control of the necessary policy measures. It took several years for the Riksbank to gain credibility for the flexible inflation targeting regime. One indication of success is that inflation expectations in the Swedish economy have been quite stable and close to the target. Another fact worth mentioning is that the social partners explicitly pay regard to the inflation target in the wage negotiations.

I realise, of course, that the same monetary policy and exchange rate regime is not optimal for all countries in all phases of development and irrespective of the rate of global integration. With growth and with increasing trade and cross-border financial transactions, new risks will appear. What kind of risks these will be, exchange rate risks or inflation risks, depends among other things, upon the monetary and exchange rate regime chosen.

The private sector needs appropriate instruments to manage risks. The development of such facilities must be in tandem with global integration. In Sweden, for example, exchange rate risks are greater now than in the old regime and it is quite common for exporters and importers to hedge their cross-border payment flows.

The IMF study shows that an intermediate regime may be favourable for a developing or an emerging market economy. When there are still capital controls and before the necessary financial infrastructure is in place, it might be necessary. But judging from, for example, the Swedish experience, when financial markets become more complex and more sophisticated, it is also much more difficult to effectively control capital flows. Since almost all advanced countries have chosen a monetary union or a float, there are good reasons to believe that other countries will do the same when their capital flows are free and their financial infrastructure is complex and rich.

References

Bank for International Settlements (2009). "Fallout for the Emerging Economies", *79th Annual Report Committee on the Global Financial System.*

CGFS (2009). "Capital Flows and Emerging Market Economies", *CGFS Paper* No. 33 January.

Filardo, Andrew and Hans Genberg (2009). *Targeting Inflation in Asia and the Pacific: Lessons from the Recent Past.* Bank for International Settlements: Representative Office for Asia and the Pacific.

Fisher, Stanley (2008) "Mundell-Fleming Lecture: Exchange Rate systems, Surveillance and Advice," *IMF Staff Papers* 55(3): 367-383.

Ghosh, Atish R. and Jonathan D. Ostry (2009). "Choosing an Exchange Rate Regime", *IMF Finance & Development.* December.

Ghosh, Atish R., Jonathan D. Ostry and Charalambos Tsangarides (forthcoming). "Toward a Stable System of Exchange Rates", *IMF Occasional Paper.* Washington DC: International Monetary Fund.

Gyntelberg, Jacob and Peter Hördal (2009). "Overview: Continued Record Low Rates Spur Markets", *Bank for International Settlements Quarterly Review.* December.

Hannoun, Hervé (2007). *Policy Responses to the Challenges Posed by Capital Inflows in Asia*. Speech on July 28. *www.bis.org*

International Monetary Fund (2009a). *World Economic Outlook*. October.

———. (2009b). *Regional Economic Outlook: Asia and Pacific*. October.

Mohanty, Deepak (2009). *Global Financial Crisis and Monetary Policy Response in India*. Speech on November 12. *RBI Monthly Bulletin.* December.

Mussa, Michael, Paul Masson, Alexander Svoboda, Esteban Jadresic, Paolo Mauro, and Andrew Berg (2000). "Exchange Rate Regimes in an Increasingly Integrated World Economy", *IMF Occasional Paper* No. 193. Washington DC: International Monetary Fund.

Rogoff, Kenneth and others (2003). "Evolution and Performance of Exchange Rate Regimes", *IMF Working Paper* 03/243. Washington DC: International Monetary Fund.

Subbarao, Duvvuri (2009). *Global Financial Crisis: Questioning the Questions*. Speech on July 31. *RBI Monthly Bulletin.* August.

10.1
DISCUSSION

What if the Globally Traded Asset is not Debt, but Equity?

BENJAMIN M. FRIEDMAN

I have very few objections to what Irma Rosenberg has said. Instead of criticising her point of view directly, therefore, I will comment on what I think are open issues in the economics of the relationships that she is describing. The first one has to do with the lack of possible downward movement in the interest rate, once the crisis like the one that we have just experienced puts interest rates at the lower bound. Irma assumes that the logic of the so-called 'Impossible Trinity' suggests that when the capital account of an economy is open, monetary policy can set either the interest rate or the exchange rate, but not both.

The question I would pose is—what happens if the interest rate is at the zero lower bound? In that case, can monetary policy, which is not able to affect the interest rate at this point, affect the exchange rate? And if so, how? I suspect that the answer is yes, it can. The influence, however, takes place through non-conventional means, which are normally excluded from the kind of analytics we have in mind when we discuss this subject.

A subsidiary issue in this regard is—what happens if the countries, whose cross-exchange rate is in question here—are both at the zero bound? What happens then to the exchange rate between their respective currencies? Is there indeterminacy? Presumably not. But I think this is a subtle matter that merits more attention.

My second question pertains to the nature of internationally traded assets in these models. The usual notion of influence of monetary policy on interest rates and exchange rates (not just in the 'Impossible Trinity' literature but more broadly in the Mundell-Fleming literature), assumes

Comments by Benjamin M. Friedman on the paper presented by Irma Rosenberg 'The Impossible Trinity and Constraints on Policy Options'.

that the internationally traded asset is a kind of debt instrument. As a result, the standard logic prevails.

If, for example, one country increases its interest rate and another country does not, then the country that increases its interest rate has made its assets more attractive to international investors relative to assets in the other country. The outcome will be an incipient movement of capital out of the other country's assets to the assets of the country that has just raised its interest rates. An increase in the exchange rate will, therefore, occur.

Think, however, how this logic plays out if the asset that international investors are trading is not a debt instrument but equity. In that case, the country that tightens monetary policy by raising its interest rates, thereby slows its economy and consequently, causes its equity returns to fall. One could, of course, imagine a world in which the decline in the equity price is instantaneous, so that there is no implication for the forward-looking return on the equity as an investment. We do not live in such a world, however. As a result, we frequently see the apparently anomalous result that when a country tightens its monetary policy, its exchange rate will depreciate—because tightening monetary policy, increasing interest rates and slowing the economy, together make investment in that country's equities less attractive. It is worth bearing in mind, therefore, as the composition of international assets that are traded internationally changes, the logic of these aspects of macroeconomic behaviour changes as well.

A third question: When countries keep their exchange rates fixed—which usually means artificially too low—and, therefore, accumulate large foreign exchange reserves as some major countries are doing today, what obligations does the rest of the world have towards them for their losses, when this policy ends? The correct answer, I would argue, is none. The countries that follow policies I have described, are owed nothing in that regard by the rest of the world.

I believe, therefore, that the attempt by some of these countries today to call for a change in the rate of compensation on international reserve asset holdings, is merely a distraction.

These demands aim to draw attention away from what even students of elementary economics know: If a country freezes its exchange rate at an artificially low value, two outcomes will follow. The first is that as long as the exchange rate is kept too low, that country will accumulate even more assets denominated in foreign currencies.

Second, when the policy is finally abandoned and the exchange rate allowed to rise to its appropriate equilibrium level, that country will incur losses on the foreign-currency-denominated assets that it has accumulated. Nothing in this process is at all surprising, or at variance with the standard economic theory. Hence, the answer to what other countries owe a country that has been accumulating foreign exchange reserves as a result of holding its exchange rate fixed at an artificially low level is—nothing.

I do disagree with Irma on a small issue. She says, at one point, 'lack of products and markets for hedging risks may be a reason for preventing full exchange rate flexibility. But, on the other hand, there are no good excuses for not working hard to develop such markets, i.e., markets for products that allow hedging risks.' Well, there may not be excuses, but there certainly are reasons.

One reason is that, even though we may want to construe markets for these products as enabling market participants to hedge themselves against risks, what we now know from experience (most dramatically, the recent crisis!) is that for every market participant who uses these products to hedge risks, there will be other market participants who use them as a way of gratuitously taking on risk. By 'gratuitously' I mean that they are not required to take on the risk in question, but they do so merely to earn excess returns.

If the hedgers outweigh the speculators, or the speculators do not themselves pose systemic risks to the economy, there is, of course, nothing wrong with all this. But we also learned from the crisis that this is not the case either. As a result, the presumption that there are no good reasons for not working hard to develop markets for new risk-bearing (as opposed to risk-sharing) markets, does not wash.

I think that countries are well-advised to think very carefully about which of these markets they would like to have and whom they would like to see participating in them. It is not at all obvious that working hard to develop such markets is what all countries should want to do.

11 The Future of Public Debt

Prospects and Implications

STEPHEN G. CECCHETTI,
M.S. MOHANTY and
FABRIZIO ZAMPOLLI

Since the financial crisis, public debt levels have increased dramatically in industrial countries and are set to keep rising in the foreseeable future. A number of countries face the prospect of large and rising future costs related to the ageing of their populations. We examine what current fiscal policy and expected future age-related spending imply for the path of debt/GDP ratios over the next several decades.

Our projections of public debt ratios lead us to conclude that the path pursued by fiscal authorities in a number of industrial countries is unsustainable. Drastic measures are necessary to check the rapid growth of current and future liabilities of governments and to reduce their adverse consequences for long-term growth and monetary stability.

The financial crisis that erupted in the middle of 2008 led to an explosion of public debt in many advanced economies. Governments were forced to recapitalise banks, take over a large part of the debts of failing financial institutions and to introduce large stimulus programmes to revive demand. According to the OECD, the total public sector debt of industrialised countries is expected to exceed 100 per cent of their gross domestic product (GDP) in 2011—something that has never happened before in peacetime.[1]

1. Public finances in emerging market economies are generally in a much better shape. With their financial systems and economies remaining relatively immune to the crisis, public debt levels have grown much less rapidly, and are on an average around 40 per cent of GDP. One notable exception is India—a country with a history of fiscal problems—where public debt remains high by today's emerging market standards.

Bad as these fiscal problems may seem, the official figures too are somewhat misleading. Rapidly ageing populations present a number of countries with the prospect of enormous future costs that are not wholly recognised in current budget projections. The size of these future obligations is anybody's guess. As far as we know, there is no definite and comprehensive account of the unfunded, contingent liabilities that governments have currently accumulated.

Should we be concerned about high and sharply rising public debts? Several advanced economies have experienced higher levels of public debt than we see today. In the aftermath of World War II, for example, government debts in excess of 100 per cent of GDP were common.[2] None of these led to default.[3] In more recent times, Japan has been living with a public debt ratio of over 150 per cent which has not caused any adverse effect on its cost.

So, it is possible that investors will continue to have strong faith in the ability of industrial countries' to repay, and that worries about excessive public debts are exaggerated.[4] Indeed, with only a few exceptions, during the crisis nominal government bond yields had fallen and remained low. So far, at least, investors have continued to view government bonds as relatively safe.

But bond traders are notoriously short-sighted. Assuming that they can get out before the storm hits, their time horizons are days or weeks, not years or decades. We take a longer and less benign view of current developments, arguing that the aftermath of the financial crisis is poised to bring a simmering fiscal problem in industrial economies to boiling point. In the face of rapidly ageing populations, for many countries the path of pre-crisis future revenues was insufficient to finance promised expenditure.

The politics of public debt vary from country to country. In some countries that have been seared by unpleasant experiences in the past, a

2. In the United States debt/GDP peaked at close to 121 per cent, while in the United Kingdom it rose to about 300 per cent.
3. According to Reinhart and Rogoff (2008, Appendix Table 3), the last defaulters in the industrial world were Japan and Germany in the immediate aftermath of World War II. There have been no advanced country defaults for more than half a century.
4. As a matter of macroeconomic theory, as long as the debt/income ratio is constant, an economy could live with any level of debt.

culture of frugality prevails. In others, profligate official spending is commonplace. In recent years, consolidation has been successful on a number of occasions. But fiscal restraint tends to deliver stable debt; rarely does it produce substantial reductions. And, most critically, swings from deficits to surpluses have tended to come along with either falling nominal interest rates, rising real growth, or both.

Today, interest rates are exceptionally low and the growth outlook for advanced economies is at best modest. This leads us to conclude that the question is when markets will start putting pressure on governments, not if. When, in the absence of fiscal actions, will investors start demanding a much higher compensation for the risk of holding the increasingly large amounts of public debt that authorities are going to issue to finance their extravagant ways? In some countries, unstable debt dynamics, in which higher debt levels lead to higher interest rates, which then lead to even higher debt levels, are already evident.

The fiscal problems now faced by industrial countries, therefore, need to be tackled soon and resolutely. Failure to do so will increase the chance of an unexpected and abrupt rise in government bond yields of medium and long maturities, which would threaten the nascent economic recovery. It would also complicate the central banks' task of controlling inflation in the immediate future, and may ultimately threaten the credibility of prevailing monetary policy arrangements.

Fiscal problems need to be tackled soon. The key challenge for fiscal authorities is how to do so, without seriously jeopardising the incipient economic recovery. We do not actually address this issue, but we do note that an important part of any fiscal consolidation programme is measures to reduce future liabilities, such as an increase in the retirement age.[5] Announcements of changes in future programmes would allow authorities to wait till the recovery from the crisis is assured, before reducing discretionary spending and improving the short-term fiscal position.

5. See Giavazzi (2009) for a discussion. Measures to tackle long-term liabilities should be such as to minimise their impact on current saving behaviour.

Before plunging into our analysis, we first examine the recent build-up of public debt. We then turn to a forward-looking examination of the public debt trajectories in industrial countries and discuss the challenges these possible debt levels pose to both fiscal and monetary authorities, before concluding our argument.

The facts

After a big increase during the recent financial crisis and recession, public debt ratios are set to rise continuously over the next few years. How far this increase in public debt will go depends on several factors. Some of the factors that will influence public debt are the ultimate costs of the financial crisis, the rate of real growth and the level of interest rates, as well as political decisions about spending and taxes.

The fact that structural deficits have a tendency to linger in industrial countries and the large long-term age-related liabilities, together make the prevailing policy in a number of countries unsustainable. We now summarise the factors that influence long-term fiscal imbalances, before going on to present projections of the path of debt/GDP ratios in large industrial countries.

Current and projected fiscal deficits

We start with Table 11.1. A key fact emerging from the table is that over the past three years public debt has grown rapidly in countries where it had remained relatively low before the crisis. This group of countries includes not only the United States and the United Kingdom, but also Spain and Ireland. Although the rise in debt levels is comparatively small in countries with a history of debt problems (such as Italy and Greece), the crisis has, nevertheless, added fuel to their problems.

It is important to realise that, while the direct costs of financial crisis on governments may appear large, they are in fact relatively small compared to the indirect costs arising from losses of tax revenues and increased expenditure to provide demand stimulus. Financial rescue programmes, including capital injection, treasury purchase of assets and lending as well as upfront government financing (but not debt guarantees), amount to 6.2 per cent of GDP in advanced economies so far (see IMF, 2010)[6]—and a significant part of this may be recovered.

Table 11.1

Fiscal situation and prospects[1]

	Fiscal balance			*Structural balance*[2]			*General government debt*[3]		
				As a percentage of GDP					
	2007	*2010*	*2011*	*2007*	*2010*	*2011*	*2007*	*2010*	*2011*
Austria	–0.7	–5.5	–5.8	–1.4	–3.3	–3.6	62	78	82
France	–2.7	–8.6	–8.0	–3.5	–6.8	–6.3	70	92	99
Germany	0.2	–5.3	–4.6	–0.8	–4.0	–3.7	65	82	85
Greece	–4.0	–9.8	–10.0	–4.5	–6.9	–6.8	104	123	130
Ireland	0.2	–12.2	–11.6	–1.3	–9.0	–9.0	28	81	93
Italy	–1.5	–5.4	–5.1	–2.2	–2.6	–2.8	112	127	130
Japan	–2.5	–8.2	–9.4	–3.4	–7.4	–9.0	167	197	204
Netherlands	0.2	–5.9	–5.3	–0.6	–3.6	–3.1	52	77	82
Portugal	–2.7	–7.6	–7.8	–2.8	–6.1	–6.8	71	91	97
Spain	1.9	–8.5	–7.7	1.6	–5.2	–4.5	42	68	74
United Kingdom	–2.7	–13.3	–12.5	–3.4	–10.5	–9.9	47	83	94
United States	–2.8	–10.7	–9.4	–3.1	–9.2	–8.2	62	92	100
Asia[4]	0.1	–3.5	–3.6	...	...	...	37	40	41
Central Europe[5]	3.7	–4.4	–3.9	...	...	...	23	28	29
Latin America[6]	–1.5	–2.4	–2.0	...	...	...	41	37	35

Note: 1. Regional averages calculated as weighted averages based on 2005 GDP and PPP exchange rates. 2. Cyclically adjusted balance. 3. For Argentina, the Philippines and Thailand, Central government debt. 4. China, Hong Kong SAR, India, Indonesia, Korea, Malaysia, the Philippines, Singapore and Thailand. 5. The Czech Republic, Hungary and Poland. 6. Argentina, Brazil, Chile and Mexico.

Sources: IMF, *World Economic Outlook* (emerging market economies); OECD, *Economic Outlook* (advanced economies).

In contrast, overall fiscal balances have been deteriorating sharply, rising by 20–30 percentage points of GDP in just three years. And, unless action is taken almost immediately, there is little hope that these deficits will decline significantly in 2011. Even more worrying is the fact that most of the projected deficits are structural rather than cyclical in nature. So, in the absence of immediate corrective action, we can expect these deficits to persist even during the cyclical recovery.

---

6. According to Laeven and Valencia (2008), in the previous 49 crises the average net direct resolution cost borne by the government has been 13 per cent of GDP.

Based on a very comprehensive dataset, Reinhart and Rogoff (2009a) report that three years after a typical banking crisis the absolute level of public debt is on an average about 86 per cent higher than prior to the crisis. In countries where the crisis was most severe, debt almost trebled. This time around, several countries are beyond this historical average.

Ireland, for instance, witnessed a 98 per cent increase in public debt between 2007 and 2009. In the United Kingdom public debt is projected to increase by 111 per cent by 2011. The United States and Spain are not far behind and by 2011, public debt in these countries is expected to increase by 75 per cent and 78 per cent, respectively.

We doubt that the present crisis will be typical in its impact on deficits and debt. The reason is that in many countries, employment and growth are unlikely to return to their pre-crisis levels in the foreseeable future.[7] As

Figure 11.1

Government gross debt and primary fiscal balance in industrial economies[1] as a percentage of GDP

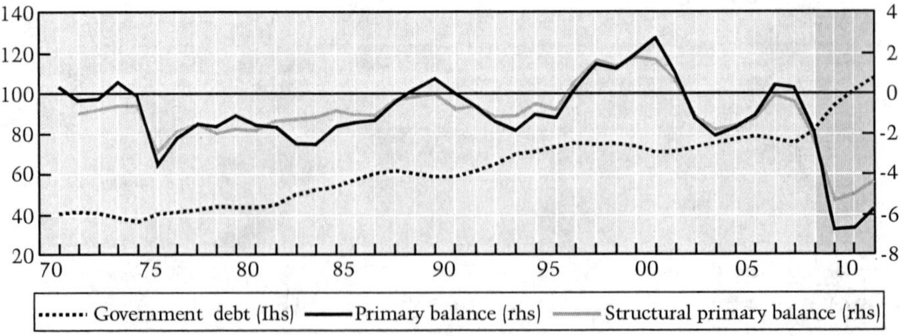

Note: Shaded areas represent forecast.

1. Weighted average based on 2005 GDP and PPP exchange rates of economies cited and data availability; Australia, Austria, Belgium, Canada, Denmark, France, Finland, Germany, Greece, Ireland, Italy, Japan, the Netherlands, New Zealand, Norway, Portugal, Spain, Sweden, Switzerland, the United Kingdom and the United States.

Sources: OECD; authors' calculations.

---

7. For instance, based on the experience of past banking crises, Knotek and Terry (2009) predict that the US unemployment rate may stay above 10 per cent up to 2011, drifting down only gradually to 8 per cent by 2014 and about 6 per cent in 2018. OECD (2009a) projects a similar path for the Euro area unemployment rate, with a return to the 9 per cent level only in 2017.

a result, unemployment and other benefits will need to be paid for several years, and high levels of public investment may also have to be maintained.

The permanent loss of potential output caused by the crisis also means that government revenues may have to be permanently low in many countries. Between 2007 and 2009, the ratio of government revenue to GDP fell by 2 to 4 percentage points in Ireland, Spain, the United States and the United Kingdom. It is difficult to tell how much of this will be reversed as the recovery progresses. Experience tells us that the longer households and firms are unemployed and underemployed and the longer they are cut off from credit markets, the bigger the shadow economy becomes.[8]

These concerns also need to be put into historical context. Many countries have a clear deficit bias. To see this, note in Figure 11.1 the relationship between public debt and two major indicators of the budgetary stance in advanced economies—the primary balance (the deficit excluding interest payments on the outstanding debt) and the structural primary balance (the primary balance adjusted for cyclical increases in expenditure and cyclical decreases in revenue).

The figure shows that primary deficits in industrial countries have a life of their own, staying high or low for a number of years running. Such persistence is clearly evident in the 1970s and 1980s and again, to a lesser extent, in the early 2000s. To investigate this tendency, we perform a panel regression of the structural primary balance on its own lag, the lagged value of the debt/GDP ratio and the contemporaneous value of the output gap, using the past 30 years as a sample period.

The estimates in Table 11.2 confirm that, on average, the structural primary balance is highly persistent and allow us to conclude that it responds positively to the lagged debt/GDP ratio. In particular, the short-term response of the structural primary balance to a one percentage point increase in the debt/GDP ratio is between 1 and 2 basis points. Taken at

8. There is some evidence to suggest that VAT non-compliance among firms tends to worsen during an economic downturn; see Brondolo (2009). Schneider (2009), for instance, predicted that the share of the shadow economy in OECD countries could rise, on average, by 0.5 percentage points of GDP in 2009 over the previous year, reversing a declining trend since the early 2000s.

face value, these results imply a long-term response of approximately 6 to 9 basis points.[9]

Moreover, we find no evidence that fiscal authorities behave opportunistically, taking advantage of improvements in the output gap to tighten the stance of fiscal policy. Taken together, all this suggest to us that fiscal policy is likely to remain highly expansionary in the near term. In addition, if past behaviour is any guide to the future, fiscal authorities might find it difficult to adjust quickly—unless, that is, they are left with no choice.

Table 11.2

Structural primary balance regressed on a constant, lagged debt/GDP ratio, lagged structural primary balance and contemporaneous output gap[1]

	R^2	*Constant*	*Debt/GDP ratio (–1)*	*Structural primary balance (–1)*	*Output gap*
Panel estimation 1[2]	0.76	–1.20***	0.02***	0.77***	0.05
Panel estimation 2[3]	0.76	–1.24***	0.02***	0.76***	0.06
Panel estimation 3[4]	0.74	–0.59***	0.01***	0.84***	0.02

Note: *, ** and *** denote coefficients significantly different from zero at the 10 per cent, 5 per cent and 1 per cent level, respectively.

1. Sample period is 1970–2008. Countries in the sample: Austria, Australia, Belgium, Canada, Denmark, Finland, France, Germany, Greece, Ireland, Italy, Japan, the Netherlands, Norway, New Zealand, Portugal, Spain, Switzerland, Sweden, United Kingdom and the United States. 2. The panel regression has been estimated by OLS with White cross-section standard errors and fixed effects. 3. The panel regression has been estimated by generalised method of moments (GMM) with White cross-section standard errors and fixed effects (using as the instruments regressors and lags of dependent variable (from –1 to –3). 4. The panel regression has been estimated by GMM with White cross-section standard errors (using as the instruments regressors and lags of dependent variable (from –1 to –3).

Sources: OECD; authors' calculations.

Long-term fiscal imbalances

What is more worrying is that the current expansionary fiscal policy has coincided with rising, and largely unfunded, age-related spending (pension and health care costs). Driven by the countries' demographic profiles, the ratio of old-age population to working-age population is projected to rise

9. A short-term response of 1–2 basis points is sufficient to offset the immediate rise in interest payments that the extra debt would generate if the difference between the interest rate paid on debt and GDP growth is smaller. Yet, because of the sluggish response, any large negative values of the structural primary balance (as brought about, for example, by a recession) would narrow only slowly over time.

sharply. Interestingly, this rise is concentrated in countries such as Japan, Spain, Italy and Greece, which are already laden with relatively high debts (Figure 11.2(a)). Added to the effects of population ageing is the problem posed by rising per capita health care costs.

Figure 11.2

Projected population structure and age-related spending

(a) Old-age population (ratio to working-age population)[1]

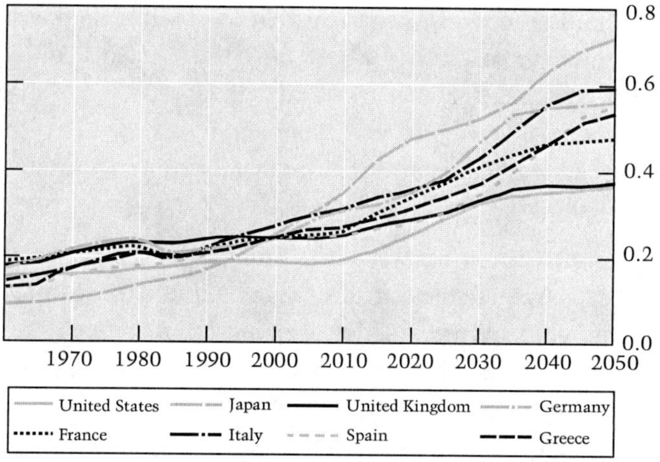

(b) Estimated increase in age-related government expenditure from 2011 to 2050[2]

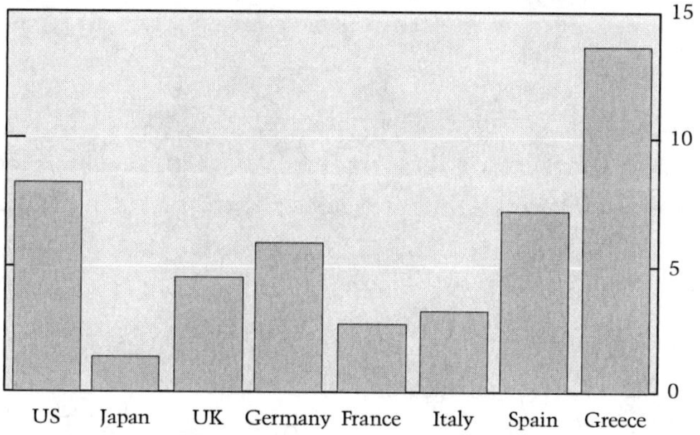

Note: 1. Working-age population is between 15 and 64 years of age. 2. In percentage points of GDP.

Sources: IMF, *World Economic Outlook*, April 2007; UN Secretariat; European Commission; Congressional Budget Office; authors' calculations.

This leads us to the obvious conclusion that any assessment of the government fiscal situation based on a short-term perspective is incomplete and at best misleading. A key question is to what extent such accrued liabilities should be reflected in debt estimates. Concerns about both fiscal sustainability and intergenerational equity demand that the accumulated net discounted value of all future revenues and expenditure commitments scheduled in current laws be added to the current debt stock.

At present, however, there is no unique source that provides such estimates. Moreover, uncertainty about future policy, demography and productivity growth raises issues about how this information should be presented and used (see for example, Auerbach, 2008, for a discussion). That said, existing studies report that the magnitude of the long-term fiscal imbalance—the present value of unfunded liabilities arising from ageing—is very large.

Hauner *et al.* (2007) estimate the change in the primary balance required to equate the net present discounted value of all future revenues and non-interest expenditures to the debt levels prevailing at the end of 2005 for seven major industrial countries (Canada, France, Germany, Italy, Japan, the United Kingdom and the United States).

The authors report that if these countries were to pay off all their financial liabilities, they would require an average improvement in their budget balance excluding interest payments of 4.5 per cent of GDP. For the United States and Japan, the estimate is 6.9 per cent and 6.2 per cent, respectively.

Other estimates are similar in magnitude. For example, Gokhale (2009) presents a measure of the long-term fiscal imbalance faced by 23 industrial countries. His estimates suggest that for financing future benefits without future tax increases, the United States and major European countries would be required to generate an annual present value surplus of the order of 8 to 10 per cent of the 2005 GDP over the period to 2050.

The US Congressional Budget Office (CBO, 2009) provides official projections of long-term fiscal gaps associated with age-related spending. These suggest that the United States would need a permanent improvement in its budget balances of the order of 2.6 per cent of the 2009

GDP in the next 50 years and 3.2 per cent in 75 years to stabilise the federal debt/GDP ratio at its 2009 level.

Because of the large uncertainties involved, we do not attempt to make our own projections of age-related liabilities, but instead rely on recent projections of age-related expenditure by the European Commission, the CBO and the IMF (Japan). Figure 11.2(b) reports the estimated incremental age-related outlays between 2011 and 2050.

We note that these numbers suggest that the distribution of age-related spending is uneven across countries, with the burden considerably higher in Germany, Greece, Spain, the United Kingdom and the United States than in other countries. At the level projected, US health care expenditures as a percentage of GDP would double from about 5 per cent today to 10 per cent by 2035 and more than treble to 17 per cent by 2080.

Interest rate and growth rate

The differential between the real interest rate and real output growth is a critical input parameter in determining the future evolution of public debt.[10] When this differential is positive, so that the interest rate is greater than the growth rate, the debt ratio will explode in the absence of a sufficiently large primary surplus.

So far, the build-up of public debt in industrial countries has taken place against the backdrop of an exceedingly low interest rate environment. Despite low inflation, the real interest rate (in effective terms) at which governments are able to finance their deficits and roll over outstanding debt obligations has been falling since the late 1990s, reaching almost zero in some countries in the wake of the monetary policy response to the financial crisis (Figure 11.3(a)).

However, as the graph reveals, the situation is changing quickly even without a change in monetary policy-controlled interest rates. Real borrowing rates rose through 2009, and are poised to continue increasing with the reversal of the current zero interest rate policy. Added to this is the

10. The Appendix contains a brief primer on the arithmetic of debt dynamics and the rationale behind our projections.

fact that the crisis is likely to reduce the potential output growth rate for some time to come (Cecchetti and Zhu, 2009).

Figure 11.3

Government borrowing and interest rate growth differentials

(a) Real government borrowing rates[1]

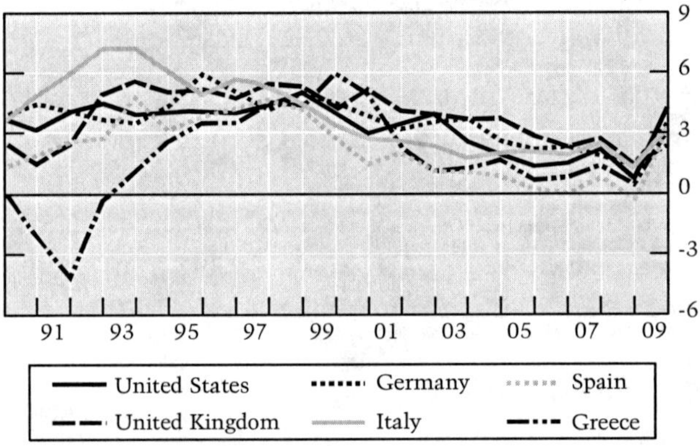

(b) Interest rate growth differential and primary balance

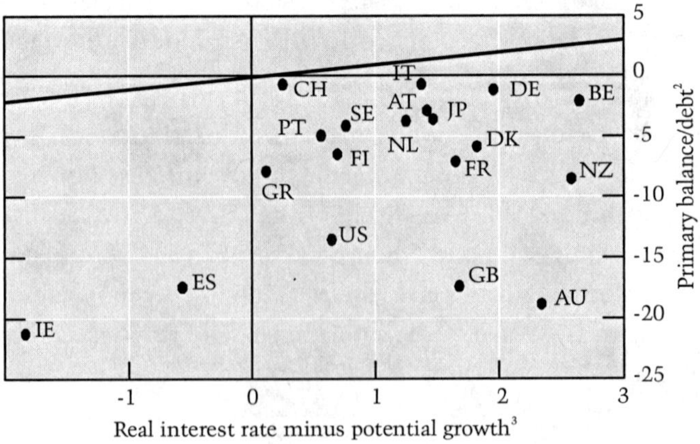

Note: AU = Australia; AT = Austria; BE = Belgium; CH = Switzerland; DE = Germany; DK = Denmark; ES = Spain; FI = Finland; FR = France; GB = United Kingdom; GR = Greece; IE = Ireland; IT = Italy; JP = Japan; NL = Netherlands; NZ = New Zealand; PT = Portugal; SE = Sweden; US = United States.

1. Effective real interest rate on public debt computed from government gross interest payments at period (t) divided by government gross financial liabilities at period (t–1) minus inflation rate; in per cent. 2. Government primary balance at period (t) divided by government gross financial liabilities at period (t–1) in 2009; in per cent. 3. Effective real interest rate on public debt (average 1998–2007) minus OECD-estimated real potential GDP growth for 2012–2017; in percentage points.

Sources: OECD; authors' calculations.

Figure 11.3(b) is indicative of the severity of the problems that governments face. It plots a measure of the difference between the real interest rate and real growth on the horizontal axis and the ratio of the primary surplus to total debt on the vertical axis. The higher the differential between the real interest rate and potential output growth, the larger the required structural primary surplus as a proportion of the previous-period debt level needed to maintain a stable debt/GDP ratio.

Turning to the graph, for debt/GDP to remain stable, a country must be above the 45-degree line on the graph (which appears relatively flat owing to the differences in the horizontal and vertical scale). The data show that the current fiscal policy is unsustainable in every country in the graph. Drastic improvements in the structural primary balance will be necessary to prevent debt ratios from exploding in future.

The future public debt trajectory

We now turn to a set of 30-year projections for the path of the debt/GDP ratio in a dozen major industrial economies (Austria, France, Germany, Greece, Ireland, Italy, Japan, the Netherlands, Portugal, Spain, the United Kingdom and the United States). We choose a 30-year horizon to capture the large unfunded liabilities stemming from future age-related expenditure without making overly strong assumptions about the future path of fiscal policy (which is unlikely to be constant).

In our baseline case, we assume that government total revenue and non-age-related primary spending remain a constant percentage of GDP at the 2011 level, as projected by the OECD. Using the CBO and European Commission projections for age-related spending, we then proceed to generate a path for total primary government spending and the primary balance over the next 30 years.[11] Throughout the projection period, the real interest rate that determines the cost of funding is assumed to remain constant at its 1998–2007 average, and potential real GDP growth is set to the OECD-estimated post-crisis rate.[12]

11. Note that the European Commission provides projections for age-related expenditure between 2008 and 2060. Using these projections, we interpolated an annual series for age-related expenditure for the next 30 years.

12. The real interest rate is computed as the effective nominal interest rate on public debt minus CPI inflation (see definition in Figure 11.3). Potential real GDP growth is taken from OECD (2009a).

Debt projections

From this exercise, we are able to come to a number of conclusions. First, in our baseline scenario, conventionally computed deficits will rise precipitously. Unless the stance of fiscal policy changes, or age-related spending is cut, by 2020 the primary deficit/GDP ratio will rise to 13 per cent in Ireland, 8–10 per cent in Japan, Spain, the United Kingdom and the United States and 3–7 per cent in Austria, Germany, Greece, the Netherlands and Portugal. Only in Italy do these policy-settings keep the primary deficits relatively well contained—a consequence of the fact that the country entered the crisis with a nearly balanced budget and did not implement any real stimulus over the past several years.

But the main point of this exercise is the impact that this will have on debt. The results plotted as (▪▪▪▪▪▪) in Figure 11.4 show that, in the baseline scenario, debt/GDP ratios rise rapidly in the next decade, exceeding 300 per cent of GDP in Japan, 200 per cent in the United Kingdom and 150 per cent in Belgium, France, Ireland, Greece, Italy and the United States.

As is clear from the slope of the line, without a change in policy, the path is unstable. This is confirmed by the projected interest rate paths, again in our baseline scenario. Figure 11.5 shows the fraction absorbed by interest payments in each of these countries. From around 5 per cent today, these numbers rise to over 10 per cent in all cases and to as high as 27 per cent in the United Kingdom.[13]

13. In our projections, we consider gross rather than net public debt, the latter being gross debt minus financial assets. Our preference for focusing on gross debt hinges on a number of considerations. First, government financial assets are more difficult to identify and accurately value than government liabilities. Second, the definition and range of assets included in net debt vary across countries, making comparisons more difficult. Third, from the point of view of a creditor, it is reasonable to assume that some or all of the fiscal authorities' financial assets, such as 'soft loans' granted to firms with a high probability of default, may not be available to repay debt when needed. Fourth, including financial assets in our analysis would require accounting not only for interest payments on gross debt but also for revenue accruing to those assets. While use of net debt numbers would have made the absolute levels of the debt/GDP ratios somewhat lower, it would have complicated the analysis significantly without changing the profile of the projections.

Figure 11.4

Public debt/GDP projections

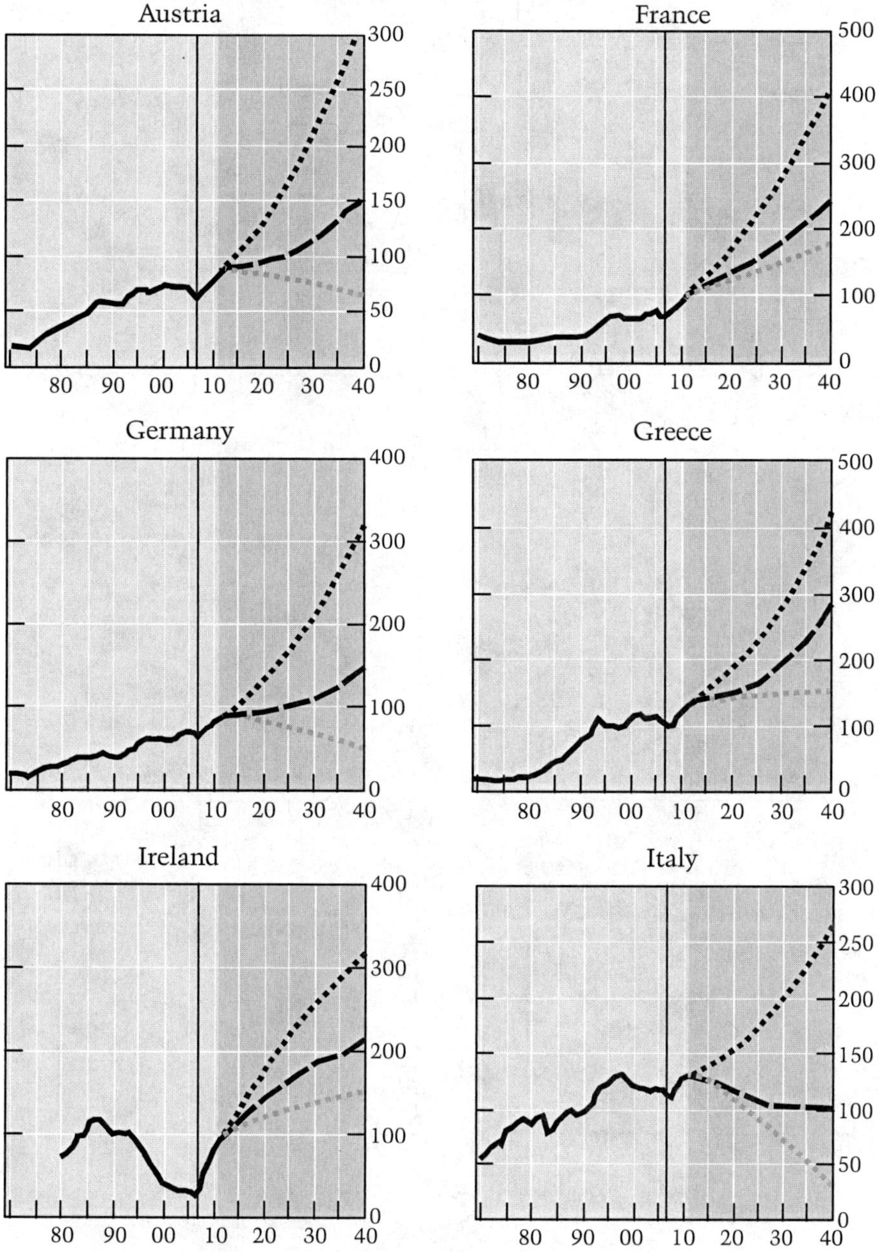

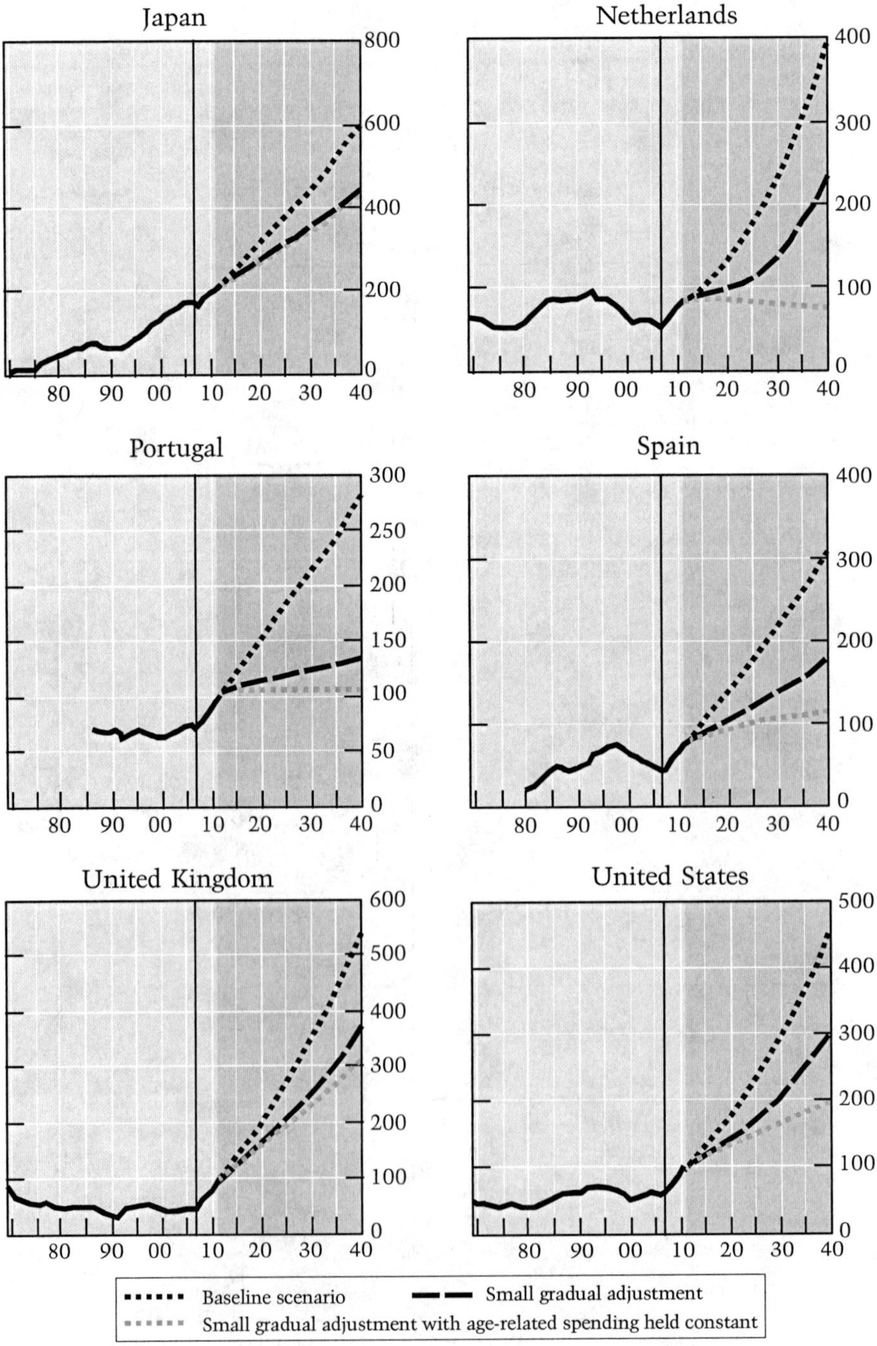

Sources: OECD; authors' projections.

Figure 11.5

Projected interest payments as a fraction of GDP (in per cent)

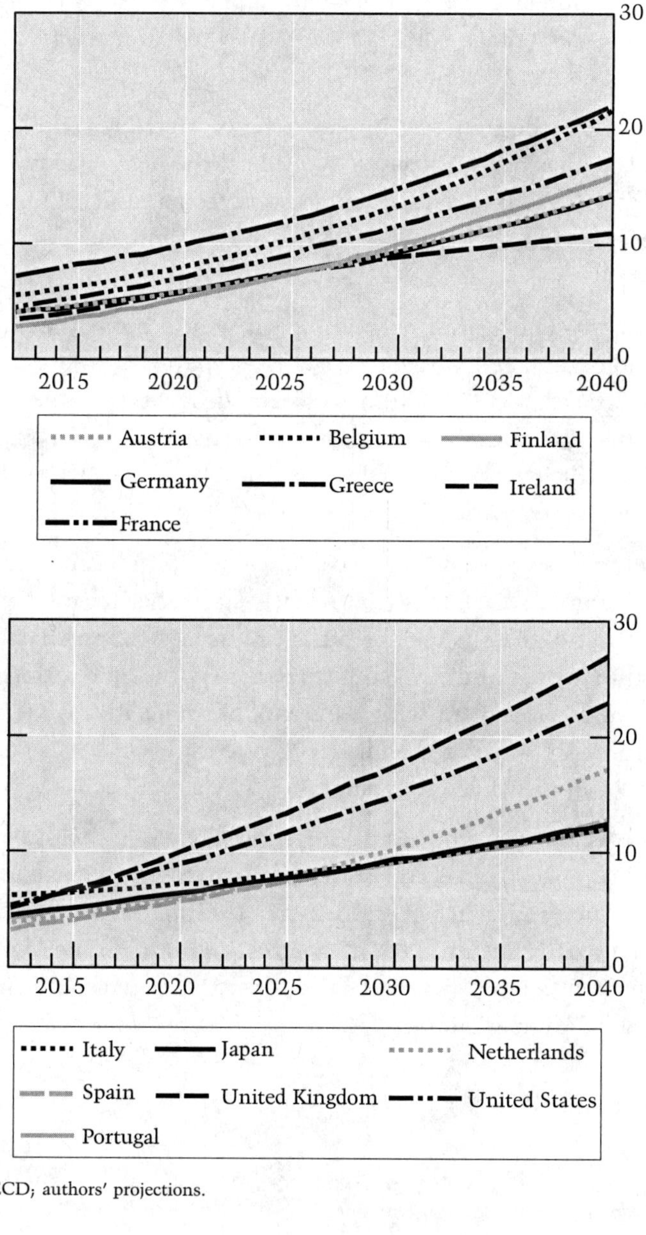

Sources: OECD; authors' projections.

Seeing that the status quo is untenable, countries are embarking on fiscal consolidation plans. In the United States, the aim is to bring the total Federal budget deficit down from 11 per cent to 4 per cent of GDP by 2015. In the United Kingdom, the consolidation plan envisages reducing budget deficits by 1.3 percentage points of GDP each year from 2010 to 2013 (see for example OECD, 2009a).

To examine the long-run implications of a gradual fiscal adjustment similar to the ones being proposed, we project the debt ratio assuming that the primary balance improves by one percentage point of GDP in each year for five years beginning 2012. The results are presented as (▬ ▬) in Figure 11.4.

Although such an adjustment path would slow the rate of debt accumulation compared with our baseline scenario, it would leave several major industrial economies with substantial debt ratios in the next decade. This suggests that consolidations along the lines currently being discussed will not be sufficient to ensure that debt levels remain within reasonable bounds over the next several decades.

An alternative to traditional spending cuts and revenue increases is to change the promises that are as yet unmet. Here, that means embarking on the politically treacherous task of cutting future age-related liabilities. With this possibility in mind, we construct a third scenario that combines gradual fiscal improvement with a freezing of age-related spending-to-GDP at the projected level for 2011. (▪▪▪▪▪▪) in Figure 11.4 shows the consequences of this draconian policy.

Given its severity, the result is no surprise. What was a rising debt/GDP ratio reverses course and starts heading down in Austria, Germany and the Netherlands. In several others, the policy yields a significant slowdown in debt accumulation. Interestingly, in France, Ireland, the United Kingdom and the United States, even this policy is not sufficient to bring rising debt under control.[14]

14. Such a policy path is unlikely to reduce Japan's debt ratio substantially because of only a small increase in projected age-related spending in future.

Table 11.3

Average primary balance required to stabilise the public debt/GDP ratio at the 2007 level[1]

	Over 5 years	*Over 10 years*	*Over 20 years*	*Memo: Primary balance in 2011 (forecast)*
Austria	5.1	3.0	2.0	–2.9
France	7.3	4.3	2.8	–5.1
Germany	5.5	3.5	2.4	–2.0
Greece	5.4	2.8	1.5	–5.3
Ireland	11.8	5.4	2.2	–9.2
Italy	5.1	3.4	2.5	0.0
Japan	10.1	6.4	4.5	–8.0
Netherlands	6.7	3.7	2.3	–3.4
Portugal	5.7	3.1	1.8	–4.4
Spain	6.1	2.9	1.3	–6.6
United Kingdom	10.6	5.8	3.5	–9.0
United States	8.1	4.3	2.4	–7.1

Note: 1. as a percentage of GDP.

Sources: OECD; authors' calculations.

All of this leads us to ask, what level of primary balance would be required to bring the debt/GDP ratio in each country back to its pre-crisis level as in 2007? Granted that countries which started with low levels of debt may never need to come back to this point, the question is an interesting one nevertheless. Table 11.3 presents the average primary surplus target required to bring debt ratios down to their 2007 levels over horizons of 5, 10 and 20 years.

An aggressive adjustment path to achieve this objective within five years would mean generating an average annual primary surplus of 8–12 per cent of GDP in the United States, Japan, the United Kingdom and Ireland, and 5–7 per cent in a number of other countries. A preference for smoothing the adjustment over a longer period (say 20 years) reduces the annual surplus target at the cost of leaving governments exposed to high debt ratios in the short to medium-term.

Risks from fiscal imbalances

The future profile of public debt presents major risks and challenges for both fiscal and monetary policy. Here we focus on the real implications of living with a higher level of debt. Further below we will turn to challenges facing monetary authorities.

When a country starts from an already high level of public debt, the probability that a given shock will trigger unstable debt dynamics is higher. This risk is increased when public debt is already on a steep upward trajectory, as it is now in several countries. Knowing this, we would expect investors to demand a higher risk premium for holding the bonds issued by a highly indebted country.

Studies of the impact of debt on risk premia are rather limited for advanced economies. Whatever evidence is available, suggests that the impact is relatively small. For each percentage point of additional public debt, researchers estimate a risk premium increase of between 1.2 and 1.6 basis points.[15]

With the advent of the market for credit default swaps (CDS),[16] we now have an additional source of information about investor attitudes towards highly indebted advanced economies. Data plotted in Figure 11.6(a) leads to the unsurprising conclusion that CDS spreads, and hence credit risk premia, are positively correlated with debt/GDP ratios. But we note that there is substantial heterogeneity, suggesting that other factors are important as well. For example, the higher the fraction of debt that is short-term, the lower the risk premium (Figure 11.6(c)). A higher ratio of incremental debt to private saving (Figure 11.6(d)) is associated with a

15. Using the difference between government bond yields and yields on corporate bonds denominated in the same currency as a proxy for credit risk premia, Alesina *et al.* (1992) find an impact of 1.6 basis points for each extra percentage point of public debt. Since these measures can be affected by changes in private sector credit risk, using the spread between the government bond yield and the return on interest rate swaps of corresponding maturity and currency, Goodhart and Lemmen (1999) find a slightly smaller effect (1.5 bp). However, these spreads are also affected by liquidity premia besides credit risk premia. In a study that attempts to disentangle the two effects, Codogno *et al.* (2003) find that debt levels can explain yield differentials *vis-à-vis* Germany only in Italy and Spain.

16. A CDS contract is a credit derivative that, for a specified bond issuer, protects the buyer against a default or debt restructuring.

Figure 11.6

Sovereign CDS spreads[1] and fiscal indicators[2]

(a) General government debt/GDP[3]

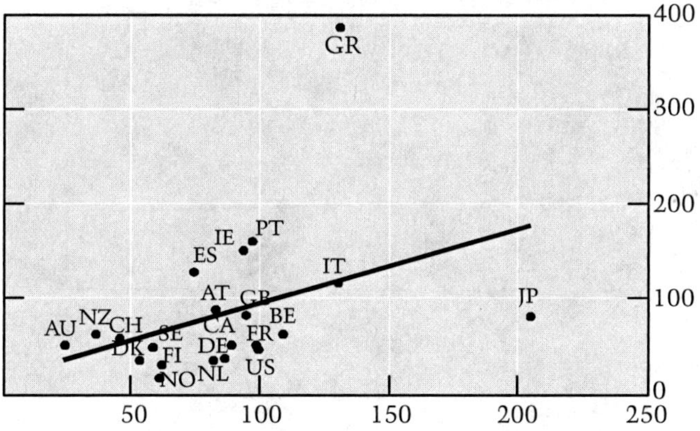

(b) General government revenue/GDP[3]

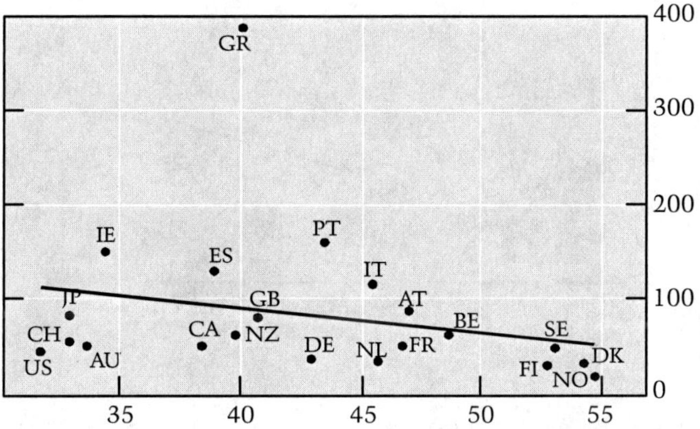

(c) Share of short-term debt[4]

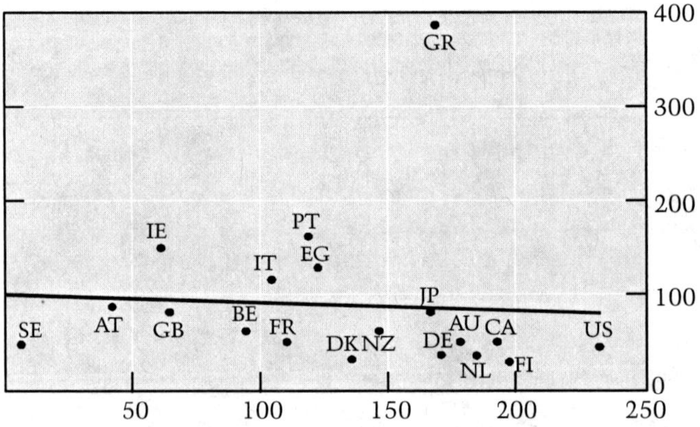

(d) Change in general government debt/savings[5]

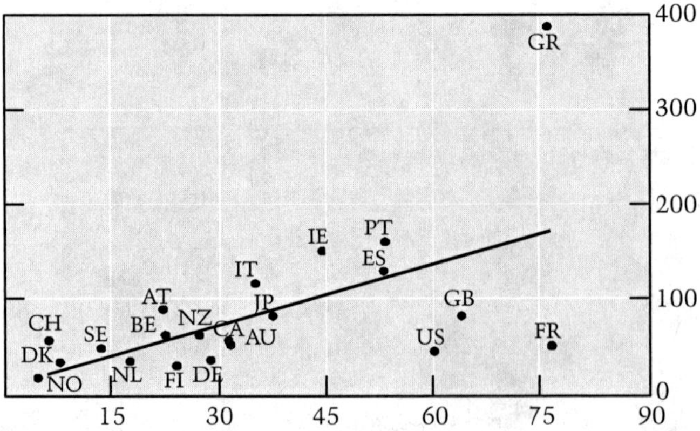

Note: AU = Australia; AT = Austria; BE = Belgium; CA = Canada; CH = Switzerland; DE = Germany; DK = Denmark; ES = Spain; FI = Finland; FR = France; GB = United Kingdom; GR = Greece; IE = Ireland; IT = Italy; JP = Japan; NL = Netherlands; NO = Norway; NZ = New Zealand; PT = Portugal; SE = Sweden; US = United States.

1. Vertical axis: spread as of end of January 2010; in basis points. 2. Horizontal axis. 3. Forecast for 2011. 4. Domestic government debt with a remaining maturity of 1 to 3 years as a percentage of total domestic government debt. 5. Average change in general government debt as a percentage of average private savings; forecast average for the period 2009–2011.

Sources: IMF, *World Economic Outlook*; OECD; JP Morgan Chase; Markit.

higher risk premium. And risk premia are generally lower for countries with a high average revenue share in GDP (Figure 11.6(b)).[17]

In addition to higher risk premia and increased cost, a second risk associated with high levels of public debt comes from potentially lower long-term growth. A higher level of public debt implies that a larger share of society's resources is permanently being spent servicing the debt. This means that a government intent on maintaining a given level of public services and transfers must raise taxes as debt increases. Taxes distort resource allocation and can lead to lower levels of growth. Given the level of taxes in some countries, one has to wonder if further increases will actually raise revenue.[18]

The distortionary impact of taxes is normally further compounded by the crowding out of productive private capital. In a closed economy, a higher level of public debt will eventually absorb a larger share of national wealth, pushing up real interest rates and causing an offsetting fall in the stock of private capital.[19] This not only lowers the level of output but (since new capital is invariably more productive than old capital) it also reduces the rate of capital accumulation. It can eventually lead to a persistent slowdown in the rate of economic growth.

In an open economy, international financial markets can moderate these effects as long as investors remain confident of a country's ability to repay. But, even when private capital is not crowded out, larger borrowing

17. It is not clear exactly how this should be interpreted. On the one hand, an already high level of average taxation may indicate that a country is close to its fiscal limit—that is, it has less room for increasing taxes further. So, other things being equal, one could expect risk premia to be lower for countries with lower average tax rates. On the other hand, countries with high taxation might also be countries with a low level of debt or with strong social and political cohesion, which should reduce risk, all else being equal. Further econometric analysis would be required to uncover partial correlations.

18. Recent estimates by Trabandt and Uhlig (2009) show that the EU 14 can increase tax revenue by 8 per cent by raising labour taxes and by 1 per cent by raising capital income taxes. In contrast, these figures stand at 30 per cent and 6 per cent, respectively, for the United States, indicating a greater fiscal capacity to tolerate higher public debt levels.

19. Estimates of the impact of public debt levels on real interest rates vary substantially. For the United States, Chinn and Frankel (2005) find an impact as low as two basis points per percentage point of the debt/GDP ratio. For Europe, EC (2004) provides a range estimate rising to 16 basis points.

from abroad means that domestic income is reduced by interest paid to foreigners, increasing the gap between GDP and GNP.

Last but not least, the existence of a higher level of public debt is likely to reduce both the size and the effectiveness of any future fiscal response to an adverse shock. Since policy cannot play its stabilising role, a more indebted economy will be more volatile. This was evident during the latest crisis.

Countries saddled with very high levels of public debt did not expand fiscal policy as much as other countries. And, although these countries benefited somewhat from the effects of foreign fiscal expansion, a larger domestic fiscal stimulus could have helped reduce the severity of the recession actually experienced.

The challenge for central banks

Steeply rising public debt levels and the uncertainty associated with future fiscal consolidation plans pose at least two important challenges for monetary policymakers. First, deteriorating public finances can trigger a sudden increase in long-term inflation expectations. Second, uncertainty about the timing and extent of fiscal consolidation plans complicates the forecasting needed to set policy interest rates at their appropriate level. Here we only focus on the inflation risks.

Is there a risk that inflation expectations may rise? What can monetary policymakers do to reduce this risk? To answer these questions, it would be helpful to review the mechanisms by which persistently high fiscal deficits could lead to inflation.[20]

A first mechanism stresses the ultimate impossibility of continuing to roll over ever increasing levels of public debt when monetary and fiscal authorities are pursuing inconsistent objectives. When the public reaches its limit and is no longer willing to hold public debt, the government would have to resort to monetisation. The result, consistent with the quantity theory of money, is inflation.

20. A main distinction in the literature is whether the quantitative theory of money holds (in which case inflation is always and everywhere a monetary phenomenon) or whether fiscal variables have a direct influence on the price level in addition to money (fiscal theory of the price level).

Anticipation that this will happen may also lead to an increase in inflation today as investors reassess the risk from holding money and government bonds. In such an environment, fighting rising inflation by tightening monetary policy would not work, as an increase in interest rates would lead to higher interest payments on public debt, leading to higher debt, bringing the likely time of monetisation even closer.[21]

Thus, in the absence of fiscal tightening, monetary policy may ultimately prove impotent in controlling inflation, regardless of the fighting credentials of the central bank.[22] Conflicts between the goals of fiscal and monetary authorities can explain a number of inflationary outbursts in emerging market economies. Notable examples include the Brazilian inflationary boom in the early 1980s, when monetary policy started to act more aggressively against inflation (Loyo, 1999) in the face of persistent fiscal deficits. Other examples are the big jump in Israeli inflation in October 1983 (Sargent and Zeira, 2008) and the Indian inflation of the 1970s and 1980s in which fiscal deficits were monetised (Rangarajan and Mohanty, 1997).

A second mechanism stresses the political and economic pressures that a monetary policymaker may face to inflate away the real value of debt. The payoff of doing this is larger, the bigger the debt, the longer its average maturity, the larger the fraction denominated in domestic currency and the bigger the fraction held by foreigners.

---

21. This 'paradox of tight money' is the striking finding of Sargent and Wallace's analysis (1981). Note that in their example debt is perfectly indexed in real terms. This rules out the case that inflation arises from the monetary authorities' attempt to reduce its real value. Inflation, instead, arises because at a certain point bond investors refuse to hold debt and the government is, therefore, forced to issue money, short of an outright default.

22. The mechanism emphasised here requires that, when the fiscal authority does not restore fiscal sustainability through changes in its fiscal instruments, the intertemporal budget constraint of the government will eventually be met through the issuance of money. In contrast, the fiscal theory of the price level stresses that the intertemporal budget constraint may also be met by a change in the market value of debt. In its more stylised form, the theory predicts that the general price level will adjust to bring about the required reduction in the value of bonds (e.g., Sims, 1994; Woodford, 1995; Cochrane, 1998). In reality, how this change in the price level should occur in the presence of a wide array of assets, nominal rigidities and rational expectations is unclear. The theory is still untested and controversial (for criticism, see Buiter, 2002).

Moreover, the incentives to tolerate temporarily high inflation rise if the tax and transfer system is mainly based on nominal cash flows and if policymakers see a social benefit in helping households and firms to reduce their leverage in real terms. It is, however, worth emphasising that the costs of creating an unexpected inflation would almost surely be very high in the form of permanently high future real interest rates (and any other distortions caused by persistently higher inflation).[23]

Discussions of inflation risks abound in the financial media. Yet, there is little evidence that fiscal prospects are materially affecting inflation expectations. While US and Euro area market-based inflation expectations became volatile immediately before and after the recent financial crisis, Figure 11.7 shows that they have reverted to the average levels of the past five years or so. Meanwhile, survey-based measures of inflation expectations in both areas have been more stable than market-based ones.

Although the possibility of governments being forced or tempted to tolerate higher inflation is rather remote in the short-run, that does not mean that it may not happen in future.[24] Therefore, the risk that long-term inflation expectations could suddenly become unanchored today is a possibility that should not be discounted. The most likely manifestation of this risk is an unexpected and abrupt rise in government bond yields at medium and long maturities, as negative news about the state of the economy and public finances lead investors to reassess the risks of unsustainable fiscal situation and future inflation.

---

23. Persson *et al.* (1996) estimate that, given the state of public finances and the economy in Sweden in the early 1990s, the benefit of an increase of 10 percentage points in the inflation rate could have been substantial (an annual real flow of 3 to 4 per cent of GDP). Most of this benefit would have arisen not from seigniorage or the devaluation of outstanding debt but from the nominal character of the tax and transfer system in Sweden. Most importantly, the authors also found that the costs of the increase in inflation, including those arising from permanent real interest rates, would have been even higher.

24. History shows that countries that ran high public debts eventually ended up with high inflation because governments were unwilling to pay high interest rates. Makinen and Woodward (1990) provide an account of the experience of the European countries during the interwar period. Following funding crises, governments in many countries (Belgium, Spain and Italy) pegged interest rates and resorted to debt monetisation. Germany's hyperinflation is also an important reminder of this risk.

Figure 11.7

Inflation expectations (in per cent)

(a) Break-even inflation rates (five-year-ahead)

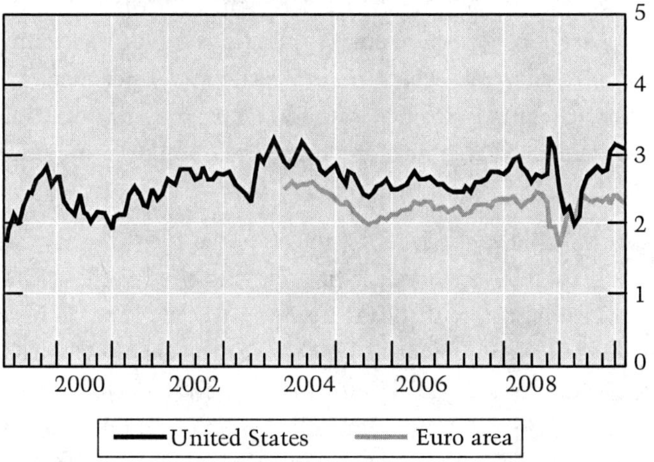

(b) Mid-term inflation expectations (10-year-ahead)[1]

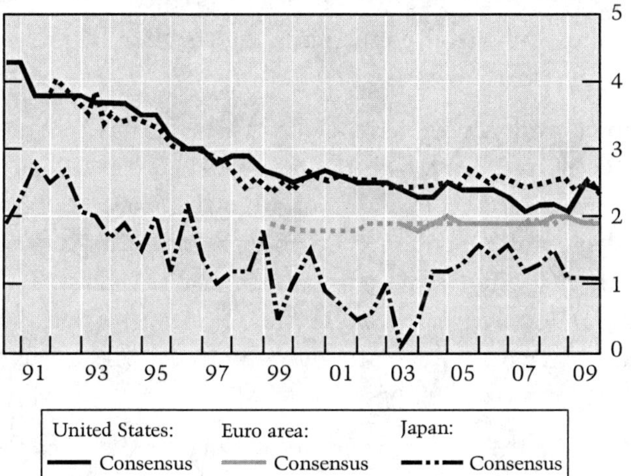

Note: 1. for survey of professional forecasters (SPF); Euro area, five-year-ahead.

Sources: ECB, *Survey of Professional Forecasters*; Federal Reserve Bank of Philadelphia, *Survey of Professional Forecasters*; © Consensus Economics; national data; authors' calculations.

Conclusion

Our examination of the future of public debt leads us to several important conclusions. First, fiscal problems confronting industrial economies are bigger than suggested by official debt figures that show the implications of the financial crisis and recession for fiscal balances. As frightening as it is to consider public debt increasing to more than 100 per cent of GDP, an even greater danger arises from a rapidly ageing population. The related unfunded liabilities are large and growing, and should be a central part of today's long-term fiscal planning.

It is essential that governments not be lulled into complacence by the ease with which they have financed their deficits thus far. In the aftermath of the financial crisis, the path of future output is likely to be permanently below where we thought it would be just several years ago. As a result, government revenues will be lower and expenditures higher, making consolidation even more difficult. But, unless action is taken to place fiscal policy on a sustainable footing, these costs could easily rise sharply and suddenly.

Second, large public debts have significant financial and real consequences. The recent sharp rise in risk premia on long-term bonds issued by several industrial countries suggests that markets no longer consider sovereign debt low-risk.

The limited evidence we have suggests that default risk premia move up with debt levels and down with the revenue share of GDP, as well as the availability of private saving. Countries with a relatively weak fiscal system and a high degree of dependence on foreign investors to finance their deficits, generally face larger spreads on their debts. This market differentiation is a positive feature of the financial system, but it could force governments with weak fiscal systems to return to fiscal rectitude sooner than they may like or hope.

Third, we note the risk that persistently high levels of public debt will drive down capital accumulation, productivity growth and long-term potential growth. Although we do not provide direct evidence of this, a recent study suggests that there may be non-linear effects of public debt on growth, with adverse output effects tending to rise as the debt/GDP ratio approaches the 100 per cent limit (Reinhart and Rogoff, 2009b).

Finally, looming long-term fiscal imbalances pose significant risk to the prospects of future monetary stability. We describe two channels through which unstable debt dynamics could lead to higher inflation—direct debt monetisation and the temptation to reduce the real value of government debt through higher inflation. Given the current institutional setting of monetary policy, both risks are clearly limited, at least for now.

The key challenge facing policymakers today is how to tackle these fiscal dangers without seriously jeopardising the incipient recovery. Although we do not offer advice on how to go about this, we believe that any fiscal consolidation plan should include credible measures to reduce future unfunded liabilities. Announcements of changes in these programmes would allow authorities to wait till the recovery from the crisis is assured, before reducing discretionary spending and improving the short-term fiscal position.

An important aspect of measures to tackle future liabilities is that any potential adverse impact on today's saving behaviour be minimised. From this point of view, a decision to raise the retirement age seems a better option than a future cut in benefits or an increase in taxes. Indeed, it may even lead to an increase in consumption (see for example, Barrell *et al.* (2009) for an analysis applied to the United Kingdom).

References

Alesina, A, M. De Broeck, A. Prati, G. Tabellini and M. Obstfeld (1992). "Default Risk on Government Debt in OECD Countries", *Economic Policy* 7.

Auerbach, A. (2008). "Long-term Objectives for Government Debt". Berkeley: University of California. *mimeo*.

Barrell, R., I. Hurst and S. Kirby (2009). "How to Pay for the Crisis or Macroeconomic Implications of Pension Reform", National Institute of Economic and Social Research, *Discussion Paper* No. 333.

Brondolo, J. (2009). "Collecting Taxes During an Economic Crisis: Challenges and Policy Options", *IMF Staff Position Note* SPN/V09/17.

Buiter, W. (2002). "The Fiscal Theory of the Price Level: A Critique", *The Economic Journal* 112, July.

Cecchetti, S. and F. Zhu (2009). "Real Consequences of Financial Crisis", Paper presented at the Bank of Mexico conference on *Challenges and Strategies for Promoting Economic Growth*. Mexico City. October 9–20.

Chinn, M. and J. Frankel (2005). "The Euro Area and World Interest Rates". University of California, Santa Cruz. *mimeo*.

Cochrane, J. (1998). "A Frictionless View of US Inflation", *NBER Macroeconomics Annual* 13: 323-421.

Codogno, L., C. Favero and A. Missale (2003). "Yield Spreads on EMU Government Bonds", *Economic Policy*. October.

Congressional Budget Office (2009). *The Long-Term Budget Outlook*. June.

European Commission (2004). *Public Finances in EMU*, No. 3/2004.

———. (2009). "2009 Ageing Report: Economic and Budgetary Projections for the EU-27 Member States (2008–2060)", *European Economy* 2 (provisional version).

Giavazzi, F. (2009). "Panel Discussion on 'Monetary and Financial Policy Responses to the Crisis'", Presentation at the 13th Annual Conference of the Central Bank of Chile. Santiago. 19 November.

Gokhale, J. (2009). "Measuring the Unfunded Obligations of European Countries", *National Centre for Policy Analysis Policy Report* No. 319. January.

Goodhart, C. and J. Lemmen (1999). "Credit Risks and European Government Bond Markets: A Panel Data Econometric Analysis", *Eastern Economic Journal* 25.

Hauner, D., D. Leigh and M. Skaarup (2007). "Ensuring Fiscal Sustainability in G7 Countries", *IMF Working Papers* 07/187.

International Monetary Fund (2010). "Navigating the Fiscal Challenges Ahead", *Fiscal Monitor*. May.

Knotek, E. and S. Terry (2009). "How will Unemployment Fare Following the Recession?", *Federal Reserve Bank of Kansas City Economic Review*. Third Quarter.

Laeven, L. and F. Valencia (2008). "Systemic Banking Crises: A New Database", *IMF Working Papers* 08/224.

Leeper, E. (1991). "Equilibria under 'Active' and 'Passive' Monetary and Fiscal Policies", *Journal of Monetary Economics* 27(1).

———. (2009). "Anchoring Fiscal Expectations", *NBER Working Papers* No. 15269.

Loyo, E. (1999). "Tight Money Paradox on the Loose: A Fiscalist Hyperinflation". J.F. Kennedy School of Government. Harvard University. June, *mimeo*.

Makinen, G. and G. Woodward (1990). "Funding Crises in the Aftermath of World War I", in R. Dornbusch and M. Draghi (eds.), *Public Debt Management: Theory and History*. Cambridge: CUP.

OECD (2009a). *Economic Outlook* No. 86. November.

———. (2009b). "The Effectiveness and Scope of Fiscal Stimulus", Chapter 3, *OECD Interim Economic Outlook*. March.

Persson, M., T. Persson and L. Svensson (1996). "Debt, Cash Flow and Inflation Incentives: A Swedish Example", *NBER Working Papers* No. W5772.

Rangarajan, C. and M.S. Mohanty (1997). "Fiscal Deficit, External Balance and Monetary Growth: Evidence on the Indian Economy", *RBI Occasional Papers* 18(9).

Reinhart, C. and K. Rogoff (2008). "This Time is Different: A Panoramic View of Eight Centuries of Financial Crises". Harvard University. *mimeo*.

———. (2009a). "Banking Crisis: An Equal Opportunity Menace", *CEPR Discussion Papers* DP/7131.

———. (2009b). "Growth in a Time of Debt". December. *mimeo*.

Sargent, T. and N. Wallace (1981). "Some Unpleasant Monetarist Arithmetic", *Federal Reserve Bank of Minneapolis Quarterly Review* 5(3).

Sargent, T. and J. Zeira (2008). "Israel 1983: A Bout of Unpleasant Monetarist Arithmetic", *CEPR Discussion Papers* DP/6792.

Schneider, F. (2009). "Influence of the Global Economic Crisis on the Underground Economy in Germany: A (renewed) increase", *Discussion Paper*. Linz. Austria: Institute of Economics, Johannes Kepler University. March.

Sims, C. (1994). "A Simple Model for the Study of the Determination of the Price Level and the Interaction of Monetary and Fiscal Policy", *Economic Theory* 4.

Trabandt, M. and H. Uhlig (2009). "How Far Are We from the Slippery Slope? The Laffer Curve Revisited", *NBER Working Papers* No. 15343.

Woodford, M. (1995). "Price Level Determination Without Control of a Monetary Aggregate", Carnegie-Rochester Conference Series on *Public Policy* 43.

Appendix

Budget accounting and debt dynamics

This appendix provides a summary of the main budget accounting identities that underpin our discussion in the main text and that have been used to generate projections of future public debt/GDP ratios in different scenarios.

Our starting point is the consolidated government sector budget identity:

$$G_t + iD_{t-1} = T_t + (D_t - D_{t-1}) + (H_t - H_{t-1}) \qquad (1)$$

where G is the nominal level of primary government expenditure and i is the nominal interest rate paid on nominal public debt D. The variables on the right indicate that total nominal expenditure (on the left) can be funded through taxes T, new debt issuance (the second term on the right) and the change in the stock of central bank liabilities or monetary base (the third term on the right).

The last term is also called seigniorage. In economies in which long-term inflation is low and stable—as it has been in major advanced economies since at least the mid-1980s—this source of public finance has been relatively small.

Dividing through by nominal GDP and rearranging terms, (1) can be rewritten as:

$$d_t - d_{t-1} = \hat{r}_t d_{t-1} + \omega_t + s_t \qquad (2)$$

$$\hat{r}_t \equiv \frac{1+i_t}{(1+\pi_t)(1+\eta_t)} - 1 \cong i_t - \pi_t + \eta_t$$

$$\omega_t \equiv g_t - t_t$$

where now the small letters represent ratios of the original variables to GDP. According to (2), the change in the public debt/GDP ratio depends on real interest payments (adjusted for real output growth η), the primary deficit and seigniorage s (all expressed as a share of GDP). If the real interest rate on debt is higher than real output growth, then the debt/GDP ratio increases, even if a government manages to match its primary expenditure with revenue. In this case, new debt needs to be issued simply to cover the interest payments on the outstanding stock of debt.[25]

25. Ignoring seigniorage, it follows from (2) that the condition for the debt/GDP ratio to remain constant over time is that:

$-\omega_t / d_{t-1} = \hat{r}_t$; or (after simple manipulation): $-\Omega_t / D_{t-1} = \hat{r}_t$ (*)

that is, the primary surplus scaled by debt needs to be identical to the difference between the real return on public debt and real output growth. Relation (*) is plotted as a 45-degree line in the right-hand panel of Figure 11.3(b). If a country's primary surplus lies below such a line, then it will experience an increase in its debt/GDP ratio, and vice versa. How far a country is from the line provides a visual representation of how fast its debt/GDP ratio will increase at a given point in time.

As new debt is added, interest payments will increase even further, leading to the issuance of ever greater amounts of debt. Roughly speaking, when a government 'indefinitely' issues new debt to pay interest on the stock of debt (and any additional non-funded expenditure), it is said to be running a Ponzi scheme, and its debt is set to grow without limit. (This statement will be made more precise below.)

However, a country does not have an unlimited capacity to borrow. The best way to see this is to solve (2) forward and rewrite it as an intertemporal budget constraint. For simplicity, we assume that both the nominal interest rate and nominal income growth are constant over time (so that we can drop the time subscript from them). We obtain:

$$d_{t-1} = \sum_{j=0}^{\infty} \frac{-\omega_{t+j} + s_{t+j}}{(1+\hat{r})^{j+1}} + \lim_{j\to\infty} \frac{d_{t+j}}{(1+\hat{r})^{j+1}} \quad (3)$$

A government is said to satisfy the intertemporal budget constraint when the last term on the right is equal to zero (no Ponzi condition):

$$d_{t-1} = \sum_{j=0}^{\infty} \frac{-\omega_{t+j} + s_{t+j}}{(1+\hat{r})^{j+1}} \quad (4)$$

If so, a government's debt must equal the present discounted value of all future primary surpluses and any future seigniorage revenue.

The seminal analysis of Sargent and Wallace (1981) has shown how fiscal and monetary policies are inextricably linked through the government's intertemporal budget constraint (4). If the fiscal authority does not adjust the primary surplus, then the monetary authority will have to issue more money to satisfy (4). If money financing implies that agents are flooded with money that they do not desire to hold, they may adjust their behaviour by spending it on goods, thus pushing up the price level.

Hence, a fiscal imbalance has the potential to cause inflation when the fiscal authority fails to behave in accordance with the goal of price stability. The 'unpleasant monetarist arithmetic' of Sargent and Wallace (1981) derives from the fact that a tightening of monetary policy will, through higher interest payments, cause a larger increase in public debt.

Greater debt, in turn, brings forward the time at which money financing will be the only means left to finance the debt as the public refuses to hold further debt. In other words, an inflation-fighting central bank may paradoxically succeed in reducing inflation today but cause higher inflation tomorrow if the fiscal authority persists in its fiscal profligacy.[26]

Any gap between the left and right side variables indicates that the current debt level is not on a sustainable path, and that an adjustment in the primary surplus is, therefore, required. Failure by the fiscal authority to adjust would inevitably lead, short of outright default, to higher inflation. To the extent that agents anticipate that an adjustment will ultimately take place, the fiscal imbalance should have no consequence for inflation.[27]

The interpretation of (4) as an intertemporal budget constraint, which must hold at any time for all values of the price level, is not the only one. The other interpretation is that (4) is an equilibrium condition that determines the price level. Depending on the interpretation given, the literature has proposed two distinct types of theory for explaining how a fiscal imbalance could lead to a higher price level.

One is that the quantity theory of money holds, so that the only way fiscal variables can affect the price level is by affecting the supply of money (as discussed above) and the real demand for money (via changes in the ratio of public debt held by the private sector). The other type of theory, instead, allows for the possibility that there could be more than one price level consistent with a given nominal amount of money. In this case, fiscal variables will determine the price level for a given level of money supply.[28]

The problem with (4) as a condition to assess the sustainability of current public debt levels is that it does not say anything about the time in which the required fiscal adjustment will or ought to take place. In principle, an adjustment could take place in the distant future. For example, it could take place so far in the future that it might not sound credible to bond investors. So, alternative benchmarks or criteria to judge fiscal sustainability are also used.

One is to estimate the amount of debt that a country could sustain over a long period of time without facing too high a risk of default. Such an estimate of the sustainable debt level will take into account, among other factors, the fiscal capacity

26. Sargent and Wallace (1981) also provide an example in which inflation may rise immediately as a result of a monetary tightening if money demand depends on expected future inflation.

27. Things are more complicated when agents discount the possibility of failure to adjust. In this case, the possibility of unstable dynamics or multiple equilibrium price levels open up. Inflation expectations might no longer be pinned down; see Leeper (2009).

28. See Leeper (1991), Sims (1994), Woodford (1995) and Cochrane (1998).

of a country (for example how far the government can raise tax revenues without causing the tax base to shrink, or how far it can cut public expenses without causing major social and political disruptions) and the response of financial markets to the state of the economy and the state of public finances.

Other approaches look at the magnitude of primary surpluses that a government needs to produce over time for its debt ratio to be stabilised at current levels or at some (lower or higher) level at some point in the future. An advantage of this approach is that it is to some degree less arbitrary than other approaches mentioned above, as the amount of assumptions and information required as an input is kept to a minimum.

In this paper, we adopt this simpler approach. Specifically, we use (2) to project debt/GDP ratios into the future in different scenarios concerning the profile of primary surpluses. To keep things simple, we also assume that in (2) the real interest rate and real output growth are time-invariant. And we also assume that seigniorage remains zero throughout—an assumption justified by the fact that, in advanced economies with low inflation, seigniorage has been rather small.

11.1
DISCUSSION

Where is the Hero Who Saves the Day?

ESWAR PRASAD

The message the authors convey is very simple. Things are bad on the fiscal front in industrial countries and they are worse than they seem. From this very cheerful premise, the authors then go on to make point number three—that things will get even worse. Do not read this before you go to bed.

Yet, what the authors have to say is very important. They point out the implications of the accumulation of public debt in advanced economies for the international financial system and for the growth of advanced and emerging market economies. I am going to talk a little bit about the numbers, a little about the overall global implications of what Steve has put up and then about the possible resolution.

The numbers do look scary. There is a minor quibble about the numbers, though. These are gross debt numbers and if you look at the net debt numbers, they do not look quite as bad. For the United States, the Congressional Budget Office (CBO) estimates that the net debt level as a ratio of the gross domestic product (GDP) is expected to stabilise at about 70 per cent of GDP relative to a gross debt ratio of 100 per cent of GDP. The difference is about $10 trillion for the net *versus* $14 trillion for the gross figure.

But these days, what is a trillion here or there? The essential point that Steve makes is that irrespective of whether public debt is 70 per cent of the US GDP or 100 per cent, the fact is that problems are building up for the future, because of the ageing of the population and a variety of other

Comments by Eswar Prasad on the paper presented by Stephen G. Cecchetti, M.S. Mohanty and Fabrizio Zampolli 'The Future of Public Debt: Prospects and Implications'.

contingent liabilities that are building up in the financial system. What are the implications?

On the global front, these piled up fiscal problems could severely set back the growth rebalancing that we have all been talking about. There is, of course, a deep and contentious debate about whether global macroeconomic imbalances were a cause, the proximate cause or mattered at all for the crisis we have been through, and are still in the midst of.

It is clear, though, that what these numbers imply is that there will be a substantial demand for resources from the advanced economies. This is going to be satisfied partly perhaps, by private savings rising in the advanced economies as it has, including in the US. The numbers, however, do not suggest that private savings in the advanced economies are going to be able to satisfy the demand. There will have to be a pull-in of resources from the emerging markets.

Another interesting issue is the implication of what this is going to imply for the advanced economy currencies. Looking at these numbers, it is hard to believe that people, especially emerging market policymakers, will want to go on putting money in the advanced economy currencies, especially in the government bonds of these currencies. Moreover, it implies a massive absorption of global savings.

Some advanced countries like Japan, are in a slightly better position. Net debt and gross debt matters for Japan too, but Japan is a high savings country domestically and they have a lot more on the asset side of their balance sheet. Yet, if you put all the advanced economies together, the amount of money they are going to suck in, in terms of their own private savings and money from the emerging markets that could use the money (in principle, more productively), suggests that we have more serious problems ahead.

All of this implies that we could be setting ourselves up for a situation where there could be trigger effects, leading to very sharp movements in these asset markets. The problem from the emerging markets' point of view is that, as in the recent financial crisis, a problem that emanates from and is the cause of the lack of political will in the advanced economies could hurt them. Of course, it could hurt them in different ways.

A movement of money away from the advanced economies towards the emerging markets could hurt them, because many of them do not have deep enough financial markets to be able to absorb these inflows. On the other hand, countries like India that still have a small financing need and other emerging markets, that have fairly large current account deficits, could get slammed against the wall as well. If you are sitting in an emerging market, the picture does not look pretty at all and there is nothing, in principle, that the emerging markets can do about it.

What about the resolution of this crisis? The financial capital of India, Mumbai, is also the home of its Hindi film industry, fondly dubbed 'Bollywood'. In Bollywood movies, a hero usually appears at the last minute to save things, because fans of Bollywood like happy endings. We have seen a variety of doomsday scenarios in various contexts in the past and not just in terms of debt—even though it is an issue that has been on the table for a long time.

We have also seen doomsday projections on other issues, like whether there was going to be food to feed the planet, whether there was going to be enough energy resources to manage the planet, or whether commodity prices were going to go through the roof. None of these things have quite happened yet. One wonders whether, in fact, these financial sector doomsday scenarios might also get sorted out.

There is a serious worry, because one could argue that there could be a resolution with, perhaps, productivity growth picking up. It has picked up in many sectors of the economy. In agriculture we have seen massive increases in productivity that got us away from Malthusian fears of world famine. Perhaps, there could be productivity increases and, in this context, the authors actually make a very important point—that this is going to be endogeneous.

In fact, Steve points out that the sort of savings absorption implied by the large government deficits and the distortionary costs potentially arising from the very large tax implications thereof, could actually reduce growth of productivity. So, unfortunately, productivity growth is not going to be the white knight that saves us.

So, how could the impending crisis be resolved? If you think about what sort of transfers this implies, there are two types. One is massive inter-generational transfers within countries, but there are also very large cross-country transfers. This simply cannot go on. So, where is the political will going to come from? It looks like, right now, there is no political will in the advanced economies to tackle these problems.

At least in the US, any mention of tax increases, even on those with incomes of over a quarter of a million dollars, is toxic. Republicans bark against revenue increases. The Democrats are going to make it difficult to make any expenditure reductions. The path towards reducing the fiscal deficit, therefore, is very unclear, especially in the US—which, of course, is the big gorilla in the room.

What could happen? One way to resolve this is to have scare tactics—basically, to have Steve go out and tell the rest of the world how bad the numbers look. But we have been told how bad the numbers look for a while. The alternative is a debt crisis. This is again potentially very, very scary!

If you think about it, the lack of financing of the advanced economy debt that could trigger a tremendous amount of instability in international financial markets and how that is going to resolve or play out, is potentially a very scary phenomenon. The reality is that advanced economies are going to have to get their acts together to solve this problem. Otherwise, the global implications are going to be very large.

Another possible scenario is that the adjustments that were imposed on the economies by the financial crisis, especially in the West, continue. In fact, the US economy did adjust to some extent. The problem is that the emerging economies also need to come on board, in particular, countries like China that have not exactly been helping foster the adjustment. In fact, the growth model in China is, if anything, going to become even more unbalanced because of the way they are getting out of the crisis.

China is investing in its economy, which is going to lead to even more excess capacity being built up in industries, where there is already excess capacity. So, the world at large is looking at exports for growth. China, many of the other emerging markets, Japan, Germany—everybody is looking towards the export market and, of course, President Obama wants the US to increase exports as well.

I see this becoming a very contentious set of issues. Emerging market economies will have to persuade themselves and persuade some of their compatriots, especially China, to make moves to shift this global imbalance. Unless adjustment is forced on the US economy from outside, it is going to make rectifying the global imbalance much harder.

In summary, I think, it will be very important for policymakers around the world to take the messages of this discussion seriously—and not just policymakers in the advanced economies. Otherwise, we are all in deep trouble.

12 The Great Recession and International Policy Coordination

CARLOS A. PRIMO BRAGA[1]

Introduction

The Great Recession of 2008-09 has been often compared to the Great Depression of the 1930s. No doubt there are many similarities between these two episodes (and other financial crises) in terms of the destabilising role played by financial innovation, the bursting of asset price bubbles, and the deterioration of financial institutions' balance sheets. The differences, however, in terms of policy response and international coordination also merit attention. After all, in spite of all the talk about the 'return of depression economics' and the ineffectiveness of monetary policies in promoting a recovery of economic growth, the global economy in early 2010 seems to contradict doomsday scenarios. But there is also broad consensus that the ongoing economic recovery is fragile and many dangers remain ahead in terms of its sustainability, not to mention the challenges in implementing exit strategies.

This paper discusses the role that international coordination has played in avoiding a global depression, the different stances in terms of policy environment and financial fragility in developed and developing countries at the start of the crisis, and some of the implications for central banks. The paper argues that *ex post* international coordination should get 'good' marks in terms of crisis response. The 'bad' news, however, is that the underlying economic situation of different economies, not surprisingly,

1. Research assistance from William G. O'Boyle as well as comments from A. Manoel, A. Prasad, E. Favaro, E. Togo, F.L. Hernandez, H. Blommestein, J. Pradelli, and R. Van Doorn are gratefully acknowledged. The views expressed here are those of the author. They do not necessarily represent the views of the World Bank, its Executive Directors, or the countries they represent.

was quite varied in 2008 and as a consequence not all of them could respond from a position of strength when addressing the crisis. Moreover, the political economy of unwinding government interventions in a global environment poses major challenges that will only be compounded over time by structural trends associated with the fiscal implications of ageing populations in many OECD countries.[2] This, in turn, underscores the potentially 'ugly' long-term implications of the Great Recession, in particular, with respect to public debt accumulation.

In what follows, a brief description of the causes of the financial crisis and related policy responses is presented. The paper goes on to describe the evolution of international policy coordination to date, pointing out that in view of the mounting fiscal and debt imbalances there are significant challenges ahead for international coordination. It concludes by arguing that there is no room for complacency, that the danger of postponing exit from exceptional fiscal and monetary interventions may soon overshadow the costs of a premature exit, and that it would be dangerous to accept unconventional balance-sheet measures by central banks in response to the crisis as the 'new normal' in the post-crisis era.

The financial crisis in a nutshell

The financial crisis was 'nurtured' by global macroeconomic imbalances, lax monetary policies in the developed world, and regulatory failures amid growing international financial integration. The burst of an asset price bubble associated with excess investment in real estate in industrialised countries unleashed the process. Additional factors which have contributed to the dimensions and impact of the crisis include the increased opaqueness of financial innovations, the reckless use of collaterised debt obligations,[3] as well as poor corporate governance of the financial system.

---

2. For a discussion of the fiscal implications of ageing and its impact on public debt accumulation see Cecchetti, Mohanty and Zampolli (2010).

3. The evolution of securitised assets associated with home mortgages in the United States captures well this dramatic process. Over the course of a few years, they 'exploded' from a level of roughly 6 per cent of GDP (2003) to close to 19 per cent of GDP by the end of 2007. The unwinding of this phenomenon—and its implications for the world financial system—will require significant deleveraging and major economic adjustments around the world. See Blundell-Wignall, Atkinson and Lee (2008).

In spite of the first signs of attenuation of the crisis in the third quarter of 2009, economic indicators still point to significant levels of unemployment and social distress around the world. The crisis has caused the sharpest decline in global growth since the 1930s. In the last quarter of 2008 and the first two quarters of 2009, economic activity in both high income and developing countries fell sharply. The most dramatic declines occurred in countries that specialised in the production of durable and investment goods and in countries already suffering from serious macroeconomic vulnerabilities before the onset of the crisis.

The World Bank estimates that global output declined 2.2 per cent in 2009 and although the world economy is expected to return to a positive growth path in 2010 (2.7 per cent), there is no denying that prospects remain uncertain. Developing countries are estimated to have grown by only 1.2 per cent in 2009, after 8.1 per cent growth in 2007 and 5.6 per cent growth in 2008.[4] Moreover, two developing regions—Europe and Central Asia and Latin America and the Caribbean—ended 2009 with negative growth rates, while output growth in other developing regions also decelerated considerably. In sub-Saharan Africa, for example, growth in 2009 was 1.1 per cent, down from 5.7 per cent, on average, over the past three years.[5]

International trade is a good leading indicator for trends in economic output. World trade volumes contracted by about 14.4 per cent in 2009, the first time since the 1982 global recession. Most developing countries are experiencing lower export proceeds as the credit crisis and recession in developed countries has curbed demand and severely disrupted trade financing. This, in turn, has impacted government revenues due to lower commodity prices and trade volumes. There is, however, a 'silver-lining'. Trends have already reversed to show a more positive outlook in the second

4. Actually, if China and India are excluded, the growth rate of the developing world was -2.2 per cent in 2009. See World Bank (2010).

5. The crisis poses a serious threat to the hard-won gains in boosting economic growth in many developing countries, particularly in Africa, and for meeting the Millennium Development Goals. Past experience shows that a decline in the average GDP growth rate in developing countries by one percentage point can trap as many as 20 million more people in poverty. See World Bank/IMF (2009).

half of 2009, and outward-oriented economies are the ones emerging faster from the global economic downturn.

The financial crisis has directly impacted the domestic financial sector (and some large firms with significant exposure to sophisticated financial instruments) in some developing countries. There has also been an increase in the external borrowing costs resulting from the liquidity squeeze and low-risk appetite affecting both sovereign and private sector borrowers.

Most developing countries have also been affected by the dramatic reduction in capital flows. In particular, private capital flows to developing countries have seen their sharpest decline in a long period of time with net flows dropping to $707 billion in 2008 (down from their peak of $1.2 trillion in 2007) and are projected to be around $364 billion in 2009. These averages, however, hide significant variance across countries—e.g., Brazil and China experienced significant rebounds in capital flows in the second half of 2009 after the seizure of capital markets in the last quarter of 2008.

On the debt front, many emerging economies have reduced the vulnerabilities of their debt portfolios over the past decade. Average maturities have increased, reflecting increases in the maturities of new debt issuances. As a consequence, many countries have entered the crisis with a lower rollover risk. Others, however, were less able to transform their portfolios during the good years and may be forced into an earlier exit from expansionary fiscal policy. In any case, as emerging market domestic debt composition increasingly encompasses a variety of indexed and floating rate instruments, the importance of effective coordination between debt management and fiscal and monetary policies gains additional relevance.

Policy responses

Countries around the world have taken measures to address the impact of the financial crisis. The most notable policy actions included easing of monetary policies, recapitalisation of financial systems, bailout of the household and corporate sectors, overhaul of financial regulatory systems and fiscal stimulus packages. With respect to monetary policies, central banks around the world significantly lowered their policy interest rates and several of them (e.g., the Fed, the ECB, the Bank of England and the Bank of Japan) approached the zero lower bound constraint. Most central banks also adopted aggressive balance-sheet policies (credit policies to affect interbank and nonbank credit markets, purchase of government bonds, and purchase of foreign currency securities).

In addition to these monetary actions, governments adopted aggressive counter-cyclical fiscal policies. In the G20 advanced economies, for example, the average discretionary fiscal expansion in 2009 has been about 1.9 per cent of GDP while the financial sector support extended so far averaged about 5.5 per cent of GDP. In the G20 emerging economies, the average discretionary fiscal expansion in 2009 is estimated at about 2.2 per cent of GDP with marked variations (and an average 0.4 per cent of GDP in terms of support extended to the financial sector).[6]

These extraordinary policy responses have helped save the global financial system from systemic collapse, though it is still early to predict the precise impact of the achieved financial stability on global economic recovery. The need to continue to restructure the banking system and the emerging limits to expansionary policies in high-income countries, combined with concerns about debt and fiscal sustainability, may prevent the current global rebound from gaining traction and paving the way for a sustained recovery.

Moreover, the impact of these policy responses on public debt around the world merits particular attention. The rapid accumulation of public debt in OECD countries will have significant implications for the evolution of interest rates and the future dynamism of the world economy. With respect to interest rates, for example, we have already witnessed a significant shift in yields—for example, the 10-year US treasury bond increased from roughly 2 per cent in December 2008 to 3.59 per cent by December 2009. This development illustrates the state of debt markets in OECD countries. Yields are returning to levels similar to those that prevailed immediately before the crisis. There are, however, two very different ways to look at this increase. An optimist would basically explain this recovery as an indicator of the bottoming out of the recession, increase in risk appetite, and a return to more conventional inflation expectations

6. For details about the state of public finances around the world see IMF (2009).

over the long-term. A pessimist, in turn, could interpret this as a sign of increasing market disquiet about the ability of governments to carry an increasing debt burden in a sustainable way without significant additional inflationary pressures or the need for debt restructuring. Needless to say, both optimists and pessimists would have also to factor in their expectations about the unwinding of quantitative easing in large economies, a topic that is discussed further below.

Figure 12.1 captures some of the key debt and fiscal variables for a relevant set of countries in 2007, immediately before the onset of the crisis. As illustrated by the location of a large number of economies in the right quadrant of the figure—with fiscal surpluses and debt/GDP ratios below 60 per cent—many countries were able to respond to the crisis from a position of strength. Figure 12.2, in turn, shows that by the end of 2009 the picture had changed significantly with many countries now displaying fiscal deficits of more than 5 per cent and debt/GDP ratios well above 60 per cent. In other words, the scope for further expansionary interventions, be it on the monetary or on the fiscal fronts, is now much more limited. At the same time, confidence in the stability of the affected economies remains a question mark and the process of deleveraging of the private sector in many OECD economies is still in its initial stages.

Accordingly, although most analysts agree that it is too soon to unwind public interventions, it is also recognised that a late exit may pose new challenges for the stability of the world economy.[7] In what follows, some of the key aspects of international policy coordination amid the crisis are discussed and the point is made that coordination of exit policies will pose major challenges for governments around the world.

Policy coordination

As pointed out in the introduction, although there were some examples of coordination failures at the onset of the crisis (e.g. inward-oriented regulatory reactions to the bankruptcy of Lehman Brothers), there is broad consensus that policymakers achieved a good degree of international

7. See, for example, Hannoun (2009).

Figure 12.1

2007-Overall fiscal balances and general government debt (% of GDP)

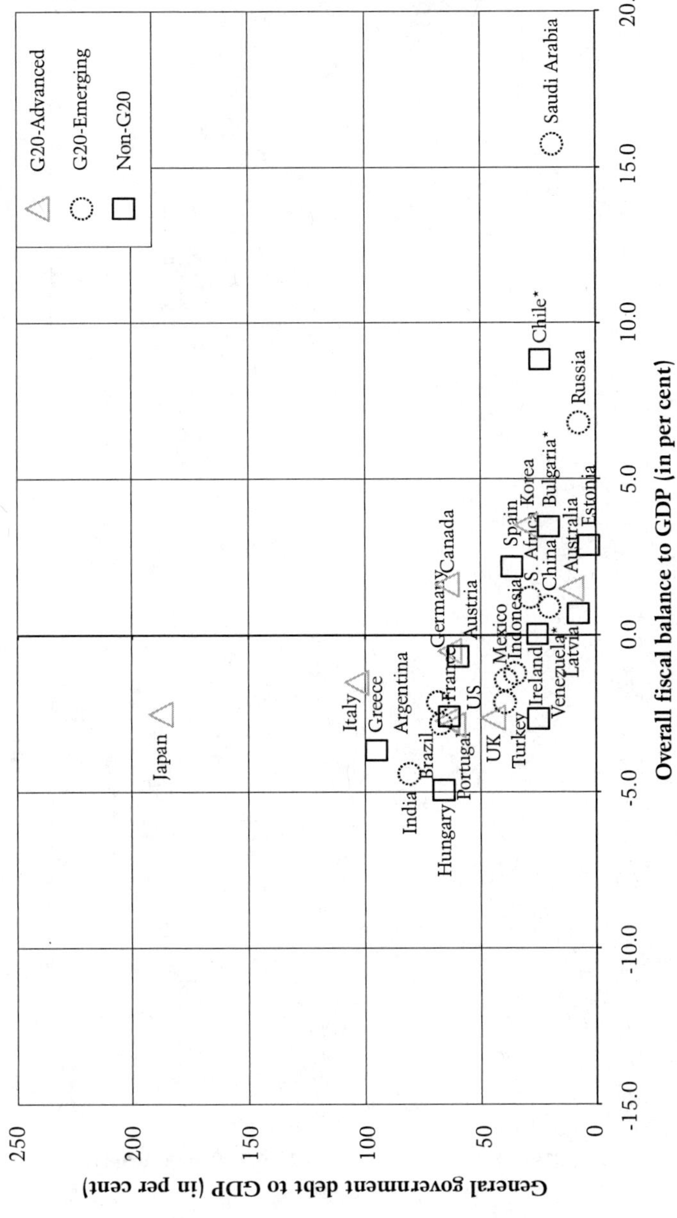

Note: * Debt measures for Bulgaria, Venezuela and Chile are Gross Public Debt, External Debt and Public Sector Gross Debt, respectively.

Sources: 'The State of Public Finances: Cross-Country Fiscal Monitor', IMF, 11/09 and 7/09; IMF WEO database and Article IV reports; IIF.

Figure 12.2

2009-Overall fiscal balances and general government debt (% of GDP)

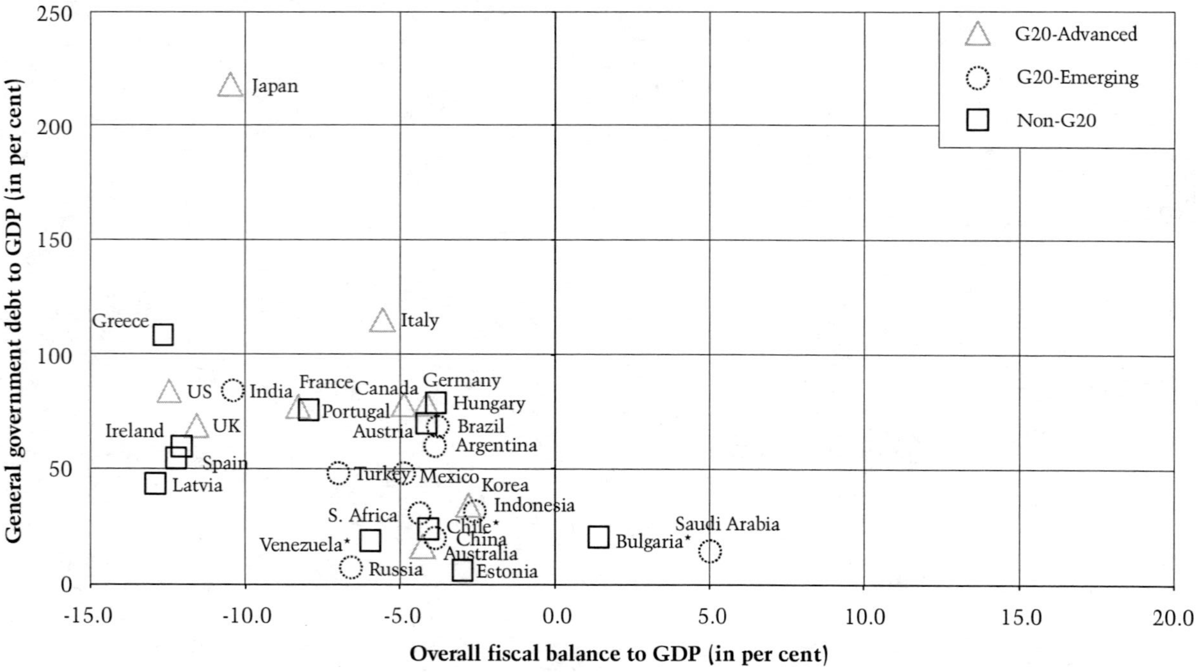

Note: * Debt measures for Bulgaria, Venezuela and Chile are Gross Public Debt, External Debt and Public Sector Gross Debt, respectively.

Sources: 'The State of Public Finances: Cross-Country Fiscal Monitor', IMF, 11/09 and 7/09; IMF WEO database and Article IV reports; IIF; Greek deficit figure for 2009 revealed by government sources in November 2009, reported by the *Financial Times*, 2/3/2010.

coordination on key macroeconomic fronts (particularly with respect to monetary and fiscal policy). The G20 played a positive role in this process.

A comparison with policy reactions in the aftermath of the 1929 crash is illustrative. In the 1930s, policy coordination was initially 'imposed' by adherence to the gold standard and the prevailing economic orthodoxy that prescribed balanced budgets even in the face of economic downturns. Against this background, as discussed in Eichengreen and Irwin (2009), the longer countries kept their allegiance to the gold standard (maintaining fixed exchange rates), the greater was the temptation to resort to trade controls as a mechanism to administer their balance of payments. In other words, policy coordination operated in a perverse fashion to the extent that contractionary monetary policies in the United States (the dominant economy behind the prevailing gold-exchange standard) and the related price deflation 'contaminated' other economies in the gold-standard bloc. As the effects of the depression were propagated around the world, the political-economy incentives to adopt 'beggar-thy-neighbour' policies—in particular, trade protectionism—increased, adding insult to injury and further depressing world trade and economic activity.

The experiences with international policy coordination in 2008-09 were much more positive. The prevailing 'conventional wisdom' recognised the importance of avoiding monetary contraction in the aftermath of the financial crisis. Moreover, most countries were willing to embrace fiscal activism in counteracting the effects of the economic downturn and to resist calls for trade protectionism.

On the monetary front, some of the highlights of international policy coordination were the unprecedented coordinated cut in policy rates (by 50 basis points) implemented by six major central banks in October 2008 and the introduction of temporary foreign exchange swaps by the US Fed involving 14 monetary authorities as a mechanism to address liquidity concerns with respect to dollar funding.[8]

On the fiscal front, the IMF played an important role, going public in support of discretionary fiscal expansion in countries with appropriate fiscal space. A target of a global fiscal stimulus of 2 per cent of GDP was

8. See Strauss-Kahn (2009).

used as a point of reference, and, as already mentioned, G20 economies delivered a fiscal stimulus of this order of magnitude in 2009. Although the coordination in this case was not explicit, the support of the IMF (and the G20) for this course of action was instrumental in supporting the global effort. Moreover, notwithstanding the protectionist bias (e.g., 'buy-national' provisions) of some of these fiscal packages, in broad terms these interventions were non-discriminatory. Figure 12.3 summarises the counter-cyclical fiscal stance adopted by G20 countries in response to the crisis.

The record for coordination on the regulatory front, in turn, was less positive. Initial reactions by regulatory authorities focused—as was inevitable—on the needs of domestic financial systems and did not pay much attention to the potential negative externalities of such interventions *vis-à-vis* other jurisdictions. Expansion of deposit protection and other bank guarantees, for example, led to international tensions in the initial stages of the crisis. Since then, regulatory coordination has been enhanced mainly in the context of the G20 process that has put emphasis on the strengthening of prudential regulation (by endorsing measures recommended by the Basel Committee designed to adjust international standards of capital and liquidity regulation), as well as on the identification of mechanisms to reduce the systemic risk posed by large and interconnected financial firms. Efforts to improve the quality and convergence of accounting standards, and to strengthen the Financial Stability Board (as a key forum to monitor adherence to international financial regulatory standards) have also been high on the G20 agenda.

International coordination and exit strategies

The debate on fiscal policy is now getting additional attention as the dimensions of the concerted stimulus (in terms of discretionary interventions) and the impact of automatic stabilisers increase the realisation that many economies have entered unsustainable fiscal paths with potential destabilising implications for debt markets in the medium to long-term. Several countries have already announced consolidation plans as illustrated by the numbers in Figure 12.4.

Figure 12.3

G20 fiscal balances—2007, 2009 (% of GDP)

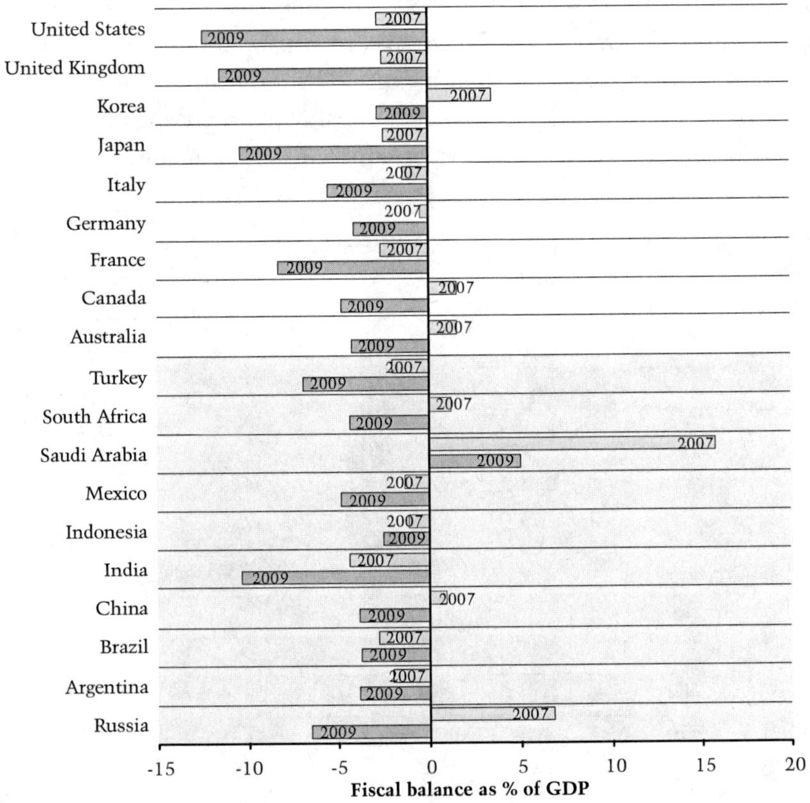

Source: 'The State of Public Finances: Cross-Country Fiscal Monitor', IMF, 11/09.

The debate, however, seems to continue to be dominated by the view that given the high levels of unemployment (particularly in advanced G20 economies), it is too early to tighten fiscal policies. Accordingly, announcements on fiscal consolidation tend to take a medium-term perspective, focusing on the temporary character of most fiscal stimulus measures introduced in 2008-09 and the intent of pursuing sustainability-enhancing measures in the near future.

Simultaneous fiscal consolidation is likely to constrain the dimensions of economic recovery at least in the initial stages of fiscal retrenchment. A case can be made that if the fiscal consolidation is focused on stabilising entitlement-spending-to-GDP ratios (a must for countries facing demographic pressures) and letting discretionary interventions expire, the required adjustment can be achieved. The difficulties of dealing with entitlement reforms (e.g., pension and health reforms) and the temptation to postpone adjustment in view of continued weaknesses in the private

Figure 12.4

G20 fiscal balances—2010, 2014 (% of GDP)

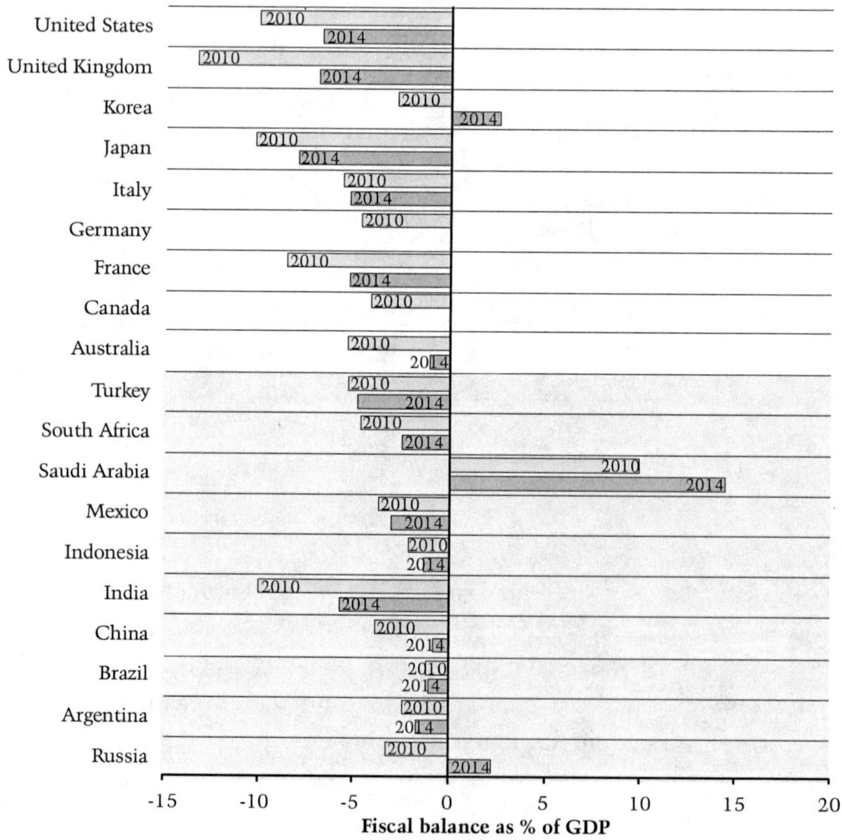

Source: 'The State of Public Finances: Cross-Country Fiscal Monitor', IMF, 11/09.

sector (reflecting the ongoing deleveraging process), however, underscore how challenging the political economy of fiscal consolidation will be. Markets will be monitoring closely the evolution of fiscal positions around the world and those economies that are not able to implement their consolidation plans will face increasing difficulties in financing their debts. In this context, international coordination (and monitoring) can play a positive role in helping enhance the credibility of national strategies and by giving 'ammunition' to financial authorities to resist short-term pressures associated with political cycles.

In the same vein, central banks will have to begin to consider when to tighten monetary policies to avoid igniting inflationary expectations. This may sound like a theoretical concern in view of the still-prevailing large output gaps in most advanced G20 economies. If, however, one accepts the proposition that monetary authorities often follow a dual mandate of price stability and high employment, then, at least in advanced G20 economies, the timing of exit from easy monetary policies may be delayed.[9] The problem, however, is that in emerging markets, inflationary pressures are resurfacing. Most countries followed monetary easing in a synchronised manner in response to the crisis, but it is unlikely that exit will be as well-synchronised. As a consequence, the intensity of destabilising carry trades on currency markets is bound to increase. This, in turn, will require central banks to pay special attention to asset prices in calibrating their interest rate policies.

Additional areas where international coordination will be important in the context of exit policies concern prudential regulation and the unwinding of unconventional balance sheet policies. With respect to prudential regulation, the focus has been on the adoption of stronger capital requirements for financial institutions. Deliberations at the Basel Committee on this topic, as well as in the context of the G20 and the Financial Stability Board, favour a gradual phase-in of stronger capital requirements with a view to avoid disruptions in financial intermediation. This gradualism, however, has not avoided regulatory uncertainty as the debate about what structure of capital cushion would be acceptable (e.g. the role of debt instruments with equity-like features) is still evolving.

9. See, for example, Bordo and Landon-Lane (2010).

Last but not least, the unwinding of exceptional financial sector support poses additional coordination challenges. It is true that some of these measures were introduced with clear expiration dates (e.g. the reciprocal currency swap lines among central banks to minimise foreign currency liquidity shortages) and others were not used (e.g. Brazil's central bank's adoption of a broader definition of eligible collateral to include foreign exchange loans). In other words, in these cases exit is unlikely to be disruptive. Weak forms of coordination (e.g. prior notification) among monetary authorities may be enough to minimise the potential for market disruptions. When, however, markets are closely integrated, individual actions may be constrained by strategic behaviour of economic agents: for example, the danger of deposit outflows between countries, if one country alone removes extraordinary financial support in an integrated market. In this context, Singapore, Malaysia and Hong Kong, China, for example, have established a working group to coordinate the unwinding of exceptional depositor guarantees in 2010.[10]

Where things get a little bit more complicated is with respect to outright asset purchases and the impact of these activities by central banks (under the broad characterisation of quantitative easing) on long-term bond yields. Needless to say, those that believe that central banks can (and should) control the entire length of yield curves may be faced with unpleasant surprises in the medium-term. The surge in gross borrowing needs of advanced economies—from US $9 trillion in 2007 to roughly US $16 trillion in 2009, with an expected similar level for 2010[11]—and the growing level of public debt suggests that the spread between long-term and short-term interest rates is bound to increase over time, even though quantitative easing may delay such a trend. The pace and the communication strategy of central banks in unwinding such interventions will play a key role in the sustainability of debt markets.

Concluding remarks

The effects of the Great Recession will continue to influence the world economy for years to come. As the private sector in advanced G20

10. See Financial Stability Board (2009).

11. See Blommestein and Gok (2009).

economies goes through the pain of deleveraging, public debt has been increasing massively. Although it is hard to predict the exact point where concerns about fiscal and debt sustainability may force drastic adjustments (be it via draconian fiscal adjustment or debt restructuring), one thing is clear: the longer corrective actions on the fiscal front and the unwinding of exceptional financial interventions are delayed, the higher the probability that governments will face challenges in addressing their financing needs.

The recognition that the public debt dynamics of many OECD countries poses significant challenges for policymakers is an important first step. It is true that 'smart' debt management can postpone the 'day of reckoning', but policy options—particularly for highly-indebted countries in monetary unions—will become increasingly unappealing (e.g. deflation as a competitiveness option). And developing countries will be affected not only by the implications of these developments for the cost of capital and by less dynamism in the world economy, but also because the massive public interventions of the last two years—in the absence of an orderly unwinding—will foster asset bubbles and speculative waves.

Exchange rates misalignments can also contribute to the tensions in the system. Speculative attacks against currencies in highly leveraged economies can add insult to injury by further contributing to the deterioration of private-sector balance sheets and may evolve into sovereign debt crises.

International coordination can ameliorate some of these problems. But in the 'new normal' of a post-crisis world characterised by lower economic growth and growing doubts about the ability of governments to implement required fiscal adjustment, the only certainty is that the future is bright for debt managers.

References

Blommestein, H.J. and A. Gok (2009). "The Surge in Borrowing Needs of OECD Governments: Revised Estimates for 2009 and 2010 Outlook", *Financial Market Trends*. Vol. 2009/2.

Blundell-Wignall, A., P. Atkinson and S.H. Lee (2008). "The Current Financial Crisis: Causes and Policy Issues", *Financial Market Trends* 1-21.

Bordo, M.D. and J.S. Landon-Lane (2010). "Exits from Recessions: The U.S. Experience 1920-2007", *NBER Working Paper Series*, Working Paper 15731.

Cecchetti, S.G., M.S. Mohanty and F. Zampolli (2010). "The Future of Public Debt: Prospects and Implications", Paper prepared for the Reserve Bank of India's International Research Conference *Challenges to Central Banking in the Context of the Financial Crisis*. Mumbai, India. February 12-13. *mimeo*.

Eichengreen, B. and D.A. Irwin (2009). "The Slide to Protectionism in the Great Depression: Who Succumbed and Why?", *NBER Working Paper Series*, Working Paper 15142.

Financial Stability Board (2009). "Exit from Extraordinary Financial Sector Support Measures". Note for G20 Ministers and Governors Meeting (*mimeo*).

Hannoun, H. (2009). "Unwinding Public Interventions After the Crisis", IMF High Level Conference, *Unwinding Public Interventions–Preconditions and Practical Considerations*. Washington, D.C. *mimeo*.

IMF (2009). "The State of Public Finances: Cross-Country Fiscal Monitor: November 2009", *International Monetary Fund Staff Position Note*, SPN/09/25.

Strauss-Khan, D. (2009). *Crisis Management and Policy Coordination: Do We Need a New Global Framework?*. Speech delivered by the IMF Managing Director at the Oesterreichische Nationalbank. Vienna. May 15.

World Bank (2010). *Global Economic Prospects: Crisis, Finance, and Growth*. Washington, D.C.: The World Bank.

World Bank and IMF (2009). *Global Monitoring Report 2009: A Development Emergency*. A report prepared jointly by staff of the World Bank and the International Monetary Fund. Washington D.C.

13 Summing-up

LARS E.O. SVENSSON

I had one reflection about Irma's paper. We all know that some emerging market economies (EMEs) face an inflow of capital with international investors exploiting the positive interest-rate differential between the EMEs and the country the investors borrow from. This results in a tendency towards appreciation of the currency. I understand that the response by the central banks of these EMEs often is to intervene and prevent the appreciation. I am not sure that is good policy. I wonder whether that makes things worse in the end. Eventually, the central bank may have to give in and allow the currency to appreciate. Meanwhile, there is even more capital inflow that benefits from the interest-rate differential. In the end, the central bank has more accumulated capital inflow and therefore a bigger problem—more hot money having come in that might suddenly leave.

The alternative, textbook response by a central bank that conducts flexible inflation targeting would be first to just sit there and watch the currency appreciate, and then, if it appreciates too much—if the appreciation becomes too contractionary and inflation and resource utilisation falls—lower the interest rate to make monetary policy more expansionary. The currency would then normally depreciate back a bit. The lower interest rate also makes it less attractive for international investors to exploit the interest-rate differential, and some of the capital may flow out. Why would that be a worse policy? It is not clear to me. In the end, the EME ends up in a new equilibrium with a stronger currency and a lower interest rate. The tradable sector, the export sector, may be hurt somewhat relative to the non-tradable sector. But maybe the EME has to live with that, and maybe that is a better policy than the alternative of intervening to prevent appreciation for a while. I do not know—this is a question.

Summing-up by Lars E.O. Svensson, Chairman, Session II: Globalisation, Market Failures and Challenges Posed to Central Banks.

As for the paper by Steve and co-authors, I agree with Eswar that it was a pretty gloomy, almost scary, paper. Recall that in many countries we have seen a strong trend towards more independent central banks with price-stability mandates and strong commitments by their leadership to maintain their independence and achieve price stability. At the same time, as the paper shows, you see developments towards unsustainable fiscal policy in several countries. One can easily imagine that a kind of war of attrition between fiscal authorities and central banks will start, and who knows how that might end? It could be that the central bank has to give in and allow inflation and the monetising of the deficit, or we get extreme fiscal austerity or default on public debt. The risks and outcomes would obviously vary from country to country.

Sweden faced similar problems in the early 1990s, problems that were eventually solved with a sustainable fiscal policy, including pension reform, and an independent central bank. The budget deficit was 13 per cent of GDP in the early 1990s, a fixed exchange-rate regime with an overvalued currency had collapsed and been replaced by inflation targeting. The new monetary policy regime lacked credibility, with inflation expectations for the next few years at 5 per cent when the inflation target was 2 per cent. Mats Persson, Torsten Persson, and I wrote a paper about whether it was possible to inflate away the public debt, which was growing very fast. To our relief, such a policy did not seem effective. The reason was that the maturity structure of the debt was relatively short and inflation does not jump—it takes a while for inflation to reach very high levels. So, in the end such policy would not reduce the real value of the debt very much. Furthermore, the economy would get stuck with high inflation, high inflation expectations, and high interest rates. It would be very costly to get down to low inflation again.

Instead, the problem was solved with fiscal austerity and tight monetary policy. The Social Democrats conducted a most restrictive fiscal policy—increased taxes and decreased expenditure. A stubborn Riksbank defended its inflation target with tight monetary policy and managed to get inflation expectations down. In the end, we are where we are now, with a sustainable fiscal policy and a fiscal policy framework that is a model for the rest of the world and flexible inflation targeting by an independent central bank.

14 Summing-up

SHYAMALA GOPINATH

Well, of course, the paper by Rosenberg did indicate the trade-offs emerging out of the Impossible Trinity. Besides the impact on exchange rates and independent monetary policy, carry trades and huge capital inflows also affect domestic credit and monetary growth and could lead to asset prices increase and, therefore, not just affect monetary stability but also financial stability. And that is what we have problems dealing with—'we' means all emerging market economies (EMEs)—capital flows that cannot be absorbed. I also liked the point made by Ben making a distinction between the impact of monetary policy tightening on exchange rates if the capital flows are predominantly into debt *vis-à-vis* equity assets. He argues that if the capital movement was predominantly on account of an asset which was a debt instrument, the currency may appreciate while if it was equity, it may anomalously depreciate. But sometimes, we do find that the interest rate element in earnings of companies is so insignificant that an interest rate tightening may not materially impact its future earnings potential. Therefore, this factor alone may not lead to exchange rate depreciation if interest rates go up.

The other interesting point was on the issue of hedging and products being made available for hedging, which Rosenberg made and Ben commented on. It is true that more hedging products increase the ability of the real economy to manage the exchange rate volatility but there is a limit up to which the real economy can actually absorb excessive volatility. Unlike financial market participants who can freely manage excessive volatility without much of a problem, in the case of the real sector, if excessive losses lead to the closure of companies, they cannot just come back if the exchange rate turns in a different direction. So, that is the

Summing-up by Shyamala Gopinath, Co-Chair, Session II: Globalisation, Market Failures and Challenges Posed to Central Banks.

difference between the real economy and the markets. The other issue is that the exchange risks actually remain in the system. It depends on who bears the risk—whether it is borne by the hedger or the speculator. In EMEs, we would certainly not like to face the prospect of high volatility in capital flows.

On public debt, Eswar mentioned about many doomsday scenarios in the past and I am glad many of them have not come true. I am sure solutions will be found and, hopefully, countries will manage their fiscal problems more responsibly.

Section III

Disruptions in Financial Systems and Challenges to Regulation and Supervision

Section III

Disruptions in Financial Systems and Challenges to Regulation and Supervision

This section corresponds to Session III of the First International Research Conference on 'Challenges to Central Banking in the Context of Financial Crisis', Reserve Bank of India, Mumbai.

Chairman: Jaime Caruana

Co-Chair: Usha Thorat

15 The Post-Crisis Fix: Regulatory or Monetary Policy Remedies?

STEPHEN S. ROACH

Under the auspices of the United States Congress, the newly constituted Financial Crisis Inquiry Commission held its first hearings in Washington on January 13-14, 2010. Established by Congress in the aftermath of the Lehman Brothers bankruptcy, its function is very reminiscent of Congressionally-sponsored hearings held in 1932 by the so-called Pecora Commission.

As was the case some 78 years ago, the present generation of Wall Street captains was grilled on the specifics of the Great Crisis of 2008-2009. Like then, this high profile exchange could well be the key to driving legislation that could shape the US financial system—and an asset-dependent and debt-dependent US economy—for generations to come.

The early betting is that, post-crisis remedies will be concentrated in a new approach to regulatory oversight—specifically the imposition of new 'macroprudential' regulations aimed at the twin concerns of systemic risk and financial stability. While this approach undoubtedly has considerable merit, it may not be enough to prevent another crisis from occurring in the not-so-distant future.

Also needed, in my opinion, is a major reworking of the mandate that guides the role and conduct of monetary policy. Specifically, the addition of a financial stability mandate could go a long way in forcing central banks to face up to the destabilising perils of asset bubbles, and the imbalances they have spawned in the mix of global saving as well as on the real side of increasingly asset-dependent economies.

There is no quick fix in this post-crisis world—no silver bullet that would inoculate an ever-changing world from the inevitable next crisis. But the world can surely do a much better job of crisis prevention than it did in the free-wheeling decade before the onset of the subprime crisis in the summer of 2007. Significantly, it should avoid a backward-looking fix that addresses the problems that gave rise to the last crisis. Such a myopic approach invariably misses the excesses that sow the seeds of the next crisis. Instead, the post-crisis fix needs to be as broad-based and comprehensive as possible—in essence, throwing out a big net that would limit as many destabilising risks as possible. The broad fix should contain both regulatory reforms and a new approach to monetary policy. Only then, will there be a meaningful chance for a safer and sounder post-crisis world.

Macroprudential regulatory options

Where the Washington debate ends up is anyone's guess. Right now, the regulatory approach has the upper hand. A resurrection of a Glass-Steagall-type separation between the commercial banking function and riskier capital market activities is certainly a possibility. Senators McCain and Cantwell have introduced just such a proposal. The proposal essentially repeals the decade-old Gramm-Leach-Bliley legislation (Financial Services Modernisation Act of 1999) that effectively repealed the original Glass-Steagall (1933) framework.

Meanwhile, none other than former Federal Reserve chairman, Paul Volcker, has offered a similar proposal that would offer full government backstop support (i.e., deposit insurance and lender-of-last-resort access) to the utility—like commercial banking functions of deposit gathering and lending—but no such support to proprietary and speculative capital market activities of financial institutions.

The Volcker proposal, which has now been formally endorsed by the Obama administration, is very specific in arguing that commercial banks be prohibited from involvement in proprietary trading, hedge funds and private equity activities. In that key respect, it is the functional equivalent of Glass-Steagall II.[1]

---

1. See remarks by Paul A. Volcker before the Statutory Congress of the European People's Parties in Bonn, Germany, December 9, 2009, as well as his testimony before the Banking, Housing and Urban Affairs Committee of the US Senate on February 2, 2010.

A reinstatement of Glass-Steagall-like restrictions on the US financial system is one example of a new 'macroprudential' approach to regulatory policy that seems to have gained favour in the current post-crisis debate. The goal of such proposals is to put regulations in place that foster stability of the system as a whole. The inference is that the former approach on 'microprudential' regulations, which were directed at the stability of individual institutions, could lead to investor herding and other counter-productive trends that could be destabilising to the broader financial system.

Among macroprudential proposals under active consideration, one is for counter-cyclical capital provisioning for banks, which would require a build-up of reserves in a boom and less onerous capital requirements in a downturn. Another proposal is to revamp bonus-driven compensation schemes of Wall Street executives and risk-takers. So-called resolution authority to unwind failed financial institutions is another option in the macroprudential tool-kit—aimed, in this instance, at the critical moral hazard implications of large financial services firms that have become 'too big to fail.'

The problem with fixating post-crisis remedies on a macroprudential regulatory solution is that it ignores the 800-pound gorilla that is also in the same room—misdirected monetary policies. Yes, regulators were asleep at the switch in the 'era of excess'. So, too, were their political overseers in the US Congress. But the Federal Reserve was hardly an innocent bystander. Excessive monetary accommodation, beginning in the late 1990s, was a conscious outgrowth of the Greenspan-Bernanke view, that monetary policy should not be used to prevent asset and debt bubbles and the distortions they foster in the real economy.

The Fed believed, instead, that it had both the power and the wisdom to use monetary policy to clean up the post-bubble carnage. The breadth and depth of the current crisis and recession draws that presumption into serious question. Yet this remains a very contentious issue in the current macro policy debate. For Ben Bernanke, the debate goes to the heart of his macro philosophy—not just as a central banker but also as an academic before he came to Washington.

In an early 2010 speech, Bernanke reiterated his long-standing view that blame for the current crisis rests on the laxity of regulatory oversight rather than on inappropriate monetary policy.[2] And he underscored the standard argument that monetary policy is too blunt an instrument to deal with asset bubbles—despite the fact that bubble-related distortions on the real side of the US economy ended up engulfing nearly 80 per cent of the GDP (personal consumption and residential construction combined).

When imbalances in the real economy are that large, relying on the blunt instruments of macro-stabilisation policy might not be such a bad idea, after all. In my view, it is not a question of either/or. While some macroprudential proposals have considerable merit, the role of monetary policy during and after this crisis also needs to be examined very carefully. I reject the suggestion that post-crisis remedies should be outsourced to regulators.

The post-crisis US financial system needs to strike a balance between better regulation, more disciplined monetary policy and more responsible political oversight. Prudential regulation of financial institutions—whether it is macro or micro—still involves very specific judgment calls affecting the performance of individual companies.

While such intervention may be appropriate at times, it is not a substitute for more disciplined monetary policy. Whatever the balance between the two avenues of control of the financial system, it would be dangerous to put too many eggs in the same basket. While some macro-prudential proposals have considerable merit, the role of monetary policy during and after this crisis also needs to be examined very carefully.

As the body politic comes to grips with America's post-crisis carnage, it must also take a long, hard look in the mirror. The failures of the political oversight function were yet another weak link in the increasingly unstable pre-crisis equation. With these considerations in mind, it is important to stress that any post-crisis fix be framed in the context of a comprehensive and forward-looking approach. In contrast, the narrow and

2. See Bernanke (2010). Bernanke was even more explicit in making this point in an extended interview with the editors of *Time* that accompanied his recent selection as 'person of the year.' The Fed Chairman said, 'I don't think that monetary policy was a particularly important source of the crisis.' See *www.time.com*, December 16, 2009.

backward-looking approaches of the past are doomed to fail—and lead to the painful likelihood of yet another crisis in the not-so-distant future.

The role of monetary policy

The experience of the past 10 years underscores how difficult it is to break the habit of monetary accommodation in bubble-dependent economies. Each successive post-bubble shakeout has required increasingly loosened monetary policy. The only way out of this vicious circle is a judicious and highly disciplined 'exit strategy'—in this case, the unwinding of the unprecedented monetary stimulus that was put in place to arrest the Great Crisis and Recession of 2008-09.

Unlike the fairly mechanistic withdrawal of the special liquidity (and capital) injections of quantitative easing that have been put in place in the past year and a half, there is nothing neat and easy about a post-crisis normalisation of the policy interest rate. That is not to say that central banks lack the tools and skills to restore benchmark interest rate to pre-crisis conditions. The issues in this case boil down to judgment and will—especially, political will. That is because the policy rate holds the keys to the kingdom of the financial system—and the support that system provides to the real side of the global economy.

The biggest risk to the exit strategy, in my opinion, remains an asymmetrical response pattern of the policy interest rate—quick to slash in a downturn, a crisis, or a post-bubble shakeout, but slow to normalise in the subsequent healing and recovery. The post-equity bubble profile of the US Federal funds rate in the early part of this decade is perhaps the best—and most relevant—illustration of this bias.

Over the 12 months of 2001, the benchmark short-term interest rate was cut 11 times from 6 to 1.75 per cent by a total of 425 basis points. It was then reduced by another 75 basis points to 1 per cent in two additional installments by mid-2003. A year later, with its mission presumably 'accomplished', the Fed embarked on the road to post-bubble normalisation—taking the funds rate up in 17 separate incremental installments of 25 bps per move—from 1 per cent in June 2004 to 5.25 per cent in June 2006.

This underscores the asymmetrical biases of the Fed's post-bubble reaction function. Once the normalisation process finally began in mid-2004, it took the US central bank twice as long to bring the policy rate back to its appropriate post-bubble setting as it did to slash the funds rate in the aftermath of the bursting of the equity bubble. Putting it another way, the speed of the normalisation—averaging out to 18 basis points per month over a 24-month interval—was less than half the speed of the easing—an average of 40 basis points per month over a 12-month period (see Table 15.1).

Table 15.1

The asymmetries of Fed policy

Date	*Fed funds target*
January 2001	6.50%
December 2001	1.75%
Reduction	475 bps
Number of cuts	11 over 12 months
Average reduction	43 bps
Speed per month	-40 bps
June 2004	1.00%
June 2006	5.25%
Increase	425 bps
Number of hikes	17 over 24 months
Average increase	25 bps
Speed per month	+18 bps
August 2007	5.25%
December 2008	0 to 0.25%
Reduction	500 to 525 bps
Number of cuts	10 over 17 months
Average reduction	51 bps
Speed per month	-30 bps

This asymmetry was justified by two key considerations—persistently low inflation and the ongoing fragility of a post-bubble jobless recovery. Yet, in retrospect, the delayed normalisation was not without serious unintended consequences. As seen through the lens of the real Federal funds rate, it meant that the US central bank maintained an extremely accommodative policy stance long after the emergency of the post-bubble shakeout had run its course (see Figure 15.1).

Notwithstanding the *ex post* justification for monetary accommodation in recent years, the numbers speak for themselves. Since 2000, the real Federal funds rate has been less than its long-term average of 1.9 per

Figure 15.1

The Fed's policy rate

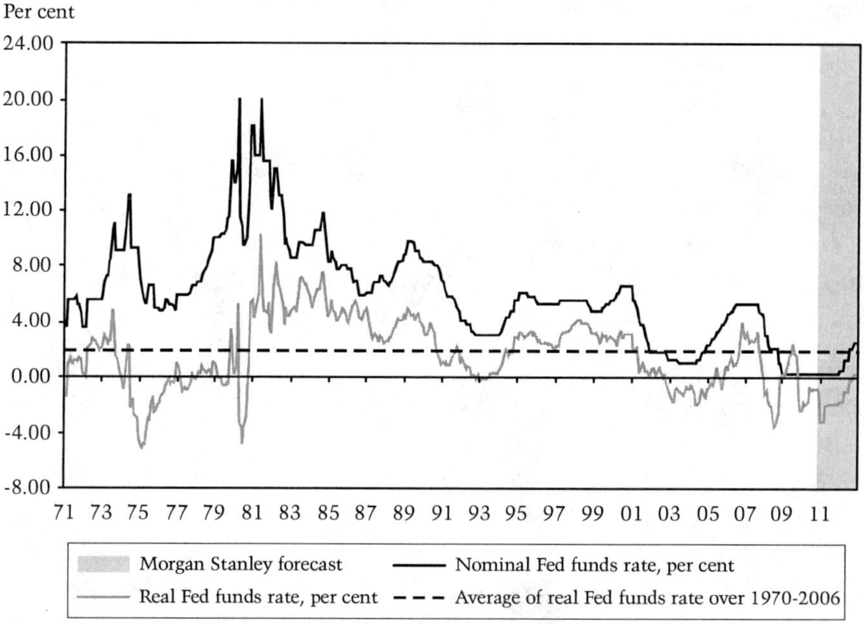

Source: Haver Analytics, Morgan Stanley Research.

cent in all but one year. Over this same period, the real funds rate has been less than zero about half the time. In short, for whatever reason, in the decade just ended, the Fed ran the most accommodative monetary policy since the 1970s—hardly a comforting precedent.

Notwithstanding the recent contentions of Ben Bernanke, it is hard to believe that the 'era of excess' leading up to the Great Crisis did not draw considerable sustenance from such easy money. With the benefit of hindsight, it now appears that the Fed's asymmetrical reaction function kept US monetary policy in a highly accommodative stance well into 2006. That, in my view, played a key role in fuelling the next round of even larger bubbles—twin bubbles in both property and credit markets.

Unfortunately, the same movie appears to be running in the current cycle. Going into the bursting of the subprime bubble in the summer of 2007, the Federal funds rate stood at 5.25 per cent. Then, beginning in September of that year, it was slashed to its current level of near 'zero' in 10 separate moves over a 17-month period. And now the Fed—once again citing sustained low inflation and a shaky post-crisis economic recovery and making explicit reference to an 'indefinite' period of monetary accommodation—is sending very clear signals of another delayed normalisation.

With a striking sense of *déjà vu*, America's central bank has once again been quick to ease aggressively—hardly surprising in the midst of the Great Crisis and Recession—but also equally reluctant to restore policy settings to pre-crisis norms. This approach can and has been repeatedly justified by a risk management approach to monetary policy. After all, history demonstrates that the bursting of asset and credit bubbles typically takes a lasting toll on the real side of underlying economies.

As a result, central bankers have opted repeatedly to err on the side of caution in implementing normalisation strategies in the context of fragile recoveries of post-bubble economies. At the same time, this rationale is very much at odds with the 'emergency' feature of aggressive crisis-driven policy responses. This raises the key question of the post-trauma reaction syndrome. If extraordinary circumstances cause policy rates to be slashed to unusually low levels, once those same circumstances have been resolved and the emergency is effectively over, why should there not be an equally prompt suspension of the emergency measures?

Putting it another way—if the US economy is in a weak recovery as the Fed seems to indicate, should the policy rate not be set at least at weak-recovery levels? Given the long lags of monetary policy, such forward-looking concerns seem especially relevant. This critical balancing act lies at the heart of the asymmetries of discretionary monetary policy adjustments. There is another key factor that drives the asymmetrical post-crisis reaction function of central banks—the desire to foster a steep yield curve that then enables crisis-torn banks to 'earn' their way back to prosperity.

By allowing, if not encouraging, banks to play the spread between rock-bottom short-term borrowing rates and higher yielding intermediate and longer term market-based investments, central banks can accelerate the healing of earnings-constrained financial institutions. In the US, the Fed discovered this approach in the early 1990s in the aftermath of the savings and loan crisis. It was even more effective in boosting earnings for beleaguered banks in the aftermath of the bursting of the equity bubble in 2001 and 2002.[3]

However, the bank earnings subsidy of a steep yield curve is hardly costless in the broader macro sense—especially if it tempts central banks to stay 'too easy for too long' in a recovery and sets up asset-dependent economies for yet another fix from the next bubble. And it is a key aspect of the moral hazard dilemma—providing banks with the comfort that the central bank will do everything in its power to allow surviving post-crisis financial institutions to earn their way back to recovery. Unwinding the yield curve subsidy is yet another critical consideration in evaluating the efficacy of the asymmetrical post-crisis pattern of the policy interest rate.

A new policy mandate

This financial crisis has unmasked some of the most serious policy blunders by central banks since the 1930s. While the so-called subprime crisis and the severe global recession it spawned, have many culprits, none have been more derelict in carrying out their responsibilities than the custodians of the financial system. Any post-crisis fix must address this glaring fault head on.

Adding a 'financial stability' provision to the policy mandates of central banks would go a long way in avoiding this type of problem in the future. Notwithstanding a predictable outbreak of post-crisis remorse, central banks cannot be relied on to break bad habits on their own. Experience suggests that they have a hard time saying 'no' to the siren song of the latest untested theory that is invariably concocted to explain away asset and credit bubbles. Recent history is littered with false claims of those in denial over the twin perils of asset bubbles and macro imbalances.

3. This shows up very clearly in the income statement of US banks over the 1999 to 2002 period. Over that timeframe, loan-provisions for Federal Deposit Insurance Corporation (FDIC)-insured commercial banks surged from $21.8 billion in 1999 to $48.2 billion in 2002. However, that $26.4 billion increase in loan write-offs was more than offset by a $44.4 billion increase in net interest income from $192.0 billion in 1999 to $236.4 billion in 2002. This earnings buffer was very much an outgrowth of the Fed's post-equity bubble yield curve steepening tactics. In the current cycle, it is much more of an uphill battle. While yield curve steepening helped boost net interest income by $16.7 billion in 2008, that was more than offset by a $95.0 billion spike in loan-loss provisions from $57.4 billion in 2007 to $152.4 billion in 2008.

Discretionary policymaking has failed in this important respect. It got caught up in an ideological debate over the risks of bubbles and imbalances. Such temptations can only be avoided by more of a rules-based approach—specifically by a financial stability mandate that is hardwired into the legal obligation between central banks and the body politic. This is especially the case for America's Federal Reserve—so far the most powerful central bank in the world, yet at the same time, the one monetary authority that played the greatest role in condoning and nurturing the 'era of excess' that nearly brought the world to its knees.

Over the past 75 years, the US Congress has intervened on several occasions to refocus America's monetary authority and now needs to do so again. For example, Fed policy blunders are widely viewed as central to the Great Depression. In response, the Employment Act of 1946 was enacted that required the Fed to aim its policy arsenal towards avoiding a repetition of the massive unemployment that occurred in the 1930s.

Then came the double-digit inflation of the1970s—another outgrowth of poor monetary policy—and the Congress passed the Humphrey-Hawkins Act of 1978, which added price stability to the Fed's mandate. Now, after a decade of asset bubbles and related saving and current-account imbalances, the Congress needs to step in again—this time adding 'financial stability' to the Fed's existing dual mandate.[4]

How would this work? Like full employment and price stability, the concept of financial stability is very much open to interpretation. One thing it should not entail would be setting price targets for key asset markets. Instead, financial stability criteria should reflect a combination of quantitative asset pricing and valuation metrics, along with an assessment of asset-related linkages to the expansion of debt and the risks of imbalances in the real economy.

4. Not surprisingly, the US Congress has now weighed in with a major legislative initiative that would, in effect, punish the Federal Reserve for its dereliction of duty in the years leading up to the Great Crisis. While the bill proposed by US Senator Christopher Dodd, Chairman of the Senate Banking Committee, would strip the Fed of much of its existing regulatory authority, it does not address the need for a financial stability mandate in shaping monetary policy decisions.

There were little doubts of an equity bubble in the late 1990s, or more recently of a confluence of property and credit bubbles. Nor were there any doubts that such bubbles had important spillover effects into the real side of the US economy? Should such situations arise in the future, as they undoubtedly will, a financial stability mandate would require the central bank to 'lean against the wind'—in effect, setting its policy rate higher than price stability and/or full employment mandates might otherwise require.[5]

In such frothy climates, the monetary authority would also be required to exercise greater regulatory discipline to manage the capital adequacy of financial institutions, as well as the leverage of return-seeking borrowers. Central bankers typically object to this approach. Both Ben Bernanke and Alan Greenspan have argued that the surgical precision of regulatory policies is more appropriate to deal with asset bubbles than the blunt instrument of the policy interest rate.

In the end, it may not be a question of either/or—but more of a strategy of using both. Regulatory action—to say nothing of the central bank's bully pulpit—can send an important message to market participants. But the policy rate is a far more powerful enforcement mechanism. The point is not to prick every bubble that arises, but to intervene when excesses in asset markets give rise to dangerous distortions to the real side of asset-dependent economies.

And that, of course, was precisely the case in the period leading up to the subprime crisis, when bubble-dependent US consumption and home-building activity ended up surging to nearly 80 per cent of total GDP. In such instances, using the blunt instruments of monetary policy to arrest the outsize excesses of bubble-prone economies, is both appropriate and desirable. Yes, such pre-emptive moves could well entail a 'growth sacrifice'—an economy that would grow slower than a more free-wheeling approach might otherwise suggest. But the growth that would be sacrificed was artificial from the start.

Moreover, if handled correctively—namely, early enough—such a sacrifice need not entail a recession. The resulting growth shortfall would be far preferable to the severe downside of wrenching post-bubble

5. See White (2008).

adjustments in financial markets and asset-dependent economies such as those that are now playing out. A financial stability mandate offers a far more robust framework than the current *ad hoc* scheme for evaluating the hows and whens of the exit strategy. Under the prevailing asymmetrical approach that plays to the downside of post-bubble growth and inflation risks, exit strategies are invariably delayed—thereby setting the stage for yet another round of ever-mounting excesses.

Under a financial stability mandate, there would undoubtedly be more symmetry to the exit strategy—forcing the authorities to weigh the perils of asset and credit bubbles against the costs of the growth sacrifice. That may well mean a quicker normalisation of monetary and fiscal policy than previous policy regimes might have otherwise suggested. While that is not exactly a riskless approach in today's fragile post-crisis climate, I believe it is worthy of serious consideration.

Global implications

The financial stability mandate would also empower central banks to take on the new and important responsibility of systemic risk regulators. This is one of the new areas of focus in the post-crisis debate on which there is a broad consensus. But the key here, like in so many macro issues, lies in execution—specifically, the mechanism by which systemic risks are identified and addressed.

In essence, systemic risks are all about spillovers—across financial institutions, asset markets, financial products, and economies. By definition, no one central bank can address these complications alone. It would be like putting pressure on one end of a water balloon. In an increasingly interconnected world, all systemic risk regulators need to be on the same page in this critical aspect of policy-setting.

To do otherwise runs the risk of a fragmented approach to global risk management and regulation—creating market-specific opportunities for 'regulatory arbitrage' that could well end up exacerbating global imbalances. Recent G20 summits in London and Pittsburgh suggest that global leaders want to get serious about establishing a new global policy and regulatory architecture.

If that were the case, then collaborative consultations between national authorities in the area of systemic risk assessment would be an important place to start. Yet it is not enough to discuss systemic risks periodically at high-profile meetings such as G20 summits. A new framework needs to be established that explicitly incorporates international policy coordination into the global architecture.

Such an effort may well require a global systemic risk manager to coordinate the surveillance and early warning responsibilities that would mitigate systemic risks. This functionality should reside in an international organisation—either the Bank for International Settlements (BIS) or the International Monetary Fund (IMF). But it should be delegated to the professional staffs of the BIS or the IMF, who would then need to be insulated from any pressures from their politically-selected boards of directors.

This could be an important transformational step for the G20—converting the rhetorical flourishes of periodic *communiqués* into ongoing operational capabilities. A robust global architecture demands nothing less if the world is ever to cope with systemic risks and the global imbalances they spawn. The global implications of the post-crisis exit strategy have recently become an increasingly contentious issue of debate.

That is especially the case these days in developing Asia, where liquidity driven surges in equity and property prices are worrisome, to say the least. This has sparked yet another global blame game. Asians pin the excesses on reckless liquidity injections made in America and Europe. The West blames it all on Chinese currency policy. While there is some validity to each line of reasoning, the dispute goes back to the deep-rooted global imbalances that lie at the heart of this crisis.

This is a classic example of why a globalised world needs a global policymaking architecture. The G20 cannot take on responsibility for avoiding crises without having a clear understanding of how to manage post-crisis exit strategies. A failure to address the global dimensions of a financial stability mandate would be a major impediment for global rebalancing. Yet that is exactly the direction in which the world is headed.

National governments are now hard at work in crafting their own individual approaches to global issues. This mismatch reflects a dangerous presumption—that the best global policies are the sum of the best national policies. Nothing could be further from the truth. A new and expanded policy mandate is not a sure-fire fix for all that ails a post-crisis world. Nor is it an inoculation against future crises. But it is an important step in the right direction.

In the rush to regulatory reform, the vengeance of a polarising populism has fixated on the compensation of risk-takers as the major post-crisis remedy. Yet it will take far more than that to create a more sound financial system. Risk-taking was excessive, not just because of misaligned bonus incentives, but also because the prices of leverage and risky assets were set far too low by misdirected central banks. New proposals for pay guidelines, regulatory consolidation, or counter-cyclical capital provisioning will work only if they are set in the context of the clearly defined goals and principles of financial stability.

Political will

Learning the lessons of this crisis is an exercise in shared responsibility. Like the rest of us, regulators, politicians and central banks hardly deserve special dispensation from this critical reappraisal. In the end, they must be held accountable for their failed stewardship of the financial system. They allowed the bedrock of policy discipline to be supplanted by the ideology of self-regulation—the very last thing that increasingly complex financial markets and asset-dependent economies needed.

Never again should the authorities have such open-ended discretion. I have argued that the rules-based approach of a new financial stability mandate for central banks and regulators must be a key piece of the post-crisis financial architecture. At the same time, I would be the first to concede that the ideological corruption of financial stewardship was a symptom of the ever-seductive excesses of the political economy of growth.

The 'era of excess' was premised on the mistaken belief that financial engineering—namely, using a credit bubble to borrow against a property bubble—could create a new and lasting period of vigorous growth in the global economy. It is easy to blame the United States, but the entire world was more than delighted to go along for the ride.

Yes, bubble-dependent American consumers led the way to the demand side of the equation. But export-dependent economies in Asia, and even Europe, were equally delighted to sustain their growth imperatives by producing the goods that fed the insatiable appetite of the American consumer. Nor was there much of a complaint from resource-dependent economies in the Middle East, Australia, New Zealand or Canada.

It was the ultimate virtuous circle—one that unfortunately depended on the folly of virtual consumption and the reckless policies that spurred such excesses. In short, this crisis arose out of the time-worn quest for a shortcut to economic growth. It did not have to happen. I categorically reject the 'inevitability excuse'—the notion that the world has once again been engulfed by the proverbial 100-year tsunami.

This all too convenient justification is nothing more than a cop-out by those who were asleep at the switch during the 'era of excess.' Yes, cycles of fear and greed date back to the inception of markets—and those powerful 'animal spirits' were very much at work this time, as well.[6] But I take strong issue with the apologists who claim that little could have been done to avoid the devastating repercussions of the so-called subprime crisis. Instead, there is a compelling reason to hold the stewards of the financial system—especially those in Washington as well as those on Wall Street—accountable for much of the blame. In free-market systems, the body politic renders the ultimate judgment on matters of governance.

The emphasis above has been on monetary policy and, specifically, on a new mandate for central banks. That is not meant to take the place of other regulatory reform proposals that have been offered in recent months. But as the debate now unfolds, I worry that too much attention is now being focused on micro remedies—ignoring the macro issues that have come to a head in this wrenching period of crisis and recession.

In that same vein, politicians and policymakers face a number of other key macro challenges. The choice between the quick fix and the heavy lifting of global rebalancing is especially critical. It is tempting to recreate the old strain of economic growth that got the world into serious trouble in the first place. Why not, for example, let Americans go back to excess

6. Akerlof and Shiller (2009).

consumption and the Chinese revert to saving and exporting? After all, as many argue, both societies are culturally inclined toward those extremes. I do not buy that logic for a second, but I certainly concede that there is a compelling political expediency in maintaining such a status quo.

Nor should politicians be let off the hook in seeking artificial insulation from mounting economic pressures through trade frictions and protectionism. These risks are particularly worrisome in the current climate. Ultimately, it boils down to a choice between the collective interests of globalisation and the self-interests of 'localisation'.

In times of prosperity and low unemployment, belligerence on trade policy can be dismissed as political posturing. But with exceptionally high unemployment rate in the aftermath of a severe recession and a weak recovery, politicians are likely to remain under serious pressure to protect increasingly beleaguered workers. The risks of protectionist policy blunders are especially worrisome in the aftermath of the Great Crisis. Only through a better understanding of globalisation—especially today's strain that is now bearing down on long-sheltered white-collar knowledge workers—can the body politic avoid such dangerous temptations.[7]

In the end, we cannot delude ourselves into thinking that the lessons of this crisis rest solely in new rules and regulations. They are a necessary—but not sufficient—condition for a more robust post-crisis architecture. Our problems also have a very important human dimension—namely, they are an outgrowth of the poor judgment that was endemic in a reckless era of self-regulation.

By purging the governance of the system of untested and misdirected ideological biases, the authorities will be much better positioned to avoid the dangerous interplay between asset bubbles and global imbalances in the future. No, I do not harbour the illusion that such steps will banish the threat of financial crises in the future. But to the extent the body politic rises to the occasion, the inevitable next crisis should be far better contained than this one.

This raises the biggest question of all. Do politicians have the vision and the courage to look beyond their normal short-term horizons and make

7. See Roach (2009).

the tough choices that could provide a longer-lasting cure for a crisis-torn world? This could well be the biggest test of all for the post-crisis world. This is not an impossible task. It takes focus and a rigorous analytical framework to pull it off—and, yes, the courage to incur enormous political risk.

I remember all too well the widely presumed impossibility of curing the Great Inflation of the late 1970s and early 1980s. Policymakers and politicians were utterly convinced that inflation was deeply entrenched in the institutional fabric of the system—a system that appeared unwilling to pay the price for the cure. Paul Volcker begged to differ—and with great courage, he led the assault that broke the back of inflation.

It will take a similar approach—and an equally heroic leader—to face up to the imperatives of the exit strategy. A failed exit strategy that is compromised by the political economy of growth only risks another—and even more serious—crisis in the future. The growth sacrifice of an early exit is the only way out.

It must be managed wisely and judiciously—and with great sensitivity to the innocent victims of this crisis and recession. But it is time to break the daisy chain of asset and credit bubbles—and the global imbalances they spawn. If we fail, there may not be another chance.

The challenge

The prominent role of Paul Volcker in the post-crisis policy debate is emblematic of what appears to be a basic flaw in the American strain of the political economy of growth. Volcker's assault on inflation some 30 years ago occurred only because the US body politic said 'enough'. Through the passage of the Humphrey-Hawkins Act of 1978, the Fed then had the political cover it needed to focus on price stability as an explicit objective of monetary policy.

The single mandate, which till then had aimed policy toward the achievement of full employment, needed to be modified in response to a major shock to the system—runaway inflation. Yet, there is nothing in the current dual mandate of America's central bank that provides comparable political cover for an assault on asset and/or credit bubbles and the imbalances that they spawn in the real economy. The mandate shaping US macro policy is in serious need of a major re-working.

With a new mandate would come a new compact between Wall Street and Washington—and that is long overdue. In the brave new era of self-regulation, the scale and complexity of Wall Street turned out to be a breeding ground for destabilising systemic risks. The policy and regulatory pendulum now needs to swing the other way. And there is good reason to believe that this process is now under way. But there is always a risk that the post-crisis response will be too extreme, shackling the US financial system and ultimately hobbling American competitiveness.

Wall Street still excels in providing effective tools for credit intermediation that are essential to productivity-enhancing allocation of capital. That role needs to be preserved at all costs. While Wall Street deserves its fair share of the blame for the Great Crisis, so does Washington. Predictably, politicians, policymakers and regulators were all delighted during the boom. Equally predictably, they are not so thrilled with the bust. Yet, the populist blame game offers little in the way of a constructive remedy. A more basic realisation is needed. Growth for the sake of growth is a recipe for instability at best, and disaster at worst. In the Great Crisis of 2008-09, the world came far too close to the once unthinkable worst-case outcome.

That takes us to that undeniably sticky point where the rubber must meet the road in the post-crisis era. Recognition of the possibility of a growth sacrifice—whether it is an outgrowth of inflation control or financial stability—must be incorporated more explicitly into political economy of growth.

That remains the most critical challenge in the aftermath of the Great Crisis and Recession—and it defines the fulcrum on which Wall Street and Washington will need to take a careful look at new approaches to both regulatory and monetary policy. A more sustainable financial system—to say nothing of a more stable and safer global economy—demands nothing less.

References

Akerlof, George A. and Robert J. Shiller (2009). *Animal Spirits: How Human Psychology Drives the Economy, and Why It Matters for Global Capitalism*. Princeton University Press.

Bernanke, Ben (2010). *Monetary Policy and the Housing Bubble*, Speech before the Annual Meeting of the American Economic Association. Atlanta. Georgia. January 3.

Roach, Stephen S. (2009). "Perils of a Different Globalization", in *The Next Asia: Opportunities and Challenges of a New Globalization*. Wiley.

White, William R. (2008). "Should Monetary Policy Lean against Credit Bubbles or Clean Up Afterwards?", Based on remarks made at the Monetary Policy Round Table at the Bank of England. September 30.

15.1
DISCUSSION

Time for a New Analytical Framework

WILLIAM R. WHITE

I first met Steve about 30 or 35 years ago, and I have agreed with almost everything he has said over the course of the years. And this is particularly true over the last dozen years or so, when we agreed on the existence of a significant credit bubble likely to have equally significant negative consequences. So, I can be brief by saying that I agree with him again. The global economy is in a big mess and, even though the analytical models do not show it, it is becoming increasingly accepted that excessive credit was somehow at the heart of this whole thing. The question is, what are we going to do to avoid such problems in the future?

There seems to be general agreement that regulation has a role to play, at least to judge by the Paulson Report (2008) or Lord Turner's Report (2009), or the Report of the de Larosière Group (2009). Where there does not seem to be agreement is on whether central banks have a role in leaning against these credit excesses. I have just two sets of comments to make on the issue. First, I want to make some technical points and then some more analytical ones.

At the technical level, the question is whether it is practically possible for monetary policy to 'lean against the credit bubble'. Those opposing this strategy have had a disconcerting tendency of referring to it as 'leaning against asset prices'. For them, this is a useful strawman, because when they say that, you are immediately going to ask, which asset price are you talking about and what is the fundamental value of that asset? Of course, there are no answers to these questions—and so you wind up by looking silly.

Comments by William R. White on the paper presented by Stephen S. Roach 'The Post-Crisis Fix: Regulatory or Monetary Policy Remedies?'.

The question ought to be phrased differently. Is there any way you can lean against the credit bubble and its associated symptoms? If credit is the underlying problem, it manifests itself in various imbalances, which show up either as asset prices, crazy spending patterns as in the United States, or crazy investment patterns as we continue to witness in China. Can you lean against these things? I think you can.

A lot of people contend that it is too difficult to know when you have a problem. Just think of the inflationary or deflationary gap. What do we know about aggregate demand? The answer at the moment is 'virtually nothing' because of the flexible balance sheet thing—which we have never seen before. What do we know about aggregate supply? The answer once again is, 'virtually nothing'.

Everyone is talking of massive changes in the potential, or perhaps the level, of the growth rate. Yet, no one really knows what these changes are. We are talking of unwinding these absolutely unprecedented policy easing measures, whose impact we have no insight into. Against such a backdrop, I think it not so hard to spot a credit bubble.

Is it possible to clean up afterwards? We have heard so often that the models say that it is possible. I will turn to the models too, for what I think they are worth or not. The second argument we hear is that it has always worked in the past. But the problem is, it has always worked in the past through a process which logically has to have a finite endpoint.

During the bust that followed, a boom in asset prices in 1987, 1991, during 1997-98 and once again between 2001 and 2003, low interest rates led to an asset price boom of some sort as we are witnessing now. The asset price boom leads to more spending and gets the whole economy going. Beneath it all, however, is there a growing 'headwind' of debt, of the kind Federal Reserve chairman Greenspan referred to in the early 1990s.

In the end, it is that burden of debt—both on the part of the banks, who will not lend, and on the part of the borrowers, who no longer wish to borrow—that stops the interest rate driven growth cycle. So, the monetary policy strategy of lowering interest rates works for a while, but it does not work forever. Can you learn? I think you can. Can you clean—I think what you are witnessing now is that you cannot, unless you spot another bubble which is probably (precisely!) going on at the moment.

The second broad set of points I wish to make, pertain to the analytical framework. If we are going to do what Steve wants us to do and which I think we should do, we have to get converted to the idea that the economy works differently from the way we have always been taught to believe it does. When you go through the academic stuff, be it neo-Keynesian, neoclassical, dynamic, stochastic or whatever, they are worth nothing. My apologies to Lars Svensson—but they are worth nothing.

The academic theories and models begin with an assumption that the economy is self-stabilising and follows rational expectations. These assumptions are totally incredible in the present circumstances. The kinds of models that the policymakers use are not much better, frankly. They are one-period models. They do not have any stocks or imbalances in them—but the stocks and imbalances are the crux of the matter.

I think we need to rethink the whole thing. We need to bring in more of the economics of Keynes. We need much more from Austrian theory that talks about the supply-side. At the moment, no one is talking about the supply side. All we hear is, 'we need to get demand back up again' and 'cash for clunkers' in the United States, where Steve says the household consumption ratio is 80 per cent of GDP. This is madness.

Just think of the irony of offering short-time jobs in the automobile industry in Germany—when those jobs will never come back! I know I speak almost too strongly. Yet, holding down the exchange rate in China to keep export jobs still functioning is an equally hilarious measure, when we all know that in the long-term, it is not going to be sustainable. All this talk of the supply-side potential does not cut much ice.

We need a new analytical framework to be able to ponder on these things. Once we have got that new analytical framework, I hope people will accept the fact that the problems we have to face are different from the ones we thought we were facing a few years ago. We will put in place both the monetary leg of the stool and the regulatory leg of the stool—which will prove a big analytical challenge. Then we will get them to work together.

Perhaps, things have changed since I left the BIS—but we will get these two silos of the regulatory and monetary policy people working far more closely together for a common purpose than they do today. So I finish by saying what I said at the beginning. I agree with Stephen Roach!

16 Why All Central Banks are not the Same

WILLIAM R. WHITE

Unpleasant facts and the differing responses of central banks[1]

The catalytic moment for the current economic and financial crisis is commonly said to have been August 9, 2007. On that date, Banque Nationale de Paris (BNP) ceased to allow withdrawals from three of its off-balance sheet vehicles, on the grounds that it could no longer reliably estimate the value of their assets. Since that time, most of the world's central banks have been confronted to varying degrees with three unpleasant facts. Broadly put, we have been witnessing the sharp reversal of all the remarkably positive economic and financial trends seen in some countries over previous years, and even over decades in others.[2] This, in itself, severely complicated the task of making monetary policy, since these different facts often seemed to call for conflicting responses from monetary policy. It is not surprising then that the policies followed by different central banks also differed. Further, and perhaps even more importantly, these continuing developments are increasingly calling into question the underlying reasons for the crisis, and whether monetary policy might have contributed to it in some material way. Should different central banks give

1. The focus of this paper is on the monetary policy decisions of the central banks in the largest of the advanced industrial economies.
2. The previous two decades in the United States had been characterised as 'The Great Moderation'. Both the level and volatility of inflation were low. As for output growth, while its level was high, its volatility was also low. Further, there were recurrent financial shocks but the financial system showed itself remarkably resilient. While other crisis-ridden countries in the emerging market economies (EMEs) exhibited a much worse overall performance over a similarly long period, this decade has until recently been characterised by outstanding economic performance in most EMEs.

different answers to this deeper analytical question, the conduct of monetary policy going forward might also be affected.

The first unpleasant fact, seen most evidently around the time of the onset of the crisis was that inflation had risen to higher levels almost everywhere, but particularly so in a number of important emerging market economies (EMEs). Higher prices for food and energy were a major contributing factor, but there were also fears in many countries that wages might also respond contributing to a more profound inflationary cycle. The second unpleasant fact, seen most evidently from the middle of 2008 to the middle of 2009 was that output in the real economy fell sharply and subsequently recovered only fitfully. This was particularly the case in a number of the advanced market economies (AMEs), including a number of countries thought to have quite strong domestic 'fundamentals'. And the third unpleasant fact, affecting particularly the AMEs with well developed capital markets, was that many of these markets became highly dysfunctional almost from the moment the crisis began. In addition, asset prices in most economies declined sharply, implying large losses at financial institutions and serious questioning of the adequacy of banks' capital levels. Indeed, a number of firms had to be merged and others (like Lehman Brothers) went bankrupt which only served to make the markets more dysfunctional.[3] With capital becoming evermore expensive, credit conditions tightened significantly in many countries as banks sought to deleverage. This led to concerns of a cumulative process that might feed back on to asset prices and global growth in turn.

Against this background, the response to date of different central banks has, at times, varied widely. At one end of the spectrum we have the central banks of Australia, Sweden and the European Central Bank (ECB) who continued to tighten for almost a year after the start of the crisis. In contrast, the Federal Reserve began to lower the policy rate almost immediately, and even more aggressively than in the period from 2001 to 2003. The upshot of this was that the 125 basis point rate differential in

3. Whether it was the Lehman bankruptcy itself, or the way in which it was handled, is still being discussed. The fact that, under UK law, the collateral lodged by many hedge funds at Lehman Brothers was tied up seemed to call into question a fundamental assumption that had previously underpinned market functioning; namely, that collateral is owned by the pledging agent.

favour of the United States (*vis-à-vis* the Euro area) in the summer of 2007, had turned into a negative differential of 175 basis points by August 2008. The policy easing of the Bank of England (BoE) also lagged significantly that of the Federal Reserve. Only after the failure of Lehman Brothers, was a dramatic easing of monetary policy central to the agenda of almost every central bank around the world.

Moreover, from the perspective of 2010, it appears that central banks might also have differing views about how to respond to the 'green shoots' that might be indicating a recovering global economy. Policy rates have already moved up in Sweden, Norway, Australia and Israel. Again in sharp contrast, the Federal Reserve has stated that policy rates are likely to stay near zero in the United States until at least the end of 2010. While the ECB has been less clear about its intentions, a number of statements from senior officials indicate serious reservations about maintaining the policy rate at 'unnatural' levels for long periods. The Bank of Japan (BoJ) has made similar protestations for many years, but has not, in fact, tightened policy appreciably to date.

This diversity of responses needs explanation. Evidently, the different degrees of exposure to individual unpleasant facts in different countries must be a significant part of this explanation. However, it will be argued in this paper that a number of other key differences also need consideration. In spite of the growing focus of almost all central banks in recent years on keeping consumer price index (CPI) inflation under control, central banks still differ in many other ways that can affect monetary policy decisions.

The extent to which a central bank's mandate extends beyond near-term inflation fighting matters. So too does its economic history, and how it comes to assess and give relative importance to different risks. Different assessments of the efficiency of monetary policy, in resisting both inflation and economic downturns, is also relevant. And finally, there is the issue of whether a central bank chooses to focus only on the desirable near-term implications of policy (via Keynesian effects on aggregate demand) or to put some weight as well on undesirable medium-term effects (largely arising on the supply side of the economy, or in the financial sector). This last consideration, reflecting stock and balance sheet effects, is fundamental. It raises important issues about macroeconomic theory and the usefulness of the economic models used by central bankers and academics, respectively. Should mainstream theories be complemented, or even replaced, by some of the insights of the Austrian school and Hyman Minsky?[4]

Before turning to the differences in central bank behaviour, the first part of this paper stresses the similarities. Indeed, it suggests that the commonly accepted framework for the conduct of monetary policy in recent decades might have helped cause the current crisis. In effect, it presupposes an answer to the question of theory raised just above. If this supposition is correct, it evidently leads on to the question of how that analytical framework ought be changed to avoid such problems arising in the future.

In this regard, an important practical issue is the length of the policy horizon on which policymakers should focus in their pursuit of price stability. Beginning in the 1970s, an increasing number of central banks extended their policy horizon to allow them to capture the costly inflationary implications of the real growth which they were trying to stimulate with expansionary monetary policies.[5] The similar question today, on which central banks still seem to differ widely in their views, is whether the policy horizon should be extended still further to capture other undesirable side effects (below called 'imbalances') of expansionary monetary policies. In the limit, as credit boom turns to bust, such imbalances could lead to deflation rather than inflation. Historical experience over the centuries indicates that debt-deflation is likely to be an even more costly threat to price stability[6] than moderate inflation.

It is an important corollary that this longer-term framework would actually encourage the acceptance of measured deflation over shorter time periods. Not all deflations are 'ugly',[7] although those arising from credit-

4. For a fuller analysis of the practical usefulness of New Classical, New Keynesian and Keynesian models of the economy, see White (2010).

5. For many years, monetary policy was focused almost solely on fostering near-term real growth and employment. The longer-term effects on inflation (implied by a negatively sloped long-term Philips curve) were judged to be acceptable. This view was challenged and then repudiated by the Friedman-Phelps hypothesis of the natural rate of unemployment.

6. For a very useful overview of this history, see Reinhart and Rogoff (2009).

7. See Borio and Filardo (2004) as well as Atkeson and Kehoe (2004).

driven 'booms' and 'busts' commonly are. To avoid such longer-term outcomes, assuming that forecast inflation was under control, tighter monetary policy might then, from time to time, cause inflation targets to be undershot. The likelihood of this happening would depend in part on the rate of growth of productivity which, unless resisted by monetary stimulus, tends to drive prices down. The neglect of positive supply-side shocks, in the essentially Keynesian framework used by most central banks to guide monetary policy, is a serious and, perhaps even, fatal shortcoming.[8]

Common causes for broadly common problems

It is not hard to tell a story in which easy financial conditions over many years lie at the heart of current global difficulties. With inflation kept down by positive supply shocks, particularly due to the reintegration of many EMEs back into the global economy, nominal interest rates in most of the world's major regions were kept very low for many years. For those central banks focused on the achievement of price-stability (a large and growing majority), there seemed no reason to raise policy rates, even though growth rates of global GDP were at record highs earlier in this decade. And, by the same token, there seemed no reason not to lower rates when growth slowed or financial disturbances threatened such an outcome in the future. This story essentially begins with the easing of monetary policies in the major industrial countries, particularly Japan, Germany and the United States in response to their respective 'busts' in the early 1990s and at the beginning of this decade. However, as this easing eventually put upward pressure on the currency of the major EMEs, these countries responded with massive exchange rate intervention and easier monetary policies as well. The former helped lower global bond rates, as foreign exchange reserves were invested in the major financial centres, and the latter encouraged more spending domestically.

This phenomenon can be put in a more Wicksellian perspective by noting that the aggregate global real 10-year bond rate (using Treasury Inflation Protected Securities (TIPS) rates where available) fell below the IMF's estimate of potential global growth in 1997. The former continued

---

8. For a review of an extensive pre-war literature on such issues, see Selgin (1997) and for a more recent discussion see Beckworth (2008).

to fall subsequently, and the latter continued to rise. The gap between the 'natural' rate of interest and the 'financial rate' is thus of very long standing and had reached almost 4 per cent by the middle of 2008. Since then, real policy rates have remained near zero in many regions and have often fallen significantly below zero in others. In China, given its very high rate of potential growth, the Wicksellian policy rate gap could currently be as high as 6 to 8 percentage points.

Closely related, growth rates of money and credit aggregates were unusually high in all major regions (except Japan) for many years, with such figures exceeding 20 per cent in many EMEs in the years preceding the onset of the crisis. Moreover, even these measures underestimate significantly the degree of monetary and financial stimulus at work in the global economy. This was due to the simultaneous process of innovation in the financial sector (in particular the processes of securitisation, globalisation and consolidation) which had the effect of encouraging speculation, leverage and the reduction of credit standards. One manifestation of this latter process was that credit was made available to many who were previously denied it. This would of course include 'cov-lite' corporate loans in many countries, below-prime mortgage borrowers in the United States (and to lesser degree in some other countries), but also the recently urbanised poor in many EMEs.

Low policy rates might themselves have encouraged this process of financial innovation. For example, tranched products like Collateralised Debt Obligations (CDOs) and Collateralised Loan Obligations (CLOs) were designed to make the senior tranches effectively look risk-free.[9] As is now clear, the process did not reduce expected losses, but rather reduced the probability of loss while increasing the size of the loss should the event materialise. Similarly, low policy rates seem to have encouraged the expansion of markets in which the receipts come up-front, but the prospective losses materialise only sporadically (if at all) and only in the future. Such behaviour would include the massive expansion in the writing of out-of-the-money options, credit default swaps and related instruments, and the pervasive use of carry-trade strategies funded with low-yielding currencies. Perhaps the most dangerous version of this latter trade was the

9. Rajan (2005).

growing recourse to mortgages, denominated in lower-yielding foreign currencies, by household borrowers in some countries in Central and Eastern Europe.

One did not have to be a 'monetarist', prior to the crisis, to worry that monetary and financial expansion of that long duration and large magnitude might eventually result in inflation. The record global growth rates in the years preceding the crisis did, in fact, eventually succeed in raising global demand to a level that matched the rapidly expanding near-term supply potential of the global economy. Accordingly, inflationary pressures also began to rise. Commodity price increases were the cutting-edge for these pressures, reflecting high income-elasticity of demand, particularly in EMEs, and a relatively low price-elasticity of supply, particularly for metals and energy products. However, wages and prices also began to rise more broadly, particularly in EMEs. While measured inflation in such countries showed the sharpest acceleration, inflationary pressures began to be seen in the AMEs as well. Higher import prices from EMEs were an early manifestation, but there were also other transmission channels[10] which aggravated domestic pressures on production capacities. Evidently, once the crisis began, these pressures retreated sharply with commodity prices once again leading the way. However, as will be discussed below, the full inflationary implications of the preceding period of rapid monetary and credit expansion might not yet have been fully seen in some countries. In particular, the United States and the United Kingdom have large current account deficits which could eventually lead to further exchange rate depreciation. Moreover, the pass-through effects of depreciation on domestic inflation might well be greater than what has been observed in recent years.[11]

Nor did one have to be an 'Austrian' to have worries that the prolonged and significant gap between the financial and natural rates of interest might also have other unwelcome effects. For many years preceding

10. See White (2005b).

11. See Galati and Melick (2006) who document that exchange rate pass-through declined in most countries in the years leading up to the crisis. If, however, this was largely because positive supply shocks were masking the effects of depreciation, this need not continue.

the crisis, the Bank for International Settlements (BIS) had raised concerns about four sets of interrelated 'imbalances' which they saw emerging in the global economy; where imbalances were broadly defined as sustained and significant deviations from historical norms. Two of these concerns had to do with the financial side of the economy: asset prices and the exposure of the financial system to losses of various sorts. The other two imbalances had to do with the real side of the economy; unusual domestic spending patterns and associated global trade imbalances. A constantly reiterated fear was that these financial and real imbalances would interact to dramatic effect in the downward phase of the credit cycle, as indeed they had interacted in the upward phase. These interactions lie at the heart of our current difficulties.

The first 'imbalance' identified prior to the crisis was that asset prices seemed very high, both by historical standards and also by the application of traditional evaluation metrics. These included house prices almost everywhere, the prices of long bonds, the level of the stock market in many countries, the price of high-risk and sovereign bonds (i.e., they carried unusually low-risk spreads) as well as the prices of antiques, fine art, wine and even stamps. Similarly, the price of buying insurance against risks of all sorts, prior to the onset of the crisis, was at record lows. It seemed hard at the time to explain these joint movements except in terms of the underlying and widespread availability of cheap credit.[12]

Evidently, the problem associated with these elevated asset prices was that normalcy might be restored through a reversal of earlier price trends. Indeed, this is precisely what happened in the aftermath of the crisis.[13] House prices fell sharply in a number of countries and risk spreads everywhere rose significantly, as did implied volatility and the cost of risk protection. Unable to borrow further against the collateral provided by

---

12. For example, expectations of continuing rapid growth in the economy, especially with inflationary pressures rising, would have seemed more likely to push bond prices down even as they pushed equity prices up.

13. An important caveat here has to do with house prices in the United States. They began to fall well before the summer of 2007, and also most immediately sparked an increase in delinquencies. This was very unusual as increases in delinquencies in the past were more likely to be associated with rising unemployment. The phenomenon is consistent with many houses having been purchased for speculative purposes.

rising house prices, and subjected to increasingly tight credit conditions, household spending in many countries slowed sharply in consequence. Housing starts and employment in construction also fell sharply in many countries, contributing to a sharp rise in recorded unemployment.

The second 'imbalance' said to arise from the long period of easy credit conditions was the increased risk exposure of the global banking system and the financial system more generally. So much has been written on this, that the account can be brief. What is clear is that lending standards in many countries declined over many years in a wide range of markets; think not only subprime, but also near-prime, home equity, commercial property, credit card debt, structured products, cov-lite and well beyond. What is still not clear is how big the ultimate losses will be, or who will bear them. Ultimately, and unfortunately, this must also be unknowable in advance since the final outcomes will be dependent on the unwinding of all of the imbalances identified above. In turn, the economic damage caused will depend on the extent to which credit conditions tighten. In the end, everything becomes endogeneous. On this issue of declining credit standards, it is also worth noting that at least one school of thought concluded the crisis would be catalysed by a subsequent and sudden increase in concerns about bank solvency. Hyman Minsky[14] posited three stages of credit expansion finally ending in 'Ponzi finance' when loans would be made to service the interest on previous loans. At what is now being referred to as a 'Minsky moment', a moment of joint 'recognition and revulsion', creditors would suddenly cease lending as they feared they would not be repaid. Such a crisis might look like it was prompted by a shortage of liquidity but, for Minsky, concerns about bank insolvency constituted the fundamental problem.

In addition to these two financial imbalances, real side imbalances were also expected to play an important role in explaining the magnitude of the post-crisis downturn. The influence of these factors has still not yet been fully appreciated.[15] The third of the 'imbalances' referred to above was that of unusual and potentially unsustainable spending patterns in

14. Minsky (1992).

15. Many commentators seem to feel that once the financial system has been restored to health, it will be 'business as usual'. For a contrary position see White (2009b).

domestic economies. This insight is conceptually similar to what the Austrian school refers to as 'malinvestments' facilitated by a credit system based on fractional reserve banking. While very low interest rates constituted the basic driver of credit extensions everywhere, the particular effects in different countries seemed very much related to their respective stage of financial development. In this regard, the United States was at one end of the spectrum (largely driven by market-based lending criteria) and China was at the other (largely driven by politically influenced lending criteria). These financial considerations also played an important role in explaining global trade imbalances, which are further discussed below.

In the United States and a number of other countries (many English-speaking), the 'malinvestment' associated with very low interest rates was a secular and ultimately unsustainable reduction in household saving rates to zero or even less than zero. As asset prices rose, so did the collateral available for borrowing, and the perception of increased wealth also seems to have discouraged saving.[16] In turn, as the demand for credit by households rose, banking systems refocused and made lending to households an integral part of their new business strategies. This change in orientation was further supported by the fact that lending to corporations was increasingly being done through markets. Associated with this lack of household saving was a steady increase in household debt to record levels as a proportion of income.

The problem implicit in the observed decline in household saving rates was that they might rebound with material and lasting effects on

16. On the relative importance of collateral *vs* wealth effects, see Muelbauer (2007) and White (2007). Both contend that the increase in 'wealth' resulting from higher house prices is not, in fact, an increase in wealth, if wealth is correctly defined as the capacity to enjoy a higher standard of living in the future. The fundamental reason is that higher house prices imply an identical (once discounted) increase in the cost of housing services in the future. Living standards remain the same. However, because the price effect is upfront, and the related costs distributed over the future, householders could well have the 'perception' of being wealthier. This is similar to the bias towards short-term results, and the tendency to ignore longer-term risks, that often characterises financial markets. Perhaps more importantly, higher house prices do increase collateral that can be used to borrow and to finance consumption. In the middle years of this decade, this was favourably viewed by some central bankers as a contribution to 'intertemporal smoothing' which moderated the earlier downturn. The fact that, by definition, this meant there had to be less consumption in the future, was hardly ever mentioned.

growth. Indeed, this process began shortly after the crisis hit, and was further encouraged both by the interaction of lower asset prices (particularly for houses) and the tightening of credit conditions noted above. In the United States, the initial sharp reduction in policy rates was met by an equally sharp rise in mortgage risk-premia, such that mortgage rates rose for a time rather than falling. Moreover, in the United States and to a lesser degree elsewhere, a further exposure had been generated by new instruments (like 'teaser' rates on subprime loans) which were designed to be serviceable over time only if house prices kept rising.[17] Once prices actually began to fall, a significant proportion of householders found that not only was such refinancing impossible, but also that the size of their mortgage was greater than the value of the house.[18] This could well lead to another round of foreclosures since the capacity for negotiated workouts in such circumstances currently seems very limited.[19]

In China, the 'malinvestment' arising from the especially wide gap between the natural and financial rates of interest was of a more traditional sort. The ratio of investment to GDP, prior to the global crisis, had risen to over 45 per cent of GDP. Such a level of investment was not approached even at the height of the Japanese bubble of the 1980s. Much of this investment has been conducted by enterprises which were still state-owned or heavily influenced by the state. Local and regional political authorities

17. Giving such mortgages, to people incapable of servicing them from income sources, still generated fees for the mortgage originators upfront. In most cases it was clear to the originator from the start that the borrower would not be able to service the loan after the 'reset'. In such cases, it was intended that the mortgage would be refinanced against the presumed higher value of the house, and with a second set of fees being charged at the time. As for the longer-term risks of this strategy, there were none since the mortgage was then sold to a bank (generally to be securitised subsequently) and the originator generally had no personal exposure.

18. As of end-2008, about one in eight houses in the US (with mortgages) had mortgages greater than the value of the house.

19. Many subprime and Alt-A loans were granted to people who did not reveal that they had borrowed the down payment from another lender. These 'silent second' mortgage-holders are now a significant obstacle to restructuring efforts. Even though house price declines may effectively have wiped out the value of the second mortgage, the owner of that mortgage can still try to get value by interfering in the workout process between the debtor and the first mortgagor. See Ellis (2008). In addition, many mortgages have been wrapped into structured products which explicitly (and legally) forbid changing the original mortgage terms. Finally, it appears that there are many incentive structures now in place that lead to involved parties making more money out of a foreclosure than a negotiated settlement.

had also exerted an important influence, with similar investments in fashionable industries threatening overcapacity. In both cases, the availability of low-cost finance from state-owned banks played an important facilitating role. Against this background, it is not difficult to imagine that many of these investments will in the end prove unprofitable or (for state-sponsored infrastructure) unproductive. Further, Chinese investment was particularly focused on heavy industry, ultimately directed to support production for export markets. Given that such investments tended to be extremely polluting and a particularly heavy user of commodities, their social rationality was being questioned within China even before the crisis broke.

As with the other imbalances, the primary concern raised pre-crisis was that this unusually high level of investment might be cut back significantly. If this occurred before domestic consumption, which has been falling as a percentage of GDP, could rise to offset it, then domestic growth overall would suffer. However, even then there were counter-arguments to indicate that this need not be an imminent worry. In particular, China seemed to have both the political and financial capacity to keep up investment demand as long as is required, even if it meant that the underlying problems would grow steadily worse. A second and related source of concern was the extent to which investments had been made in support of export-oriented industries. The ultimate intertemporal imbalance, feared by the Austrians, would emerge if the build-up of export capacity in Asia (and also Central and Eastern Europe) came on line just as a significant number of countries in the industrial world began to raise household saving rates in response to their past over-consumption. Thus, a slowdown in growth elsewhere in the world would have a material effect on China, and perhaps an even greater effect on those who export parts to China for assembling in that country.

The final 'imbalance' identified prior to the crisis was that of global trade imbalances. In the United States and a number of other countries, unusually high levels of consumption (with generally high import content) drove up imports as a percentage of GDP to record levels. The counterpart surplus countries were generally to be found in Germany, Japan, Southeast Asia and regional producers of commodities. One contributing factor to the surpluses was a high level of national savings in some countries; in particular, China. Another was the fact that the exchange rates (against the dollar) of many of the surplus countries were effectively pegged to the dollar (the yen tracked the dollar for different reasons) thus moderating the influence of the 'elasticity' channel for reducing current account rate imbalances. Further, massive exchange rate intervention by surplus countries resulted in a build-up of foreign exchange reserves that were largely reinvested in longer-term securities in deficit countries (especially the US). This had the effect of lowering long-term interest rates, which moderated the 'absorption' channel for reducing current account imbalances as well. The effect of these accumulating current account deficits was that the external debt of the United States had risen to unprecedented levels prior to the onset of the crisis.

It should be noted that the trade imbalance story had a worrying supply-side component as well as a demand-side. As noted above, financial systems at different stages of development in different countries (particularly the United States and China) resulted in different kinds of 'malinvestments'. In the United States, there was unusually strong investment in consumer durables (especially cars and home furnishings) and investment in housing. Investments of this sort produce services over time which are not malleable. That is, unlike a machine tool, their output cannot be redirected for sale to foreigners or for import substitution. In China and some other countries, the stock of physical capital is more malleable, but it would still require significant time and effort (to say nothing of appropriate shifts in domestic demand), to redirect sunk capital from external to domestic markets.

The first worry raised by these global trade imbalances was that they might eventually spark a dollar crisis, with a massive depreciation in the effective value of the dollar. This might lead to financial disruptions of various sorts, as foreign holders of dollar-denominated assets took big losses in domestic currencies. Further, these wealth losses might also impair aggregate demand in creditor countries, preventing domestic demand from rising to offset the depressing effects of lower levels of exports. A combination of 'J' curve effects and a non-malleable capital stock might further slow down any improvement in the trade imbalances, potentially leading to even more extreme exchange rate movements. A second worry was that these trade imbalances might lead to protectionist trade policies, particularly if global demand were to slow down for any of the reasons noted above.

In the event, these particular risks did not materialise in the aftermath of the crisis. Contrary to most anticipations, the onset of the financial crisis did not result in strong downward pressure on the US dollar. On the contrary, with rising risk aversion and with long positions in US dollar assets having been financed with short-term money, a dollar shortage emerged which (for a time) led the dollar to strengthen.[20] When the anticipated downward trend re-emerged, it was met by even more vigorous monetary easing in many creditor countries (especially China) and still heavier exchange rate intervention.[21] As for protectionist pressures, they clearly began to rise, but their incidence was by no means as great as some feared.

To summarise: The emergence of rising inflation and financial turbulence, followed by a sharp slowdown in global economic activity, was caused by a long period of excessive credit expansion driven by easy monetary conditions and financial innovation. A tipping point marked the ending of the 'boom' phase, along with its potentially inherently inflationary implications, and also marked the beginning of the 'bust' phase. This latter phase is being driven by the simultaneous and interacting reversal of a number (if not yet all) of the imbalances which had accumulated in the boom phase. If unresisted by policy, this process might well have culminated in outright deflation, made more dangerous by the magnitude of the nominal debts accumulated during the boom years.[22]

Virtually all central banks have, in the end, decided to resist these deflationary forces. In effect, they have all proved themselves 'Keynesians' in that they saw the first prerequisite in the situation was to stimulate aggregate demand. In the use of this analytical framework, they are similar

20. McGuire and McCauley (2009).

21. Perhaps most important, whereas China had previously allowed the renmimbi to drift upwards against the dollar, the dollar peg was re-established during the crisis.

22. The classic reference here is Fisher (1933).

to their respective Ministries of Finance who have generally engaged in discretionary fiscal stimulus as well.[23] Yet, as documented above, there were as well significant differences in the timing and force of the central bank resistance to the crisis. Moreover, looking forward, virtually all central banks are talking about the need for 'exit strategies', a non-Keynesian phrase which implicitly seems to recognise that there is something 'unnatural' about the current stance of policy. This need to 'exit' being generally agreed, some central banks seem clearly to worry more about this than others. The rest of this paper explores those differences further.

Why might different central banks choose to behave differently?

When the crisis hit in August of 2007, it was clear that global inflation was on the rise. While food and energy were important components, these prices movements must be treated as endogeneous at the global level. Thus 'headline' inflation should have been a concern for the monetary authorities. Moreover, the history of the industrial countries in the 1970s indicated clearly that inflationary expectations could easily rise leading to second-round effects and a future wage-price spiral. With the IMF at the time also predicting real growth in the global economy of over four per cent, there were clearly big risks to the global inflation outlook. The imbalances identified above were steadily growing as well. For both reasons, since higher inflation must eventually be resisted and larger imbalances are more dangerous than small ones, tighter monetary policies might generally have been expected. In fact, as noted above, the actual policies followed diverged significantly.

Many reasons can be suggested to explain past differences, and they also seem likely to affect policies going forward. Four sets of considerations

23. This has not been the case everywhere. For example, the economies of Hungary and Ireland were particularly hard-hit by the crisis. Nevertheless, both governments used discretionary fiscal tightening to offset, in part, the massive effect on government deficits of automatic stabilisers and the drying up of tax revenues previously thought to be structural rather than cyclical. In the former case, the fear was of a massive run on the forint, and in the latter case an unsustainable increase in the risk-premia on government debt. In effect, discretionary tightening was judged to be less contractionary than the alternative thought likely to be imposed by increased market discipline.

would seem to account for different central banks having done what they have done. First, different central banks have different objectives, in part arising from their unique histories. Second, different central banks found themselves confronted with different objective circumstances. Third, they had different views about the effectiveness of monetary instruments in different circumstances. Fourth, different central banks put different degrees of emphasis on the urgency of dealing with today's problems as opposed to the possibility of inadvertently making tomorrow's problems worse. This last difference marks a significant analytical rupture, recalling in important respects the Keynes-Hayek debate of the early 1930s.[24] It may be that a reopening of this debate will prove one of the few positive aspects of recent developments.

First, central banks have different objectives. On the one hand, there is little doubt that central banks globally have converged on a framework that gives significantly more emphasis to inflation control while remaining cognisant of the costs of real output deviating from potential. The remarkable spread of explicit 'inflation targeting regimes' is one indication of this trend, though the differences in both approach and results between implicit and explicit inflation targeters seems to be less than many believe.[25] On the other hand, the central banks of all the largest currency areas do not in fact consider themselves to be explicit inflation targeters, and this gives considerable scope for different policy choices.

The Federal Reserve has a dual mandate concerning the maintenance of both growth and price stability, and seems to have an historical bias towards the former. This is not surprising. After all, the 'Great Depression' was the defining economic event for the US in the 20th century. In contrast, the ECB must put price stability first, but can then exploit whatever leeway this provides to pursue other objectives. This is also not surprising and consistent with their history, since the defining economic event for them in the 20th century was the hyperinflation in middle Europe in the 1920s. In sum, the Fed could have a relative bias in favour of supporting growth, while the ECB has a similar bias to fighting inflation.

24. Cochrane and Glahe (1999).

25. See White (2008).

Finally, another argument supporting the need for the ECB to be relatively cautious was that it was a relatively new institution. Therefore, its credibility was more open to question, particularly since it had failed to hit its inflation targets at times in the recent past.

In China, for all practical purposes, it is the objectives of the State Council that govern the conduct of monetary policy. Moreover, these objectives could change quite quickly depending upon the assessment of whether, at any moment, slowing growth or rising inflation posed the greater threat to social stability. The mandate of the BoJ is not, in fact, clear, and they operate as well under immense pressure from the government via the Ministry of Finance. Such pressures might be expected to be especially potent in a society traditionally driven by consensus.

Second, central banks always find themselves reacting to somewhat different near-term prospects, and these differences can be widened if they put different emphasis on different 'indicators' for the conduct of monetary policy. This was clearly the case in mid-2007, as evidenced by the different reaction of the Fed and the ECB to ongoing events. One reason why the Fed eased so vigorously relative to others was that the downside risks for growth seemed much greater in the United States. There, the household spending (balance sheet) imbalances seemed very large compared to the problems faced by European households and US house prices had already begun to fall significantly. In addition, and closely related, was the fact that the US financial system seemed more exposed, and evidence was accumulating that US credit conditions were tightening sharply. Such considerations would help explain the relatively greater degree of easing in the United States.

As further support, it could also be argued that the Fed's focus on core inflation, in contrast to the ECB's emphasis on headline inflation, gave very different impressions of the seriousness of the inflationary problem. Further, it might have been thought that inflationary expectations were more stable in the United States, and that the relative absence of unionisation and wage indexation would also work in the same direction.[26]

26. Union membership in the US has fallen to around 7 per cent of the workforce, and most of this is in seriously troubled industries (automobiles, airlines, construction, etc.). In Europe, union members make up around 25 per cent of the workforce.

Rising inflation in the United States was then thought to be both less likely and more tolerable in the United States than in Europe.

The third reason why central banks might differ in their policy responses would be different assessments of the effectiveness of monetary policy. Again, a comparison of the Fed's views with those of others might provide some insights. The Fed clearly felt, not only that their objective was to resist a potentially serious downturn, but also that the monetary instruments they had at their disposal would be effective in doing so. Chairmen Greenspan and Bernanke stated repeatedly that, while it was not effective to use monetary policy to lean against asset price bubbles, monetary instruments would be effective in cleaning up afterwards. Evidence from simulations with economic models were commonly cited,[27] as was the successful and repeated use of such policies in the past. Recall that interest rates were lowered sharply in response to financial and economic shocks in 1987, 1990, 1998 and 2001 and were kept on hold in 1997 during the Asian crisis. In every case, recovery (or continued expansion) followed. Finally, spokesmen for the Board stated repeatedly that it was the failure of monetary policy to ease aggressively in the US Great Depression (in the 1930s) and at the beginning of the Japanese Great Stagnation (in the 1990s) that was fundamentally responsible for these outturns. In short, the Fed did what it did because it thought it was necessary, and because they thought that it would work.

There is not a great deal of evidence for or against the proposition that other central banks shared the Fed's strong views on this. Only the Bank of Japan made it clear, on the basis of its own experiences, that cleaning up after a boom-bust cycle was by no means easy. What is also clear is that there were plausible counter-arguments to each of the arguments presented by the Fed.[28] Moreover, these arguments gained force with each day that the economic downturn gained momentum in spite of the (eventual) vigorous monetary policy easing on the part of almost everyone. The fact that traditional means of monetary easing had in the end to be supplemented with 'quantitative' and 'credit easing', respectively,[29] testifies further to the

27. See, for example, Mishkin (2007).

28. White (2009a).

29. See Borio and Disyatat (2009).

ineffectiveness of traditional monetary easing. Of course, the zero lower bound problem might be introduced logically as a separate constraint necessitating such unusual monetary measures. However, it had been pointed out much earlier[30] that a central bank would inevitably be driven to such a point if (like the Fed) it followed a monetary policy that was asymmetrically easy in the downward phase of successive economic cycles.

The fourth set of explanations for divergent policy reactions is that different central banks might give different weights to solving the problems of 'today' as opposed to worrying about the problems of 'tomorrow'. Again, there seems to be something of a trans-oceanic divide.[31] The approach of the Federal Reserve is to focus almost wholly on setting policy to have the desired effect on growth and inflation over a relatively short policy horizon, say two or three years. In this one-period context, the domestic output 'gap' plays a dominant role in assessing the prospects for inflation. Very little concern is given to the possibility that such policies might, even though they work effectively within that timeframe, create 'imbalances' which would make policymaking more difficult in subsequent periods.

Reference was made above to the various occasions in which monetary easing in the United States (and elsewhere) did seem to lead to subsequent recovery or continued economic expansion. But the same experiences can also be viewed through a different lens. Arguably, the easy monetary conditions which followed the sharp easing of monetary policy in 1987 contributed to the property price boom in the late 1980s and the crisis which subsequently affected the saving and loans associations. The easing of policy through the early 1990s led to a further decline in the US dollar, and the Asian currencies which chose to peg to it. The excessive lending and investment which followed, culminated in the 1987 Asian crisis. Putting US policy rates on hold, in spite of all traditional indicators pointing to overheating,[32] then encouraged the position taking which led to

30. White (2005a).

31. From the perspective of the history of economic thought, the divide is between the 'Keynesians', whose views are essentially summarised in the one-period IS/LM model, and the Austrians who tell a much more dynamic and forward-looking story. See Laidler (1999) and White (2010).

32. The decision was also justified in terms of 'New Era' increases in potential, which would further lower inflationary pressures. However, if 'bubbles' were possible problems as well, then failing to raise rates exacerbated these problems.

the Long-Term Capital Management (LTCM) crisis in 1998. Subsequent interest rate decreases then contributed to the momentum of the NASDAQ 'boom-bust'. Finally, the monetary easing from 2001 to 2003 contributed significantly to the build-up of the imbalances referred to earlier in this paper.

It is also noteworthy that the easing phases of US monetary policy over this 20-year period became evermore aggressive. Not only were the peak-to-trough movements larger, but the speed of the movements increased. The easing in 2007-08 was more dramatic than 2001-2003, which was itself more dramatic than in earlier cycles. One plausible reason for this was the increasing need to offset the growing 'headwinds' of debt and associated problems in the financial system. Chairman Greenspan recognised the problem of headwinds as far back as the recession of the early 1990s, and they grew steadily stronger over the years. In effect, each phase of easing not only set the scene for the next financial bubble, but it ensured that the following bust in the real economy would be still more resistant to monetary easing. If this logic can be followed to its limit, monetary easing would in the end have no stimulative effects on the real side of the economy at all. Indeed, this may be the point at which the US economy has already arrived.

The European Central Bank seems somewhat more open to such forward-looking (multiperiod) considerations, though perhaps still not being totally convinced. Europeans have traditionally worried more than North Americans about 'moral hazard', and in recent years some Europeans have raised specific concerns that the 'Greenspan Put' was creating serial bubbles in the United States and elsewhere. The ECB also has its second 'pillar', which lets policy be influenced by a presumed long-run relationship in which monetary growth leads to inflation. However, it is actually the Bank of Japan (BoJ) that seems most worried about the longer-run side effects of policies that seem perfectly sensible in a short-term context. Indeed, the second 'perspective' guiding the policy of the BoJ is an implicit vow to conduct policy such that the mistakes made in Japan in the 1980s are never repeated. Note, however, that this is a very different concept to the second 'pillar' of the ECB. The Japanese worry is that excessive monetary and credit creation might well lead to deflation (after the bubble bursts) rather than inflation. Such concerns presumably underlie the BoJ's continuing frustration in not being able to 'normalise' the level of policy rates.

Another indication that different central banks might have different policy horizons can be found in their assessment of the implications of 'Quantitative Easing'. On the one hand, the Fed's view has a decidedly one-period flavour. There can be no inflationary upsurge as long as the output gap is negative. Thus, close monitoring of the gap and its projected behaviour, which would prompt, in turn, an appropriate monetary response, would suffice to head off future inflation.[33] On the other hand, it could be suggested that, over time, a more direct link (bypassing the real economy) might be forged between monetary easing, inflationary expectations, and then inflation itself. Should fears of monetisation raise inflationary expectations, even with a negative output gap, inflation could rise and potentially quite quickly. As noted above, currency depreciation in countries with large external deficits could play a crucial role in this regard. Such processes have been seen repeatedly in history, particularly in Latin America,[34] and cannot be ruled out of hand.

All of the concerns raised above, about the negative longer run effects of monetary easing during a downturn, have to do with implications for the demand-side of the economy. However, the effects of extended monetary easing on the supply-side of the economy can be no less important. While most central banks tend to underplay the importance of such effects, those taking a longer term view of the implications of monetary policy are evidently more sympathetic to such arguments. It is now increasingly accepted that financial crises (mostly driven by preceding credit excess) can lead to permanently lower levels of 'potential output' going forward.[35]

33. Of course, this still leaves open the possibility of policy error. Going forward, the levels of both projected demand (due to balance sheet effects) and potential supply (for reasons noted in the text) are open to unusual degrees of forecast error. Moreover, many central banks will be trying to reverse policy measures of unprecedented character and magnitude. Given this reality, it will not be easy to avoid error. In addition, there will be very substantial political pressure, especially from governments with high debt levels, to keep policy rates low. This will not help to stabilise inflationary expectations.

34. Most Latin American economies have been were traditionally relatively closed to external trade. Nevertheless, exchange rate depreciation traditionally sparked much more inflation than in the much more open Asian economies.

35. See Cerra and Saxena (2008) and Reinhart and Rogoff (2009).

Monetary easing might well exacerbate such tendencies. Low interest rates lead to lower saving rates, and capital accumulation in turn. Further, low interest rates can encourage the survival of 'zombie companies' and even the 'zombie banks' that finance them.[36]

These tendencies are even more pernicious if the 'boom' has encouraged an unsustainable degree of production capacity to be built up in certain industries or regions. At the global level, a number of industries (construction, banking services, transportation, ship-building, wholesale distribution, steel, concrete, etc.) currently look to be in such a situation. Further, as noted above, all of Asia is now geared up to produce goods and services that traditional importers can no longer afford to buy. These situations must be rectified through factors of production being re-allocated to more profitable endeavours. If low policy rates actually impede such a reallocation, then they have supply-side costs as well as demand-side benefits.

Should there be more convergence in policy settings?[37]

In the previous section, four sets of explanations were given for why central banks might decide to do different things with their policy rates. However, to explain differences is not to validate them. On the one hand, if different countries find themselves in different objective circumstances in an assumed one-period model (described above as 'different worries about today'), or if they have different views about the effectiveness of monetary policy in given circumstances, then it might be appropriate to have different policy settings. On the other hand, the other explanations for different policy settings (different objectives, different degrees of concern about prospective future problems) raise the question of why those differences exist in the first place.

---

36. Some commentators, particularly in Japan, would ascribe the length of the Japanese period of stagnation more to supply-side rigidities of this sort (following the misallocations caused by the boom of the 1980s) than to policy mistakes on the demand side. See Toyama and Sato (2006).

37. This discussion will be strictly limited to questions of principle. Whether 'exit strategies' for monetary policy need to be coordinated could be the subject for a separate paper.

One possibility is that they are justified by different economies having different structures, in which case different policies might again seem warranted. However, another possibility is that some central banks simply discount too much the future costs of their current policy actions. Given this possibility, the question of whether concerns about rising 'imbalances' should or should not play a central role in the setting of domestic monetary policies becomes a crucial question. So too is the assertion that the aftermath of such imbalances (the bust after the boom) can be easily cleaned up with appropriate macroeconomic policies. If the current global slowdown is subject to a 'second dip', and if expansionary global monetary policy in the end proves ineffective, debate on these issues will surely intensify.

References

Atkeson, A. and P.J. Kehoe (2004). "Deflation and Depression: Is there an Empirical Link?", *American Economic Review, Papers and Proceedings* 94(2), May.

Beckworth, D. (2008). "Aggregate Supply Driven Deflation and its Implications for Macroeconomic Stability", *Cato Journal* 28(3), Fall.

Borio, C. and P. Disyatat (2009). "Unconventional Monetary Policies: An Appraisal", *BIS Working Paper* 292. Basel. November.

Borio, C. and A. Filardo (2004). "Looking Back at the International Deflation Record", *North American Journal of Economics and Finance* 15: 287-311.

Cerra, V. and S. Saxena (2008). "Growth Dynamics: The Myth of Economic Recovery", *American Economic Review* 98(1): 439-57.

Cochran, J.P. and F.R. Glahe (1999). *The Hayek-Keynes Debate: Lessons for Current Business Cycle Research.* Lewiston, New York: Edwin Miller Press.

Ellis, L. (2008). "The Housing Meltdown: Why did it Happen in the United States?", *BIS Working Paper* 259. Basel.

Fisher, I. (1933). "The Debt-Deflation Theory of Great Depressions" *Econometrica* 1(4): 337-57.

Galati, G. and W.R. Melick (2006). "The Evolving Inflation Process: An Overview", *BIS Working Paper* 195, February.

Laidler, D. (1999). *Fabricating the Keynesian Revolution*. Cambridge: Cambridge University Press.

McGuire, P. and R. McCauley (2009). "Dollar Appreciation in 2008: Safe Havens, Carry Trade, Dollar Shortage and Overhedging", *BIS Quarterly Review.* Basel. December.

Minsky, H. (1992). "The Financial Stability Hypothesis", in E. Arestis and M. Sawyer (eds.), *Handbook of Radical Political Economy, WP* 74. Aldershot: Edward Elgar.

Mishkin, R. (2007). "Housing and the Monetary Policy Transmission Mechanism", Paper presented at a symposium sponsored by the Federal Reserve Bank of Kansas City, Jackson Hole, Wyoming. August.

Muelbauer, J. (2007). "Housing, Credit and Consumer Expenditures", Paper presented at a symposium sponsored by the Federal Reserve Bank of Kansas City. Jackson Hole, Wyoming. August.

Rajan, R.G. (2005). "Has Financial Development made the World Riskier", Paper presented at a symposium sponsored by the Federal Reserve Bank of Kansas City. Jackson Hole, Wyoming. August.

Reinhart, C.M. and K. Rogoff (2009). *This Time is Different*. Princeton and Oxford: Princeton University Press.

Selgin, G. (1997). "Less than Zero: The Case for Falling Price Level in a Growing Economy", *IEA Hobart Paper* No 32. London.

Toyama, K. and S. Sato (2006). "Creative Destruction and Reorganization: Overcoming the Nash Equilibrium". Industrial Revitalization Corporation of Japan. (*mimeo*).

White, W.R. (2005a). "Is Price Stability Enough?", *BIS Working Paper* 205. Basel. April.

———. (2005b). "Globalisation and the Determinants of Domestic Inflation", *BIS Working Paper* 250. Basel. Also, paper presented at a symposium organised by the Bank of France, *Changes in Productivity and Competitiveness: Impact on the International Allocation of Capital and Global Imbalances*. Paris. November.

———. (2007). "Measured Wealth, Real Wealth and the Illusion of Saving", Paper presented at the Irving Fisher Conference on *Measuring the Financial Position of the Household Sector*. Basel. August.

———. (2008). "The Future of Inflation Targeting", Comments on a panel at a conference organised by the Bank of Canada. Ottawa. July.

———. (2009a). "Should Monetary Policy Lean or Clean?", *Globalisation and Monetary Policy Institute Working Paper* No. 34. Federal Reserve Bank of Dallas.

———. (2009b). "Is Financial Stability Enough?", *OECD Observer*. Paris. December.

———. (2010). "The Mayekawa Lecture: Some Alternative Perspectives on Macroeconomic Theory and Some Policy Implications", *Monetary and Economic Studies* 28. IMES Studies. Tokyo: Bank of Japan. November.

17 Managing Financial Innovation in Emerging Markets

JOHN LIPSKY

My colleagues at the International Monetary Fund (IMF) and I have watched with great interest—and satisfaction—the strides that India has made in its economic policy management in recent years. That has been reflected in the economy's impressive progress. I would particularly like to underscore the Reserve Bank of India's (RBI) adept handling of monetary and regulatory policy in the current financial crisis. This is a testimony to the professional qualities of the Reserve Bank's skilled senior staff and to the leadership of Governor D. Subbarao and former Governor Y.V. Reddy. As is recognised widely, India is well-positioned to continue on its path of strong and inclusive growth, thanks in no small measure to the RBI's stewardship.

I will focus on the importance of finance for rapid and sustainable growth. While some may consider this topic odd in the light of the current crisis, I will seek to draw out some key lessons of recent events for the appropriate policy stance toward financial innovation. Many critics (although notably not policymakers in India or in most other major emerging markets) have concluded that such innovation should be actively discouraged. I would claim, though, that this is precisely the wrong lesson to draw.

Despite the unsettling and even dramatic recent global experience with 'cutting edge' finance, I believe that without a renewed effort to foster financial innovation in the global economy, all countries—including emerging market economies—will underperform their potential. The principal challenge for policymakers then, is to strike an appropriate balance between financial openness that supports growth-enhancing innovation, while implementing regulations and effective supervision that limits the potential risk of financial instability.

This does not mean that we should return to the exuberant pre-crisis approach to financial innovation. Neither does it suggest a 'one-size-fits-all' approach to the issue. In fact, I agree very much with Reserve Bank's Deputy Governor Shyamala Gopinath, that innovation 'needs to be pursued in the broader context of financial stability and has to necessarily correspond to the level of maturity of the financial system and the needs of the real economy....'

Great strides have already been made in the development of the Indian financial system. As the recent Rajan report (2009) noted, 'India's financial sector is at a turning point. There are many successes—the rapidity and reliability of settlement at the National Stock Exchange (NSE) or the mobile phone banking being implemented around the country indicate that much of the system is at the Internet age and beyond. There is justifiable reason to take pride in this. Yet much needs to be done.'[1]

Growth and the financial sector

There is a clear connection between economic growth and the state of development of the financial sector. Speaking late last year at the Bank of Mexico[2], I reviewed the economic literature on the relationship between finance and economic growth. At that time, I highlighted that for many decades the financial sector largely was ignored in theories of economic growth. In fact, only since the 1990s has the important role of the financial sector been widely accepted.[3]

In modern market-based economies, financial intermediation is a critical determinant of performance. As economies develop and mature, so do financial markets. The accompanying infrastructure has also evolved to meet the wide range of needs of households, businesses and government.

Looking forward from the current juncture, financial innovation has at least three principal tasks. First, it should address the challenge of missing

1. Planning Commission (2009).
2. Remarks by IMF First Deputy Managing Director John Lipsky at the Bank of Mexico Conference, 'Challenges and Strategies for Promoting Economic Growth', Mexico City, Mexico, October 19, 2009.
3. Rajan and Zingales (1998).

markets, such as those for the long-term financing that is required for creating long-lived assets, or for efficient risk-sharing, by providing appropriate insurance and hedging products.

Second, it should deepen liquidity in existing markets, for example, by reducing excessive reliance on a narrow base of depositors for funding. Finally, it should raise the quantity and quality of investment. Only then can financial innovation increase efficiency in the economy as a whole.

The limits of traditional banking systems

A key challenge faced by many emerging markets is their heavy reliance on traditional commercial banking. While such a system may be more than adequate during the early stages of a country's development, it may act as an unintended constraint on growth, as the real economy becomes more complex and, as the demand for financial services expands.

There are several reasons for this. First, in the absence of robust debt and money markets, the ability of banks to grow their loan portfolio is limited by their access to deposits. Second, banks are not well-placed to meet the significant needs in emerging and developing countries for long-term infrastructure financing. The size, maturity and illiquidity of such loans make them unsuitable for traditional commercial bank financing.

The danger in such operations is that banks take on inappropriate levels of credit and interest rate risk or else operate under a system where the government provides a financial backstop and, hence, passes on the risk to taxpayers. Finally, commercial banks are often not well-placed to diversify the credit risk in their loan portfolios—their financial performance, therefore, typically mirrors the underlying condition of their borrowers and of the local economy.

Implications for India

While India's financial system is multifaceted, with some world class segments such as its equity market, other segments—notably, the corporate bond market—remain less developed. The limited size of India's debt capital markets makes banks the main source of loans for both firms and households.

Moreover, India has enormous infrastructure needs, but infrastructure financing remains largely dependent on bank financing, with all its attendant inadequacies and risks. There are also important issues of access to credit and financial services for Indian corporations, but especially for small and medium enterprises (SMEs) and households.

A recent IMF staff study found that Indian firms have become increasingly reliant on borrowed funds (as opposed to retained earnings) to fund their investments. The study also found that there are important inefficiencies in debt financing. In fact, firms in industries that are more dependent on such financing have tended to grow more slowly.[4] A lack of financial instruments has also limited the ability of firms to manage risks.

The limited availability of derivative products compels corporations to shoulder risk-related costs that they would otherwise not bear, which in turn could stymie their ability to expand. At another level, only 40 per cent of India's population benefits from a bank account, as a large number of households still remain outside the formal financial sector.

These issues are well-understood here. Thus, several steps are being taken to meet the growing needs for more diverse sources of finance. Notably, the Reserve Bank has taken important initiatives to promote financial inclusion, with the aim of having a banking outlet in every village of more than 2,000 residents by 2011.

Moreover, Indian authorities are targeting an increase in infrastructure spending of some $500 billion during the current five-year plan. With fiscal space limited, meeting this need in a prudent fashion will require a more developed capital market, especially a more developed long-term corporate bond market. The India Infrastructure Finance Company Limited (IIFCL) has been established with a mandate to co-finance projects and issue local currency-denominated bonds. In addition, repos for corporate bonds have been introduced along with interest rate and currency futures.

Fortunately, there are several successful models of capital market development in emerging markets. The growth of corporate bond markets in Mexico and Malaysia, for instance, has been closely linked to the development of domestic institutional investors. Mobilising such investors

4. Oura (2008).

through the gradual liberalisation of portfolio guidelines of insurance companies and pension funds would help transform India's large pool of savings into investible funds for long-term financing.

However, liquidity may need to be generated in other ways, as these institutions typically are 'buy-and-hold' investors. In India, increasing foreign participation in the local debt market would provide additional liquidity and more robust pricing of local bond market issues. A recent IMF study[5] of 10 emerging markets suggests that foreign participation has lowered borrowing costs. Of course, unfettered access of foreign investors to India's large government securities market would create concerns, hence it would be reasonable to proceed in an orderly manner.[6]

Similarly, further progress in the development of an active securitisation market for consumer and small business loans would facilitate greater access to credit, by enabling risks to be shared by banks and other investors. Such securitisations, executed prudently, would help broaden the investor base and allow for the conversion of longer term amortising loans into instruments more suitable for institutional investors. This development would have the added benefit of facilitating better diversification by banks of their credit and maturity risks, while providing institutional investors with the opportunity to earn higher yields by taking on some of the risks of underlying loans. Of course, it is important that securitisation include appropriate safeguards—I will say more about that later.

Facing up to risks

I recognise that there is a growing skepticism about the merits of moving towards a more modern financial system and away from bank-centric financial systems. It has been widely noted that major emerging markets

5. Peiris (2010).

6. As background, there is currently a limit for foreign institutional investors (FIIs) of $5 billion in the government debt market and $15 billion in the corporate debt market. The Fund has advised that these limits be merged as currently the one on the corporate bond market has very little utilisation, while that on the government debt market is close to its limit. This will mainly help develop the government bond market in the first instance, but by improving liquidity in this market, it will also provide a benchmark for the corporate bond market.

have avoided the current problems being experienced in the United States and Europe. Some would argue that financial innovation ended up wreaking havoc on advanced economies—and indirectly on the rest of the world—and therefore, should be avoided in emerging markets at all costs.

In my view, however, the financial crisis in the advanced economies was not primarily a function of asset securitisation or the general growth of securitised capital markets. Rather, the crisis reflected a toxic mix of factors, including excessive complacency among both borrowers and investors about risk—including systemic risks. This led to an extended period of exceptional economic performance and low market volatility.

Poor governance and risk management at overly leveraged financial institutions was another factor. It resulted in the development and spread of excessively complex instruments and of unexamined and unrecognised interconnectedness and fragility. The failure of some institutional investors to exercise the due diligence responsibilities inherent in their fiduciary duties and regulatory arrangements that did not adjust effectively to financial market developments also led to the crisis. As did the failure of supervision to enforce standards effectively.

Happily, India is in a favourable situation in this regard. First, complexity of instruments is not currently a problem. Second, governance and risk management seem adequate in the current circumstances and bank leverage is appropriate. Third, both the Reserve Bank and capital markets regulators have fostered a robust financial sector. This suggests that India has significant opportunities for productive and prudent financial innovation, leaving it in the enviable position of learning from the experience of others.

Lessons from the crisis

Perhaps, the key lesson of the current crisis is that traditional virtues—like maintaining adequate capital, avoiding excessive reliance on short-term funding, maintaining proper loan underwriting, following sound risk management and effective corporate governance—remain as critical as always. We have been reminded again by recent events that securitisation—an innovation that has the capacity to enhance systemic efficiency and effectiveness—must be developed within a sound regulatory and supervisory framework, especially when facilitated by intermediation paths outside the formal banking sector.

In the United States and some other markets, it is clear that the fundamentals underlying some forms of securitised mortgages and other complex instruments were simply inadequate. Underwriting standards in many markets had become lax and were not properly regulated, ultimately harming both consumers and investors.

The role in this process of the United States' so called 'shadow banking sector', also highlighted weaknesses in regulatory cooperation and in the construction of the regulatory perimeter. Complexity was an element that contributed to the crisis, but excessive instrument complexity in some cases—and the lack of a clear economic function of some of the most exotic products—was more a reflection of systemic weaknesses than an underlying cause.

It is painfully evident that many institutional investors failed in their most basic fiduciary duties by purchasing instruments whose risks they simply did not understand on the basis of third-party recommendations and ratings. The lack of attention to risk management practices and the lack of understanding of liquidity risks being accumulated played an important role in creating, overpricing and overleveraging complex assets.

Unfortunately, the consequences were nearly catastrophic. Some aspects of the crisis reflected a lack of transparency in products and markets. A principal example of this is the credit default swap market—an enormous market that developed almost entirely over-the-counter. In the event, some of the key participants in this market simply failed to assess counter-party risks adequately, with disastrous results.

The move to standardise and centrally clear a substantial portion of derivative trading will help address these risks, as will redrawing the regulatory perimeter and an improvement in supervisory effectiveness. Even in the extraordinarily deep and broad crisis of the last two years, not all major firms and not all advanced financial systems were affected equally.

Canada and Australia, for instance, escaped most of the problems affecting the United States and Europe. While their financial institutions were exposed to the same disruption in global capital markets, they weathered the crisis well, underlining the importance of ensuring that, as financial systems become more complex, prudential supervision and regulation remains appropriate.

The role of international cooperation

This crisis has had at least one beneficial effect. It has galvanised international cooperation in economic policymaking in general and, specifically, in seeking to build a global financial system that can contribute to strong and sustainable growth. The G20 leaders (including India's Prime Minister Dr. Manmohan Singh), agreed at last year's Pittsburgh Summit to establish a 'Financial Inclusion Experts Group (FIEG)' to identify innovative approaches to enhance financial access, financial literacy, and consumer protection.

At the same time, efforts are underway at an international level to reduce the likelihood that the current financial sector crisis will be repeated. Regulatory reform, spearheaded by the G20 leaders, is being implemented both at the national level and internationally. The London Declaration (2009) on strengthening the financial system included a series of recommendations on overhauling the financial sector's regulatory framework. It also established the Financial Stability Board (FSB) (with both India and the IMF as members) that has the mandate to implement the agreed recommendations.

Many of the proposals being considered—notably those on the quality of bank capital, liquidity metrics and leverage ratios—have been in discussion for several years. The crisis has created a powerful incentive to forge a consensus on these as well as newer initiatives, such as focusing on macroprudential supervision and on aligning compensation with firms' risk management objectives.

Creativity is called for in these reform efforts. An example of this is the request by the G20 Leaders to the IMF to prepare a report on policy options for the financial sector itself to cover costs associated with crisis-related government intervention in the sector. We are exploring options for a financial sector levy that would create appropriate incentives for reducing risks, while providing the required anti-crisis funding.

Modernising financial systems

Ultimately, each country will develop its own approach to foster appropriate and useful financial innovation. I would, however, like to offer a few general suggestions for emerging market countries looking to realise the benefits of financial innovation. My first suggestion is to keep it simple.

Introduce products that are relatively straightforward and that offer clear value-additions. Thus, new financial products should be understood by regulators, by sellers and by prospective buyers. Investors should be able to calculate the risks being undertaken without undue reliance on credit rating agencies or other outside advisors.

Close attention should be paid to ensure adequate disclosure. In this regard, long-term institutional investors, including insurance companies, mutual funds and pension funds, are vital to securitisation markets, because they can and should form a stable and sophisticated investor base.

My second suggestion is, keep incentives aligned throughout the process. In approving new products, ensure that the interests of the originators of loans and securitised assets are aligned with the interests of investors. As you know, the Reserve Bank has adopted a retention rule and a lock-in period for securitised instruments designed to align incentives—although it will be important to see what impact these will have on issuers. After all, the most seriously affected advanced economy firms in the current crisis were grievously damaged by excessive retention of toxic assets —reflecting their substandard risk management and exacerbated by weak supervision.

Third, ensure that banks' risk management systems and the regulatory system keep up with the pace of innovation. The recently released Senior Supervisors Group (SSG) report[7] highlighted ongoing problems in the governance, firm management, internal control programmes and risk management in many of the world's largest financial institutions. Notably, many boards of directors seemed to be largely uninformed about the risks their institutions were undertaking, or simply did not understand them.

---

7. SSG (2009).

It is critical that governance be reformed and boards include members with experience to take a useful role in monitoring and controlling the level of risk taken by their institution. Regulation and supervision must also keep up with innovation. This requires both adequate resources to hire skilled professionals, along with political support to ensure that regulations and supervisory recommendations are taken seriously.

Indian regulators have been a part of the global standard-setting process and will continue to be early adopters of new standards. This should help India prepare for ongoing and even accelerated modernisation.

My fourth suggestion to emerging market countries is that they develop a robust resolution scheme. It is inevitable that in every financial market, some financial firms eventually will experience difficulties. A key policy conclusion highlighted by the crisis is that, an effective resolution scheme must be created for systemically important firms, so that governments are able to act promptly and effectively when an institution becomes troubled. Such regimes should minimise potential market disruption as well as dampen moral hazard.[8]

Of particular importance in our globalised financial world is dealing with cross-border dimensions of large institutional failures. Progress in this important task is taking place through development of contingency plans for global financial institutions by their home and host supervisors, along with efforts to identify and address barriers to implement plans for the recovery or orderly resolution of these institutions. This is a complex undertaking, but it is extremely important.

In conclusion

Despite the current difficulties and challenges, financial innovation will continue to play an important role in promoting global growth, especially in emerging markets and developing countries. The current crisis can provide important lessons and I am confident that India too will draw useful conclusions. We all share the responsibility of ensuring that the

8. Calomiris (2009).

global financial system evolves in a manner that supports strong, sustainable and balanced growth.

References

Calomiris, Charles (2009). "Financial Innovation, Regulation and Reform", *Cato Journal* 29(1). Washington DC (Winter).

Oura, Hiroko (2008). "Financial Development and Growth in India: A Growing Tiger in a Cage?", *IMF WP/08/79*.

Peiris, S.J. (2010). "Foreign Participation in Emerging Markets Local Currency Bond Markets", *IMF Working Paper* 10(88). April.

Planning Commission (2009). *Report of the Committee on Financial Sector Reforms*. New Delhi: Government of India.

Rajan, Raghuram G. and Luigi Zingales (1998). "Financial Dependence and Growth", *American Economic Review* 88(3).

Senior Supervisors Group (2009). *Risk Management Lessons from the Global Banking Crisis of 2008*. Federal Reserve Bank of New York. October 21.

17.1
DISCUSSION

Regulate the Subatomic Fragments of Finance

STEPHEN G. CECCHETTI

John Lipsky's analysis of the risks and rewards of financial innovation leaves little scope for criticism or even expansion. Even so, I will emphasise and expand on some key points he has made, focusing on financial instruments and financial markets. As justified as the work to improve the regulation and supervision of financial institutions is, I believe that we must give equal weight to the two other parts of the financial system. I strongly believe that regulation and monitoring of securities issuance and trading are essential complements to regulating and supervising institutions.

In paying close attention to instruments and markets, we make some progress in addressing the systemic risks that can arise should institutional regulation turn out to be porous. Before I begin, I would like to note that in thinking about financial innovation and its risk in the context of a place like India, we need to keep in mind that developing countries have a tendency to 'leap-frog' technologies. In the same way that countries that do not have landline telephone networks are unlikely to ever install them, financial systems that are now less developed, will quickly adopt sophisticated mechanisms for trading risk—or, at least, that is what I suspect.

Moving on to the substance of what I have to say, I believe that everyone would agree that innovation has transformed the operation of financial markets and financial intermediaries. The ability to separate finance into its most fundamental parts—the financial analogue to physics'

Comments by Stephen G. Cecchetti on the paper presented by John Lipsky 'Managing Financial Innovation in Emerging Markets'.

subatomic particles—has had profound implications for the way payments are made and risk is bought and sold.

In advanced economies, we take the ability to transfer risk for granted. Without it, a variety of things would not or could not be done. How many of us would drive a car without liability insurance? Mortgage lenders in the United States require borrowers to obtain fire insurance on the homes that form the collateral for the loan. Without fire insurance, there would be no mortgages.

The basic idea behind subatomic finance is that markets will allocate risk to those who are most able to bear it. As a result, we can insure virtually anything and engage in many activities we would not have undertaken in the past (at least in principle). As John correctly notes, this completes and deepens markets and improves efficiency.[1]

The ability to sell risk easily and cheaply has two unfortunate side effects—more aggregate risk and the ability to accumulate it in almost arbitrarily large amounts. Along with compensation schemes, in which portfolio managers share the gains but not the losses of their investment strategies, this creates incentives to take on huge amounts of risk. Without risk there is no reward and without big risks, there are never big rewards.

The result is that small groups of individuals have the potential to jeopardise the stability of the entire financial system.[2] They do this not because they fail (the right to succeed in the capitalist system comes along with the right to fail) but through the knock-on effects of their failure. The interconnectedness of the system is the biggest challenge. And the more complex the system becomes, the greater this risk.

Like pollution, systemic risk is a classic externality—a case in which an individual's actions impose costs on others that he or she does not bear.[3]

1. I am convinced that the development of the financial system is an important source of the Great Moderation—the reduced volatility of real growth in the developed world over the past 20 years. Faced with income volatility, individuals today can use the financial system to insure that their consumption remains smooth. Amazingly, this adds up to macroeconomic stability.

2. Limited liability and traditional compensation systems provide an incentive for this.

3. The following discussion is largely based on Chapter 7 of the BIS's *79th Annual Report* (2009).

Two externalities are key to systemic risk. The first is the systemic consequences of the failure of institutions. Joint failures are the outcome of common exposures to shocks that come from outside the financial system or from linkages among intermediaries.

The second externality is what has come to be known as procyclicality, the fact that the dynamics of the financial system and of the real economy reinforce each other, increasing the amplitude of booms and busts and undermining stability in both the financial sector and the real economy. The objective of regulation and supervision is to mitigate the systemic risk arising from all three elements of the financial system—instruments, markets and institutions. I focus on the first two elements, for they receive far less attention than they deserve.

Beginning with financial instruments or securities, opacity, complexity and sheer quantity can lead to systemic problems. The most recent examples of such instruments were the various structured products, including securitised subprime mortgages, which were difficult to evaluate and sell. As Lipsky notes, it is difficult—if not impossible—to properly evaluate certain complex and opaque instruments. And when valuation is imprecise, it not only complicates risk management within individual institutions, but also makes the already difficult task of evaluating common exposures even more difficult.

Instruments also have the capacity to exacerbate procyclicality. Typically, booms are periods of financial innovation. When things are going well, firms and individuals feel secure in experimenting. As we saw, however, flourishing financial innovation can create hidden, underpriced risks. Balancing safety and innovation in financial instruments requires providing for innovation, while limiting the capacity of any individual security to weaken the system as a whole.

The solution is to require product registration that limits the use of instruments according to their degree of safety. In a scheme analogous to the hierarchy controlling the availability of pharmaceuticals, the safest securities would, like non-prescription medicines, be available for purchase by everyone. Less safe financial instruments should be available for use only to those with a licence, like prescription drugs. The third category of securities would be those available in limited amounts to highly qualified individuals and institutions, like drugs in experimental trials. The last category would include securities deemed illegal.

An instrument could move to a higher category of safety only after successful tests as in clinical trials—which would combine issuance in limited quantities in the real world, with simulations of how the new instrument would behave under severe stress. Such a registration and certification system creates both transparency and pressure for standardisation.

As in the case of pharmaceutical manufacturers, there must be a mechanism for holding securities issuers accountable for the quality of what they sell. This will amount to issuers taking on increased responsibility for risk assessment of their products. Turning to financial markets, the crisis showed that they can fail to self-correct, putting the entire financial system at risk.

I agree completely with John that by shifting trading to central counter-parties (CCPs) and organised exchanges, we will address key aspects of the systemic risks created by over-the-counter (OTC) financial markets. A CCP is an entity that interposes itself between the two sides in a transaction, becoming the buyer to every seller and the seller to every buyer.

While the CCP appears to be perfectly hedged—that is, it has bought exactly what it has sold—it still faces the risk that someone will default when a payment is due. The CCP addresses that risk by requiring participants to hold balances in a margin account based on the value of its outstanding contracts. More volatile the market, larger the required margin balance and the more expensive it becomes to hold large positions.

Forcing all transactions to occur on the same platform or set of platforms brings transparency to the process of collecting and disseminating information that both market participants and authorities can use to monitor the concentration of individual exposures. The linkages that market participants and authorities create also become straightforward.

As an aside, I would like to point out that financial innovation makes it much more difficult to regulate and supervise institutions in keeping with their legal framework. Inevitably, since regulation and supervision act as a tax on what happens inside the perimeter, they create an incentive for regulatory arbitrage with innovation that moves risky activities outside the perimeter. Focusing on instruments and markets prevents activities from escaping from the regulatory perimeter.

The CCPs and exchanges are in a position to mitigate the procyclicality that arises from the tendency of individual counter-parties to demand increased margin during financial stress. As the financial crisis revealed, increased price volatility, combined with uncertainty about counter-party creditworthiness, leads to demands for higher margin.

Meeting the request means finding funds, which can prompt forced selling at the worst possible time. With a CCP or an exchange, margin requirements would be set centrally (or by policymakers), not by the counter-parties themselves, so that they need not rise during periods of market stress. This feature creates at least the possibility of moderating the increases in margin that naturally accompany market stress, reducing procyclicality.[4]

I strongly favour pushing trading beyond CCPs to organised exchanges. The primary advantage of taking this final step is that it would ensure price transparency with less reliance on market-makers—and generally cheaper trade execution for customers. As such, the market would be more stable—something suggested by the fact that exchanges are among the markets most likely to continue operating in a crisis.[5]

I am sure we would all agree that ideally any innovation that creates new securities that are not spanned by existing ones, or that reduces the cost of obtaining such a security, is a good thing. I must say that I find it

4. For an instrument to be in a CCP, it must have a certain degree of standardisation and documentation and reliable prices must be available to allow regular marking to market of participants' margin accounts. Since many derivatives currently traded over-the-counter meet these criteria, or could meet them with only slight changes, the requirements do not seem to be much of an impediment.

5. But they do have their limitations. Price transparency reduces the incentives for individuals or institutions to devote capital to making markets, which potentially increases the difficulty of transacting in large volumes. That problem has led the market to create securities exchanges or trading platforms for large transactions with a reduced level of transparency.

impossible to argue, as the late John Kenneth Galbraith did, that all financial innovation is counterproductive. But, as John Lipsky writes, we need to, 'strike an appropriate balance between financial openness that supports growth-enhancing innovation while implementing regulations and effective supervision that limit the potential risks of financial instability'. And doing this means making sure that we think not only about institutions, but also about markets and instruments.

18 Systemic Risk

How to Deal with it?

JAIME CARUANA

The international financial crisis has made us all think much harder—not only about what systemic risk means, but also about what it means for policy. Systemic risk was underestimated across the board before this crisis. We were faced with the unthinkable when a number of very large institutions failed, despite their previous reputation for balance sheet strength and leadership in risk management. Coming to grips with systemic risk is vital because the aggregate risk facing the system is much higher than the simple sum of the individual risks attending financial institutions, products and markets.

The work of the International Monetary Fund (IMF), Financial Stability Board (FSB) and the Bank for International Settlements (BIS) for the G20[1] now enables a definition of systemic risk. Systemic risk can be defined as 'a risk of disruption to financial services that is caused by an impairment of all or parts of the financial system and has the potential to have serious negative consequences for the real economy.' If a bank loses money from a risky investment, that is not systemic.

Institutional failure, market seizure, infrastructure breakdown or even a sharp rise in the cost of financial services can, however, have serious adverse implications for many other market participants. Such cases have a systemic dimension. It is such negative externalities and the significant spillovers to the real economy that are the essence of systemic risk that make a case for policy intervention.

1. Guidance to Assess the Systemic Importance of Financial Institutions, Markets and Instruments: Initial Considerations, October 2009.

Translating this general insight into practical policies is, of course, very difficult. What I would like to do is outline some of the thinking at the BIS and suggest what this might mean for policy. First, from a conceptual point of view, systemic risk has two dimensions, i.e., a cross-sectional dimension and a time dimension. In the cross-sectional dimension, the structure of the financial system influences how it responds to and possibly amplifies shocks.

Such spillover effects can arise, for instance, from common exposures across institutions or from network interconnections. The policy problem is how to address such common exposures and interlinkages among financial institutions. In the time dimension, the build-up of risk over time interacts with the macroeconomic cycle. The associated policy problem is how to address the procyclicality of the financial system.

Second, and from a policy point of view, financial regulatory policies are an essential part of the solution, but they alone will not suffice to address systemic risk in all its complexity. Other policies—especially monetary and fiscal policy—also have a role to play. Third, policy coordination is essential—not just nationally among monetary policy, fiscal policy and macro- and microprudential policies—but also internationally.

Finally, there is a fourth group of very important measures bearing on market discipline, transparency, governance, incentives, market integrity, consumer protection, etc., that would also be very relevant to supporting confidence, fostering market and institutional resilience, and curbing excesses in risk-taking. I do not dwell on these measures here, though.

A key message is that a lot of progress has already been achieved, but the reform agenda is still large and its implementation will speed up this year. In the first section, I briefly discuss the concept of systemic risk. The second section focuses on the regulatory policies in the pipeline to address that risk. The third and fourth sections deal with monetary and fiscal policy approaches to the same risk, while the fifth section outlines the role of international coordination. The last section concludes with a few final remarks.

Concepts of systemic risk[2]

Systemic risk has two dimensions, cross-sectional and time. Each has different policy implications. The first dimension of systemic risk—the common exposures/interlinkages in the cross-section—relates to how a specific shock to the financial system can propagate itself and become systemic. The focus is on how risk is distributed within the financial system at a given point in time.

A shock may take two main forms. The first kind occurs because the financial system is a network of interconnected balance sheets. As a result, an increasingly complex web of daily transactions means that a shock hitting one institution can spread to the other institutions that are connected to it and become systemic. The Herstatt and Continental Illinois crises both started with problems in one specific financial institution. Because of settlement and interbank linkages, the failure of each of these specific firms threatened wider problems for connected institutions that were otherwise sound.

Alternatively, a shock can have wide ramifications and become systemic because of direct common exposures. By its nature, a nationwide downturn in commercial real estate or housing markets tend to have this character. As the recent crisis has shown, such common exposure can have a profound international sweep. A negative exogeneous shock or, metaphorically speaking, a meteor strike or perfect storm, is indeed how many practitioners viewed this crisis, at least initially.[3]

The procyclicality dimension of systemic risk relates to the progressive build-up of financial fragility and how aggregate risk evolves over time. Over the economic cycle, the dynamics of the financial system and of the real economy reinforce each other, increasing the amplitude of booms and busts and undermining financial and macroeconomic stability. Typically, booms are periods of financial innovation. When things are going well, firms and individuals feel (over)confident in experimenting with and taking on risk. They create new, untested instruments that are difficult to understand and value. Credit grows rapidly, based on and contributing to

2. Borio and Drehmann (2009).

3. Alfaro and Drehmann (2009).

higher asset prices. In this way, the common exposures/interlinkages dimension concerns the various interconnections among the network of financial institutions. In contrast, the procyclicality dimension of systemic risk highlights the underlying build-up over time of risks that are hidden and underpriced. As strains develop, previously unseen risks materialise, deepening the retrenchment that is already under way.

In this procyclicality dimension, the financial sector endogeneously generates systemic risk and this risk can be highest precisely when it looks lowest. It is precisely then that credit is extended most freely and that low volatility encourages the greatest leverage. Complacency regarding risk itself turns into a source of risk. Normal margins of safety, whether down payments in real estate lending, haircuts in securities financing or covenants in corporate loans, are seen as unnecessary hindrances to profit. Policies to deal with systemic risk must operate in both dimensions.

Policies for dealing with system-wide interlinkages[4]

Turning first to the cross-sectional dimension of systemic risk, the policy task is to capture system-wide risk and to adjust prudential tools based on individual institutions' contribution to that risk.[5] It is a continuous approach, which does not require one to draw up a list of systemic institutions. Let me highlight six key building blocks in setting policies to mitigate this common exposures/interlinkages aspect of systemic risk.

More and better capital/liquidity

Firms that contribute to systemic risk must internalise the externalities that they create. Higher prudential standards would be one way to do this. Capital and liquidity buffers need to be higher across the board. The Basel Committee's recent reform package aims at improving the banking sector's ability to absorb shocks arising from financial and economic stress—whatever the source—thus reducing the risk of spillover from the financial sector into the real economy.

The Committee's proposals include a series of measures to raise the quality, consistency and transparency of the regulatory capital base. In

4. Caruana (2009) and BIS (2009).
5. Tarashev *et al.* (2009).

particular, they aim to strengthen the component of the Tier 1 capital base that is fully available to absorb losses on a going concern basis. This will contribute to a reduction of systemic risk from the banking sector.

The Committee's proposals also seek to strengthen the capital framework's risk coverage. Failure to capture major on- and off-balance sheet risks, as well as derivatives related exposures, was a key destabilising factor over the past two and a half years. Therefore, in addition to the trading book and securitisation reforms announced in July 2009, the Committee is proposing to strengthen capital requirements for counterparty credit risk exposures arising from derivatives, repos and securities financing activities.

What is more important, the reforms also have the necessary macroprudential focus, addressing both system-wide risks and their procyclical amplification over time. One way to get systemically important institutions to internalise the risks that they pose is to require them to hold more capital and more liquidity than other firms.

Such additional charges should be calibrated to a given institution's contribution to systemic risk on a continuous basis, with a view to reducing its probability of default and related knock-on effects. In addition, a straightforward leverage ratio will serve as a backstop to risk-weighted capital measures.

Resolution regime

The failure of a systemically important institution should be managed in an orderly manner.[6] Adequate resolution regimes should be put in place to hold down the system-wide loss that arises when such an institution fails. One important aspect is to ensure that the counter-parties of an important institution are not sheltered from loss in the event of failure, so that market discipline is strengthened *ex ante*. This can further help limit the probability of default.

Setting up adequate resolution regimes is no easy matter, however. Progress has been limited, and work by the FSB and the Basel Committee

6. Basel Committee (2009a).

continues.[7] One reason is that the legal problems are complex, as the ongoing Lehman Brothers liquidation reminds us. Another difficulty highlighted by the recent crisis in Iceland relates to the problem of cost-sharing across countries. Nevertheless, new standards for cross-border resolution frameworks have already been developed. Concrete proposals to facilitate the orderly resolution of a failing firm are actively being worked on and progress can be expected this year.

Structure of the financial industry

The recent financial crisis was a sign of market failures within the financial industry. Measures must be adopted to avoid perverse incentives that spur leverage and the pursuit of short-term profit. Bank supervisors are working on proposals to strengthen governance within firms and to encourage sound compensation practices. In addition, a number of countries are considering steps to limit the size/structure of financial groups, or to place curbs on some of their business activities.

We have to accept that there will never be total agreement across borders on what banks should and should not be allowed to do. There have always been differences in the business lines permitted to banks in different countries and there probably will always be. Hence, there can be a wide range of approaches, depending on the particular circumstances. All measures should be consistent with internationally agreed standards, though, to ensure that the playing field is levelled and that systemic risk is reduced.

More robust market infrastructure

A key way to lessen the systemic risks created by large, interconnected firms is to put in place more resilient market structures. Trading of financial derivatives on organised exchanges is one way. Another is to replace the web of bilateral exposures with robust central counter-parties (CCPs). This can reduce the risk of common exposures in several ways.

A CCP is an entity that interposes itself between the two sides of a transaction, becoming the buyer to every seller and the seller to every

7. Basel Committee (1992).

buyer, thereby contributing to greater liquidity in the market and reducing contagion effects. A CCP also addresses default risk by requiring each participant to hold a margin account in which the balance is determined by the value of the participant's outstanding contracts.

The more volatile the market, the larger the required margin balance and the more expensive it becomes to hold large positions. Moreover, channelling transactions on a single platform enhances the collection and dissemination of information. This in turn allows market participants and the authorities to monitor the concentration of individual exposures and the linkages that they create.

Taxation

Another building block added recently to the debate is the idea of taxing bigness or interconnectedness. While this deserves study as a classic means of dealing with an externality, many questions arise. Would the tax end up being paid by customers, or even by shareholders if their control over management is weak? Would higher capital and liquidity requirements for systemic institutions or prudential incentives for simpler structures not be preferable?

Supervision

Finally, more proactive supervision of systemic institutions is necessary to ensure that the perimeter of financial regulation is wide enough for supervisors to be able to see right through a financial institution, no matter what the legal configuration is. An interesting question thrown up by the recent crisis is why the same regulation produced different results in different countries.

Banking systems in Australia and Canada, for instance, remained relatively resilient during the recent crisis. There were obviously many reasons for the differences seen across various jurisdictions, including differences in the structure and business models of the financial system. Another relevant factor that led to the crisis was that regulation was not implemented across countries with the same rigour. So, a key lesson is that good regulation will not work without adequate supervision that looks through both the business cycle and the structures of financial institutions.

But this is easier said than done. The recent crisis has highlighted the difficulties of setting a consistent perimeter of regulation over time and across jurisdictions. Moreover, the problem of the shadow banking system remains a challenge.[8] Ongoing work to ensure greater consistency across sectors and jurisdictions in the key respects of capital, liquidity and resolution regimes will be essential to address these issues.

Policies to deal with procyclicality[9]

Let me now turn to policies that deal with systemic risk in the time dimension, the so-called procyclicality aspect. The first and obvious lesson is that capital and liquidity buffers need to be higher on average over time, as was outlined in the previous section. A second element of the macroprudential response to procyclicality consists in building up and running down buffers over the cycle.

The guiding policy principle must be to build up safety margins of capital in good times, when it is easier and cheaper to do so.[10] These can restrain risk-taking. In bad times, the margins can be run down, allowing the system to absorb emerging strains more easily and dampening the feedback mechanisms.

At the level of individual banks, appropriate buffers can be maintained through capital conservation measures when the buffers are inadequately replenished, including actions to limit excessive dividend payments, share buybacks and compensation. These buffers can then be used during periods of stress. At the macroprudential level, an operational framework has to be set up that relies on adequate indicators signalling the build-up of risks in the financial system.

A third element is to encourage banks to use forward-looking provisioning based on expected losses instead of more backward-looking provisions based on realised losses.[11] This will promote early identification and recognition of credit losses in a more robust manner. It will better

8. Tucker (2010).
9. Caruana (2009). op cit; Bank for International Settlements (2009). op cit.
10. BIS (2009).
11. Basel Committee (2009b).

reflect the reality of the financial performance and risk of financial institutions, by incorporating a broader range of credit information, both quantitative and qualitative. This should be done in a transparent way and be subject to appropriate internal and external validation by auditors.

Finally, it should be acknowledged that other macroprudential policy tools can be used to limit or prevent the emergence of macroeconomic and financial imbalances.[12] Indeed, they have long been part of the arsenal, particularly—but not only—in Asia. For example, tighter provisioning norms against rapid credit expansion have been used in China to counter potential vulnerabilities from excessive credit growth or asset price bubbles.

Other prudential tools have been used as automatic stabilisers, that is, to forestall the emergence of such imbalances. In India, for instance, a long-standing prudential requirement is that banks must hold a relatively large part of their assets in risk-free liquid securities. Several other Asian economies place limits on credit exposures or otherwise restrict concentration risks towards banks. Korea, for instance, has announced loan-to-deposit (LTD) requirements that aim to limit the exposure of its banks to wholesale funding markets.

Because it can be difficult to set general rules that cut across all sectors, some countries have also used sectoral policies to regulate credit terms, as well as capital or provisioning requirements for loans to specific borrowers or sectors. For instance, loan-to-value (LTV) ratios and restrictions on mortgage lending have often been used by Asian authorities to address concerns about real estate bubbles. In India, the central bank has actively used differential risk weighting in capital regulation and countercyclical provisioning norms to slow the pace of growth of bank credit to specific sectors.

One must, however, recognise that some of these measures can be intrusive and can have unexpected distortive effects. In addition, significant uncertainty remains about how and under what circumstances these measures are likely to be effective. While discretionary sector-based prudential measures taken by Asian policymakers have proved quite successful in containing financial system damage as asset prices fall,

12. BoE (2009).

generally they have been less effective in preventing or constraining asset price booms.

It remains to be seen whether and how rule-based measures might counter the effect of distorted incentives and so prevent boom-bust cycles. Effective rules need to take into account the endogeneous behaviour of financial institutions and their impact on credit extension, as well as the relationship between the financial and real sectors of the economy.

Regulation is not enough: Monetary policy

This brings me to my next point that better regulation is essential, but even with the new macroprudential focus it may not be enough to prevent the build-up of systemic risks. Other policies, particularly monetary policy, must play a supporting role. The question is not whether monetary policy should target asset prices. It is rather what role monetary policy should play in leaning against the build-up of imbalances that contribute to systemic risk which can derail the economy.

It is tempting to make a neat Tinbergian assignment in which we would assign a single policy instrument to each policy objective. In such a world, interest rate policy is assigned to stabilise prices, while prudential policies, be they capital requirements or credit restrictions, are assigned to maintain financial stability. In reality, however, prudential policies will not suffice to maintain financial stability and should be supported by monetary policy.

A key element is that monetary policy should take into account its effect on financial stability, for instance, on financial innovation and the quest for yield. The current crisis has highlighted the hitherto neglected channel of monetary transmission, the 'risk-taking' channel—the link between monetary policy and the perception and pricing of risk by economic agents.[13]

Such self-reinforcing dynamics were detected empirically in Spain, where lower short-term interest rates led Spanish banks to loosen their

13. Borio and Zhu (2008); Gambacorta (2009).

lending standards and to grant riskier loans.[14] This and other research at the ECB suggests that this effect is related to the impact on the banks' appetite for credit risk when interest rates are low.

As a result, the interest rate can affect the supply of credit through the bank lending channel and risk-taking through the search for yield, thereby influencing the pace of financial innovation. Asset price and credit cycles cannot be treated as exogeneous when they are, in fact, inherently influenced by the monetary policy stance.

A more symmetrical approach is needed. Monetary policy should not act only when the bubble bursts, leading to a macroeconomic downturn. It should also act pre-emptively to limit the preceding phase of expansion.[15] This suggests that the reaction function of the monetary authorities should not be narrowly understood as aiming to control inflation over the short-run.

Rather, it must also take account of credit growth and asset information with the goal of promoting financial and macroeconomic stability over the medium-term. In some circumstances, central banks may need to respond directly to this additional information, even if inflation deviates from its objective in the short-run. This is because the trade-off between financial stability and monetary stability may be more apparent than real when the appropriate time horizon is considered.

In the long-run, the two goals are indeed likely to be complementary. For example, some restraint on the build-up of financial imbalances today may mitigate the severity of a subsequent financial crisis, preventing a future economic contraction and the undershooting of inflation targets.[16]

Several recent experiences suggest that central banks are becoming more alert to developments in asset markets. In 2003, for instance, the Reserve Bank of Australia's (RBA) interest rate policy quite appropriately erred on the side of tightness in the face of strong credit growth and

14. Jiménez *et al.* (2009).

15. Caruana (2005).

16. Borio and Lowe (2002).

housing price increases, even though consumer price inflation remained muted.

The RBA also made public statements highlighting the risks in the rise in housing prices.[17] There is little doubt that this subsequently contributed to the levelling out of house prices. In the Euro area, the monetary pillar—that is, broad money and credit growth—also helped the ECB take difficult interest rate decisions in 2004 and 2005.

Regulation is not enough: Fiscal buffers and tax policy

Fiscal policy can also be called upon to promote financial stability, not least because of the sheer scale of the financial resources that the public sector can call upon in times of stress. One obvious mechanism is to let fiscal automatic stabilisers play their part in difficult times, alleviating the impact of economic weakness on business activity and employment.

Moreover, government can play the role of a kind of insurer by building fiscal room for manoeuvre in good times. When bad times come, these 'reserves' can be used for financial stability. Governments have mobilised massive resources in the financial rescue programmes set up in response to the recent financial crisis. This implies that government debt should be maintained at reasonably low levels in good times, so that additional debt can be taken on in times of stress without unsettling financial market conditions.

As with monetary policy, it is also important to take into account how fiscal policy affects financial stability. In good times, procyclical policies can serve to heighten complacency and encourage the build-up of financial imbalances. This is even more the case when rapid credit growth and high asset prices flatter the fiscal accounts during the upturn.

All this implies that fiscal policy may have to err more on the side of tightness, preparing for the realisation that part of what appears to be sustainable revenues may be subject to a payback. Of course, this strongly reinforces the case for reducing government debt in relation to gross domestic product (GDP) in good times. That said, we should recognise the

---

17. Cagliarini *et al.* (2010).

political economy problem that Adam Smith highlighted in his treatment of public debt.[18]

Lastly, tax policy could also be used to address sectoral developments with potential financial stability implications. We have seen how macroprudential tools can be used to limit excessive credit growth in specific areas such as housing. Tax policy could also be of use here. A key way to ensure that the tax code worked for rather than against financial stability would be to reduce or eliminate its bias towards debt and against equity.

The recent crisis has shown the unfortunate results this bias can have on asset prices and leverage, especially in housing markets. This is not the place to explore in detail how the tax code might be made more even-handed. Suffice it to say that getting rid of the tax incentive to leverage could make a handsome contribution to financial stability.

The institutional framework of systemic regulation

To summarise, we need to ensure that all public policies—especially monetary, fiscal and macro- and microprudential policies (complemented by adequate supervision)—become part of a consistent macrofinancial stability framework designed to pre-empt financial excesses and serial boom and bust cycles.

To make this framework effective, careful thought must be given to the institutional setup and to international coordination. It is crucial to align goals, know-how and control over the various policy instruments, precisely because the responsibilities for financial stability are so widely distributed. The institutional setup should, therefore, be based on clear mandates and accountability. It will need to rely on close cooperation between central banks and supervisory authorities, both within and across borders.

Having said that, let me acknowledge that some important questions remain open. A first open question pertains to the governance structure and flow of information in systemic risk regulation. The crisis has shown that central banks play a decisive role in systemic regulation.

18. Smith (1937).

It is not entirely clear, though, how central banks need to be equipped to play this role. Especially where the central bank is not the bank supervisor, it is important that the goal be well-defined, the instruments-understood and the exchange of information with other authorities be appropriate—including detailed supervisory information on individual firms.[19] Financial supervisors can also benefit from information collected by central banks in the context of their liquidity operations.

A second open question is how to balance rules and discretion. In principle, we should rely as far as possible on rules and automatic stabilisers rather than discretion. Rules can help avoid errors that can stem from difficulties in identifying threats to financial stability contemporaneously—dynamic provisioning is a good example of a rule that can help in dealing with procyclicality.

In addition, clear rules can allow the authorities to commit themselves *ex ante* to responses, thereby facilitating international coordination and enlisting the understanding, and even the anticipation, of market participants. For instance, market participants, including rating agencies, may not necessarily permit capital and liquidity that is built up in good times to be used in bad times.

In this case, clear rules communicated by supervisors will help drawdowns be accepted in the marketplace. Lastly, and perhaps more importantly, rules reduce the enormous political pressures on policy-makers to refrain from intervening against booms. However, rules may not be enough. Discretion has a role to play as it can help tailor intervention to varying and often unpredictable, circumstances. That is the reason why we should accept that some degree of discretion is inevitable.

While these open questions still have to be dealt with, I would like to emphasise that important progress has been made in the international coordination of systemic regulation. Indeed, we emerge from the global financial crisis with a brand new structure. The crisis gave further evidence that financial stability cannot be assured by each neighbour only keeping his own house in order. This is necessary, but not sufficient. Exposures to a neighbour's losses can bring down one's own house too.

---

19. Caruana (2010).

The FSB has taken up a key role in coordinating the work of national authorities and standard-setters to ensure international consistency. New mechanisms have been developed to support the development of the IMF-FSB early warning exercises, to increase cooperation across borders and between supervisors and to conduct peer review exercises. Comprising both thematic and country-by-country approaches, such exercises are a new instrument that will strengthen adherence to international standards.

Key input into the coordinating work of the FSB comes from the expanded Basel Process, which internationally coordinates standard-setting. Whatever be the differences at the national level on the scale and scope of financial firms, international agreements on minimum capital and liquidity are being refined. Peer-review exercises have been launched to ensure adherence to these standards in each jurisdiction.

New institutional arrangements are being explored to enhance cooperation among supervisors both at the national level and across borders. Let me just give some examples. In the case of the biggest firms operating across borders, colleges of supervisors are supplementing the Basel Concordat that sets out the respective roles of home and host supervisors.

Another example, but of a different nature, is the proposed European Systemic Risk Board (ESRB), which will help to coordinate micro and macro approaches and enhance international cooperation. This body would take charge of macroprudential supervision at the European level, issuing risk warnings and making recommendations on policy measures.

Lastly, the G20 is playing an increasing role to enhance the necessary coordination of macroeconomic policies and to ensure political support for financial regulatory reform. The mutual assessment process reinforces the commitment of national leaders to joint and coordinated action. Just as financial stability needs help from monetary and fiscal policy at the national level, international financial stability cannot be achieved in the face of inconsistent policies at the global level. It is very important that leaders remain engaged in and committed to this effort.

No doubt this international structure will continue to evolve. The challenge is to maintain the intimate cooperation that has characterised the Basel Process even as it widens the effort in terms of both participants and issues. As it approaches the end of its 80th year, the BIS pledges to continue its support for this cooperative project to tame systemic risk.

In conclusion

The issue of systemic risk is probably the most important and most difficult that we confront. Progress will require a combination of better regulation, a more macro-orientation of prudential tools, better macroeconomic policies, enhanced international coordination and greater market discipline. A lot of work has been done and much progress made. In some areas, such as capital and liquidity, the convergence of minds has already been substantial. In others, such as the handling of systemically important institutions, work is well under way.

Many ideas and proposals are on the table and we need to make sure that this work does not lose sight of the wood for the trees. The BIS will fully support the Basel Committee and the FSB in their comprehensive assessment of the impact of the various proposals to strengthen the financial system before they are implemented. This assessment will clarify the new regulatory framework and will ensure that transition to this new and more demanding framework is achieved with minimal interference to the ongoing recovery process.

References

Alfaro, R. and M. Drehmann (2009). "Macro Stress Tests and Crises: What Can We Learn?", *BIS Quarterly Review*: 29–41. December.

Bank for International Settlements (2009). "Addressing Financial System Pro-cyclicality: A Possible Framework". Note for the FSF Working Group on Market and Institutional Resilience. April.

Bank for International Settlements (2009). *79th Annual Report*. Chapter VII. June.

Bank of England (2009). "The Role of Macroprudential Policy", *Discussion Paper* 21. November.

Basel Committee on Banking Supervision (2009a). *Report and Recommendations of the Cross-border Bank Resolution Group*. September.

———. (2009b). *Strengthening the Resilience of the Banking Sector*. Consultative Document. December.

———. (1992). *The Insolvency Liquidation of a Multinational Bank*. December.

Borio, C. and H. Zhu (2008). "Capital Regulation, Risk-taking and Monetary Policy: A Missing Link in the Transmission Mechanism?", *BIS Working Papers* 268.

Borio, C. and M. Drehmann (2009). "Towards an Operational Framework for Financial Stability: 'Fuzzy' Measurement and its Consequences", *BIS Working Papers* 284: 5–8. June.

Borio, C. and P. Lowe (2002). "Asset Prices, Financial and Monetary Stability: Exploring the Nexus", *BIS Working Papers* 114.

Cagliarini, A., C. Kent and G. Stevens (2010). "Fifty Years of Monetary Policy: What have We Learned?", Paper presented to the *Reserve Bank of Australia Symposium*. February 9.

Caruana, J. (2010). "Financial Stability: Ten Questions and About Seven Answers", Speech to the *Reserve Bank of Australia Symposium*. February 9.

———. (2009). "The International Policy Response to Financial Crises: Making the Macro-prudential Approach Operational", Panel remarks, Jackson Hole. August 21–22.

———. (2005). "Monetary Policy, Financial Stability and Asset Prices", *Documentos Ocasionales* No. 0507, Bank of Spain.

Gambacorta, L. (2009). "Monetary Policy and the Risk-taking Channel", *BIS Quarterly Review*: 43–53. December.

Jiménez, G., S. Ongena, J. Peydrò and J. Saurina (2009). "Hazardous Times for Monetary Policy: What Do Twenty-three Million Bank Loans say about the Effects of Monetary Policy on Credit Risk-taking?", *Bank of Spain Working Papers* 833.

Smith, Adam (1937). "Of Public Debts", in *The Wealth of Nations*. Book V. Chapter III. New York: Modern Library.

Tarashev, N., C. Borio and K. Tsatsaronis (2009). "The Systemic Importance of Financial Institutions", *BIS Quarterly Review*: 75–87. September.

Tucker, P. (2010). "Shadow Banking, Financing Markets and Financial Stability", Speech to BGC Partners Seminar. January 21.

19 Summing-up

JAIME CARUANA

Let me just say three things by way of summary. One, on financial sector regulation, I believe that recent regulatory reforms are moving in the right direction. Substantial efforts have been under way over the past year to develop key building blocks of the new regulatory regime: reforms to avoid excessive build-up of leverage in the financial system; better capital and liquidity standards; robust domestic and cross-border resolution; policies to deal with externality problems associated with bigness or inter-connectedness; and more proactive supervision of particularly large, systemically important financial institutions. And these efforts have been combined with initiatives to develop new macroprudential tools to reduce procyclicality in bank lending.

Second, I would like to emphasise that prudential regulatory reforms, even with this macroprudential approach, are not going to be enough. Monetary policy must also be a part of the solution. Both Steve Roach and Bill White highlighted what went wrong in the past and why changes to monetary policy should form a critical part of the reform strategy to reduce the risk of future crises. For this reform we will have to analyse and study the tools and the approaches of monetary policy. I think there is now greater awareness among monetary policymakers about the need for a new approach to the conduct of monetary policy, particularly by taking into account developments in asset prices and their implications for the stability of the financial system.

Finally, John Lipksy spoke on innovation, and he put it very nicely that we need innovation with adequate safeguards. I agree with John that

---

Summing-up by Jaime Caruana, Chairman, Session III: Disruptions in Financial Systems and Challenges to Regulation and Supervision.

the crisis was more the result of poor risk-management systems than simply the growth of financial innovation. Governor Subbarao put it very clearly in the case of India. So I will stop here. Let me just mention that I have delivered a paper to all of you where I explain my position on many of these topics.

20 Summing-up

USHA THORAT

I think we have really had a very strong case made for central banks to lean against credit bubbles through whatever means they can. I think the essential point that Bill really focused on, whether it is through banks or otherwise, is that it is really the credit bubble that we are dealing with; it is the excessive credit growth, and one does not have to fine-tune the measurement. You know when it is there and you can recognise it and, therefore, the need to do something about it. What is it that central banks can do? Should it be monetary policy or should it be regulatory policy? This has obviously been the debate that we have had the whole day. I guess what my colleague is saying is that it has to be a bit of both. I think as far as the regulatory policy is concerned, clearly when there is excessive credit growth, the international regulatory system is looking for more capital in the form of more credit capital buffers, curbing excessive leverage and implementing macroprudential measures as well. Whether it is countercyclical capital and provisioning, it would really be worked through credit instruments and through the measurements of credit. I think this is the right way to go.

In emerging market economies (EMEs), the need of the day is actually more credit penetration and more credit linked to growth. Therefore, in that context, the implications of the enhanced capital credit requirements and the leverage proposals on the requirements of credit for growth for EMEs like India becomes a very important point to assess.

Second, the paper that we had from Mr. Lipsky and the comments—I think the important point is that to arrive late on the block is really learning from the mistakes elsewhere, especially in the area of financial

---

Summing-up by Usha Thorat, Co-Chair, Session III: Disruptions in Financial Systems and Challenges to Regulation and Supervision.

innovation and regulation. Countries like India have a huge requirement of infrastructure and we do have problems of asset-liability management. We have basically a bank-dominated system. Most of the pressure is on the banks to fund infrastructure. The fiscal headroom is very little and there is a huge concentration risk. So how do we provide instrumentalities through market innovation so that long-term players like pension funds and insurance funds really come into these markets and are able to leverage on the financial instruments and diversify the risk amongst the larger group of savers? We have a high savings ratio but the penetration in terms of financial savings is something that does not give us much headroom to meet the requirements of growth, particularly inclusive growth. These are the challenges that we are trying to address.

Section IV

Financial Stability as an Objective of Monetary Policy

Section IV

Financial Stability as an Objective of Monetary Policy

This section corresponds to Session IV of the First International Research Conference on 'Challenges to Central Banking in the Context of Financial Crisis', Reserve Bank of India, Mumbai.

Chairman: Michael Foot

Co-Chair: K.C. Chakrabarty

21 Two Cheers for Bagehot

JOHN C. WILLIAMS*

The global financial crisis and ensuing recession that began in 2007 have tested and stretched the traditional roles of central banking. The Federal Reserve, in particular, has undertaken a multipronged attack on the sources and consequences of the crisis. This has included conventional and 'unconventional' monetary policy actions, including lowering interest rates effectively to zero and greatly expanding its balance sheet holdings of Treasury and mortgage-related securities. It has joined forces with other regulatory agencies and the Treasury department in conducting the 'stress tests' of the largest bank holding companies with the goal of assuring that these institutions hold adequate capital to see them through the economic storm. Finally, it has acted as a lender-of-last-resort for much of the financial system, greatly expanding the provision of liquidity and support to banks and to other key distressed sectors of the financial system. This paper focuses on the third aspect of the Fed's attack on the crisis.

As emphasised by Madigan (2009), modern central bank lender-of-last-resort policies are guided by the dictum laid down by Walter Bagehot over a century ago, that is, to lend freely to solvent institutions on good collateral and at a high interest rate. Economic theory shows that lender-of-last-resort policies of this type can be very powerful at mitigating the effects of liquidity crises (see, e.g. Kiyotaki and Moore, 2008). During the crisis the Fed, as well as other central banks, applied this principle again and again, often in new and innovative ways. The experiences of the crisis have highlighted the critical need for lender-of-last-resort liquidity policies as well as their limitations.

---

* The views expressed in this paper are solely those of the author and should not be interpreted as reflecting the views of the management of the Federal Reserve Bank of San Francisco or the Board of Governors of the Federal Reserve System.

In examining the use and effects of lender-of-last-resort policies, it is useful to divide the financial crisis into two stages. The first stage began in the summer of 2007, when disruptions in interbank lending markets emerged. The Fed's actions during this stage were focused on providing liquidity to the commercial banking sector through various forms of discount window lending.

The second stage began in the spring of 2008 when stresses developed in the funding markets for investment banks. In the fall of 2008 matters took a sharp turn for the worse, when two large financial institutions failed—the investment bank, Lehman Brothers and the savings and loan institution, Washington Mutual. Several others threatened to go under.

The danger of the failure of other systemically important financial institutions threatened the entire financial system and caused parts of the commercial paper market and the asset-backed securitisation market to freeze up. In response to these events, the Fed extended discount window lending to non-depository institutions in support of key segments of non-bank funding markets. At its peak in late 2008, Fed's lending programmes (including swaps with foreign banks) totalled over $1.5 trillion (Figure 21.1).

Bagehot and black swans

Starting in early 2007, the downturn in housing prices and the rising number of delinquencies on sub-prime mortgages was a wake-up call to market participants that many residential mortgages were not nearly as safe as was once believed. Investors and financial institutions became increasingly nervous about their own exposure to risk and the financial health of firms with which they did business.

It became difficult to determine the value of many loans and mortgage related securities. In addition, the widespread use of complex and exotic financial instruments made it even harder to figure out the vulnerability of financial institutions to losses. As a result, financial institutions became increasingly reluctant to lend to each other. In August 2007, these fears about the financial health of counter-parties and the banking system as a whole led to disruptions in the wholesale bank lending market.

Figure 21.1

The asset side of the Fed's balance sheet

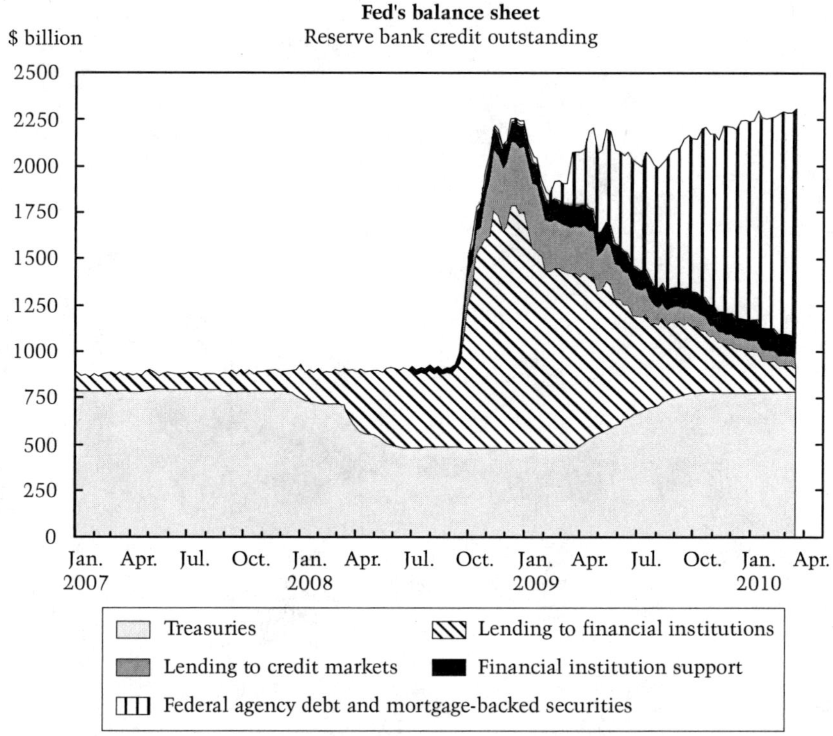

Note: Lending to financial institutions includes repurchase agreements, term auction credit, discount window lending, primary dealer credit, central bank liquidity swaps, and other Federal Reserve assets.

Source: Federal Reserve Board, Haver Analytics.

As shown in Figure 21.2, the 'Libor' interbank lending rate for a term of three months rose significantly above the overnight federal funds rate in August 2007. The rise in term lending rates relative to corresponding overnight rates was a sharp departure from past experience, causing Taylor and Williams (2009) to label it a 'black swan' event. Spreads on other term interbank loans similarly rose.

The predominant explanation for the rise in term lending spreads was the unwillingness of banks to tie up funds for even a month despite the existence of otherwise profitable loans. This appetite for hoarding cash was traced back to uncertainty about the future availability of, and need for,

Figure 21.2

A black swan in the money market

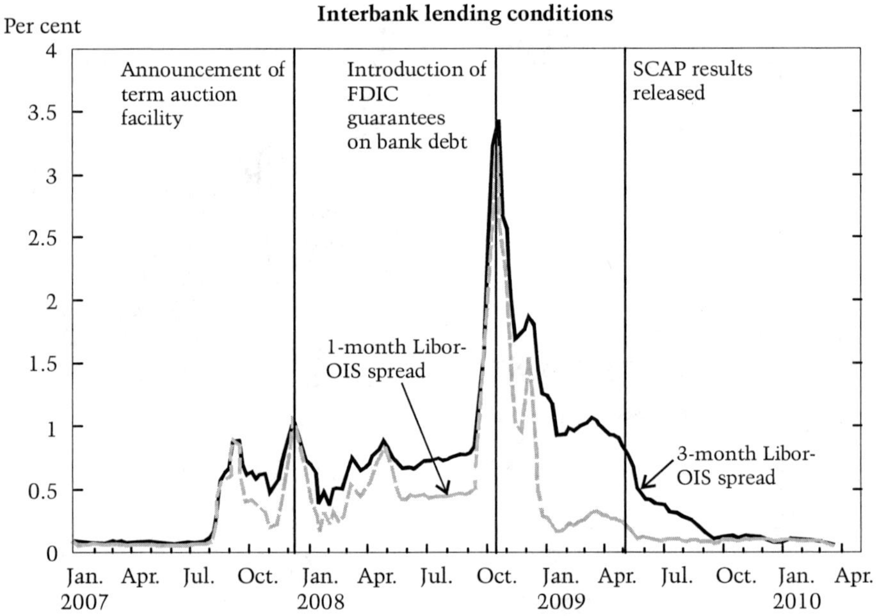

Sources: *Financial Times*, Federal Reserve Board, Haver Analytics.

funds in the light of the mortgage market meltdown. In this view, there was a shortage of 'liquidity' for term interbank lending, despite ample liquidity for overnight lending.

In theory, the presence of the Fed as a lender-of-last-resort should have been very effective at limiting stresses in the interbank market resulting from a shortage of term liquidity that emerged in the summer of 2007. After all, healthy banks with good collateral can borrow from the Federal Reserve's discount window whenever they wish, just as Bagehot advised. Moreover, banks can rollover overnight discount window loans or borrow at terms of up to a month, so the presence of the discount window should have been effective at addressing stresses in term lending markets as well.

However, banks initially shunned the discount window, evidently in part owing to the perceived stigma associated with borrowing from the Fed. There was a perception that the Federal Reserve prefers banks to use private sources for liquidity rather than the discount window. In addition, borrowing at a high penalty rate—initially 100 basis points above the federal funds target rate—could be perceived as a sign of weakness if discovered by market participants. (At the time discount window transactions were not made public, but borrowing totals in each of the 12 Federal Reserve districts are released on a weekly basis.)

The Fed took a number of steps aimed at overcoming stigma and any other impediments interfering with the use of the discount window. In August 2007, it publicly encouraged use of the discount window through a Press release. It also lowered the 'penalty' on discount rate loans from 100 basis points to 50 basis points. (It later lowered it further to just 25 basis points.) In December 2007, the Fed began regular auctions of one-month discount window loans to banks through the newly created term auction facility (TAF). The conditions for participating in the TAF were the same as for primary credit loans at the discount window. The key innovation was the auction format. The initial quantity of TAF credit put up for bid was relatively small, but it was expanded several times over the following year and extended to three-month loans. (See Taylor and Williams, 2009 for details on the TAF).

At the same time, the Fed also created swap lines with several foreign central banks to increase the availability of dollar-denominated loans to banks in those countries. TAF auctions were also set up in Switzerland and the European Central Bank (ECB). Owing to its auction format, the TAF is generally thought to have been effective at reducing banks' reluctance to borrow at the discount window.

However, despite the Fed's concerted efforts to reduce stigma through the TAF, central bank-provided liquidity alone proved insufficient to remove all signs of stresses in the interbank market. Although spreads on term interbank loans declined following the announcement of the TAF, they remained elevated relative to pre-crisis levels and in fact, reached all-time highs in late 2008 after the crisis intensified.

The Fed's discount window programmes could only do so much in reducing term interbank spreads because they are designed to address liquidity shortages, not problems caused by potential insolvency. Evidence for the increase in counter-party risks is seen, for example, in the sustained rise in the rates on credit default swap rates for major banks and the rise in the spread between rates on unsecured and secured loans. Of course, liquidity and solvency are inextricably bound and it is an impossible task to separate the two. A number of research papers have investigated the behaviour of term interbank spreads during the crisis (McAndrews *et al.*, 2009; Christensen *et al.*, 2009; Taylor and Williams, 2009; Wu, 2009). A consistent finding in the literature is that counter-party risk, not only liquidity, was an important factor in explaining the rise in term interbank spreads during the crisis.

Skyrocketing financial losses potentially threatened the viability of many financial institutions. As the mortgage meltdown intensified, the magnitude of anticipated losses rose dramatically. In October 2007, shortly after the onset of the US housing bust, the International Monetary Fund (IMF) estimated that financial institutions' losses related to US residential mortgages would total $240 billion.

By April 2009, the IMF's estimate was nearly six times larger, exceeding $1.4 trillion. Because millions of US mortgages were repackaged as securities, these losses spread across the globe. The IMF's estimates of losses of all types of loans and loan-related securities, originated in the United States and abroad, skyrocketed as well, as seen in Figure 21.3. The IMF's (2009) most recent estimate is that global losses over 2007-2010 will total an astounding $2.8 trillion.

Indeed, term interbank spreads did not return to relatively low levels until other interventions directed at the health of the banking system were enacted as seen in Figure 21.2. These included capital injections from troubled asset relief programme (TARP), the temporary liquidity guarantee programme (TLGP) introduced by the Federal Deposit Insurance Corporation (FDIC) in October 2008 (that provided guarantees on newly issued bank debt and expanded deposit insurance coverage) and the regulatory stress tests conducted in the spring of 2009. These interventions improved the stability and helped rebuild confidence in the banking system.

Bagehot for the 21st century

In early 2008, the tentacles of the crisis spread further throughout the financial system. Amid a widespread collapse of confidence in early 2008,

Figure 21.3

Estimated losses skyrocket

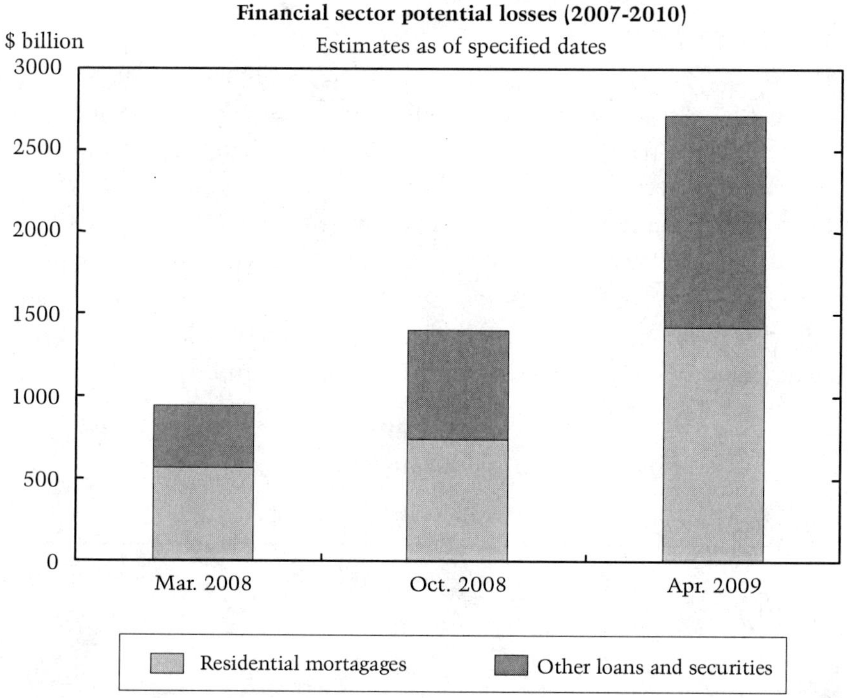

Source: International Monetary Fund.

investment banks, including those that were primary dealers of government securities, had trouble obtaining short-term funding. These institutions, which rely on repurchase agreements for short-term funding, proved to be vulnerable to liquidity shortages very similar to bank runs (Adrian *et al.*, 2009). The crucial differences being that investment banks are not covered by deposit insurance and do not have access to the discount window.

In response to the impairment in this market, the Federal Reserve expanded its own collateralised lending to primary dealers to ensure that they had access to the critical funding needed for day-to-day operations. Normally, the Federal Reserve provides collateralised discount window loans only to institutions that take deposits, such as commercial banks. But, in March 2008, the Fed exercised its authority, in cases of 'unusual and exigent circumstances', to expand discount window access beyond depository institutions for the first time in many decades (see Fettig, 2002, for a history of the Fed's authority to lend to non-depository institutions). It created the primary dealer credit facility (PDCF; see Adrian *et al.*, 2009, for a detailed discussion.)

The Fed also introduced the term securities lending facility (TSLF), which provided term loans of Fed holdings of Treasury securities for certain types of collateral (see Fleming *et al.*, 2009, for a description and analysis). These facilities were designed to improve access to liquidity and to reduce fears of future liquidity shortages. As seen in Figure 21.4, the PDCF was used during the spring of 2008, but then rose sharply following the intensification of the crisis in September 2008. Like the discount window programmes for commercial banks, the purpose of the PDCF was to provide liquidity, fully consistent with Bagehot's dictum.

Figure 21.4

The primary dealer credit facility (PDCF)

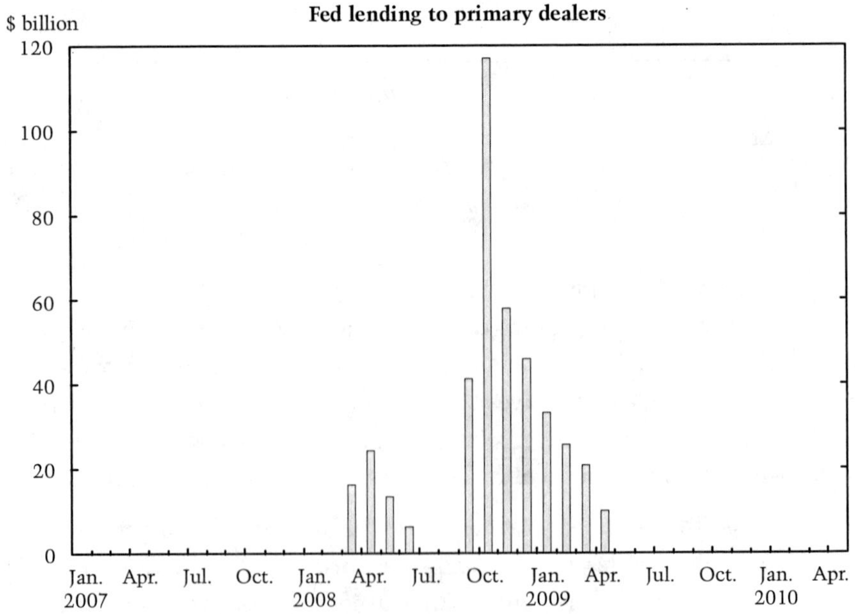

Note: Reflects credit extended through the primary dealer credit facility and certain other dealers.
Sources: Federal Reserve Board, Haver Analytics.

The next stage of the widening of the use of the discount window occurred in the fall of 2008, in the wake of the failure of Lehman Brothers.

Large losses at a big money market mutual fund extended the crisis to a part of the financial system previously regarded as safe, prompting investors, that held commercial paper, to pull their money out. Short-term lending to financial corporations in the commercial paper market froze and spreads on commercial paper shot up, as seen in Figure 21.5.

In October 2008, the Fed provided secured loans to institutions in the money market mutual fund sector and high-quality segments of the commercial paper markets. These programmes, the money market investor funding facility (MMIFF) and the commercial paper funding facility (CPFF), were designed to restore functioning to these markets that had frozen (See Covitz *et al.*, 2009; Schnabel and Kacperczyk, 2009; Adrian *et al.*, 2010).

Figure 21.5

The commercial paper market

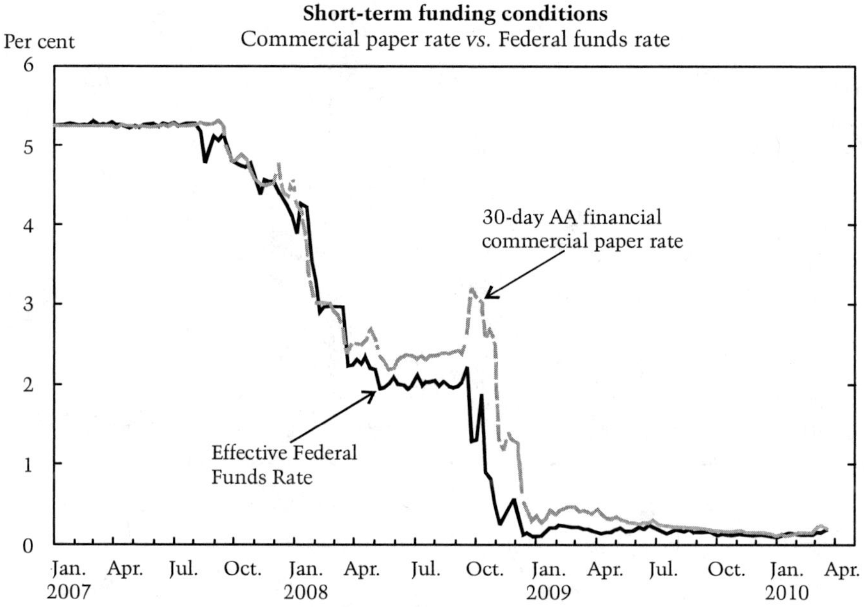

Sources: Federal Reserve Board, Haver Analytics.

These facilities made non-recourse loans to special purpose vehicles for the purchase of very high-quality commercial paper. To limit the possibility of losses from the CPFF, the Fed limited the investments to the highest-rated securities, which restricted the reach and benefits of the programme. The Fed was explicitly taking on a small amount of tail-event risk through the CPFF.

Some default risk is always present in lender-of-last-resort operations. But, in practice, the haircut on the collateral and the short term of a discount window loan to a bank makes a loss highly unlikely. The structure of the programmes directed at capital market funding sources differs from those for banks. To ensure minimal risk to the Fed, the programme was limited to only very high quality commercial paper.

Figure 21.6

Differential effects in the commercial paper market

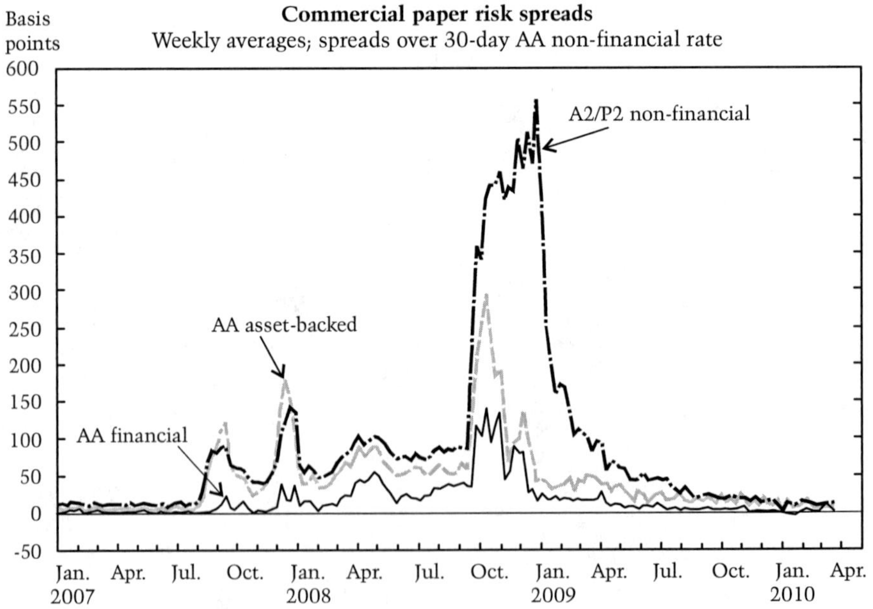

These programmes were highly effective in bringing commercial paper spreads of high quality paper, back down, as seen in Figure 21.6. But spreads on lower quality paper excluded from the programme remained extremely elevated for several months. In the end, the Fed did not suffer any losses on the loans made through these programmes. The intensification of the crisis in late 2008 also saw a freezing up of asset-backed securitisation markets. As seen in Figure 21.7, issuance of asset-backed securities for tried-and-true products such as credit cards, auto loans, and students loans came to a grinding halt. In November 2008, the Fed announced the creation of the TALF that provides loans to help finance the issuance of asset-backed securities.

Figure 21.7

Term asset-backed securities loan facility (TALF)

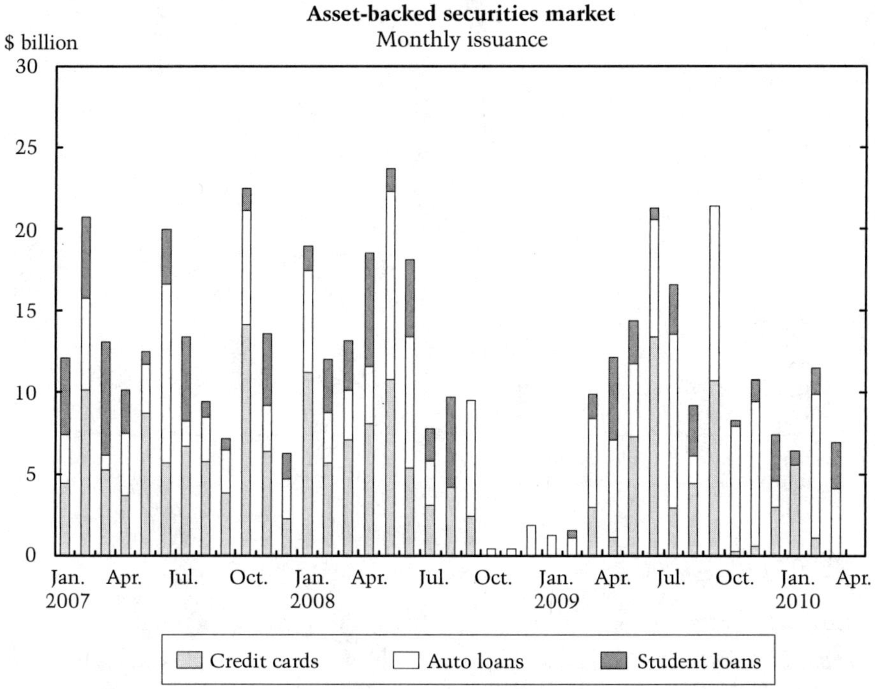

Source: Bloomberg.

Like the CPFF described above, the reach of this programme was limited by the requirement that the Fed's loan be adequately safe, which limited its loans to only the highest quality segment. One innovation is that the Treasury department took on some of the risk of the TALF loans, expanding the availability of credit under the programme.

After a slow start, issuance of asset-backed securities for these types of loans picked up in 2009. Issuance of other segments that did not receive support from the TALF, such as private-label mortgage-backed securities

(MBS) shown in Figure 21.8, remained moribund through 2009. In July 2009, the TALF included some categories of commercial real estate MBS.

Figure 21.8

Private-label real estate MBS markets remain moribund

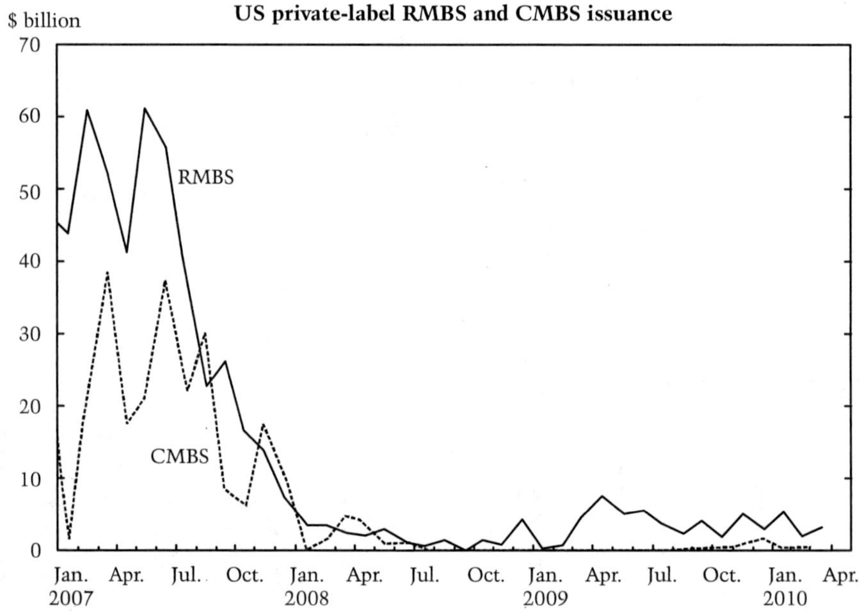

The limits to Bagehot

The recent crisis has highlighted both the importance and limitations of central bank lender-of-last-resort policies. The Fed acted quickly and creatively to provide liquidity to the banking sector and critical financial markets. These actions significantly reduced the fallout from the financial crisis from what it might have otherwise been. Importantly, they were conducted as part of a concerted international effort to reduce stresses in funding markets.

But, recent events also demonstrate the limitations of Bagehot's principles. Like Irving Kristol's (1978) withholding of one cheer for capitalism, Bagehot's principles, although valuable, can only go so far in averting panics and crises in the 21st century. In particular, the liquidity crises were often the proximate causes of market disruptions and stresses, while the ultimate cause was the possibility of insolvency of major financial institutions owing to massive losses associated with the mortgage meltdown and the global recession. Of course, issues of insolvency cannot be solved by central bank liquidity policies. These are properly the domain of the fiscal authority.

A key lesson of the crisis is the need for fiscal and supervisory interventions that deal with insolvency issues more directly, such as capital injections. As seen in Figure 21.9, market perceptions of the default risk of major US banks fell sharply after the introduction of the FDIC guarantees on bank debt and the release of the results from the bank stress tests (formally known as the Supervisory Capital Assessment Program, or SCAP). These programmes directly addressed the uncertainty and risks of insolvency of key banks.

Figure 21.9

Perceptions of major bank default risk

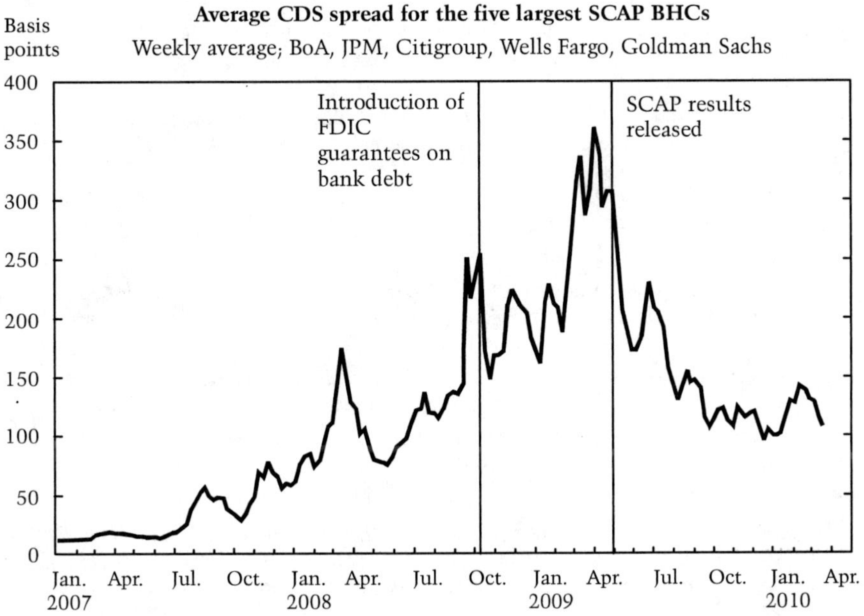

The crisis also demonstrated the risk of runs on the capital market-based funding system. Like traditional commercial banks, investment banks and commercial paper markets are susceptible to panics and contagion, absent a lender-of-last-resort or insurance. The Federal Reserve acted boldly to avert a far worse crisis, but absent regulatory changes, these actions have increased the moral hazard problem regarding liquidity management. A key issue for the future is how to reduce the risks and consequences of runs in these markets. Experience from the crisis suggests that lender-of-last-resort policies will be more effective if the fiscal authority also plays a role by taking on risk, given the limitations on central bank risk-taking. The TALF provides an excellent example where the Fed provided liquidity at minimal risk while the United States Treasury and market participants were exposed to risk.

References

Adrian, Tobias, Christopher Burke and James McAndrews (2009). "The Federal Reserve's Primary Dealer Credit Facility", Federal Reserve Bank of New York Current Issues in *Economics and Finance* 15(4).

Adrian, Tobias, Karin Kimbrough and Dina Marchioni (2010). "The Federal Reserve's Commercial Paper Funding Facility", *Federal Reserve Bank of New York Staff Reports* No. 423, January.

Christensen, Jens H.E., Jose A. Lopez and Glenn D. Rudebusch (2009). "Do Central Bank Liquidity Facilities Affect Interbank Lending Rates?", *Federal Reserve Bank of San Francisco Working Paper* No. 2009-13. June.

Covitz, Daniel, Nellie Liang and Gustavo Suarez (2009). "The Evolution of a Financial Crisis: Collapse of the Asset-Backed Commercial Paper Market", *Finance and Economics Discussion Series* No. 2009-36. Washington, DC: Board of Governors of the Federal Reserve System.

Fettig, David (2002). "Lender of More than Last Resort", *The Region*, Federal Reserve Bank of Minneapolis. December. pp.14-47.

Fleming, Michael, Warren Hrung and Frank Keane (2009). "The Term Securities Lending Facility: Origin, Design and Effects", Federal Reserve Bank of New York Current Issues in *Economics and Finance* 14(2).

International Monetary Fund (2009). *Global Financial Stability Report: Navigating the Financial Challenges Ahead*. Washington, DC: International Monetary Fund. October.

Kiyotaki, Nobuhiro and John Moore (2008). *Liquidity, Business Cycles, and Monetary Policy*. US: Princeton University. April.

Kristol, Irving (1978). *Two Cheers for Capitalism*. New York: Basic Books.

Madigan, Brian F. (2009). "Bagehot's Dictum in Practice: Formulating and Implementing Policies to Combat the Financial Crisis", Presented at the Federal Reserve Bank of Kansas City's *Annual Economic Symposium*. Jackson Hole. Wyoming. August 21.

McAndrews, James, Asani Sarkar and Zhenyu Wang (2008). "The Effect of the Term Auction Facility on the London Inter-bank Offered Rate", *Federal Reserve Bank of New York Staff Reports* No. 335. July.

Schnabel, Isabel and Marcin Kacperczyk (2009). "When Safe Proved Risky: Commercial Paper During the Financial Crisis of 2007-2009". Unpublished *Working Paper*. NYU Stern School of Management.

Taylor, John B. and John C. Williams (2009). "A Black Swan in the Money Market", *American Economic Journal: Macroeconomics* 1(1): 58-83, January.

Wu, Tao (2009). "The US Money Market and the Term Auction Facility in Financial Crisis of 2007-2009", *Review of Economics and Statistics.* Federal Reserve Bank of Dallas.

21.1
DISCUSSION

New Research Agenda of the Central Banks

STEPHEN S. ROACH

John Williams has provided an excellent description of the Federal Reserve's extraordinary actions during the Great Crisis. The only issue I have in this regard is his depiction of the so-called Bagehot notion of lending freely on good collateral. I don't want to belabour this point—I think Paul Volcker has raised that question early on in addressing this collateral issue, certainly in the context of both the Bear Stearns and American Insurance Group (AIG) bailouts where the collateral turned over to the Fed was far from good quality. John, in this instance, is of course referring to the various quantitative easing programmes which were of a different calibre.

What I would like to do in this brief comment is to use John's paper to segue into a much bigger question. Do we want central bankers to excel in the art of post-crisis damage control by using the types of tools that John has described on a regular basis or do we want proactive central bankers to rethink their role by trying to be out in front of a crisis in the future so they do not have to use these same tools again? I guess what I am really asking is whether we want John or his successor to write another paper like this ever again? For reasons that I articulated earlier, I have a strong preference for the latter, specifically for a proactive Fed, empowered by a new financial stability mandate that leans against asset bubbles and their destabilising impacts on the real side of the US and the global economy.

John is a research director, at one of the 12 district banks in the Federal Reserve System. I honestly think that the issue I have raised bears critically on the central bank research functions. That is true not just of research departments at the District banks but also of the Board of

Comments by Stephen S. Roach on the paper presented by John C. Williams 'Two Cheers for Bagehot'.

Governors in Washington where I spent six of my greatest years. I think it is absolutely essential for the research functions of central banks to come up to speed with the new responsibilities that central banks say they deserve to have in dealing with systemic risks. I am not sure that the Fed or other central banks around the world have research programmes that are well-aligned with this key responsibility.

I would be so bold as to recommend four specific ingredients that will be needed for the new systemtic risk research agenda of the central banks: One, central bank researchers need to develop a deeper understanding of the hows and whys of an asset-dependent economy—specifically the link between asset markets and real economies.

Two, central bank research departments need to focus much more on savings flows as by-product of asset-dependent economies. They especially need to understand the linkages between asset markets and the potentially destabilising shifts in the mix of global savings flows. The corollary agenda focuses on the potentially lethal mix of current account disparities between deficit and surplus nations around the world.

Three, I think central banks and their research departments need to work hard with international authorities, including those of the BIS to develop a good, solid macro-analytic capability to assess the incidence of counter-party risk. That is especially the case in so far as the recent unmonitored derivatives explosion was concerned. We operated under the theory, or presumption, that this was not a major risk. But we had no data to validate that assertion and, of course, the theory turned out to be dead wrong. I think central banks can do a much better job in grounding their assessment of systemic risks in facts and data rather than in ideology.

Four, I think, in order to handle the responsibilities of a systemic risk regulator, central banks will need to get out of their silos and integrate research functionality with that of other central banks. In the case of the Fed, I think that each of the 12 district banks need to become better integrated with the research function in other districts as well as that which resides at the Board. It is my impression—maybe this is dated and incorrect, and you can certainly correct me on this, John—that there is not a lot of integration across the system in research functionality at the Fed.

So, in short, central banks need a research agenda that is compatible with a much deeper understanding and the pitfalls of systemic risk. Central banks, in my opinion, are not well-equipped to take on the new responsibility that they say they want to have. Still, I believe they are best positioned to take on this responsibility. But we need to bring the research function up to speed before they are entrusted with the most daunting challenges of the post-crisis era.

22 Crisis and Implications for Central Bank Balance Sheets

Policies, Effectiveness and Designing an Exit

KRISHNA SRINIVASAN*

Policymakers across major advanced and key emerging economies adopted large-scale and wide-ranging measures to combat the financial crisis and the associated slump in the global economy that some have described as the 'Great Recession'. These measures have yielded tangible benefits.

The policy actions have included significant fiscal stimulus, amounting to around two per cent of the gross domestic product (GDP) in the G20 countries, extraordinary credit and quantitative easing by major central banks and large-scale public sector support for the financial sector. These policy actions have contributed in stabilising financial market conditions and global economic activity.

As the global economy begins to recover, policymakers will need to transcend from extraordinary short-term support to medium-term policy requirements, through credible and coherent exit strategies. The key challenge is to map a course between exiting from public interventions too early, which would jeopardise progress in securing financial stability and economic recovery. Exiting too late, on the other hand, would distort private incentives and create new risks.

Recovery in most advanced economies is expected to be weak and there are no signs of a sustained pickup in private demand as yet. Policy stimulus will, therefore, need to be maintained in these economies at least

* The views expressed in this paper are my own, and should not be attributed to the staff, Management or the Board of the IMF.

through 2010. On the other hand, some major emerging economies are already growing rapidly and may have to unwind stimulus faster than the advanced economies.

Against this backdrop, this paper focuses on key central bank policy actions aimed at alleviating the financial crisis and bolstering aggregate demand. It assesses the effectiveness of such measures and examines issues related to the timing and exit from the wide-ranging policy actions. Clearly, there are broader issues concerning the timing and sequencing of exit from all crisis-related intervention policies, including whether fiscal consolidation should take priority over monetary tightening or not.

However, a substantive discussion on these issues is beyond the scope of this paper. Section II of the paper will discuss central bank policy actions at different stages of the crisis, followed by a discussion on the diversity in approaches pursued by central banks across major advanced and emerging economies. Section III will assess the effectiveness of these policy actions. Section IV will discuss issues pertaining to designing an appropriate exit strategy from extraordinary central bank actions. Section V will wind up the discussion with my conclusions.

The crisis and central bank actions

In the initial stages of the recent financial crisis, central banks in advanced countries faced difficult choices. Even as signs of stress appeared in the financial system in the second half of 2007, the problems were perceived to be limited to a few isolated markets and the main concern at the systemic level was about liquidity.

Few called into question the solvency of the financial system as a whole. Major central banks reacted to the ensuing financial stress by raising the scale of their liquidity providing operations, while seeking to bolster demand through conventional means, notably by adjusting policy interest rates. Central banks sterilised their liquidity provision to individual institutions through open market operations, altering primarily the composition, but not the size of their balance sheets (Figure 22.1).

Figure 22.1

Evolution of central bank assets and policy rates

US Federal Reserve

(Per cent of 2008 GDP)

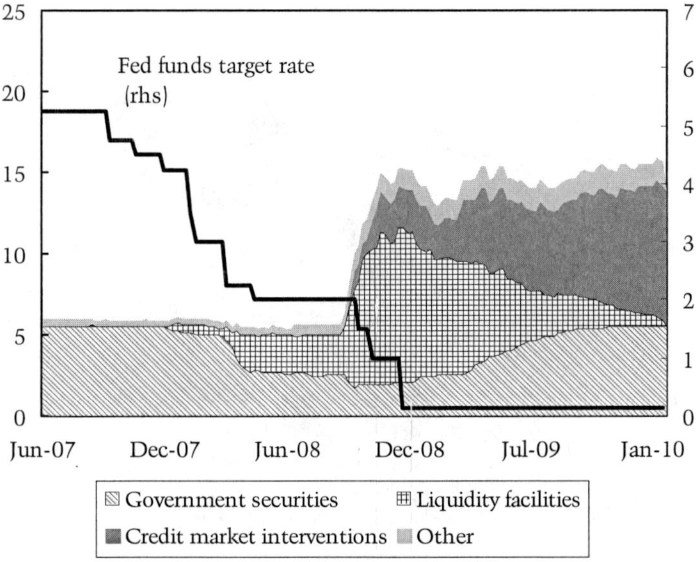

European Central Bank

(Per cent of 2008 GDP)

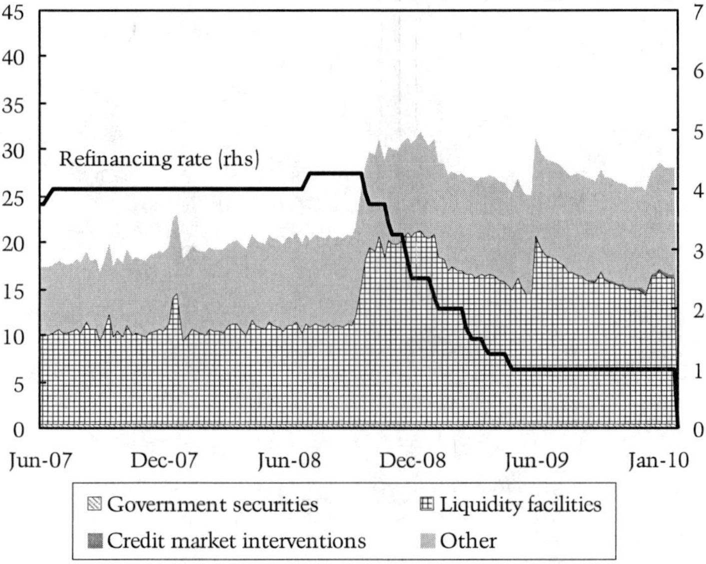

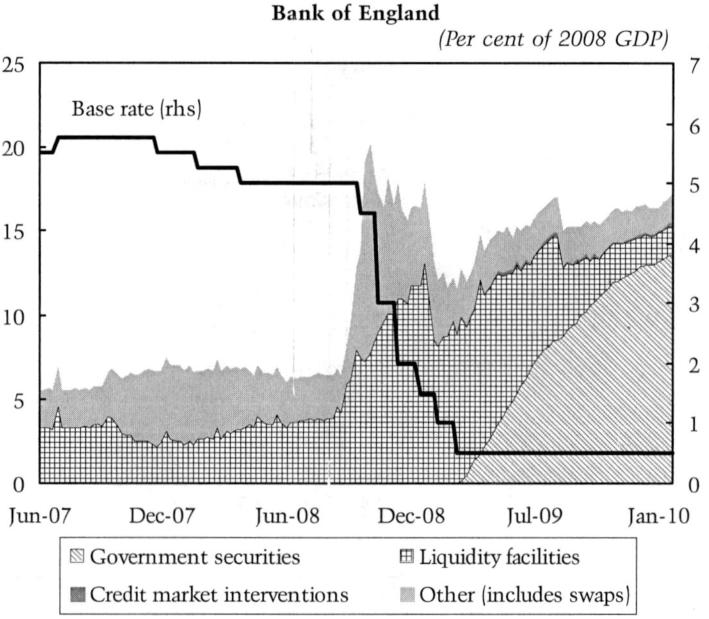

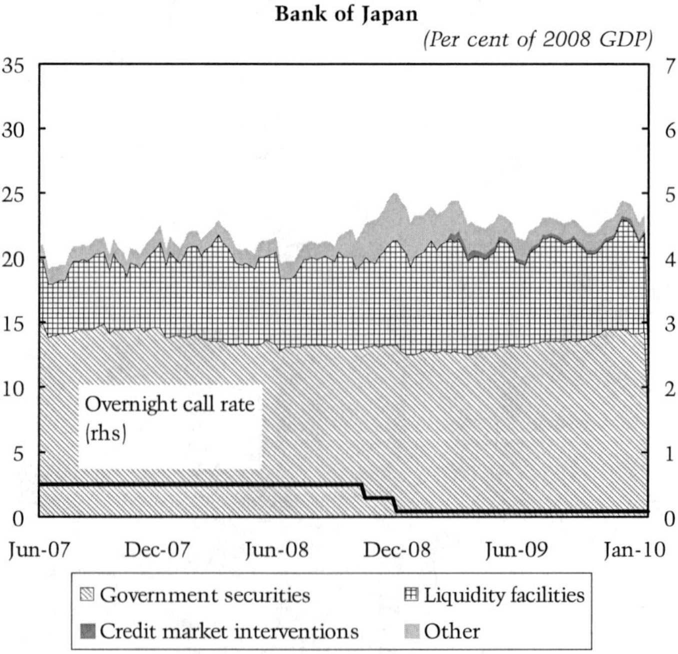

Sources: Haver Analytics and Bank of England.

Actions on the policy rate front diverged substantially during the first year of the crisis. This reflected the differences in central banks' assessment of relative risks to growth and inflation and the impact of the financial crisis on the cost and availability of credit. At one extreme, the US Federal Reserve (Fed) cut its policy rate quite aggressively[1] to offset the impact of elevated spreads on market rates. At the other extreme, the European Central Bank (ECB) raised its main refinancing rate ¼ percentage points in July 2008, because of concerns about rising inflation (Trichet, 2009b).

Central banks, however, quickly recognised the insufficiency of their traditional tools, in both dealing with the collapse of aggregate demand and the freezing of key credit markets, as the financial crisis intensified in September 2008. The size of the shock, the offsetting impact of a drop in inflation expectations on the real rates and the disruptions in the transmission mechanism from policy rates to private borrowing rates and the real economy were too big for the conventional tools. The sharp reduction of policy rates to close to effective lower bounds particularly proved insufficient in stimulating economies.

With the capital adequacy of systemically important financial institutions being called into question and wholesale funding markets under stress, commercial banks tightened their lending. At the same time, non-bank financing, particularly via private-label securitisation, virtually came to a halt. Access of households and businesses to credit was severely curtailed, while its cost ratcheted up.

Under these circumstances, policymakers undertook a number of decisive measures to stabilise financial markets and institutions and prevent a severe and prolonged contraction in real activity. Steps were taken to guarantee bank liabilities, recapitalise financial institutions and limit portfolio losses. Large fiscal stimulus packages were adopted to bolster aggregate demand. Central banks acted nimbly, decisively and creatively in

1. The target for the federal funds rate was reduced by 325 bps to 2 per cent between September 2007 and April 2008. Also, the spread between the primary discount window rate and the policy rate was cut to 25 bps from the usual 100 bps within this time period.

their response to the deepening of the crisis. They embarked on a number of unconventional policy measures, some of which had been tried before, while others were new.

Monetary stimulus when policy rates are at 'zero bound'

With policy rates close to the zero bound in key advanced economies, central banks provided additional monetary stimulus through several complementary means, all of which differed in their mechanics and underlying economics. They also had their respective advantages and drawbacks.

First, some central banks were explicitly committed to keeping policy rates low for an extended period. Amidst rapidly rising market perceptions of policy uncertainty, such action was aimed at anchoring market expectations that monetary stimulus would not be withdrawn until durable recovery took effect. Such a commitment was expected to keep inflation expectations from declining, which would, in turn, prevent a rise in real interest rates and bolster demand.

It was recognised that the effectiveness of such actions hinged on the credibility of the central banks and would have value only to the extent to which they restricted future options. If inflationary pressures were to rise earlier than expected, they could damage the credibility of the central bank, both reneging on the commitment and sticking to it when interest rate hikes were possibly needed.

Second, central banks across major advanced and emerging economies provided broad liquidity support to financial institutions. When concerns about counter-party credit risk was high as was uncertainty about an institution's own short-term financing needs and the value of assets that could be used as collateral along with the limited supply of high quality collateral, banks were both unable and unwilling to lend. They were even unwilling to lend to each other, beyond the shortest maturities.

Central banks aimed to alleviate these constraints by enhancing the scale and scope of their liquidity-providing operations. This included lending at longer maturities, broadening the quality of collateral and expanding the access of their operations to a wider set of financial institutions. Increasing bank reserves through central bank liquidity facilities could be implemented easily, as it relies on the ordinary channel of credit creation, does not expose the central bank to significant credit risk and reduces the risk of bank runs and, if appropriately designed, could be self-unwinding.

Central banks in major reserve currency countries facilitated foreign exchange funding. To cope with the significant constraints in the availability of cross-border foreign exchange funding, several central banks expanded access to their lender-of-last-resort facilities. For instance, the Fed entered into reciprocal currency swap arrangements with other central banks to increase the availability of dollar funding outside the United States. The ECB also signed similar agreements with the central banks of several European countries to improve the provision of Euro liquidity to their banking sectors.

Third, some central banks tried to reduce long-term interest rates across a wide range of financial assets, independent of their risk. To reduce the risk-free rate, central banks purchased longer term government securities. This was intended to reduce private borrowing rates, particularly when short-term policy rates were near their lower bound and commitment of keeping policy rates low was not effectively translating into lower long-term interest rates.

Because long-term treasuries serve as benchmarks for pricing a variety of private sector assets, it was expected that interest rates on privately issued securities and loans would also decline, as government bond yields decline. While there was merit in such action, there was a risk that central bank purchases of government securities may not have a significant impact on long-term yields, notably if they accounted for a small share of the government bond market. It was also perceived that even if treasury yields fell, they may not have much impact on private borrowing rates and credit market risk premiums, as heightened risk aversion reduces the substitutability between government and private assets.

Fourth, some central banks intervened directly in specific segments of the credit markets. This was led by purchasing private assets and by providing loans to financial institutions against private sector assets that were used as collateral. Credit market interventions involved direct support by the central bank in specific segments of credit markets that were experiencing dislocations.

Such intervention was aimed at alleviating illiquid trading conditions, reducing liquidity premiums and establishing benchmark prices. It was also aimed at encouraging origination in the targeted market, including through the purchase of commercial paper, corporate bonds and asset-backed securities. Credit market interventions can generally be useful not only at near-zero, but also at above-zero levels of the short-term nominal interest rate, if continued dislocations in the targeted markets are deemed to pose wider threats to the financial or credit system.

Some central banks were of the view that providing credit directly to end borrowers may be more effective than going through banks when banks' capacity and/or willingness to lend was impaired. Central banks were selective, targeting particularly important and distressed markets. Credit market interventions, however, exposed central banks to greater credit risk, although some risk-sharing mechanisms were included in these operations.

How did individual central bank actions differ?

Since the early days of the financial crisis, all major advanced and emerging country central banks took resolute steps to enhance the provision for liquidity to the financial system. Their initial reaction was to dramatically increase the size of liquidity operations, followed by steps to broaden the scope of current operations and the introduction of new ones to address specific stresses.

Central banks particularly extended the maturity of their lending operations to alleviate stress in term markets. They expanded the list of eligible collateral for repurchase operations[2] to help overcome market fragmentation and shortage of high-quality collateral triggered by a flight to quality. In the initial phase of the crisis, even as monetary authorities

2. The ECB—which had a large list of counter-parties for its liquidity facilities and the least restrictive collateral rules even before the crisis—was at the forefront of these efforts and made enhanced liquidity provision a linchpin of its approach to deal with the crisis.

sought to improve money market functioning, their liquidity-providing efforts were offset by liquidity-draining over the course of their respective maintenance periods, so that no significant net new base money was added to the financial system.

This approach had implications for the composition, but not the size of central bank balance sheets and had a flavour of a large scale lender-of-last-resort action.[3] However, after the intensification of the crisis in the fall of 2008, central banks accelerated policy rate reductions and began expanding their balance sheets to support credit more directly. Other than in the provision of liquidity, there was considerable diversity in approaches taken till date among the G7 central banks (Figure 22.1).

The Fed advanced far ahead in terms of intervening in impaired credit markets, having employed a variety of unconventional measures on a large scale. It has been purchasing government bonds as well as the debt and mortgage-backed securities (MBSs) issued by the US government-sponsored enterprises (GSEs) to bring down their yields and encourage investors to switch to riskier assets.

These actions were aimed at reducing long-term funding costs, especially residential mortgage rates. The Fed also set up facilities to support the commercial paper market by buying such paper directly from issuers or through money market mutual funds. Finally, through the term asset-backed securities lending facility (TALF), the Fed sought to enhance liquidity and jump-start the private sector securitisation market by providing funding and limiting the downside risk of investors in asset-backed securities.

Through its diverse tools, the Fed has not only provided ample resources for banks to lend, but also in some cases bypassed them to give credit directly to lenders and investors, or facilitated credit flows by making funding contingent on lending. In addition, the Fed has stated that the policy rate is likely to stay exceptionally low 'for an extended period'.

---

3. Central banks were also involved in more direct rescue operations for several large banks and other financial institutions.

The Bank of England (BoE) rivalled the Fed in the size of the balance sheet expansion, but its approach has been quite different.[4] Although it has put in place a programme for purchasing private sector securities to alleviate stress in particular markets, efforts to stimulate the economy are based largely on money creation through government bond purchases (Figure 22.2). In particular, the BoE was authorised by HM Treasury to purchase up to £150 billion of assets, including a maximum of £50 billion of private sector assets, financed through the issuance of central bank reserves.

Figure 22.2

*Outright holdings of securities by central banks**

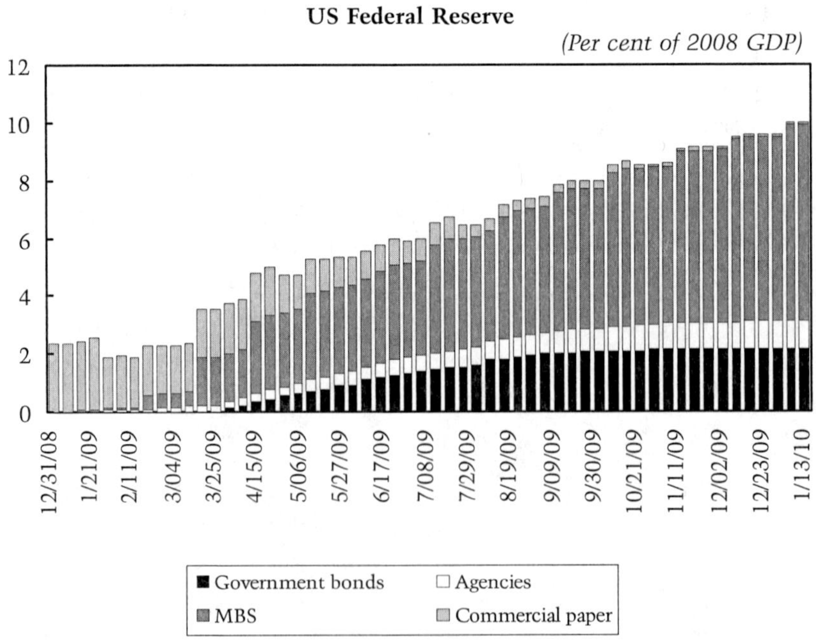

4. See Meier (2009) for an in-depth analysis of the BoE's unconventional policies.

Bank of England

(Per cent of 2008 GDP)

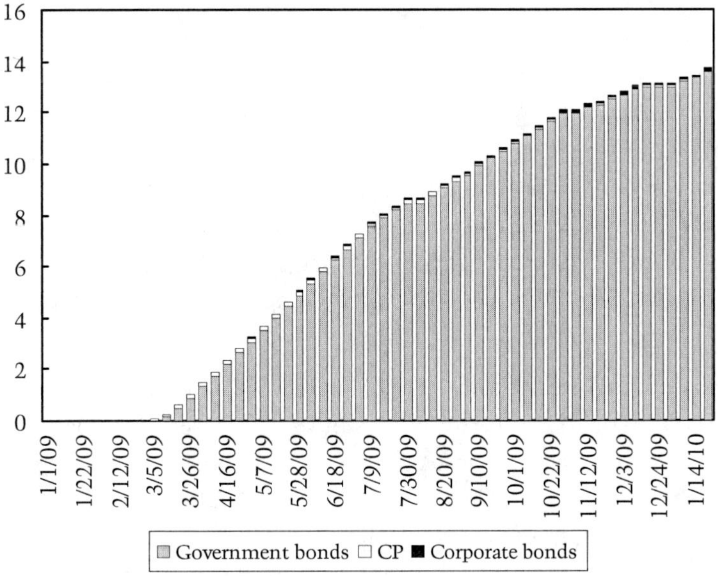

Bank of Japan

(Per cent of 2008 GDP)

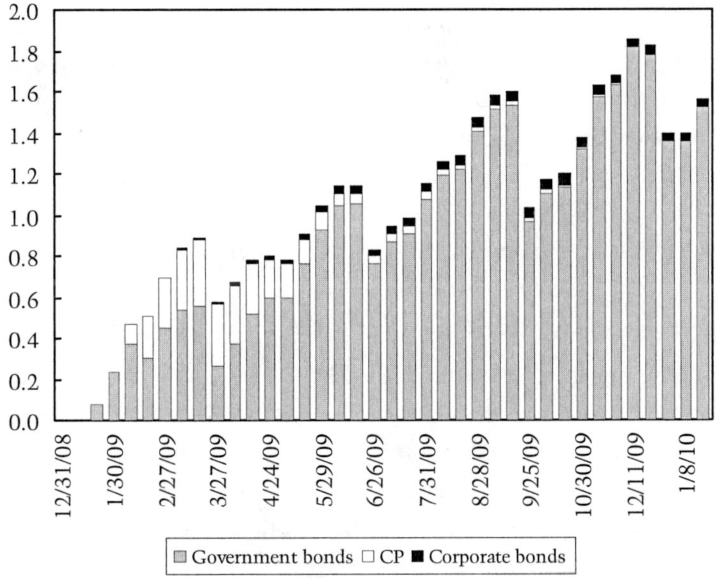

Note: * Government and agency bonds: change since end-2008.

Sources: Haver Analytics and Bank of England.

On that authority, the BoE announced a three-month asset purchase programme (APP) to purchase £75 billion worth of assets, mostly medium and long-term UK government notes and bonds (gilts). Subsequently, it extended the term and scaled up the target amount twice to around £175 billion. This amounted to 41 per cent of outstanding gilts in the relevant maturity range and nearly 80 per cent of planned debt issuance in the financial year 2009. The £50 billion credit easing component of the Bank's unconventional policy authorised the BoE to purchase a broad range of high-quality private assets, including commercial paper, corporate bonds, paper issued under the credit guarantee scheme (CGS), syndicated loans and asset-backed securities created in viable securitisation structures.

The Bank of Japan's (BoJ) approach is similar to that of the BoE, in that it has undertaken some purchases of private assets, but focused largely on money creation via purchases of government bonds. However, the scale of operations is much smaller. The BoJ has gradually scaled up the size of its outright purchases of government bonds from ¥1.2 trillion per month (the level set in October 2002) to ¥1.4 trillion in December 2008 and then to ¥1.8 trillion per month starting in March 2009.

At the latest rate, annual purchases would amount to only 2.5 per cent of the Fed's debt outstanding in early 2009—but close to 50 per cent of the net bond issuance projected for 2009, providing an important source of financing for the government. On the other hand, even at that pace, BoJ's bond purchases are not much larger than amortisation. In addition to increasing bank reserves through government bond purchases in a manner reminiscent of its policy of quantitative easing in the early 2000s, the BoJ has been purchasing private sector securities to alleviate stress in particular market segments. It has purchased high-grade commercial paper and corporate bonds with maturity of less than a year.

However, these operations are rather small. The BoJ's commercial paper holdings barely exceed 1 per cent of its balance sheet (compared to nearly 18 per cent at its peak for the Fed), and the limit on these holdings (¥3 trillion) is under 3 per cent of the BoJ balance sheet size and 16 per cent of Japan's commercial paper market. The Bank of Japan's corporate bond holdings are currently negligible and the limit is set at ¥1 trillion.

In addition, in October 2008, the bank suspended divestment of stocks it had acquired to support the economy in the early 2000s. Then in February 2009, it started purchasing stocks from Japanese financial institutions to help reduce their exposure to market risk. This programme is also limited to ¥1 trillion. To further enhance easy monetary conditions, the BoJ introduced a new funds supplying operation in December 2009.

The ECB has followed a strategy of 'enhanced credit support'. It has boosted its liquidity facilities and expanded its balance sheet considerably, but has not engaged in outright purchases of government paper. Till mid-2009, the ECB had not supported credit markets directly, but it greatly facilitated issuance of private securities and provision of certain types of loans by accepting them as collateral in its refinancing operations.

It has gone the furthest among major central banks in expanding the range of acceptable collateral and the term of its liquidity providing operations.[5] It auctioned off an unprecedented €442 billion of 1-year funds at 1 per cent in late June and another €75 billion in late September. Finally, to support the housing market, the ECB has initiated a €60 billion programme to buy covered bonds over the course of 12 months, with purchases starting in July 2009.

The Bank of Canada (BoC) is the only major central bank besides the Fed to have committed itself to maintaining low policy rates till there are clear signs of recovery. Moreover, it has made a 'conditional commitment' to keep the interest rate at its effective low bound of 25 basis points till the end of the second quarter of 2010, pioneering the communication of a specific end date for this type of guidance. While expanding its liquidity operations, the BoC has taken very limited steps in the other areas, but it pre-emptively put together a framework for quantitative and credit easing and indicated that it is prepared to use such instruments, if needed to achieve its inflation objective.

Crisis intervention measures of central banks in emerging economies differed from those of advanced economies in timing, focus and magnitude. In particular, most of the intervention measures were put in place after the

5. Even before the crisis, the ECB accepted a broader range of collateral, including commercial bank loans, other than major central banks' currency liabilities.

crisis intensified in September 2008, and focused largely on the provision of foreign exchange liquidity and cuts in policy rates. Moreover, the magnitude of intervention measures were smaller, reflecting the significantly less stress experienced by the financial sectors in emerging economies, compared to those in the major advanced economies. It also reflected a concern that excessive monetary easing may exacerbate pressure on the currencies of these countries.

Emerging market central banks (EMCBs) eased the terms of existing foreign exchange liquidity facilities and introduced some new ones. This included maturity extension of foreign exchange swaps and introduction of new facilities providing foreign exchange repos, loans or swaps. In some cases, access to these facilities was widened to include non-bank financial institutions and key non-financial institutions. Many EMCBs opened foreign exchange selling auctions and relaxed foreign exchange liquidity or borrowing limits, apart from lowering the required reserve ratios for foreign currency liabilities of banks.

To support their foreign liquidity operations, a number of EMCBs entered into currency swap arrangements with reserve currency central banks. Some EMCBs acted indirectly to alleviate credit strains, by guiding banks to use the liquidity freed by lower reserves requirements for lending to the private sector, for instance.

What explains the divergence in central bank actions

What can account for the considerable difference and the unconventional approaches of the central banks? Central banks found themselves grappling with a global financial crisis, near-simultaneous bursting of several asset-price bubbles, breakdown of securitisation, collapse of confidence and a synchronised recession.

Faced with an arguably unprecedented set of issues, they had to explore measures tailored specifically for their country circumstances. They, moreover, had little support from economic theory or prior experience. So, understandably, they came up with somewhat different solutions. There also seems to be a conceptual disagreement on the usefulness of providing explicit guidance on the future path of interest rates.

Largely, however, the differences in responses can be attributed to the differences—real or perceived—in the countries' circumstances. Such circumstances include the depth and timing of recessions or slowdowns in individual countries, the relative roles played by banks and capital markets in credit allocation, the severity of the problems in the financial system, the flexibility of pre-existing institutional arrangements, political environments and structures and actions taken by non-monetary authorities.

Particularly in the early stages of the crisis, the ECB seemed to be relatively more optimistic about the economic outlook. Consequently, it focused on liquidity support for struggling banks much more than on stimulating demand through rate cuts or quantitative easing. Moreover, since the non-financial private sector in Europe relies much more on the banking system for credit than on securities markets (Figure 22.3), the authorities' efforts appropriately focused on ensuring that banks are strong and have adequate resources to lend.

Even in the United Kingdom, outstanding corporate bonds of domestic non-financial issuers total about £15 billion, with another £7 billion in commercial paper, so even the fairly small allocation for private assets under the APP amounted to a non-negligible share of these markets.[6] Moreover, with a broad access to its lending window to begin with, there was less need for the ECB to introduce new facilities.

Canada has been one of the few countries whose financial system was not damaged severely by the financial crisis. As a result, the Bank of Canada could, for a considerable length of time, afford to rely largely on conventional measures to support the economy in the face of external shocks. However, when global economic prospects weakened significantly in 2008 and risk aversion rose, Canadian banks tightened credit conditions.

With no room for interest rate cuts, the BoC sought to guide interest rate expectations and put in place a framework for quantitative credit easing. In a similar vein, although Japan's financial institutions were not highly exposed to US toxic assets, their losses on stock holdings and expected rise in delinquencies made them reluctant to lend, prompting the BoJ to initiate some limited credit easing measures.

6. However, the market is much larger if financial issuers and foreign corporations issuing sterling debt are included.

Figure 22.3

*Sources of financing for corporations**

(Per cent, average 2004-2008)

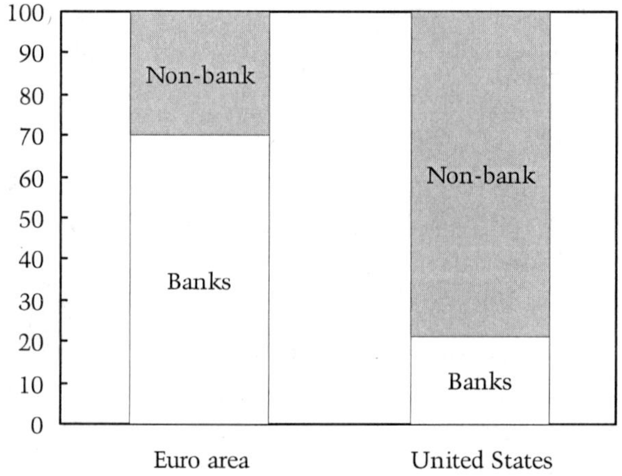

Note: * Breakdown of the sources of external financing of non-financial corporations.
Source: ECB Monthly Bulletin, April 2009.

Finally, the actions of the legislative and executive branches of government shape the environment in which central banks and financial systems operate. G7 countries have taken numerous actions to support financial institutions. Guarantees of bank debt and deposits decreased bank reliance on wholesale funding such as through commercial paper and repurchase agreements.

In some countries, governments have taken a leading role in providing support to credit markets, thereby reducing the need for central bank operations. For example, in Canada the government has been purchasing insured mortgage pools from financial institutions, as well as term asset-backed securities (ABS). In the UK, the government is leading the effort to restart residential mortgage securitisation through its guarantee programme and the Development Bank of Japan (DBJ) has started outright purchases of commercial paper.

It should be noted that while all central banks pledged prudence in their credit easing operations, there is considerable differentiation in their exposure to credit risk. The Fed has accumulated the largest portfolio of risky private sector securities among the major central banks, with the understanding, initially implicit, but later partly formalised in the setup of the CPFF and TALF and in a joint Fed–Treasury statement, that ultimately the Fed's losses, if any, will be borne by the government.[7]

In the UK, the government authorised asset purchases by the BoE in a formal exchange of letters between the Governor and the Chancellor. The Bank is explicitly indemnified by the Treasury from any losses arising from these purchases. The supranational nature of the ECB may have contributed to its reluctance to buy assets.

Effectiveness of central bank actions

Taken collectively, policy actions, notably by major advanced country central banks, contributed to the reduction in systemic tail-risks following the bankruptcy of Lehman Brothers and to improvements in market confidence and risk appetite. However, financial indicators suggest that some policies are proving to be more successful than others.

Gauging the effectiveness of central bank measures is difficult because transmission to the economy is complex and opaque. A number of factors influence market conditions and the impact of individual policies is difficult to isolate, especially from the impact of fiscal and non-central bank financial policy actions taken over the crisis period. Moreover, it is difficult to determine what would have happened had central banks not taken action, especially given the relatively low level of market confidence that prevailed with the onset of the crisis.

This analysis focuses on the observable effects of central bank interventions on credit conditions, especially on credit market interest rates, spreads and volumes. It reviews the various transmission channels of policy—broad credit, bank lending, and interest rates, as well as the impact of policies on specifically targeted markets. Central bank actions have helped reduce tail-risks and financial conditions have improved, but the bank lending channel remains strained.

---

7. The Fed is protected against losses by its focus on purchasing highly rated securities, over-collateralisation and the government's support for the GSEs.

Forceful monetary easing and virtually unlimited offers of liquidity by major central banks have helped reduce the extreme financial stress and tightness in financial conditions that prevailed after the bankruptcy of Lehman Brothers. Moreover, some authorities, like the Fed and Swiss National Bank (SNB), directly participated in the rescue efforts for specific large, highly interconnected financial institutions.[8]

As a result, the International Monetary Fund's (IMF) financial stress indices (FSIs, Figure 22.4)[9] for the major advanced economies have declined, with some falling below their pre-crisis levels. Central bank efforts have helped reduce the systemic tail-risks, including the potential for cascading insolvencies in the financial sector.

Figure 22.4

Financial stress indicators

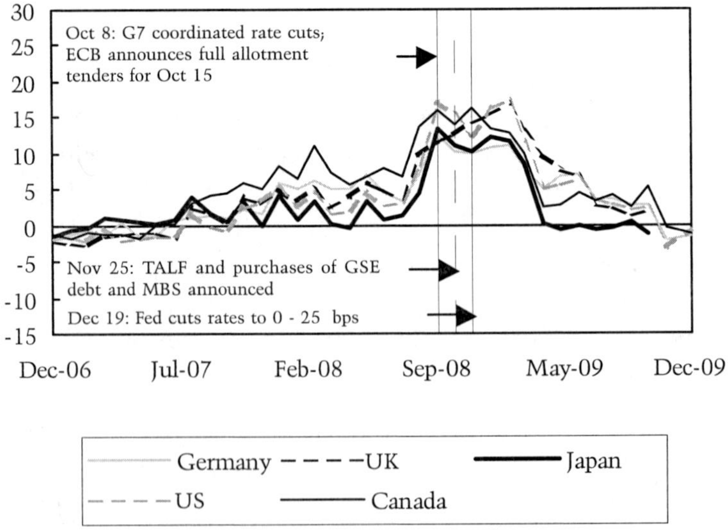

Source: IMF Staff.

8. The BoJ also stands ready to purchase equity holdings and subordinated debt of major Japanese banks.
9. The FSIs consist of seven financial market variables, including the beta of banking stocks, the TED spread, the slope of the yield curve, corporate bond spreads, stock market returns, stock market volatility, and exchange rate volatility (Balakrishnan *et al.*, 2009).

Broad measures of financial conditions (Figure 22.5) have also improved, partly due to the significant drop in real short-term rates. However, conditions remain tight relative to their pre-crisis levels, especially for some regions where higher real effective exchange rates and lower equity market capitalisation (in Europe and Japan) have offset the decline in interest rates.

Figure 22.5

*Financial conditions indices**

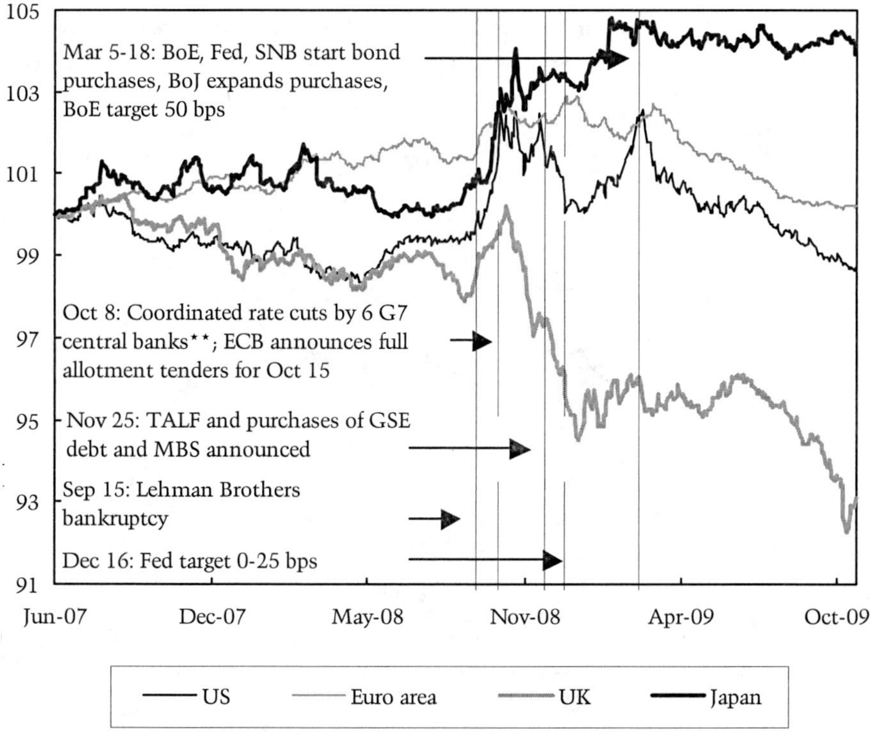

Note: * The indices combine real three-month and long-term interest rates, the real exchange rate, and equity market capitalisation to GDP.

** Bank of Canada, Bank of England, ECB, Federal Reserve, Riksbank, SNB cut rates by 50 bps with strong support by Bank of Japan. The ECB rescinded the rate cut and instead announced full allotment tenders at main refinancing rate.

Sources: Goldman Sachs and IMF Staff.

Despite the tremendous infusion of liquidity by central banks and the capital and guarantees provided by other agencies, the bank lending channel remains strained. Central banks have a more limited role in meeting the potential capital needs of banks and strengthening their capacity for new lending. Although many mature market banks have increased their capital adequacy via public and private capital raising, these efforts seem to have primarily stabilised the banking system. Not enough capital has been raised, though, to adequately support lending and economic recovery.[10]

Bank lending to the private non-financial sector remains restrained across major advanced economies (Figures 22.6 and 22.7). Still, were it not for official interventions, credit flows would probably have fallen much more and beyond comparison with any other post-war recession—given the magnitude of the shock. Surveys from the ECB and the Fed indicate that

Figure 22.6

Bank credit to the private non-financial sector

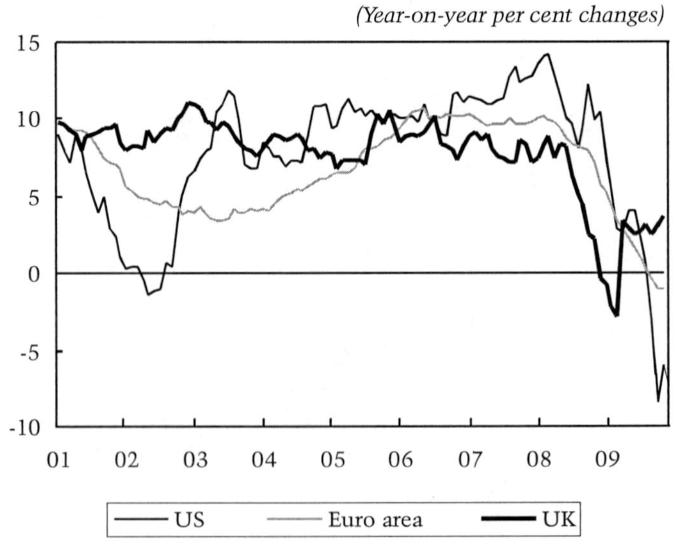

Source: Haver Analytics.

10. The October 2009 Global Financial Stability Report (GFSR) by IMF explains (p. 27) how the lending capacity of banks in the Euro area, the United Kingdom and the United States is projected to decline in both 2009 and 2010, contributing to a potential *ex ante* gap between total non-financial borrowing needs and the total capacity of the system to provide credit.

Figure 22.7

Total credit to the private non-financial sector

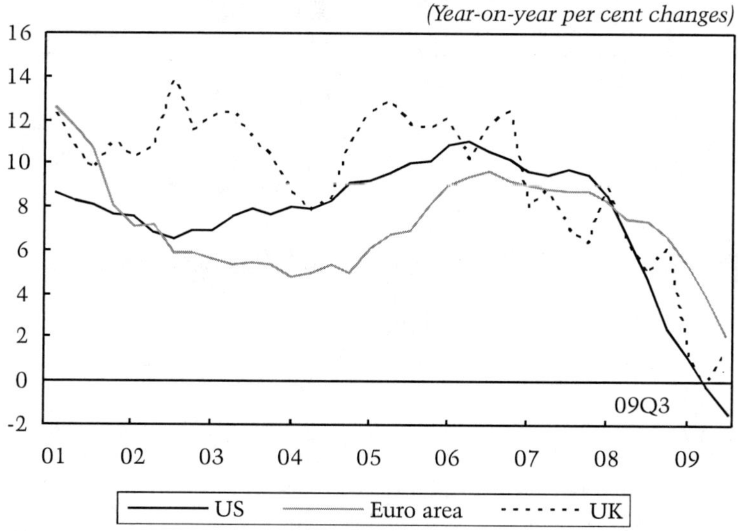

Source: Haver Analytics.

Figure 22.8

Bank lending surveys: Corporate loans

(Net survey balances; in per cent; positive responses denote tightening)

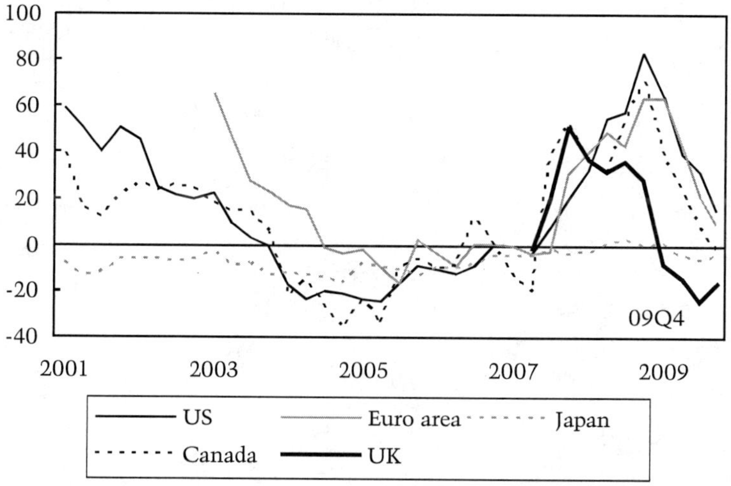

Source: Haver Analytics.

Figure 22.9

Bank lending surveys: Loans to households
(Net survey balances; in per cent; positive responses denote tightening)

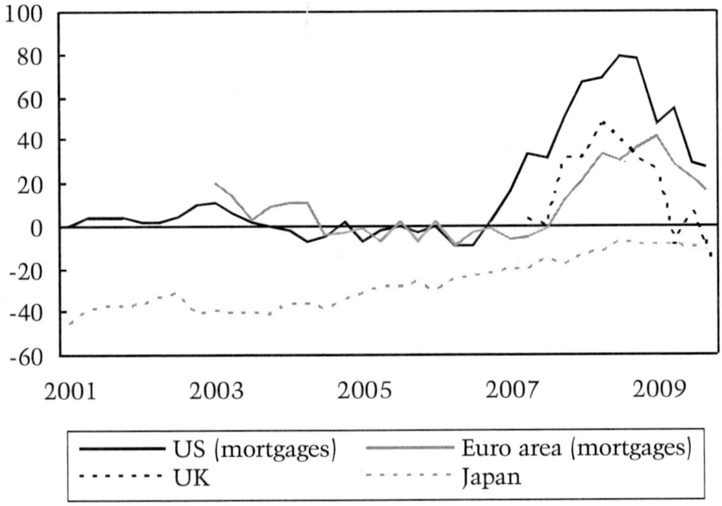

Source: Haver Analytics.

banks are still tightening lending standards to households and non-financial firms, *albeit* not as vigorously as at the peak of the crisis (Figures 22.8 and 22.9). In the United Kingdom, standards for corporate lending loosened slightly in 2009, but remain tight nonetheless.

Compared to these swings, lending standards in Japan have largely remained on the pre-crisis trajectory of moderate loosening, with standards for large corporations reaching the neutral point.

Funding strains are easing, but the money market complex is contracting

Central banks have eventually been successful in reducing term premiums in money market rates and increasing the availability of short-term financing. The record low levels of target policy rates and generous liquidity providing operations have contributed to the steep reductions in London interbank offered rate (LIBOR), repurchase and commercial paper (CP) rates and their risk premiums, as well as a narrowing in foreign exchange swap basis. Reflecting this reduction in liquidity risk, use of central bank liquidity facilities have generally been falling lately (Figure 22.10).

Figure 22.10

Fed liquidity facilities

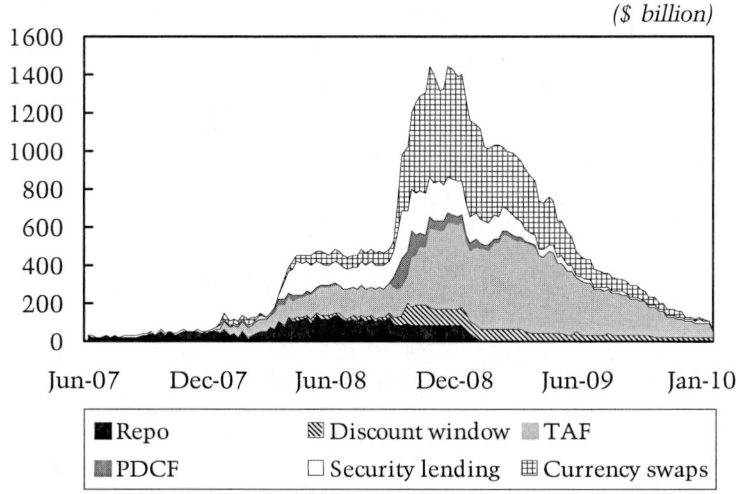

Source: Haver Analytics.

The LIBOR rates of maturities of three months or more have dropped across a number of currencies, and so have their spreads over implied overnight rates derived from overnight index swaps (OIS) (Figure 22.11). This not only means lower bank funding costs, but a decline in key indices used in setting the interest rates on a host of loans to non-financial actors and fixed income and derivative products.

However, LIBOR-OIS spreads still remain wider than their pre-crisis levels, partly reflecting the limits of central bank liquidity operations. The operations seem to have reduced liquidity risk premiums, but have had less of an impact on counter-party credit risk premiums as reflected in a greater

Figure 22.11

Three-month LIBOR-OIS spreads

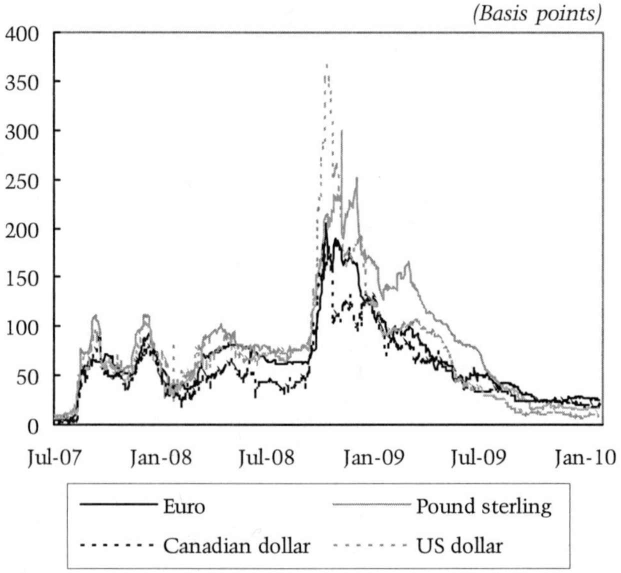

Source: Bloomberg L.P.

Figure 22.12

*US credit and liquidity strains**

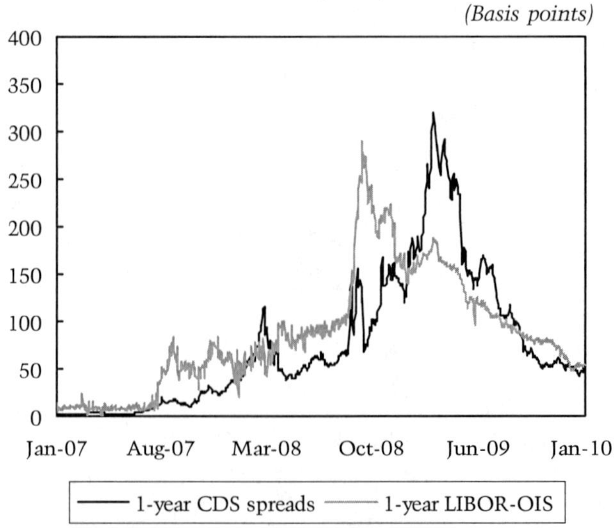

Note: * Spreads are for participating banks that fix USD LIBOR rates.
Sources: Datastream and Bloomberg L.P.

decline in LIBOR–OIS spreads than in bank CDS spreads (Figures 22.12 and 22.13).[11]

Figure 22.13

*EU credit and liquidity strains**

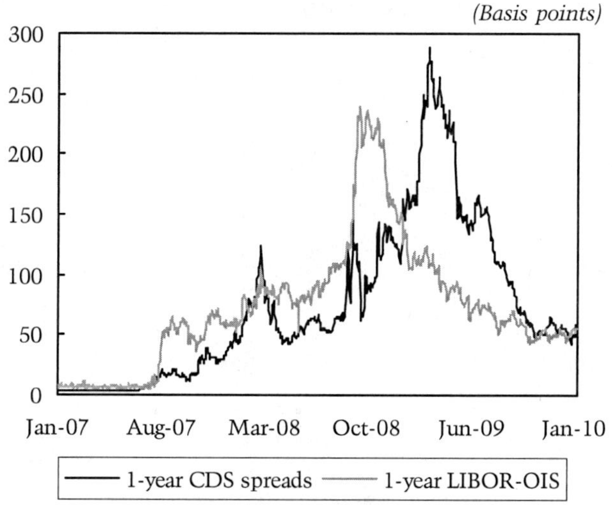

Note:* Spreads are for participating banks that fix Euro LIBOR rates.
Sources: Datastream and Bloomberg L.P.

Credit risk premiums remain high as markets still perceive banks to be vulnerable to risks from unresolved troubled asset issues and headwinds from rising unemployment. Moreover, higher premiums may also reflect a longer-lasting increase in the price of credit risk embedded in uncollateralised money market rates. The TAF[12] and currency swap

11. The LIBOR-OIS spreads can be decomposed to estimate what can be attributed to counter-party credit risk and other risks, including liquidity risk.

12. Some studies have empirically tested the effectiveness of the TAF in reducing the dollar LIBOR-OIS spread. An early study by Taylor and Williams (2009) concluded that it was not effective, but other studies by Sack and Meyer (2008) and McAndrews, Sarkar, and Wang (2008) refute that conclusion. A fourth study by Hooper and Slock (2009) concluded that the announcement effect of the TAF was the most important, whereas the TSLF was not significant in narrowing the LIBOR-OIS spread.

arrangements between the Fed and 14 central banks have helped enhance the functioning of the foreign exchange swap and forward markets. These markets, especially those without access to Fed liquidity, had become dislocated as financial institutions and attempted to garner their short-term dollar funding from other sources. At the height of the crisis, dollar funding rates implied by three-month euro and sterling forward contracts were 6.6 per cent and 7.4 per cent, respectively. By January 2010, these rates had fallen to below one per cent (Figure 22.14).

Figure 22.14

*FX forward implied US dollar funding rates**

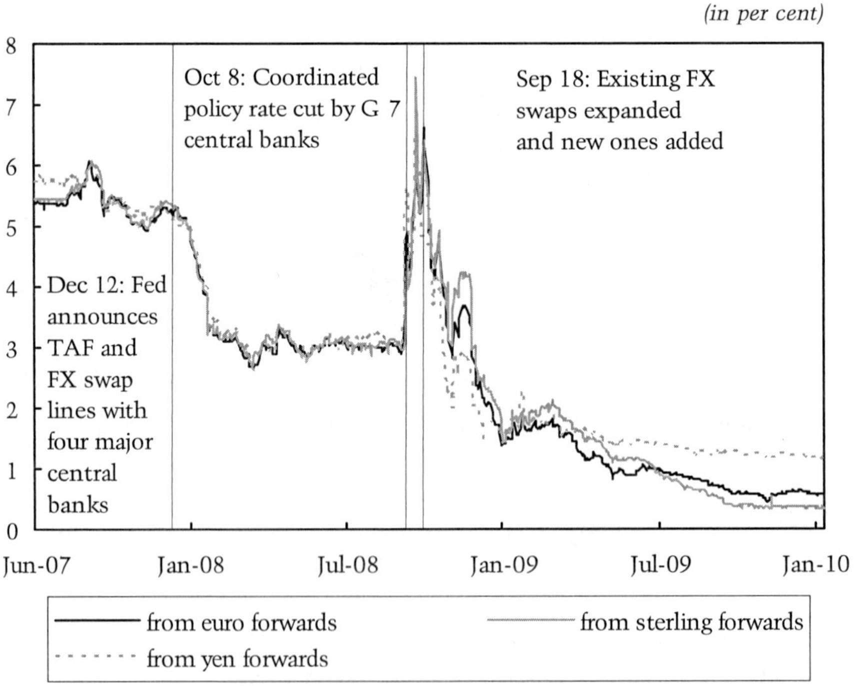

Note: * three-month US dollar funding implied by FX forward and LIBOR rates.

Sources: IMF staff calculations and Bloooomberg L.P.

Commercial paper rates have fallen in advanced economies, driven partly by direct purchases and liquidity operations by the Fed, BoE and BoJ targeted at short-term corporate financing. Both the highest and the lower tiers of CP rates are down,[13] although for several months following the introduction of intervention measures, there was a wide positive spread between the higher and the lower tiers (Figure 22.15).

Figure 22.15

US commercial paper spreads over treasury bill

(in per cent)

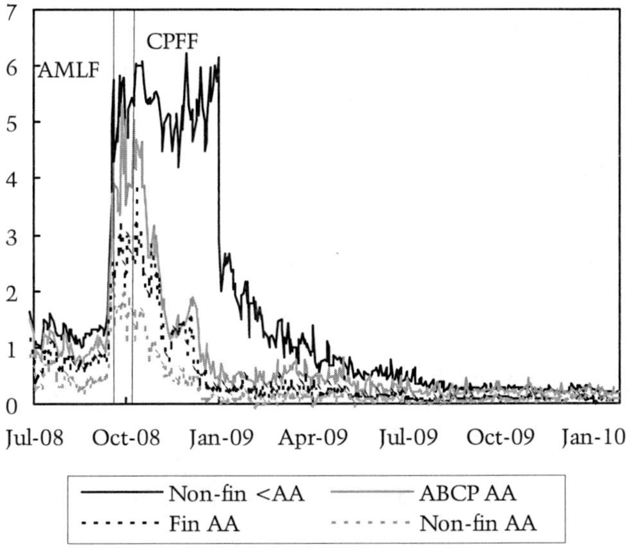

Source: Haver Analytics.

In the United States, the amount of CP outstanding has been contracting, notwithstanding temporary increases following the announcements of the asset-backed commercial paper money market fund liquidity facility (AMLF) and the commercial paper funding facility (CPFF) (Figure 22.16). This largely reflects a fall in demand for CP funding since banks have alternative funding sources via government guaranteed debt, to a lesser extent non-guaranteed note issuance and increased deposits.

At the same time, it should be noted that the Fed's facilities buttressed the CP market at the crucial time, allowing a reduction in rate and

13. In the United States, second-tier CP volumes have fallen substantially, so the decline in rates may partly reflect a survivorship bias, although the drop in broad liquidity concerns is probably a more important factor.

extension of maturities and supporting the volume. Term repurchase (repo) rates have declined in G7 countries partly owing to central bank operations to aid the functioning of the repo markets, such as the BoE's special liquidity scheme (SLS) and the Fed's term securities lending facility (TSLF). These and other central banks, particularly the ECB, freed up some of the high-quality collateral that financial institutions could use as collateral by accepting a wider range of assets to pledge at central bank auctions.

Figure 22.16

US commercial paper outstanding

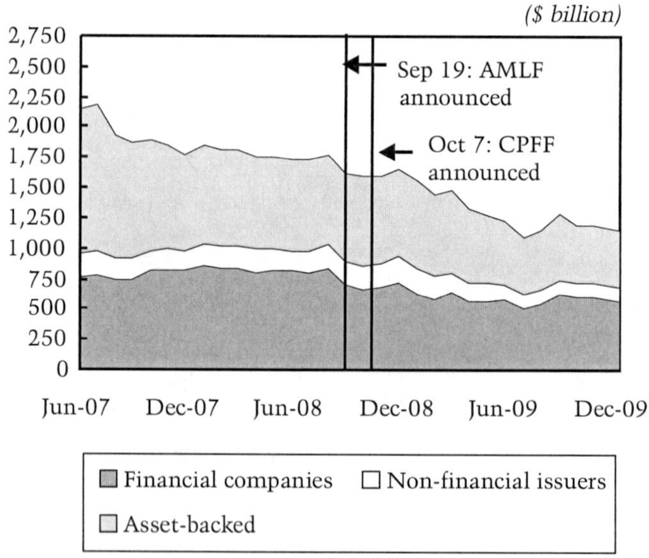

Source: Haver Analytics.

There had been a scarcity of high-quality collateral as demand for safe haven assets rose and counter-parties no longer accepted non-traditional collateral for repos during most of the crisis. Despite lower repo rates, volumes have fallen over the crisis as the number of dealers have declined and the activity of securities lenders and some other money market investors has been curtailed.

Despite the reduction in money market rates and risk premiums, the progress on money market volumes are mixed, with some segments still experiencing significant drops in outstanding amounts. The shock to the money market complex during the crisis has led to a potentially long-lasting repricing of credit risk in money market rates, the exit and significant reduction in the activity of a number of money market players and a likely tightening of regulations governing bank liquidity management and money market mutual fund investments.

In addition, ongoing deleveraging efforts by financial firms are likely to lead to a reduced demand for funding and the very low levels of money market rates are leading to early signs of reduced demand for money market investments. All of these factors have led to broad-based shrinkage in money market activity and capacity, some of which is likely to persist for a long period of time.

Central banks' efforts to reduce longer term rates having mixed results

Central bank operations directed at longer term fixed income markets, including those supporting securitisation markets, have had mixed results, with some programmes more successful at lowering rates or significantly affecting origination than others. Yields on government bonds have increased over the last several months despite sizeable purchases by some major central banks.

The spreads between private asset yields and treasuries have declined both in the markets with major central bank support, such as the US conforming mortgage market and in those with much more limited support, such as corporate bonds. This suggests that the compression in a wide variety of credit spreads since the first quarter of 2009 may be partially attributed to the broad-based fall in investor risk aversion, rather than to any particular policy interventions—although it may well be the totality of the interventions that has created a more favourable climate.

Improving views about the global economic outlook, reduced concerns about deflation, and some anxiety about increased government supply to finance anti-crisis efforts are counteracting the yield impact of quantitative easing by the Fed, BoE, and BoJ. As a result, despite a noticeable drop in intermediate-dated yields on US and UK government bonds immediately after the announcement of large bond purchase programmes by the respective central banks (Figure 22.17), most global yields are much higher than their post-announcement levels.

Figure 22.17

10-year government bond yields in the US, UK, Germany and Japan

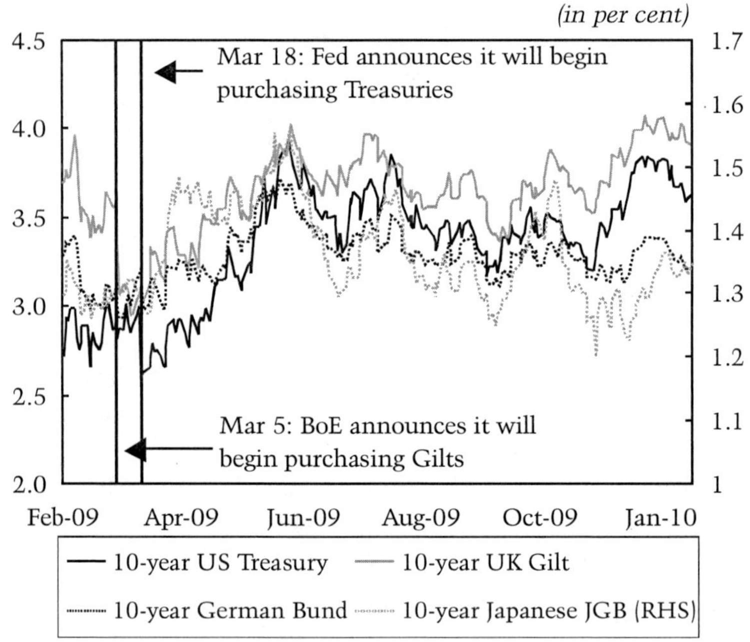

Source: Bloomberg L.P.

Particularly between the announcement date on March 18 and January 25, 2010 10-year US Treasury yields have risen by about 109 basis points (bps). In contrast, Japanese government bond (JGB) and UK gilt yields moved by much less since the BoJ and BoE first made announcements of their outright purchases of government bonds during the crisis,[14] although 5-year gilts increased 47 bps since March 4, 2009 due in part, to the BoE's announcement that it would suspend its purchases of 5-year and 12-year bonds as of late June.

14. The BoJ announced the first increase in its JGB purchases on December 19, 2008 and the BoE announced its asset purchase facility on March 5, 2009.

In Germany and Canada, whose central banks have not engaged in purchases of government bonds, 10-year yields rose about 20 and 40 bps, respectively, between the ECB's and BoC's March monetary policy meetings and January 25, 2010. Interestingly, augmented liquidity provision may have an impact on government bond yields. Cihak *et al.* (2009) estimate a yield curve model for the Euro area and find that in the recent period the actual spread between long-term and short-term interest rates has been lower than predicted—even though the ECB is not buying government bonds.

They attribute the deviation to the enhanced credit support provided by the ECB, although other explanations cannot be ruled out. The Fed's purchases of the MBSs and direct obligation of the US-GSEs seem to have had their intended effect. Most notably, the spreads of both the 30-year fixed rate mortgage and MBS to 10-year Treasuries have declined progressively since the APP was first announced in November 2008.

Figure 22.18

Effects of Fed MBS Purchases

(Spread to 10-year US Treasury; in basis points)

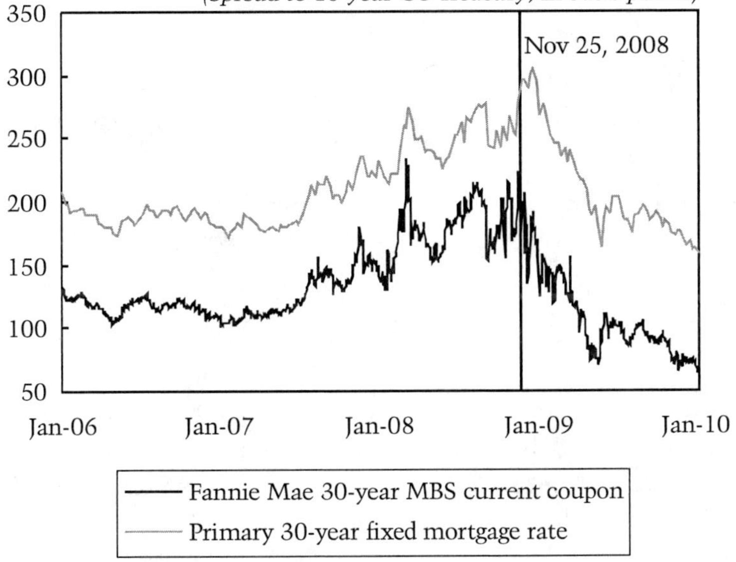

Sources: Merrill Lynch; Freddie Mac, Primary Mortgage Market Survey; Bloomberg L.P.; Board of Governors of the Federal Reserve System; and Haver Analytics.

Similarly, the prepayment option-adjusted spread to Treasuries has narrowed by 75 bps over the same period. At the height of the financial crisis and as the housing market became distressed, the spread increased to 150-175 bps. Currently, the nominal spread between agency MBS and Treasuries is around 60 bps, compared to 100 bps historically (Figure 22.18). On net, both 30-year agency conforming mortgage rates and those on non-conforming jumbo loans remain below the levels observed before the Fed announced its purchase programme and those on jumbo yields have declined more (Figure 22.19).

Figure 22.19

US mortgage rates

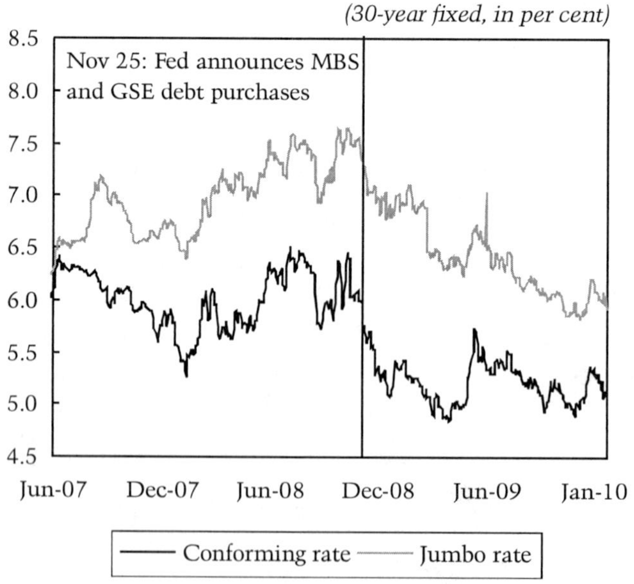

Source: Bloomberg L.P.

Additionally, there was a large jump in refinancing as conforming mortgage rates fell below five per cent, but this activity has slowed. Moreover, since November 2008, there has been very little private buying interest in agency MBS, leaving the Fed to purchase a significant share of new issuance (Figure 22.20). The corporate bond purchases by the BoE and BoJ have been small relative to the size of their balance sheets and the size of the overall markets. The BoE uses its programme primarily as a backstop to potential dislocations in the UK corporate bond market.

Figure 22.20

US agency MBS: Issuance and official purchases

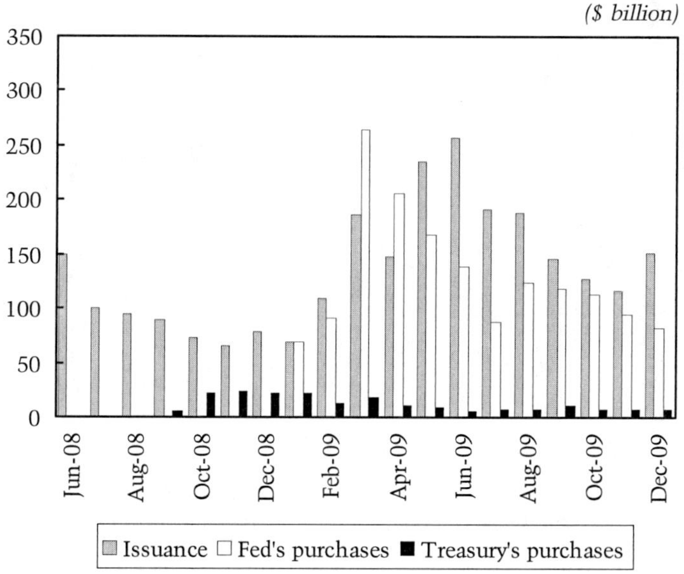

Sources: US Federal Reserve, US Treasury, and SIFMA.

Despite the small amounts purchased, the BoE's programme has contributed to the narrowing of UK corporate bond spreads on the margin. The main reason for tightening corporate credit spreads is the broader investor interest in corporate bonds globally. Given these improvements in bond market conditions, the BoE's purchases have begun to slow.

Market participants suggest that the corporate bond portion of the asset purchase programme may no longer be necessary. Greater support for other private credit markets may still be warranted, though. The BoJ focuses its purchases on bonds with up to one-year maturity. They are part of the BoJ's efforts to enhance corporate funding conditions and are not geared toward lowering long-term corporate bond yields or credit premiums.

Resuscitating securitisation markets through the Fed's TALF is proving to be challenging. Secondary market spreads on highly rated consumer ABS and commercial MBS (CMBS), and to a lesser extent mortgage-related ABS, have narrowed considerably since the announcement of the TALF and the eligibility of CMBS for TALF funding (Figure 22.21).

Figure 22.21

*AAA-rated US asset-backed securities**

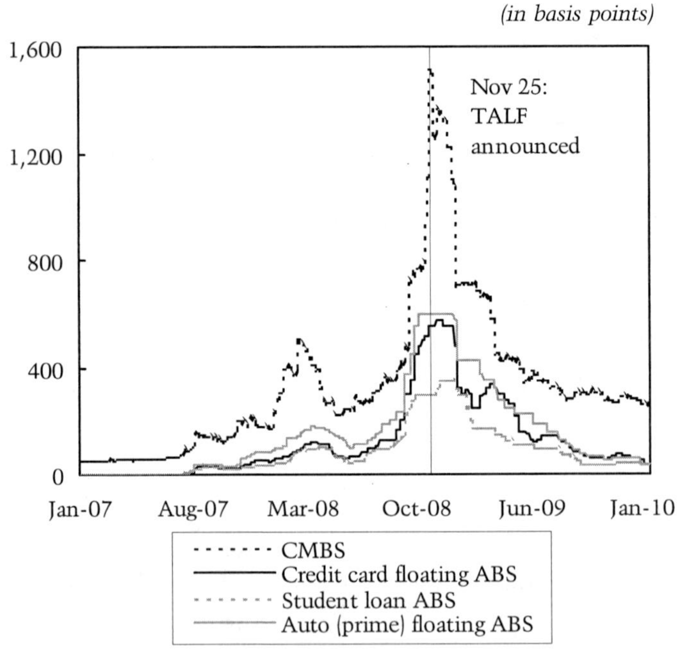

Note: * Spread to one-month LIBOR for credit card, auto, home equities, and student loan three-year ABS. Spread to synthetic three-year Treasury for three-year CMBS.

Source: J.P. Morgan.

However, the capacity of traditional buyers of consumer ABS and CMBS has diminished over the crisis and the Fed is enticing remaining players into this space with very high expected returns on their capital. The Fed's efforts have helped new issuance of consumer ABS to normalise (Figure 22.22). New CMBS issuance, however, remains virtually non-existent (Figure 22.23). TALF funding for CMBS has been used primarily for purchasing legacy CMBS instead of newly originated securities.

Figure 22.22

*Gross issuance of US consumer ABS**

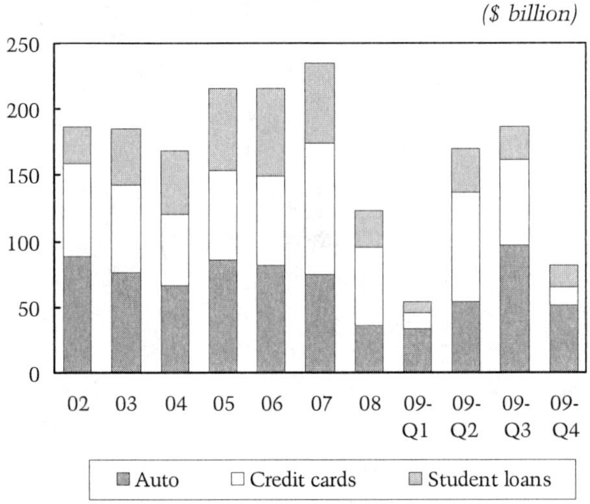

Note: * 2009 quarterly numbers are given at an annual rate.

Source: SIFMA.

Figure 22.23

*Annual change in outstanding stock of US ABS securities**

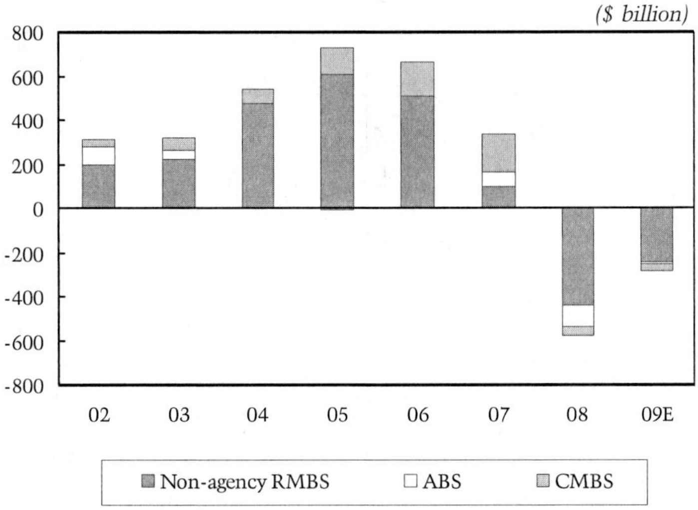

Note: * ABS include autos, student loans, and credit cards. CMBS reflect conduit issuance. RMBS include subprime, Alt-A, and prime. 2009 estimate uses 2009Q3 figures *vs* 2008Q4 for RMBS and ABS to calculate the annual change.

Sources: Thomson Financial, Bloomberg, SIFMA, Loan Performance, Trepp, and J.P. Morgan.

Securitisation markets also remain under pressure in Europe, despite the wider collateral accepted and longer terms offered by the ECB's and BoE's liquidity operations. The UK's official programme to guarantee new issuance of securitised products is run by H.M. Treasury. Secondary market spreads in UK and European ABS and residential MBS markets remained on an upward trend until the first half of 2009 amid concerns about credit deterioration in their underlying collateral.

Spreads only started to improve significantly after the ECB extended the term of its fixed rate, full allotment liquidity operations to one year (Figure 22.24), and the origination of privately distributed ABS has been limited. Total primary issuance volumes did not materially decline in 2008 and 2009, reflecting the significant amount of new issues retained by the issuer as collateral for central bank funding (Figure 22.25). For all of 2008, market participants estimate that 98 per cent of new issues were retained by issuers. However, more recently some banks have begun to issue privately distributed ABS.

Figure 22.24

European AAA asset-backed securities spreads

(Basis points)

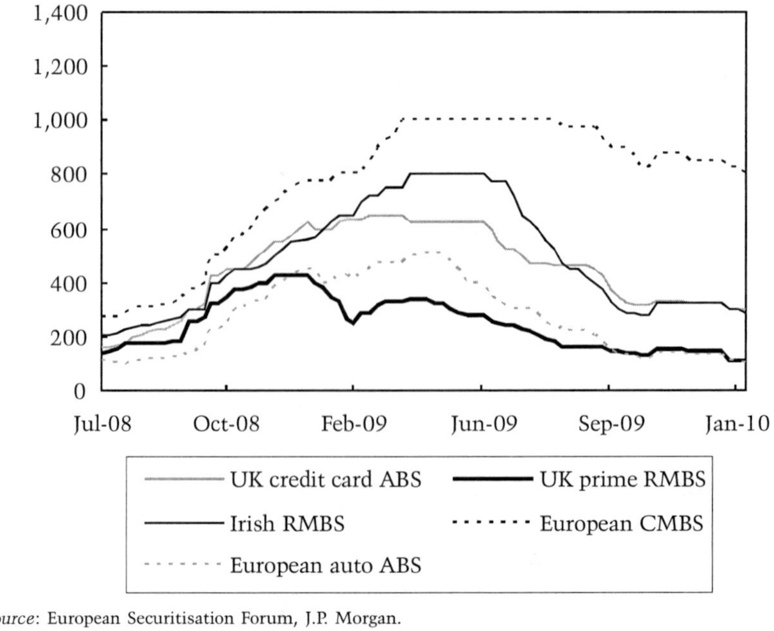

Source: European Securitisation Forum, J.P. Morgan.

Figure 22.25

European asset-backed securities issuance

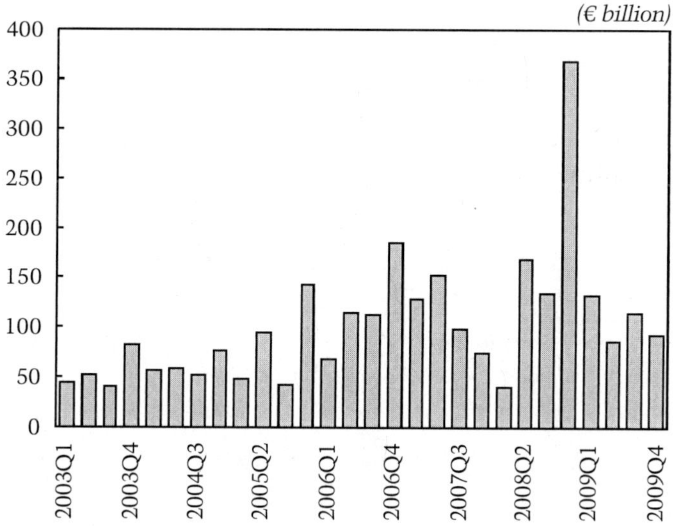

Source: European Securitisation Forum, J.P. Morgan.

The ECB's programme to purchase €60 billion of European covered bonds has led to improvements in that market. Credit spreads have narrowed since the ECB announcement in early May, and issuance volumes have risen.

Exiting from crisis-intervention measures

General considerations: Timing and sequencing

The global recovery is off to a stronger start than anticipated earlier, but is proceeding at different speeds in different regions. In the wake of the deepest global recession in recent history, economic growth returned and broadened to advanced economies in the second half of 2009. A four per cent increase in world output was anticipated for 2010.

Even early in 2010 the recovery was expected to remain sluggish by past standards in most advanced economies, in the absence of clear signs that domestic demand would be self-sustaining. On the contrary, economic activity was expected to be relatively vigorous in many emerging and developing economies, driven largely by buoyant internal demand.

A multi-speed recovery implies differentiation in the timing and sequencing of exit from crisis-related intervention policies. But policy-makers in all countries should remain proactive in preparing for exiting from extraordinary stimulus, recognising the challenge of mapping a course between exiting too early and too late. Unwinding stimulus too early could jeopardise progress in securing economic recovery, while maintaining it for too long could distort private incentives and pose risks to price, financial and fiscal stability.

Notwithstanding the recent uptick in growth prospects, recovery in the major advanced economies will remain sluggish, underpinning the need for continued policy stimulus till private demand gathers momentum on a sustainable basis. Central banks in these economies should maintain low interest rates till the end of 2010, since underlying inflation is expected to remain subdued and unemployment high for some time.

Similarly, fiscal policies need to remain supportive of economic activity in the near-term, and the fiscal stimulus planned for 2010 should be implemented fully. In contrast, in some major emerging economies in Asia and Latin America, output gaps are closing rapidly. There are also nascent signs of asset price booms and in some cases, deteriorating credit quality. In these economies, stimulus may need to be unwound soon.

There are also differences in the sequencing of exit from various intervention policies. In several of the major advanced economies, ensuring fiscal sustainability is a key priority and policy challenge, notably in the light of the surge in government debt levels. The long implementation lags in fiscal policy means that policy change will have to be initiated early rather than late.

In contrast, maintaining an accommodative monetary policy stance does not have a similar downside, because it can be reversed quickly and poses few risks in the current inflation environment. Also, a tightening of the fiscal stance may help monetary management, while a monetary tightening could contribute to a worsening of the fiscal position. Hence, fiscal consolidation should generally take priority, particularly in countries that need to raise national savings.

Achieving fiscal sustainability will be a difficult and prolonged process, making it imperative for consolidation to begin as soon as there is clear evidence of self-sustaining recovery. Given a path for fiscal policies, monetary policy can be set to achieve a desired level of overall stimulus, tightening as needed to counter inflationary risks and maintain price stability.

In major emerging (and some advanced) economies experiencing faster recoveries, including those with large fiscal space, the desirable policy mix may be different. For economies that have relied on export-led growth and with sufficient fiscal space, rebalancing from external to domestic demand may require additional measures to reduce precautionary savings, through further efforts to strengthen social safety nets, pension and healthcare systems reforms and improvements in corporate governance.

In countries with excessive current account surpluses, monetary conditions may have to be tightened relatively soon (notably through currency appreciation) and might, therefore, lead fiscal consolidation, owing to rising inflation or incipient financial vulnerabilities. Monetary tightening may be more complicated in countries with broadly balanced external positions, as it could amplify exchange rate pressures. These economies may have to consider macroprudential measures and fiscal tightening and, under some circumstances, reserve accumulation and restrictions on capital inflows.

Exiting from central bank policy actions in advanced economies

Monetary policy in the large advanced economies was justifiably accommodative as of the first half of 2010. There were no clear signs till then of a sustained recovery in private demand that could anchor a durable recovery and contain underlying inflation.

Should financial conditions normalise further and economic activity gain greater momentum, monetary stimulus will need to be withdrawn, however. Exiting from the stimulus will be necessary to maintain the economy at potential and avoid inflation. Although complex technical and conceptual issues are involved, central banks have adequate tools to control monetary conditions during the exit.[15]

15. Cottarelli and Viñals (2009).

Developing clear and effective exit strategies from exceptional monetary policy actions, involving both an unwinding of unconventional measures and a return to overnight interest-rate management as the principal tool of monetary policy, will be central to ensuring a smooth return to normal market functioning and to forestall inflation. At the same time, to limit concerns about inflation and the risk that liquidity be prematurely withdrawn while the recovery is still fragile, monetary authorities will need to communicate their exit strategies to the markets clearly.

Maintaining price stability should be a key objective. The large expansion of central bank balance sheets are mirrored in the growth of bank reserves, underpinning concerns that the excess liquidity could transform into rapid credit growth and lead to inflation (Figure 22.26). In major advanced economies, such concerns are not justified at this stage of the economic cycle, notably because of large output gaps.

Figure 22.26

Evolution of central bank liabilities

US Federal Reserve

(Per cent of 2008 GDP)

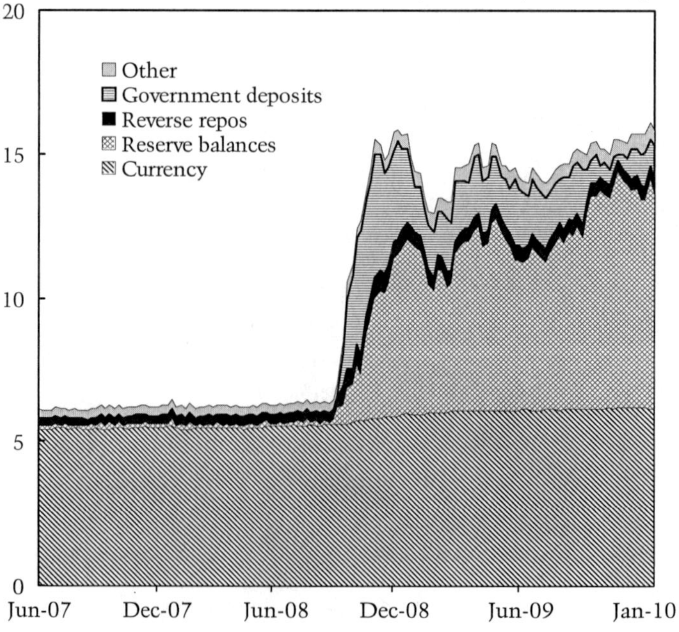

European Central Bank

(Per cent of 2008 GDP)

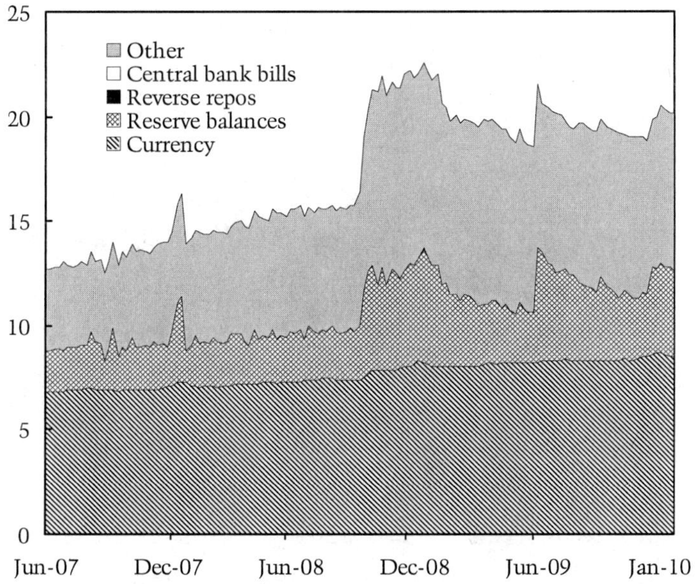

Bank of England

(Per cent of 2008 GDP)

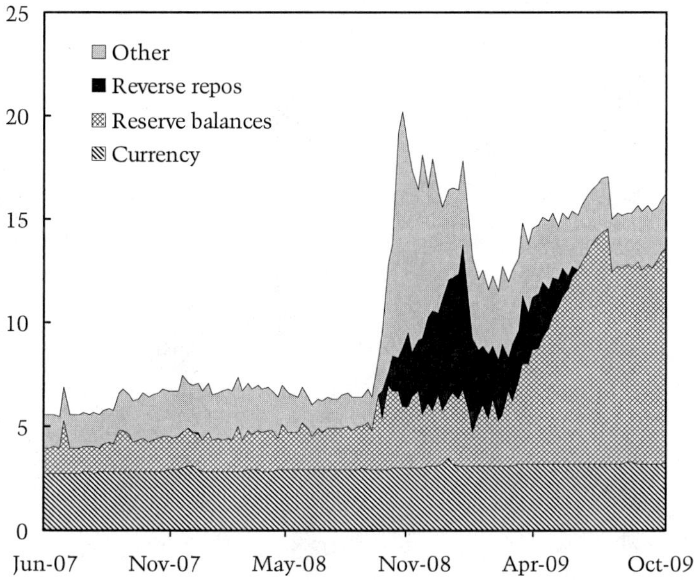

Bank of Japan

(Per cent of 2008 GDP)

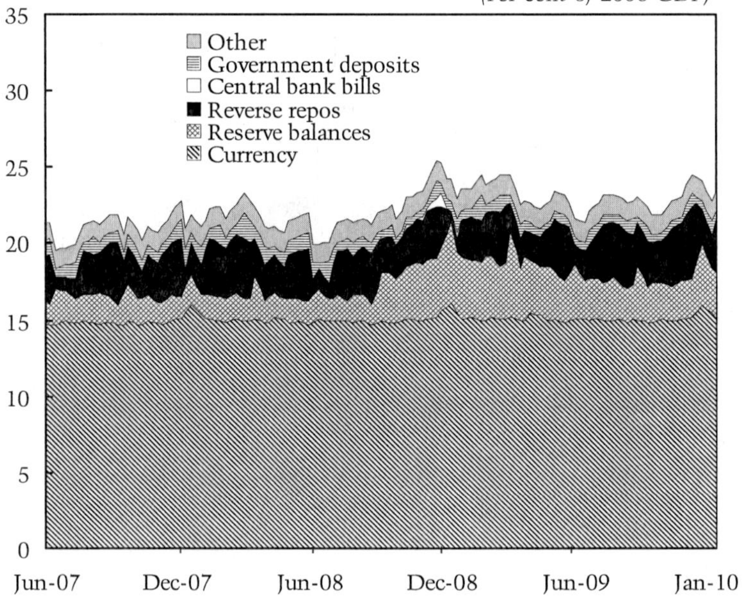

Moreover, in many advanced economies, financial stability remains fragile and/or key markets are not yet functioning normally. This condition underscores the need for central banks to maintain crisis-intervention measures or possibly introduce new ones, even within the context of an overall tightening of the monetary policy stance.

Raising policy interest rates

Raising policy interest rates need not await the unwinding of balance sheet policies. As and when the balance of risk shifts toward greater concerns about inflation, central banks can shift towards a tightening of the monetary policy stance through liability management, notwithstanding expanded bank balance sheets and large reserves in the banking system.

The rapid build-up of aggregate reserves in the banking system has led to a sharp decline in overnight rates that is consistent with broad macroeconomic objectives in the current context. If, however, inflation concerns mount, central banks could begin to raise policy rates even if their balance sheets are substantially above pre-crisis levels. Central banks could raise interest paid on reserves to discourage banks from lending their excess reserves to each other in the overnight market and push the overnight rate below the target.

Unwinding unconventional measures

Unwinding unconventional measures may be more challenging, but some of it is already happening. While the recourse to unconventional measures has exposed central banks to greater credit risk, to the extent that these policy measures were aimed at alleviating strains in individual credit markets, central banks may choose to sustain their operations, even though they are acting more broadly to tighten monetary conditions. That said, some unconventional measures will unwind naturally, as market conditions normalise, but others that are centred on purchases of assets and are long-term in nature and less liquid could be difficult to wind.

The problem is likely to be much greater for some assets, such as MBSs and agency bonds, where central banks—notably the Fed—have come to dominate the market, rather than other assets, notably treasuries, where the market is deep and central bank purchases are comparatively small (except in the United Kingdom). The composition of central bank assets will in part determine the approach to be taken.

Short-term credit operations—where the scale of intervention is determined by private demand—have already started to unwind naturally as market conditions normalise and central banks scale back access, gradually exiting facilities or introduce new liquidity-absorbing instruments.[16] The Fed announced that it would let some of its special liquidity facilities expire early in 2010 and the ECB and BoC recently announced that they would shorten the maturity of liquidity providing operations.

Financial conditions have improved, making central bank programmes increasingly unattractive, notably since lending facilities provide liquidity at

16. Central banks will want to restore much of the pre-crisis monetary operations framework, including using a single short-term interest rate. Some of the crisis measures may be worth retaining—such as the widening of counter-parties—because they addressed structural, pre-crisis inefficiencies and are unlikely to exacerbate vulnerabilities in the future.

a premium over the main policy rate or with a high haircut, applied to the required collateral. This has made interbank lending the more attractive option and banks have reduced their recourse to liquidity provision from the central banks, although the outstanding levels under various old and new facilities are still considerably higher than before the crisis.

Central bank currency swaps have shrunk as dollar funding in non-US markets improved, and the swap facilities were allowed to expire on February 1, 2010. Similarly, recourse to the discount window has declined, while some of the Fed's emergency facilities, including the primary dealer credit facility (PDCF) and the TSLF, have not been accessed in recent months. The amount outstanding under the TAF has declined.[17]

The unwinding of medium and long-term asset purchases may, however, be a slower process. Unwinding public sector security purchases involve flow and stock decisions. Ending purchases of public sector securities—the flow decision—might be taken as a signal that a robust economic recovery is under way. This step should, therefore, be taken with some caution and communications might emphasise flexibility in the face of changing market conditions.

Since purchases of public securities are aimed at influencing overall credit conditions, the decision to slow or stop them must be based not just on market information on the securities themselves, but also on broader indicators such as lending surveys and the growth of credit to the non-financial private sector. Management of central banks' increased holdings of public securities—the stock decision—will be a long-run issue.

Large-scale sales could raise the yield curve and widen market spreads. Potential disruptions could be minimised by selling excess holdings on a regular pre-announced basis. Therefore, selling these securities can be expected to take place over the long-term. If sales-risk disrupt the market and the central bank wants to absorb liquidity, these securities could be used as collateral for short-term liquidity-absorbing instruments.

---

17. The size of TAF and TSLF auctions has been reduced recently in response to flagging demand.

Unwinding private securities is likely to be more challenging, since this could adversely affect conditions in specific financial markets. Rolling back new purchases—the 'flow' decision—can be based primarily on market indicators. Credit spreads for the targeted markets, use of the facilities, and overall issuance volume (excluding central bank purchases) could be used to help guide when and how to stop purchases.

The 'flow' considerations are similar to those for public sector securities. However, the 'stock' decision is more difficult. Considering the large size of many credit-easing programmes involving the purchases of long-term assets, including corporate bonds and agency securities, it may be difficult to sell assets without a significant market impact. In the MBS market, for instance, even small sales of securities by the central bank could cause spreads to widen considerably and to undermine recovery in the housing market.

On the one hand, there may be merit in central banks holding some assets to maturity, which would help avoid capital losses and not jeopardise economic recovery, even if it implies expanded balance sheets for an extended period of time. On the other hand, however, holding these securities on their balance sheet exposes central banks to significant credit risks and transfers resources to specific economic sectors or even individual counter-parties. Central banks can pay interest on banking system reserves as a key tool to control monetary conditions, notwithstanding expanded balance sheets.

In addition to mopping up liquidity through a contraction of central bank balance sheets, monetary policy could also be tightened through substitution on the liability side. Central banks, particularly, could raise reserve requirements, accept term deposits from commercial banks, issue central bank bills or conduct reverse repos to reduce excess reserves, *albeit* subject to some constraints.

Central banks could mandate banks to hold greater statutory reserves to mop up some of the liquidity, although it is likely that the requirement would have to be raised quite dramatically to make a serious dent. Alternatively, fiscal authorities could issue financial obligations, drawing liquidity from the banking system and deposit proceeds at the central bank, as in the US supplementary financing programme (SFP).

However, the willingness of the Treasury to cooperate in such a programme cannot be taken for granted, owing to political economy considerations, notably since such action would be seen as increasing gross government debt. Political consensus would also be required to allow central banks to issue their own bills where they do not already have such authority.

Careful and consistent communication is essential

During the unwinding, there will be an unusually high premium on effective and innovative policy communication. The potential for confusion will be great. For example, reducing liquidity support for specific markets may give the erroneous impression that monetary policy is being tightened.

Conversely, raising policy interest rates could lead to a questioning of the commitment to maintain support for stressed markets. Central banks will need to lay out a general strategy to remove crisis measures and carefully explain the significance of different actions. They may also aim at a more internationally comparable terminology, while still taking account of national differences in policies and their implementation.

Ensuring that unwinding does not compromise central bank independence

Governments should design the unwinding strategy so as to assure the independence of central banks. The large and protracted increase in public debt in many countries might eventually lead to pressure on some central banks to relax their commitment to price stability. Governments may also be tempted to pressure central banks to maintain or expand market support measures taken during the crisis.

To avoid a return to damaging high inflation and preserve policy credibility, all the key dimensions of central bank independence—institutional, operational and financial—need to be respected and reinforced where necessary. Government support of central bank independence and price stability through the appropriate statements and actions will also be important, including the restructuring of central bank balance sheets, when necessary.

Addressing international spillovers of differentiated exit

Differentiation in the timing and sequencing of exit will have spillover effects, which will need to be managed. Clear differences have emerged in the pace of economic recovery and countries will need to exit from intervention policies as best suits the state of their economies. Although domestic considerations are likely to be the main determinant of exit policy choices, these also generate important international spillovers. For instance, the accommodative monetary stance of advanced countries can generate unwanted levels of capital flows into economies with higher yields.

Depending on the problems at hand and local circumstances, such inflows may be addressed through a mix of the following policies. Allowing for more flexible exchange rates could play a valuable role. Stronger currencies in economies with large surpluses could facilitate the needed shift in productive resources from tradable to non-tradable sectors, while depreciations in deficit economies would assist the adjustment away from overstretched domestic demand. Sterilised interventions may limit exchange rate appreciations temporarily, but they bring potentially large quasi-fiscal costs and, moreover, may actually promote inflows by raising expectations of large future appreciations.

Implementing new or tightening existing prudential measures could help address financial system stress resulting from capital flows. Finally, applying direct controls over capital flows (whether inflows or outflows) may reduce gains to carry-type trades. Effectiveness, however, may be temporary.

In conclusion

The financial crisis and the associated sharp contraction in economic activity compelled central banks to employ a wide range of crisis-intervention measures, which were in many cases unprecedented. This included the cutting of policy rates to near zero and the use of several unconventional measures. Such measures included commitment to keeping interest rates low for an extended period of time, dramatic expansion of liquidity provision, purchases of long-term government bonds and direct intervention in key credit markets.

The scale and scope of unconventional measures have differed substantially across major central banks. Most of them boosted significantly their liquidity operations, with the ECB being at the forefront in terms of the size, maturity, and collateral and counter-party eligibility. Massive asset purchases have boosted the size of the central bank balance sheets, the most in the United States and the United Kingdom.

The BoE has relied primarily on purchasing government bonds. The Fed, on the other hand, has acquired a variety of assets, including CP and MBSs and provided financing for acquiring other ABSs. EMCBs have largely focused on policy rate cuts and liquidity provision in response to the crisis. The reasons for this diversity include differences in institutional arrangements, in the role of the banking system, in the degree of distress in financial markets and in the assessment of economic prospects.

Central bank interventions, along with government actions, have been broadly successful in stabilising financial conditions. While stress indicators still remain at elevated levels, tail risks have declined dramatically and funding strains have eased. Ample liquidity provision helped avoid a meltdown in the financial system, while direct support of credit flows to borrowers and investors in disrupted markets and indirect support through broadening collateral eligibility requirements seems to have been successful in alleviating pressure and propping up demand.

Policymakers in all countries should remain proactive in preparing for exiting from extraordinary stimulus, recognising the challenge of mapping a course between exiting too early and too late. Central banks need to prepare and clearly communicate credible strategies for unwinding the extraordinary monetary policy support. Unwinding should be tractable and central banks have the tools needed to tighten policy, but there will be challenges.

The key objective will be to maintain price stability. However, where financial stability remains fragile, or key markets are not yet functioning, central banks may need to maintain crisis intervention measures, or possibly introduce new ones, even within the context of an overall tightening of the monetary policy stance. Central banks will need to unwind conventional and unconventional measures at different paces. Some unconventional (or 'balance sheet') measures are already being unwound, as funding markets improve and certain facilities expire or run off automatically.

Central banks can further tighten the parameters of existing facilities, or introduce new liquidity absorbing instruments, if tightening is needed before central bank balance sheets have been restored to normal levels. Reducing central banks' exposure to assets associated with credit-easing operations and private or quasi-sovereign financial instruments will depend on the state of financial markets and may take considerable time.

In designing appropriate exit strategies, there are other key considerations, which will need to be thought through and internalised, where relevant. These include effective and innovative policy communication, ensuring the independence of central banks and managing the spillovers from a differentiation in the timing and sequencing of the exit.

References

Balakrishnan, Ravi, Stephan Danninger, Selim Elekdag and Irina Tytell (2009). "The Transmission of Financial Stress from Advanced to Emerging Economies", *IMF Working Paper* 09/133. Washington, DC: International Monetary Fund.

Bank of Canada (2009). *Monetary Policy Report.* April. Ottawa.

Bernanke, Ben S. (2009). "The Crisis and the Policy Response". The Stamp Lecture at the London School of Economics. January 13.

Bernanke, Ben S., Vincent R. Reinhart and Brian P. Sack (2004). "Monetary Policy Alternatives at the Zero Bound: An Empirical Assessment", *Finance and Economics Discussion Series Paper* 2004–48. Washington, DC: Board of Governors of the Federal Reserve System.

Buiter, Willem (2008). *Quantitative Easing and Qualitative Easing: A Terminological and Taxonomic Proposal*. Available via the Internet: *http://blogs.ft.com/maverecon/2008/12/quantitative-easing-and-qualitative-easing-aterminological-and-taxonomic-proposal/*

Cihak, Martin, Thomas Harjes and Emil Stavrev (2009). "Euro Area Monetary Policy in Uncharted Waters", *IMF Working Paper* 09/185. Washington, DC: International Monetary Fund.

Cottarelli, Carlo and Jose Viñals (2009). "A Strategy for Renormalizing Fiscal and Monetary Policies in Advanced Economies", *IMF Staff Position Note* 09/22. Washington, DC: International Monetary Fund.

Decressin, Jörg and Douglas Laxton (2009). "Gauging Risks for Deflation", *IMF Staff Position Note* 09/01. Washington, DC: International Monetary Fund.

Hooper, Peter and Slok Torsten (2009). "Are the Fed's Programs Working?", *Deutsche Bank Global Economic Perspectives*, March 4.

International Monetary Fund (2009a). *Global Financial Stability Report*. April. Washington, DC.

———. (2009b). *Global Financial Stability Report*. October. Washington, DC.

Klyuev, Vladimir, Phil de Imus and Krishna Srinivasan (2009). "Unconventional Choices for Unconventional Times: Credit and Quantitative Easing in Advanced Economies", *IMF Staff Position Note* SPN/09/27, November 4.

King, Mervyn (2009). *Speech to the CBI Dinner.* Nottingham: East Midlands Conference Centre. January 20.

Meier, André (2009). "Panacea, Curse, or Nonevent? Unconventional Monetary Policy in the United Kingdom", *IMF Working Paper* 09/163. Washington, DC: International Monetary Fund.

McAndrews, James, Asani Sarkar and Zhenyu Wang (2008). "The Effect of the Term Auction Facility on the London Inter-Bank Offered Rate", *Federal Reserve Bank of New York Staff Report* No. 335.

Okina, Kunio and Shigenori Shiratsuka (2004). "Policy Commitment and Expectation Formation: Japan's Experience under Zero Interest Rates", *North American Journal of Economics and Finance* 15(1): 75–100.

Sack, Brian and Meyer Laurence (2008). "TAF and Liquidity Policies: Keeping Libor Down", *Macroeconomic Advisers*, May 15.

Taylor, John B. and John C. Williams (2009). "A Black Swan in the Money Market", *American Economic Journal: Macroeconomics* 1(1): 58–83.

Trichet, Jean-Claude (2009a). *The ECB's Enhanced Credit Support*. Keynote address at the University of Munich, July 13.

———. (2009b). "Credible Alertness Revisited", Intervention at the symposium on *Financial Stability and Macroeconomic Policy* sponsored by the Federal Reserve Bank of Kansas City. Jackson Hole. Wyoming. August 22.

22.1
DISCUSSION

Central Banks need to Find a Mid-Path

ESWAR PRASAD

Krishna Srinivasan makes a number of plausible, reasonable and balanced statements that actually would not pass the Michael Spence test, because it is very hard to disagree with them. Having said that, I do worry a little bit about making statements about how certain policies were effective or not, based simply on the outcomes. I think we need to take a look at the counterfactuals and think through them seriously, before we decide what was and what was not effective and try to draw lessons from them.

Frankly, I am a lot less concerned about what the advanced countries' central banks can do in the way of exit strategies. What I worry about are the countries caught in the middle—the emerging markets—specifically, the non-China emerging markets. What I see developing right now is a situation where low interest rates in the advanced economies (the US in particular) on the one hand and Chinese currency policy on the other, are putting emerging markets in a vice-like grip.

Emerging markets essentially have to deal with the consequences of money flowing in from the advanced economies and the loss of competitiveness that comes from an appreciation of their exchange rates, while China holds its line. The exit strategies, therefore, are really more of a concern for the emerging markets than for the advanced economies right now.

The other issue in terms of exit, although this is a slightly awkward segue, is what central banking is going to look like at the end of all of this. I echo back Reserve Bank of India Governor D. Subbarao's concern that in

---

Comments by Eswar Prasad on the paper presented by Krishna Srinivasan 'Crisis and Implications for Central Bank Balance Sheets: Policies, Effectiveness and Designing an Exit'.

the midst of this crisis, we risk a temptation to believe that all we have learnt from monetary theory was bunk and that it needs to be rejected. I fear that not only are we throwing out the baby with the bathwater, we are trying to throw out the entire bath-tub as well.

There is a serious risk here in the perceptions about monetary policy. In emerging markets, many of these issues are heightened but curiously, there is this convergence right now in the debates on central banks' independence, about monetary policy frameworks in advanced economies and emerging markets. I think in emerging markets, there is an order of magnitude increase in complexity.

So, let us take the Reserve Bank of India (RBI), for instance. What does it have to do? It is forced, in some sense, to manage the exchange rate. Now, the Reserve Bank talks about leaning against the wind, but when exchange market pressures become very high, it has no choice but to take account of them. After all, in an economy like India, which is reasonably open, the effects of an appreciation of the exchange rate on the real economy could be quite persistent.

The central bank, however, also has to worry about financial stability, about asset prices and a whole lot of other things. My concern really is that this goes against the effectiveness and independence of the central banks. The term 'independence' of central banks is, of course, used in a very specific sense by different people. I think the operational independence of central banks is all that we can hope for in emerging markets.

In reality, even if the central bank is independent by statute, that independence hangs by a thread. Especially in emerging markets, I do not think it is feasible for a central bank to not seem to be very concerned about growth and employment or financial stability. Hence, to argue that the central bank should have a very limited mandate is also a potential problem because ultimately, that could rebound in terms of a loss of independence.

In fact, we see that even in the United States these days. The notion that the central bank may not have cared about financial stability is creating pressure for greater oversight of the central bank. The risk, however, is that such pressures could make central banks much less effective in what they could be doing and one has to think very seriously about what central banks and monetary policy can accomplish.

The more we ask monetary policy to do, the harder it is going to be to do, especially if we think about a situation where we simply do not have a good idea about what it is that we should be doing about asset prices. In some cases, like in the US, where there were clear regulatory failures, I think the answers are much easier to see. Considering how difficult it is to detect asset bubbles, I think that putting the onus of managing asset-price bubbles on central banks is going to be a serious problem.

The Reserve Bank has managed this juggling act very effectively. However, over time, it is tempting for the Reserve Bank to take on these mandates and this is true of many other emerging market central banks as well. If something goes wrong here, believe me, the Reserve Bank will be blamed for it. And the institution has done a remarkable job of managing the different and difficult pressures it faces.

The general problem, however, is that in emerging markets, it becomes very tempting to give central banks much more in the way of mandates.

The central banks typically are the most effective institutions. The government is often seen as corrupt. The central bank is considered much purer and is usually staffed by more analytically oriented people. Here again, I am worried that we may be giving central banks a lot of things to do, perhaps with some more instruments, but invariably making them a lot more subject to political pressure. I think we are going to have to work hard to find the right balance.

There are big road bumps ahead. The first problem concerns the looming fiscal deficits and potential debt problems in the advanced economies, but there are other potential sources of financial instability as well. When all hell does break loose and I think, sooner or later, it is going to—the emerging markets' central banks will have to throw whatever they can at the problem.

My concern is that, before it happens, if there is no good framework in place with a limited set of objectives, central banks will find it hard to justify their actions and to fend off accusations of an *ad hoc* approach. I think the time is ripe for central banks of emerging economies to solidify the gains they have made.

It is going to be a very difficult balance, irrespective of whether it is going to be through more mandates or more focused mandates. I think, though, that the urge to swing the pendulum all the way to the other side is a potentially dangerous one and should be resisted.

23 Monetary Policy Challenges for Emerging Market Economies*

GILL HAMMOND, RAVI KANBUR
and ESWAR PRASAD

Monetary policy has become especially challenging in emerging market economies (EMEs) in the aftermath of the global financial crisis. We provide an overview of the main issues, linking them to broader debates in academic literature. We also assess how individual countries have chosen to respond to specific policy challenges and what the consequences have been.

Some key issues in this debate are as follows. Does existing economic theory provide lessons that are pertinent to designing effective monetary policy frameworks in emerging markets? What can be learnt from cross-country studies and from experiences of individual countries that have adopted different approaches? While country-specific circumstances and initial conditions matter a great deal in formulating suitable frameworks, are there clear general principles that can serve as a guide in this process?

EMEs have now become one of the most dynamic and economically important groups in the world economy. As these economies become larger and integrate more into international trade and finance, they face an increasingly complex set of policy challenges. Considering the important role emerging economies play in the world economy in terms of population and sheer economic size, addressing these challenges effectively has important economic, social and political implications that stretch beyond national borders.

---

* This essay is adapted from the introductory chapter in: Gill Hammond, Ravi Kanbur and Eswar Prasad (eds.) (2009). *Monetary Policy Frameworks for Emerging Markets*, Edward Elgar. The views expressed here are those of the authors and not necessarily those of the Bank of England (BoE).

Monetary policy is typically the first line of defence against a number of internal and external shocks that these economies are now exposed to, so it is important to get it right. EMEs, however, face a number of difficult challenges in designing monetary policy frameworks that work well in terms of promoting monetary and financial stability.

Notwithstanding their rising economic might, many EMEs still have relatively underdeveloped financial markets and institutions. They still have per capita incomes that lag far behind those of advanced industrial economies and they still have a significant fraction of their population living in poverty. These conditions put a number of constraints on the effective formulation and implementation of macroeconomic policies.

We list a more specific set of issues, which is as follows. What are the particular challenges faced by central banks in emerging markets? What are the pros and cons of different monetary policy frameworks? Has rising openness to trade and financial flows made monetary policy less effective in achieving domestic objectives? How should monetary policy respond to shocks of uncertain nature (demand/supply, transitory/permanent)?

What institutional frameworks can help in increasing the effectiveness of monetary policy transmission in less developed economies? What role do policies toward capital account liberalisation have in devising appropriate monetary policy strategies? How should monetary policy in EMEs respond to large exogeneous shocks, such as the world-wide surge in food and fuel prices, or the possible spillovers from financial shocks such as the subprime crisis in the United States?

There are unlikely to be clear or general answers to many questions confronting central bankers in these challenging times. Nevertheless, dialogue between academics and policymakers has facilitated a revealing discussion on the interaction between theory and practice. For instance, theoretical work on the optimality of an inflation target as the main objective of monetary policy has been influential in guiding the adoption of inflation targeting regimes around the world (De Gregorio, 2009). But such discussions also highlight large gaps between what can be learnt from existing theoretical and empirical research and the practical challenges that confront central bankers.

In this paper, we provide an overview of the main issues confronting monetary policy theory and practice, linking them to broader debates in academic literature, as well as an assessment of how individual countries have chosen to respond to specific policy challenges and what the consequences have been.

We discuss many controversies where there are still sharp differences in views between and among theorists and practitioners. We also delineate some key analytical issues, where yawning gaps still exist between theory and practice. In the process, we set out a broad agenda for further research in these areas.

We set the background to this discussion by reviewing the objectives of monetary policy, the particular challenges faced by central bankers in EMEs, and some recent developments that have heightened these challenges.

Objectives of monetary policy

There is a general recognition in academic literature and in advanced industrial economies (AIE) that the primary role of monetary policy is to ensure price stability (see Bernanke *et al.*, 1999). Other objectives, such as promoting growth and employment are considered secondary.

This has been reflected in increasing independence for central banks and new laws that give central banks statutory responsibility for price stability (for example, Ghana; see Sowa and Abradu-Otoo, 2009). The rationale is that the best way that a central bank can promote growth and employment is by keeping inflation low and stable.

Central banks are also responsible for financial stability—a role that has come to the fore during the global financial crisis. Even central banks that are not responsible for prudential regulation are usually responsible for maintaining the stability of the financial system as a whole. The current market turbulence has rendered financial stability as the more pre-eminent objective and monetary policy has been focused on restoring and maintaining the stability of the financial system.

Indeed, the dual role expected of monetary policy in responding to a financial stability shock (the credit crunch, a price stability shock, and rising oil and commodity prices) has posed particularly challenging dilemmas for central banks. On the institutional side, some central banks are being given a greater role in promoting financial stability.

The situation is more complex in EMEs, however. While price stability is viewed as important in these economies too, financial stability is a key responsibility, since central banks in most of the emerging markets are also responsible for prudential regulation (Nijathaworn and Disyatat, 2009; Singh, 2009). Moreover, the political economy context in these countries makes it harder for central banks to be insulated from other objectives, including promoting output and employment growth.

This is the essence of the challenge facing central bankers in EMEs. With just one instrument at it disposal—usually short-term interest rates—monetary policy in many emerging market countries is considered responsible for promoting high growth, keeping inflation low and stable and maintaining financial stability (Goodfriend and Prasad, 2009), discuss this with specific reference to China). Even this one instrument, though, is subject to a variety of constraints.

Constraints on monetary policy in emerging markets

Central banks in emerging markets face a unique set of challenges. These are in part institutional and in part technical, but both act as severe constraints on monetary policy implementation.

The key institutional constraint is the lack of central bank's independence. In some countries, this takes the form of the central bank being statutorily under the purview of the finance ministry. In some countries, where the central bank is in principle independent, there is still the reality that it can be buffeted by various political forces, especially the finance ministry (as argued by Dragutinovic (2009), in the case of Serbia). Hence, central banks are always treading a fine line in their endeavour to maintain their legitimacy and independence in difficult circumstances.

Moreover, irrespective of the degree of statutory independence, operational independence of the central bank is in some cases circumscribed by constraints, such as an exchange rate objective. Maintaining the exchange rate at a particular level or within a specific range can often limit the room that the central bank has, in using policy instruments such as the interest rate to pursue an independent domestic monetary policy aimed at managing domestic activity and inflation (Goodfriend, 2004).

Fiscal dominance is another key problem facing emerging market central banks (EMCB). In many of these countries, fiscal discipline is lacking and monetary policy is often an adjunct to fiscal policy, particularly since the latter is seen as having important redistributive functions.

An unsound fiscal policy, characterised by high levels of government budget deficits and public debt acts as a severe constraint on monetary policy. The central bank then has to take account of the government's debt management objectives in setting interest rates, instead of focusing exclusively on the price stability objective. It also makes it harder to manage inflation expectations (see Sims, 2005).

Moreover, monetary policy is often hampered by a weak transmission mechanism, related to the underdevelopment of the financial system (for example, the case of Zambia; see Kalyalya, 2009). A fragile banking system can make it particularly difficult for a central bank to aggressively use policy interest rates to achieve domestic objectives, as large changes in interest rates can have potentially devastating consequences on the balance sheets of weak banks.

The lack of well-developed financial markets means that the interest rate channel of monetary policy transmission is less effective. Moreover, the lack of market integration within these countries means that there are asymmetrical regional responses to monetary policy, as shown by Fielding (2009). Consequently, the lags in the effects of monetary policy on economic activity are even more long and variable than in industrial economies.

The absence of deep and liquid financial markets also means that there is limited feedback from the market about monetary policy. Central banks in industrial economies rely on these market signals for feedback about the effects of their policy actions on market sentiment and expectations. Other institutional rigidities can also undermine the effectiveness of monetary policy. For instance, inflexible labour markets can lead to persistent inflation, which again makes it harder for monetary policy to reliably manage economic activity.

Other challenges

One structural change that is making it more difficult to isolate monetary policy from external influences, is the increasing openness of the capital account in EMEs. Even in countries that have *de jure* capital controls, financial flows are increasingly able to find their way around those controls. Greater trade openness, the rising sophistication of domestic and international investors and the sheer volume of financial flows, have all made it increasingly difficult to keep capital bottled up when the incentives for it to cross national borders are strong enough.

A prime example is that of China where, despite the determined efforts of the authorities to tighten controls on inflows, money has been pouring in through different channels in recent years (see Prasad and Wei, 2007). An open capital account, of course, makes it much harder to maintain an independent monetary policy, when the central bank is also trying to manage the exchange rate (this is the Mundell-Fleming 'Impossible Trinity'.

A different type of problem of capital flows arises in heavily aid-dependent low-income economies, particularly in Africa. Aid flows are significant, but can be volatile, depending on political and other factors. How should governments and monetary policy respond to these volatile flows to the government? Buffie *et al.* (2009) argue that a key aspect is how credibly the government can commit to time paths of expenditure and absorption.

If an aid boom is perceived to be temporary, the markets' fear of the looming fiscal problems can lead to capital outflows and inflation. An appropriate strategy, it is argued, could be to reduce deficits to some extent, along with purchases of internal debt. Adam *et al.* (2009) further support the case for temporary reserve accumulation in the face of aid-driven capital flows.

Recent circumstances have made monetary policy formulation even more challenging in emerging markets. Rising food and energy prices worldwide have created a dilemma for central bankers in these economies. These central banks are endeavouring to manage inflationary expectations, even as they are under political pressure to avoid stifling growth by tightening monetary policy.

This episode highlights the difficulties in formulating strategies for responding to commodity price shocks. Existing theoretical models provide somewhat naïve and simplistic solutions. Central banks are expected to target only the core component of the price index and let prices of food and energy (which tend to be flexible prices), adjust to market conditions. In less developed economies, expenditures on food tend to constitute a large share of total consumption expenditures. Central banks in these economies, therefore, find it difficult to leave these prices to market conditions.

In addition to institutional constraints, central banks in EMEs face a number of technical challenges in implementing monetary policy and targeting inflation. In an inflation targeting regime, the central bank needs the technical capacity to model the economy, understand the transmission mechanism, and forecast inflation and output.

Structural changes in the economy, such as greater openness, mean that modelling and forecasting techniques must evolve and that the past can be a less reliable guide to the future. These issues are discussed by Aron and Muellbauer (2009) in the case of South Africa. Central banks also need good macroeconomic data to inform their decisions. Finally, they need a communication strategy as an integral part of their inflation targeting framework, as argued, for example by Niedermayer (2009) for the Czech Republic.

Options for monetary policy frameworks

Each country has specific institutional features and circumstances that determine how monetary policy decisions are formulated and implemented. Nevertheless, it is possible to identify a set of broad frameworks that have been used by emerging market and other economies. We begin by evaluating these options, in terms of their durability and effectiveness in achieving monetary policy objectives.

Managed exchange rate

The exchange rate provides a nominal anchor that is quite useful for some countries, especially those with low levels of financial and institutional development and/or central banks that lack credibility (Husain *et al.*, 2005). For economies that are highly open to trade, which is the case with many emerging markets, high nominal exchange rate volatility complicates domestic macroeconomic management and can have adverse effects on investment, employment and output growth. Because of these potential advantages, many emerging markets have chosen to use the exchange rate as a nominal anchor to varying degrees.

A strict version of a managed exchange rate is hard peg (currency board or dollarisation), although there are a variety of other intermediate versions (for an early discussion of exchange rate regime options for emerging markets and the constraints on some of these regimes in a world of mobile capital, see Williamson, 1998).

The common feature is that this option involves the loss of monetary autonomy and the 'importing' of monetary policy from abroad. The virtue is that pegging the domestic currency to the currency of a country whose central bank has credibility in maintaining low and stable inflation helps keep domestic inflation low. Experience has shown, however, that even with a hard peg, good inflation and growth, fiscal discipline and sound structural policies are necessary to deliver outcomes. Otherwise, currency pegs quickly become unsustainable.

Other forms of a hard peg include monetary unions, such as the Euro area. The logic of this approach is that linking monetary policy among a group of similar countries may facilitate a common response to common shocks, while acting as a disciplining mechanism on other policies in individual countries. There is also some evidence that currency unions promote trade and investment flows within the union.

Some argue that the benefits from currency blocs means there will be an inevitable move by regional countries to monetary unions and far fewer individual currencies in the future. The downside is that, in periods when business cycles across countries in the union are not well-synchronised, or when they get hit with different shocks, navigating a common monetary policy could be difficult.

A different option is to have an exchange rate that is tightly managed against one currency or a basket of other currencies. This arrangement can coexist with an open capital account only in countries like Singapore that have high levels of financial development and other good policies. This is not an easy combination for most emerging markets to manage, though.

In general, managed exchange rate regimes require a large array of capital controls, since large volumes of flows can make exchange rate management very difficult, apart from stripping away monetary policy autonomy. There are, of course, currency boards in Hong Kong and countries with exchange rate targets and well-disciplined macro policies (as in Singapore) that are able to manage their exchange rates effectively, while keeping their capital accounts fully open. In most other developing economies, especially those with weak macro policies and underdeveloped financial markets, capital controls are seen as an important buffer required to mitigate exchange rate volatility.

Flexible exchange rate and monetary targeting

A flexible exchange rate usually involves a managed float, where the currency is managed within a relatively tight band, although the size of this band varies across countries and within countries over time. Examples are Bangladesh, Sri Lanka, Tanzania, Uganda and Zambia (Kalyalya (2009), discusses the Zambian case). Monetary aggregates provide visible targets that are relatively easy to measure, making them appealing to economies with underdeveloped financial systems.

One complication is that monetary aggregates are increasingly distorted by financial integration and globalisation. Moreover, in economies where the rate of productivity growth is highly volatile, there is no stable relationship between monetary aggregates, on the one hand, and economic activity and inflation, on the other.

Consequently, many of these countries are in fact, trying to move towards an alternative regime such as inflation targeting, but lack the institutional and technical pre-requisites. Goodhart (2009) challenges the view that money does not matter, arguing that a strong empirical relationship continues between money and prices.

Inflation targeting with managed float

Many countries have adopted inflation targeting but manage the exchange rate, ostensibly to 'lean against the wind' in smoothing out short-term volatility in exchange markets. In practice, this approach often involves substantial exchange market intervention, as countries have a fear of letting their currencies float freely. Examples of countries that the IMF classifies as 'inflation targeters with managed float' constitute a diverse group, including Colombia, Ghana, Indonesia, Romania and Thailand (see Sowa and Abradu-Otoo (2009) on Ghana; Nijathaworn and Disyatat (2009) on Thailand).

A variant of this is the approach adopted by the Reserve Bank of India (RBI), which does not have a formal inflation objective but whose senior officials, nevertheless, mention the range of inflation that they are comfortable with in an attempt to anchor inflationary expectations. The RBI also manages the exchange rate quite actively at times and its senior officials have argued that this is a pragmatic approach that gives them a degree of freedom in running monetary policy effectively (Mohan and Patra, 2009).

Inflation targeting with exchange rate flexibility

More and more countries, both from the group of Advanced Industrial Economies (AIEs) as well as the EMEs, are moving towards this monetary regime. Even a number of countries that, at present, have one or the other regimes discussed above, have indicated that they view this regime as the end game for the evolution of their own monetary frameworks.

Indeed, part of the apparent inevitability of moving to this regime is that, in every country, capital accounts are becoming more open over time in *de facto* terms, whatever the capital control regime in place. This makes it harder to manage exchange rates for any sustained period, without exposing the exchange rate regime to speculative attacks. The Chinese experience suggests that it may yet be possible to maintain a tightly managed exchange rate while the capital account is becoming more open, but only by maintaining extensive financial repression, which in turn has large welfare costs (see Prasad, 2009).

In tandem with the moves by central banks to adopt some form of inflation targeting, the academic literature has, by and large, come around to the view that this alternative is the best one for most advanced and middle-income economies. The inflation target provides a clear anchor for monetary policy, while exchange rate flexibility provides room for an independent monetary policy and a buffer against certain external shocks.

Rose (2006) marshalls evidence that this regime seems to deliver the best outcomes in terms of output growth, low inflation and lower exchange rate volatility than alternative regimes. He also notes that this regime is the most durable of the lot. However, it may be premature to declare that this is the best alternative. After all, it has not been around for very long and may not have been tested sufficiently under conditions of extreme duress.

Moreover, many countries introduced inflation targeting during the last two decades, a period when inflation had generally been moderate around the world. In terms of durability, the fact is that many countries lack credible alternatives since many of them turned to this regime after the breakdown of alternatives, such as a fixed exchange rate regime. Nevertheless, experience indicates that in countries that have adopted inflation targeting, inflation expectations are better anchored and inflation persistence is lower.

Is the shift towards inflation-targeting regimes well advised? We now provide a critical review of the theoretical and empirical evidence of the appropriateness of this regime for EMEs and the potential complications faced by central banks that do adopt inflation targeting (see Mishkin (2000), for an excellent alternative summary of these issues).

Benefits of an explicit inflation objective

There is a great deal of evidence, both from individual country experiences and cross-country studies that a central bank focused on price stability can be most effective at delivering good monetary and macro outcomes.[1] Low and stable inflation has large macroeconomic benefits.

It stabilises GDP growth, helps households and firms to make long-term plans with confidence, increases investment and thereby, allows monetary policy to make its best possible contribution to long-term employment and output growth. It also has financial market benefits, by enabling the development of a long-maturity bond market, for instance, which would assist in infrastructure financing and public debt management.

1. The general discussion in this section draws on material from the volume edited by Bernanke and Woodford (2005). For a more specific discussion of these issues for emerging markets, see Jonas and Mishkin (2005) and, for a skeptical view on the relevance of inflation targeting for these economies, see Blanchard (2005).

Monetary policy that has a single clearly-defined objective may be the best contribution that monetary policy can make to macroeconomic and financial stability and, therefore, to long-term growth. In contrast, trying to do too much with one instrument is a recipe for ineffectiveness, especially in difficult times.

Moreover, the notion that monetary policy can itself raise long-term growth through activist policies has been shown to be demonstrably false. As a matter of fact, faith in that belief led to stagflationary episodes (economic stagnation coupled with high inflation) in the United States in the 1970s and 1980s (see Broaddus and Goodfriend, 2002).

Monetary policy, nevertheless, has a key role to play in encouraging investment in physical capital and galvanising productivity gains, mainly by ensuring macroeconomic stability. Transparency and predictability of monetary policy are essential ingredients for achieving liquid financial markets, reducing fragility of financial firms and stabilising capital flows.

A stable macroeconomic environment helps make cross-border capital flows more stable by giving domestic and foreign investors more confidence in a country's fundamentals. It also helps in dealing with the inevitable vagaries of those flows.

It is sometimes argued that the process of switching to an objective of price stability entails a loss in output growth. This is true in countries where an inflation target has been used as a device to bring down inflation from a high level and to build credibility for a central bank that has lacked inflation-fighting credentials. One of the earliest inflation targeters—New Zealand—suffered this problem. An early form of inflation targeting was introduced in early 1988 in an attempt to bring inflation down from around 15 per cent in the mid-1980s.

Inflation was brought down to two per cent by 1991, although with an adverse impact on growth and employment during that period. Output losses were also experienced when inflation targeting was introduced in some Latin American economies. But in each one of these cases, inflation targeting was seen as a solution to high inflation and lack of central bank credibility. However, there is no reason why switching focus to price stability instead of multiple objectives should have output costs, provided, of course, that inflation is low and the central bank has a reasonable degree of credibility.

One lesson from these episodes is that inflation targeting may not necessarily be the best monetary policy framework for bringing inflation down from high levels. This is because it depends on the ability to forecast inflation, which is more difficult when inflation is high and volatile. So, a central bank risks losing credibility by getting the forecast wrong and having large target misses.

Nevertheless, some countries like Chile and Israel have still used inflation targeting successfully in purging entrenched high levels of inflation from their economies. More generally, inflation targeting is regarded as a good framework for keeping inflation low (Mishkin and Schmidt-Hebbel, 2005).

It is also argued by some that making low and stable inflation the objective of monetary policy creates a deflationary anti-growth bias, wherein inflationary pressures would be dealt with swiftly and decisively, but deflationary pressures would not be resisted as aggressively (McKinnon, 2006, implicitly makes this point in his discussion of Chinese exchange rate policy). In fact, there is no reason why there should be an asymmetric approach to inflation *versus* deflation.

The BoE, for example, explicitly has a symmetric point target for inflation. In other countries, where the inflation target is specified as a range, the norm is to treat the floor of the target range as seriously as the ceiling. Put differently, if growth falters, it is also likely to bring inflation down below the floor of the inflation objective, allowing the central bank to ease. In this case again, the ability of the central bank to move aggressively with its policy instrument to maintain price stability (and thus growth), rather than being hamstrung by an exchange rate objective, is crucial (see Goodfriend, 2004).

Inflation targeting is sometimes seen as a rigid framework that ties the hands of central bankers and constrains their decision-making in some respects. In practice, however, the monetary policy frameworks of most central banks do give them discretion in reacting to shocks, as to how quickly they aim to bring inflation back to target after a shock. The frameworks have evolved such that most are now described as 'flexible inflation targeting'.

In sum, focusing on low and stable inflation does not mean that short-term fluctuations in output and employment growth will be ignored in monetary policy formulation. This objective provides a framework for thinking about how other macro developments affect inflation and, therefore, how monetary policy should react to those developments. This provides some degree of flexibility to central bankers in reacting to different types of shocks and how persistent they are likely to be.

Moreover, it can increase the independence and effectiveness of monetary policy by setting more realistic expectations of what monetary policy can and cannot achieve. A central bank can achieve this by focusing attention on future inflation (which monetary policy can influence) rather than current inflation, which is already 'in the bag' as monetary policy can have an effect only with a lag. Finally, transparency about the monetary policy process allows financial market participants to plan for the already high volatility they need to deal with, without it being augmented by policy volatility.

One should also not oversell the benefits of this regime. In particular, it is worth making the point that adopting an inflation targeting regime by itself will not confer credibility on a central bank (Mishkin and Schmidt-Hebbel, 2005). But this regime has often been adopted as part of a package of measures aimed at building stronger institutions.

It provides a framework, in which policy makers can make a greater political commitment to price stability and, as in the case of Latin America, better fiscal policies. Thus, while inflation targeting may not be a macroeconomic panacea in itself, it can serve as a catalyst for a broader set of reforms that can increase the credibility of the central bank and deliver better outcomes on inflation and macroeconomic stability more generally.

Problems with an explicit inflation objective

In practice, inflation targeting poses a number of challenges for central bankers. One recent policy challenge for many emerging markets has been dealing with the volumes and volatility of capital inflows and outflows. Indeed, in some circumstances, these flows can drive monetary policy into a corner, as in the cases of many economies in Asia that experienced large capital inflows during 2005-2007, for instance (Singh, 2009).

This stoked domestic inflation, but central bankers in many of these countries found it difficult to raise interest rates to manage domestic inflation, as that would have drawn in more inflows. Exchange rate appreciation would, of course, serve as a shock absorber in these circumstances, but many of these economies were wary of allowing their exchange rates to fluctuate by a wide margin, which complicated matters.

A related problem other than just the sheer volume of inflows, is that it can be difficult to separate out long-term *versus* short-term speculative inflows. Unfortunately, reimposition of capital controls to control inflows, even in a selective manner, is a tried and failed option. It often ends up being not just ineffective but even counterproductive, as it injects uncertainty into an already unsettled environment. A case study of this is Thailand, which in December 2007 tried to impose a tax on short-term portfolio inflows. The market reaction was swift and brutal, with the stock market plunging by over 15 per cent in one day, forcing the government to largely rescind the controls.

What are the policy options for emerging markets facing such circumstances and how do the viable options vary for different types of economies? In the face of a surge in inflows, the central bank has few options to control inflation. One option is to allow the exchange rate to appreciate.

Exchange rate flexibility facilitates adjustment to relative prices, freeing up monetary policy to focus on the inflation objective. The downside is that the cost of hedging such exchange rate volatility falls on the private sector. In many emerging markets, financial underdevelopment means that currency derivatives and other instruments for hedging currency risk may not be available, putting an especially onerous burden on small and medium-sized enterprises that may not have easy access to hedging opportunities via international financial markets.

Another option is to intervene against appreciation. Some central banks in emerging markets have chosen to intervene aggressively in exchange markets to avoid excess volatility and also, what they perceive as divergence from fundamentals. But prolonged intervention can cause a surge in reserve accumulation, which then exposes central banks to the risks of currency mismatches on their balance sheets and potentially large carrying costs on their reserve portfolios.

In addition, this puts the onus on central banks to sterilise the intervention, as the liquidity inflows would otherwise undermine domestic price stability. Sterilisation, of course, has quasi-fiscal costs since the rate of return that has to be paid on sterilisation bonds is typically higher than that earned on liquid instruments, such as industrial country treasury bonds that reserves are kept in.

Such costs can mount very quickly as sterilisation levels increase. These problems with intervention are emphasised by Goodfriend and Prasad (2009) for China. However, the discussion of the Brazilian experience by Pires *et al.* (2009) shows that in some circumstances temporary reserve buildup through intervention need not have large costs and can be part of a strategy that incorporates exchange rate smoothing. Levy-Yeyati and Sturzenegger (2009) further strengthens the case for temporary intervention by presenting evidence on the link between relative undervaluation and growth.

A third policy option before emerging markets is to impose restrictions on capital inflows. This is becoming an increasingly unviable option, as *de facto* financial openness increases. Selective and targeted controls are a seductive option for a central bank that is concerned about specific types of flows, but these tend to be ineffective as there are inevitably large loopholes to get around these controls.

Comprehensive controls have large costs to economy and also tend to lose their effectiveness fairly quickly. But it remains an open question whether it is a viable, or ultimately counterproductive, short-run strategy for countries to hold on to whatever controls they have and thereby avoid 'unilateral disarmament' in the face of volatile capital flows (see Williamson, 2006).

A fourth option before an emerging market grappling with huge capital inflows and outflows, is to reduce restrictions on capital outflows. This is an appealing alternative to counterbalance inflows and take some of the pressure off the exchange rate. It may also have the advantage of generating many of the indirect benefits of financial openness that have been touted by various authors, including domestic financial development and opportunities for international portfolio diversification by domestic investors.

One problem is that once controls on outflows are weakened in good times, it may be difficult to turn off the taps in bad times when domestic and international investors are heading for the exits owing to a change in sentiment about an economy's prospects. This implies that opening up to outflows should be done in a controlled manner rather than as a one-shot full liberalisation (see Prasad and Rajan, 2008).

Difficult choices and outstanding analytical questions

How should an EMCB go about picking from the menu of tough choices laid out above? Monetary policy on the ground is, of course, a matter of judgment rather than mechanical rules, but academic knowledge has an important role in providing guidance on the relative merits and demerits of these choices. But only limited progress has been made so far in providing clear analytical guidance on these issues. And there are other related issues, where again much analytical work, both theoretical and empirical, remains to be done.

Many emerging markets have been experiencing rapid productivity growth relative to their major industrial country trading partners and are, therefore, experiencing pressures for real exchange rate appreciation. What then are the relative costs, for instance, of accepting real exchange rate appreciation through nominal appreciation or inflation? For example, Levy-Yeyati and Sturzenegger (2009) suggest that there are growth benefits to some undervaluation.

Is it really true that holding down the nominal exchange rate results in inflation taking on the burden of adjustment? To answer such questions, a great deal of work needs to be done to understand whether the interest rate channel or the exchange rate channel is more important in emerging markets for transmitting the effects of monetary policy actions.

One response to the sort of conundrum laid out above is to argue that it is better for central bankers to adopt a pragmatic and flexible approach, rather than a rule-bound framework. India's central bankers, for instance, have an inflation objective but do actively manage the exchange rate at times (also see Yi (2001) for a Chinese central banker's views on this issue).

Some policymakers seem to feel that this type of approach gives them a degree of operational freedom, since they can keep market participants guessing and avoid giving markets one-way bets. But there are some potentially negative effects of such an approach, which have been in evidence in the Indian context.

It makes outcomes of monetary policy actions less predictable since the market is never entirely sure of how to interpret individual policy actions, leading to market overreactions in some circumstances. This reduces the effectiveness of the monetary transmission mechanism. It also increases overall policy uncertainty, which is not good for anchoring inflation expectations, or for growth and stability.

A different set of questions enter into the complicated relationship between monetary policy and financial markets. How should monetary policy react to asset-price bubbles? Are there conflicts between the monetary policy and financial stability objectives? What are the implications for the optimal regulatory structure for banks and other financial institutions? Is it better for the central bank not to be the direct regulator of banks, freeing it up to take monetary policy decisions, without having to be constrained by worries about the repercussions on the banking system? (For a practitioner's perspective on these issues, see Reddy, 2008).

Events in 2007 and 2008 showed that faced with a looming financial crisis, a central bank cannot ignore the banking system when pursuing its monetary policy objective (see Mohan, 2007, for a related discussion). Events related to the US bailout of Bear Stearns and the failure of Northern Rock in the UK show that conventional wisdom does not always hold. The US Federal Reserve won at least a few plaudits for rescuing non-bank institutions, while the BoE's reputation was damaged, even though it was not the regulator of the bank in question.

There are also a number of practical issues that need to be confronted in the context of an inflation targeting regime. For instance, what is the right inflation rate to target? Theory tells us that monetary policy should target the inflexible component of price index, i.e., core inflation, and not attempt to offset certain relative price shifts that have no long-run implications for general consumer price index (CPI) inflation.

In practice, almost all inflation-targeting central banks target the headline measure of inflation. In EMEs, the reality is that a large part of the consumption basket of average household is accounted for by food and energy. The price of food, in particular, can rise rapidly, putting central bankers in a quandary since targeting core inflation then becomes politically unacceptable.

Moreover, rising food and fuel prices have economic consequences that a central bank cannot ignore. Food and fuel prices, may for example, create upward pressure on wages as workers strive to maintain real incomes. Such second-round effects may result in higher inflation becoming entrenched and require a larger monetary policy response to bring inflation back to target.

A different complication arises when there is a large divergence between inflation based on regional CPI or between urban and rural CPI inflation. What price index should central bankers really focus on and why? What are the trade-offs in terms of credibility and ease of communications *versus* effective monetary control of choosing different price indexes as the target? Clearly, the list of unanswered questions far outnumbers those for which we have more or less arrived at plausible answers that both academics and practitioners can agree upon.

Bridging the gaps between theory and practice

How can academic research contribute to improving the formulation of monetary policy and addressing the difficult challenges that central bankers face in a concrete way? Many practitioners feel that the academic literature has failed to come to grips with the complexities and messiness of policymaking in the real world.

Mervyn King (2005), for instance, has gently noted that in some respects monetary practice is ahead of monetary theory. The discussion in the preceding sections has laid out a number of issues where theory has not provided clear-cut answers. There are, however, challenges in another dimension as well—incorporating the knowledge from existing theory (and related empirical evidence) into the policymaking process.

We list some obvious challenges in these two dimensions. Analytical models currently used by central banks have serious limitations. For instance, neo-Keynesian models that are still widely used in many policy institutions typically have very little role for money, despite a broad consensus that in the long-run inflation remains a monetary phenomenon (Goodhart, 2009).

Dynamic stochastic general equilibrium (DSGE) models hold out a lot of promises in terms of formulating monetary policy, but often have a limited role for the financial sector and for commodity prices (see Goodfriend and King, 1997; Goodfriend, 2002; Woodford, 2003). So, the available models are not very helpful in thinking about how central banks should react to shocks, such as sharp changes in food or fuel prices, or dislocation in financial markets.

On the financial stability side, the development of macro-models with real-financial linkages that can help seriously analyse issues of financial and macro-stability in a general equilibrium context is still in its infancy. At the same time, theoretical models have not yet done a good job of figuring out how to model the formation of inflation expectations, which is a key input into monetary policy formulation.

Despite the potency of the Lucas critique, models with backward-looking expectations still dominate, in part because of their tractability relative to models with forward-looking expectations. One way of making progress on these difficult issues will be through a process of regular interactive dialogue between central bankers and academics.

Appendix

Emerging market central banks should focus on inflation

Inflation targeting has become the monetary policy framework of choice for emerging markets. Following the lead of developed countries, most EMCBs have adopted frameworks in which their priority is to maintain price rises at a target level or within a specified range. Many others are moving towards such a system.

Inflation targeting has a good track record of delivering price stability and anchoring inflation expectations. This is valuable in emerging markets, where high inflation is especially pernicious as it hits the poor very hard.

Even as its popularity has spread, inflation targeting has come under sharp attack in the aftermath of the global financial crisis. Central bankers in developed economies are being pilloried for focusing too much on price stability, ignoring asset-market bubbles and failing to prevent the worst crisis seen for a generation.

Many emerging markets have weathered the crisis quite well but their central banks also face pressure to abandon inflation targets. Critics argue that targeting inflation could be damaging in these economies, if it means ignoring sharp exchange rate fluctuations and boom-bust cycles in equity and housing markets.

There is no doubt that asset-market booms in advanced economies fuelled the global financial crisis. This has given rise to the notion that, in addition to their goal of price stability, central banks should be given a further explicit objective of puncturing asset-price bubbles to maintain financial stability.

There is however, a deep tension between central banks having multiple objectives and the operational independence needed to achieve the inflation target. Broader objectives invariably mean more political interference and less credibility in maintaining low inflation.

This tension is heightened in emerging markets, where central banks have traditionally been responsible for a broad array of social and economic goals in addition to price and financial stability. Some objectives, such as exchange rate management, already complicate the conduct of monetary policy. Capital controls provide some breathing room, but they are porous and often impose many other costs on the economy.

How should EMCBs juggle these objectives? Certainly, inflation targeting frameworks can be improved to pay heed to signs of asset price and credit booms.

This Appendix contains an op-ed article written by Ravi Kanbur and Eswar Prasad that appeared in the *Financial Times* on January 6, 2010.

Indeed, better models of inflation forecasting should incorporate the effects of market booms on financial wealth and private consumption.

But it is not realistic to expect monetary policy to prevent asset bubbles by itself. The main instrument of monetary policy, the policy interest rate, is best used to target inflation. If central banks are to be given more responsibilities to moderate credit cycles and help prevent asset-price bubbles, they will need new tools.

There are other instruments better suited to managing asset-price booms—prudential regulatory policies to make leverage in housing and other asset markets more costly, tighten up lending standards and increase capital and liquidity requirements. These instruments should be developed and better coordinated with policy interest rates to manage inflation.

The bigger concern is whether central banks can maintain operational effectiveness and their independence if they have 'mandate creep'—that is, more and more objectives. Indeed, the independence of these institutions, which hangs by a thread in the best of times, is now under assault around the world. Even the US Congress is taking steps to increase oversight of the Federal Reserve. In these circumstances, increasing the responsibilities of central banks could make them more subject to political pressures and erode their credibility, especially in emerging markets where public finances are strained and the institutional framework is weak.

In many emerging markets, central banks are among the most well-managed and trusted public institutions. It is tempting to give them more responsibilities. But this should be done with great caution for it could make them less effective at the one thing they have proven good at—controlling inflation!

References

Adam, Christopher, Stephen O'Connell and Edward Buffie (2009). "Aid Volatility, Monetary Policy Rules and the Capital Account in African Economies", Chapter 13 in Gill Hammond, Ravi Kanbur and Eswar Prasad (eds.), *Monetary Policy Frameworks for Emerging Markets*. Edward Elgar Press.

Anand, Rahul and Eswar Prasad (2010). "Optimal Price Indices for Targeting Inflation Under Incomplete Markets". Manuscript. Cornell University.

Aron, Janine and John Muellbauer (2009). "Monetary Policy and Inflation in a More Open Economy in South Africa", Chapter 15 in Gill Hammond, Ravi Kanbur and Eswar Prasad (eds.), *Monetary Policy Frameworks for Emerging Markets*. Edward Elgar Press.

Bernanke, Ben, Thomas Laubach, Fredrick Mishkin and Adam Posen (1999). *Inflation Targeting: Lessons from International Experience*. Princeton, N.J.: Princeton University Press.

Bernanke, Ben and Michael Woodford (eds.) (2005). *The Inflation Targeting Debate*. Chicago, IL: University of Chicago Press.

Blanchard, Olivier (2005). "Discussion of Inflation Targeting in Transition Countries: Experience and Prospects", in Ben Bernanke and Michael Woodford (eds.), *The Inflation Targeting Debate*. Chicago, IL: University of Chicago Press.

Broaddus, J. Alfred and Marvin Goodfriend (2004). "Sustaining Price Stability", *Economic Quarterly* 90(3): 3-20, Summer, US: Federal Reserve Bank of Richmond.

Buffie, Edward, Christopher Adam, Stephen O'Connell and Catherine Patillo (2009). "Aid Reversals, Credibility, and Macroeconomic Policy", Chapter 6 in Gill Hammond, Ravi Kanbur and Eswar Prasad (eds.), *Monetary Policy Frameworks for Emerging Markets*. Edward Elgar Press.

De Gregorio, Jose (2009). "Implementation of Inflation Targets in Emerging Markets", Chapter 3 in Gill Hammond, Ravi Kanbur and Eswar Prasad (eds.), *Monetary Policy Frameworks for Emerging Markets*. Edward Elgar Press.

Dragutinovic, Diana (2009). "Monetary and Fiscal Policy Mix in Serbia: 2002-2007", Chapter 12 in Gill Hammond, Ravi Kanbur and Eswar Prasad (eds.), *Monetary Policy Frameworks for Emerging Markets*. Edward Elgar Press.

Fielding, David (2009). "Regional Asymmetries in the Impact of Monetary Policy on Prices: Evidence from Africa", Chapter 14 in Gill Hammond, Ravi Kanbur and Eswar Prasad (eds.), *Monetary Policy Frameworks for Emerging Markets*. Edward Elgar Press.

Goodfriend, Marvin (2002). "Monetary Policy in the New Neoclassical Synthesis: A Primer", *International Finance: 165-92.* Summer. Reprinted in *Economic Quarterly: 21-45.* Summer. 2004. US: Federal Reserve Bank of Richmond.

———. (2004). "Understanding the Transmission of Monetary Policy", manuscript, Federal Reserve Bank of Richmond. Presented at Joint China-IMF High Level Seminar on *China's Monetary Policy Transmission Mechanism*. Beijing. May.

Goodfriend, Marvin and Robert King (1997). "The New Neoclassical Synthesis and the Role of Monetary Policy," in Ben Bernanke and Julio Rotemberg (eds.), *NBER Macroeconomics Annual*. pp.231-95. Cambridge, MA: MIT Press.

Goodfriend, Marvin and Eswar Prasad (2009). "A Framework for Independent Monetary Policy in China", Chapter 8 in Gill Hammond, Ravi Kanbur and Eswar Prasad (eds.), *Monetary Policy Frameworks for Emerging Markets*. Edward Elgar Press.

Goodhart, Charles (2009). "Whatever Became of the Monetary Aggregates?", Chapter 4 in Gill Hammond, Ravi Kanbur and Eswar Prasad (eds.), *Monetary Policy Frameworks for Emerging Markets*. Edward Elgar Press.

Husain, Aasim, Ashoka Mody and Kenneth Rogoff (2005). "Exchange Rate Durability and Performance in Developing versus Advanced Economies", *Journal of Monetary Economics* 52: 35-64.

Jonas, Jiri and Frederic S. Mishkin (2005). "Inflation Targeting in Transition Countries: Experience and Prospects", in Ben Bernanke and Michael Woodford (eds.), *The Inflation Targeting Debate*. Chicago, IL: University of Chicago Press.

Kalyalya, Denny (2009). "Monetary Policy in Zambia: Experiences and Challenges", Chapter 17 in Gill Hammond, Ravi Kanbur and Eswar Prasad (eds.), *Monetary Policy Frameworks for Emerging Markets*. Edward Elgar Press.

King, Mervyn (2005). "Monetary Policy: Practice Ahead of Theory". Mais lecture. *http://www.bankofengland.co.uk/publications/speeches/2005/speech245.pdf*

Levy-Yeyati, Eduardo and Federico Sturzenegger (2009). "Fear of Appreciation: Exchange Rate Policy as a Development Strategy", Chapter 5 in Gill Hammond, Ravi Kanbur and Eswar Prasad (eds.) *Monetary Policy Frameworks for Emerging Markets*. Edward Elgar Press.

McKinnon, Ronald I. (2006). "China's Exchange Rate Trap: Japan Redux?", *American Economic Review* 6(2): 427-31, forthcoming.

Mishkin, Frederic S. (2000). "Inflation Targeting in Emerging-Market Countries", *The American Economic Review Papers and Proceedings* 90(2): 105-109.

Mishkin, Frederic S. and Klaus Schmidt-Hebbel (2005). "Does Inflation Targeting Make a Difference". Manuscript. Columbia University.

Nijathaworn, Bandid and Piti Disyatat (2009). "The Pursuit of Monetary and Financial Stability in Emerging Market Economies", Chapter 2 in Gill Hammond, Ravi Kanbur and Eswar Prasad (eds.), *Monetary Policy Frameworks for Emerging Markets*. Edward Elgar Press.

Mohan, Rakesh (2007). "Recent Financial Market Developments and Implications For Monetary Policy", Valedictory Address at *IIF's Inaugural Asia Regional Economic Forum*. September 20.

Mohan, Rakesh and Michael Patra (2009). "Monetary Policy Transmission in India", Chapter 9 in Gill Hammond, Ravi Kanbur and Eswar Prasad (eds.), *Monetary Policy Frameworks for Emerging Markets*. Edward Elgar Press.

Niedermayer, Ludek (2009). "Czech Experience with Inflation Targeting", Chapter 11 in Gill Hammond, Ravi Kanbur and Eswar Prasad (eds.), *Monetary Policy Frameworks for Emerging Markets*. Edward Elgar Press.

Pires, Daniela Silva, Paulo Vieira da Cunha and Wenersamy Ramos de Alcantara (2009). "Inflation Targeting and the Exchange Rate: Notes on Brazil's Experience", Chapter 10 in Gill Hammond, Ravi Kanbur and Eswar Prasad (eds.), *Monetary Policy Frameworks for Emerging Markets*. Edward Elgar Press.

Prasad, Eswar and Shang-Jin Wei (2007). "The Chinese Approach to Capital Inflows: Patterns and Possible Explanations", in Sebastian Edwards (ed.), *Capital Controls and Capital Flows in Emerging Economies: Policies, Practices, and Consequences*. Chicago, IL: University of Chicago Press.

Prasad, Eswar (2009). "Is China's Growth Miracle Built to Last?", *China Economic Review* 20(1): 103-123.

Prasad, Eswar and Raghuram Rajan (2008). "A Pragmatic Approach to Capital Account Liberalization", *Journal of Economic Perspectives* 22(3): 149-72.

Reddy, Yaga V. (2008). "Monetary and Regulatory Policies: How to Get the Balance Right", Speech at the BIS. June 29.

Rose, Andrew (2006). "A Stable International System Emerges: Bretton Woods, Reversed", *CEPR Discussion Paper* 5854.

Singh, Sukhdave (2009). "The Nexus between Monetary and Financial Stability: The Experience of Selected Asian Economies", Chapter 7 in Gill Hammond, Ravi Kanbur and Eswar Prasad (eds.), *Monetary Policy Frameworks for Emerging Markets.* Edward Elgar Press.

Sims, Christopher (2005). "Limits to Inflation Targeting", in B. Bernanke and M. Woodford, (eds.), *The Inflation Targeting Debate*. Chicago: University of Chicago Press.

Sowa, Nii Kwaku and Philip Abradu-Otoo (2009). "Inflation Management and Monetary Policy Formulation in Ghana", Chapter 16 in Gill Hammond, Ravi Kanbur and Eswar Prasad (eds.), *Monetary Policy Frameworks for Emerging Markets.* Edward Elgar Press.

Williamson, John (1998). "Crawling Bands or Monitoring Bands: How to Manage Exchange Rates in a World of Capital Mobility", *International Finance* 1(1): 59-79.

———. (2006). "Why Capital Account Convertibility in India Is Premature", *Economic and Political Weekly*: 1848-1850, May 13.

Woodford, Michael (2003). *Interest and Prices: Foundations of a Theory of Monetary Policy*. Princeton, N.J.: Princeton University Press.

Yi, Gang (2001). "The Framework of China's Monetary Policy", manuscript, People's Bank of China (Beijing, China). Presented at the PBC-IMF International Seminar on *Monetary Policy Operations*. May. Suzhou, China.

24 Summing-up

MICHAEL FOOT

I would like to begin with what I regard as one of the most insightful speeches made in recent decades by a central bank governor. I will then focus on one particular concern it raises—a concern that I have shared throughout the global crisis and which needs to be addressed as exit strategies are being sought.

The speech was given by the man who taught me more than anyone else about central banking—Eddie George. I had the honour of working for him for some 20 years at the Bank of England (BoE), as he rose to become governor in 1993 and while he was in office. His death last year was a great personal loss to his family and many friends and a huge loss of practical central bank expertise.

On November 18, 1993 as the UK began to get over the banking crisis of the early 1990s, Eddie gave a speech at the London School of Economics.[1] The extent of covert support to banks that the BoE had provided in the early 1990's had only recently become public knowledge, though of course, the scale of this assistance was minute in comparison with what has been provided in recent years. Eddie decided that he needed to pick out some 'lessons learned', and to set some guidelines for future central bank involvement in aid to banks.

What he said then, would now no doubt attract little attention if it were said now, because much of it has passed into mainstream thinking. But at the time such a coherent and clear-sighted public statement on how bank rescues should be tackled was most unusual. Eddie's starting point was that the terms of any bank rescue that involved the central bank

Summing-up by Michael Foot, Chairman, Session IV: Financial Stability as an Objective of Monetary Policy.

1. Reprinted in The Bank of England *Quarterly Review* February, 1994.

should be, 'as penal as we can make them without precipitating the collapse we are trying to avoid'. He then set out five principles for coming to the assistance of banks in trouble.

The first principle was that every option would be explored *before* the central bank committed its own funds. The second was that there would be no public subsidy to private shareholders. It was decided that if support was provided, 'we would try to structure it so that any losses fall first on the shareholders and any benefits come first to us'. The third principle was that the central bank would not normally provide funds to a bank it knows to be insolvent. The fourth was that the central bank would always look to establish in advance a clear exit. The fifth principle for assisting banks in trouble was that support should normally be kept secret at the time.

Nowadays, I suspect the issue of what could and should be kept secret might provoke more of a debate than it did then. I am sure, though, that central bankers the world over still hanker for a life in which secrecy is possible for more than a few hours. There are also many issues wrapped up in the simple statement that, from the outset, there needs to be a clear exit in sight, but that is another issue.

The point I want to focus on is the concern that Eddie always had, that people had to take responsibility for their actions and that central bank action should always try to reinforce this principle. In particular, he thought that there should never be circumstances where depositors, shareholders or others could 'game the system', so that profits accrued to them, while losses accrued to others. In short, he was very concerned about what is generally termed 'moral hazard'.

He always argued, for instance, that deposit protection should never provide 100 per cent compensation. This was because that practice gave a perverse incentive for people to chase yield, safe in the knowledge that provided they kept their deposits below some publicly-known threshold, they would be made whole for losses by a compensation fund.

In looking at what has happened in the last couple of years, I am loathe to pass any censorious judgments on what authorities round the world did or did not do. It is only if you have lived through such events 'on the inside' that you know just how much (normally, just how little) information was available at the time the decisions had to be made!

We all have to accept that the scale and nature of some of the decisions that were made at this time were of a size and complexity that dwarfed most previous challenges. As an 'outsider' at that time, I certainly want to be very careful about passing judgments tinged with the aid of hindsight.

That said, throughout the crisis, I have worried that many authorities have failed to have sufficient regard for the risk of moral hazard, by so often providing what has been effectively a blanket 100 per cent underwriting of deposit risk. In my opinion, it is going to be extraordinarily difficult to get away from that commitment or, if it is dropped, to make people believe that a similar comfort blanket will not get thrown over the banking system again as soon as there is serious trouble. What ought to be a key part of market discipline on depositors going forward may just not be there.

We have seen before how the authorities' handling of systemic problems can generate serious major moral hazard issues. Two notable instances to my mind were the way in which the US authorities handled the savings and loan (S&L) crisis in the 1980s and how regulators and central banks handled Long-Term Capital Management (LTCM) implosion in the late 1990s. Indeed, I think some of the rescue actions taken in 2008-2009 followed directly from the way these crises were handled and the 'lessons' that stakeholders drew from those events.

Now, I think the great danger we face is that the authorities—especially the fiscal authorities—will decide that they will not be able to do without the 100 per cent safety blanket for deposits in future troubles easily. Instead, they may look for ways to slim the biggest banks down to a size where it will be possible to contemplate their 'demise'. Or, and this I think would have serious economic consequences, they may look for non-price ways to try to limit the risk of renewed failure among the large banks, in order to limit the future liability of the tax-payer.

How might this non-price intervention work and why would it carry real costs? Well, clearly, the risk of a bank failure can be reduced by demanding that higher liquidity and capital be held. Of course, the need for higher liquidity and capital requirements can be readily defended anyway, as a rational regulatory response to what has occurred.

The great danger is that these demands will be upped for political reasons to a point where the economics of banking is seriously disturbed. We have already seen in some countries, for reasons of politics, public bodies requiring banks, over whom they have leverage, to change their behaviour on executive remuneration and to amend lending practices (initially to favour small and medium enterprises).

Already, in a few cases, we have seen governments influencing where a bank does business geographically. The risk is that many governments will get a taste of such interventions. The danger is that they may then use them to further their political objectives and reduce the risk profile of their largest banks so that—if blanket deposit insurance has to be retained—it is less likely to be needed.

The increased requirements on banks already in train are going to make many forms of banking a much less attractive business proposition than hitherto, and limit new competition. That is inevitable and, if competition is seriously reduced, potentially harmful. In many countries over the last two years, we have indeed seen competition in many banking markets falling, as well as a huge reduction in the risk appetite of bank managements.

Central banks may well argue that competition policy is not their business and, in a strict sense, that is true. But the extraordinary flood of liquidity provided has helped some banks much more than others and banks as a class over other financial intermediaries. The way in which it is withdrawn and a more 'normal' yield curve re-established may help (or hinder) wider efforts to leave us with a banking system that, while prudentially sound, is still innovative, competitive and willing to take economically justifiable risks. We can only hope that the exit strategies finally chosen, when combined with other national policies (on competition, the granting of new banking licences, etc.), help rather than hinder.

25 Summing-up

K.C. CHAKRABARTY

I think I will just summarise the key take-aways distilled from the two important papers presented and also the discussions on them. The first take-away is on the liquidity support. It has been said that various conventional and unconventional liquidity support measures which have been utilised during the time of distress, *prima facie*, have shown results, though, Eswar Prasad has averred that there are medium-term and long-term implications to consider. It has also led to many other issues such as moral hazard, especially regarding whether we are providing liquidity support or solvency support. That issue remains unresolved. The basic take-away is that we need to frame some policy, and have a framework for such crisis situations on how to provide liquidity support to various types of institutions in the market. I hope that the Basel Committee on Banking Supervision (BCBS) and Financial Stability Board (FSB) will work on that and in the next crisis situation, as and when it comes, we will be able to handle it better.

Now coming to the exit policy, it is certain that we need to exit. The first take-away thus is that we need to exit. It needs to be coordinated across nations. It needs to be coordinated with the fiscal stimulus. Sequencing is also important. But nobody knows how and when it is going to happen and it will vary from country to country and between emerging markets and developed markets. I feel it has to be evolutionary because we have never passed through such a situation before and, hence, these are all extraordinary measures. I think imagination and what we call 'our own wisdom' has to be used in creating the exit strategy by different countries. May be we will learn from this crisis and, hence, the responses to the crisis

Summing-up by K.C. Chakrabarty, Co-Chair, Session IV: Financial Stability as an Objective of Monetary Policy.

need to be documented to be able to cope better in future. Subsequently, Prasad and the Session's Chairman Michael Foot have raised certain basic issues about the independence of the central banking: what is going to happen, what will be the mandate of central banks, how difficult it is to identify what is systemic risk, etc? I think this session has created a background for tomorrow's session when the Governors' panel will be discussing these issues.

Section V

Governors Speak

Section V

Governors Speak

This section corresponds to Session V of the First International Research Conference on 'Challenges to Central Banking in the Context of Financial Crisis', Reserve Bank of India, Mumbai.

Moderator: Martin Wolf, Associate Editor and Chief Economics Commentator Financial Times, London.

Panel 1: Domestic Monetary Policy

Panelists: Christian Noyer, Governor, Bank of France; Glenn Robert Stevens, Governor, Reserve Bank of Australia; Duvvuri Subbarao, Governor, Reserve Bank of India; Tarisa Watanagase, Governor, Bank of Thailand.

Panel 2: International Monetary System

Panelists: Atiur Rahman, Governor, Bangladesh Bank; Daw Tenzin, Managing Director, Royal Monetary Authority of Bhutan; Mark J. Carney, Governor, Bank of Canada; Miguel Angel Fernandez Ordonez, Governor, Bank of Spain; Duvvuri Subbarao, Governor, Reserve Bank of India.

26 Governors Speak—Panel I

Domestic Monetary Policy

Martin Wolf: Our panel discussions this morning are divided into two different themes—the present one is on the formation of domestic monetary policy in the light of the crisis and the second one will be on the international monetary system (IMS). The first topic will be centred around the themes of yesterday's discussion, focusing, in particular, on three major issues: first and most important, the lessons to be learned from the crisis, about what was right and what was wrong about monetary policy leading up to the crisis, the future of inflation targeting and so forth; second, about the crisis response and exit from the crisis and finally, about the role of central banks, specifically as regulators. Since the Panel is perfectly balanced in terms of representatives of central banks in high-income countries and in important emerging countries, it should be an exceptionally interesting debate, because I expect the perspectives to be somewhat different between these two groups of countries.

The second Panel will focus on international monetary issues, which, in fact, we have not discussed much in this Conference with very few exceptions. But I think most of us, who have looked at this issue with any care, recognise that the IMS is also an important aspect of what has been happening. There also has been immense debate about reform of the IMS.

I would like to start with you, Mr. Noyer. How far do you think this crisis indicates that the way central banks were approaching monetary policy before the crisis, particularly the focus on inflation targeting, was mistaken?

Christian Noyer: Thank you very much. I will make three series of remarks and try to keep it short. First, I think there were mainly two lessons or questions which have been raised. The first is about inflation targeting strategies as you mentioned. When central banks have gained credibility on their inflation targeting, then unsustainable economic expansion tends to show up more in asset prices rather than in the inflation of the prices of goods and services and that may lead to risk-taking, since cheap liquidity tends to foster risk appetite and leverage.

The other question or lesson drawn by a number of commentators is about the symmetric reaction of central banks to bubbles. The risk of deflation associated with this leads to a stronger reaction when the bubble bursts and when it does, the insurance against asset-price losses that were provided by monetary policy may lead to excessive risk-taking strategies.

I, personally, see at least three other factors responsible for the run-up to the current crisis. One is the global imbalances. Remember that in 2004 and 2005, monetary policy had been tightened in the advanced economies. However, long-term interest rates remained insensitive to this tightening—this was described as the 'conundrum' you may remember—and that may be related to capital inflows due to major current account imbalances.

The other one is asset shortages, sometimes described the other way around as the 'savings block'. I think the shortage of safe and liquid assets to invest savings in emerging economies may well have played a role in the build-up of bubbles. And, finally, the issue of financial market weakness. In particular, the transformation of risky and illiquid assets into AAA assets has been performed at the expense of higher sensitivity to extreme events, which obviously have been considerably underestimated by market participants.

The last series of remarks relate to what lessons we can draw from that and what central banks should do. At this stage, I would submit three ideas. One of the objectives, certainly without prejudice of the permanent price stability objective, could be financial stability and sought after by monetary policy. I think this approach is already well-encompassed by the so-called second pillar of our strategy where we examine credit and monetary developments—not only because we believe that they are key determinants of long-term inflation but they are also, as a matter of fact, leading indicators of financial imbalances.

The second idea is about the tools. It is quite clear to me that financial imbalances are better addressed by macroprudential policies. I think we, the central banks, are better endowed to contribute to such policies because we have the incentives. It is clear that monetary policy works better when financial markets function properly. We also are used to monitoring financial market developments and banks. And finally, we have the necessary independence to take away the punch bowls just when the party gets going. It is more delicate when it comes to asset price bubbles and inflation because of the difficulty of identifying a bubble. But this leads to, I think, the developmental function there. You may know that within Europe, we are trying to achieve that through the European Systemic Risk Board (ESRB).

Finally, I think there is a question about both from the policy and operational perspective. I will not elaborate a lot on the question about the interactions between monetary and macroprudential policy, not only because I promised to keep it short but also because I think we need more work to understand how they play together. I can well imagine both circumstances in which policies may have either offsetting or compounding effects on the financial system in the economy. We need to understand these interactions better if we want to deliver a better chance of financial stability in future.

Martin Wolf: Thank you very much for a very comprehensive and swift answer. I notice—perhaps we will come back to this—that you emphasised the second pillar of the European Central Bank's (ECB) monetary framework, which of course policymakers and economists, particularly in English-speaking countries, tended to regard as mildly ridiculous. So, that is actually one of the more interesting resurrections—I would not say from the dead—but it intellectually raised an interesting set of questions. I am going to stick with the high-income countries for the moment before we get to the emerging country perspective. So Mr. Stevens, how does this set of questions look to you and where, if anywhere, would you differ from the way Mr. Noyer looked at it.

Glenn Robert Stevens: Well, let me make a couple of remarks here. I think I would not regard the recent set of events as necessarily indicating a failure of inflation targeting *per se*. It is true that some countries that are formally inflation targeters have had very deep recessions and financial crisis. But it is also true that some of the countries that had crisis are not formal inflation targeters. Furthermore, there are a number of other countries—and my own is one—in which the pursued inflation targeting has, I think, been relatively successful in this period. In our own case, yes, we had a downturn, but far from this being the biggest recession since World War II, it was actually the smallest. So, in my mind, I think it would not be the right lesson to draw that inflation targeting should in any sense be abandoned or that it has comprehensively failed.

Having said that though, I think the issue is whether we are working with the right model of the economy. I think this goes beyond monitoring credit aggregates. I fully agree with the notion that it is more important than many of us in the English-speaking countries might have hitherto thought it to be. We have always tried to keep a close eye on credit. But, I think the issue goes beyond that. I think the problem is that in the models of the world, which we are working with, we have only a very crude understanding of the behaviour of financial institutions as they extend credit and the behaviour of all the risk-takers, so to speak, in the financial sector. My guess is that in all our models, be the econometric models or the ones we are carrying around in our heads, we have only a very limited assessment or capture of those dynamics. I think, that is important because if it is true, as a number of people today claim, that the setting of monetary policy influences the risk-taking behaviour of all the entities in the financial sector, then I think it is quite hard for monetary policy to escape completely the charge that it may have, however inadvertently, done something to foster the build-up of excessive leverage and risk.

I think what we need to be doing is working harder on capturing those dynamics in the way we think about the world and I think down that track lies the scope to duly take account of financial stability concerns in the setting of monetary policies. So I guess my story is: we should not throw away inflation targeting *per se*, but we need a richer, more realistic model of how the financial sector of the economy works and how monetary policy interacts with that. I suspect if we can get that richer model, the conduct of policy will be a bit different in the future.

Martin Wolf: So this is inflation targeting plus in a way, and let us come back to that in a moment, to tease out some of those issues. I would now like to turn, if I may, to Ms. Watanagase from the Bank of Thailand (BoT). How does, if at all, this crisis, this breakdown in the high-income countries' economies from the financial crisis, affect the way you look at the formation of monetary policy within your own country? Does it have any lessons for you at all, or is it actually some other's catastrophe while you have actually done rather well?

Tarisa Watanagase: Well, in fact, I have a list of questions and answers, at least five of them. I will just try to give my views on these important issues. These are short answers—probably we will have more time to come back to the details later on.

The first question: Has inflation targeting contributed to the crisis? My answer is, no. In my view, I think inflation targeting has been able to do what it decided to do and that is to maintain price stability through the anchoring of inflation expectations. I think the inflation targeting framework has been able to do that job both before and after the crisis. Now I am going to stop right there. We will come back to the details later.

Having said that, I must say that there are challenges going forward. Inflation targeting has been able to do the job simply because central banks have been able to maintain credibility. Now, going forward, there is a big question mark lying ahead whether central banks would be able to maintain credibility and anchor inflation expectations. There are a few challenges. First, we are right now concerned about fiscal dominance. Second, we are concerned about forecast uncertainty. Yesterday, we talked about uncertainties arising from the fall in potential output arising from regulatory changes, just to mention one. So basically, I think what central banks need to do is to show commitment to maintain credibility and maintain independence from fiscal dominance.

The second issue is: did monetary policy contribute to the crisis? Here, I purposefully make a distinction between inflation targeting and monetary policy. I think they are two distinct questions. And the answer here is yes. In my view, maintaining low interest rates for a long period of time set the stage for the crisis through the build-up of asset price bubble and excessive risk-taking behaviour.

The third question is: should financial stability be part of the central bank's mandate? Yes, and there is no conflict between maintaining long-term price stability and maintaining financial stability because, to me, both policies contribute to sustainable economic growth and the long-term well-being of the masses. When you maintain price stability, the ultimate objective is to make sure that you have sustainable growth and business sector and consumers are able to make the right decisions regarding investment and consumption to ensure sustainable growth. Obviously, when you maintain financial stability, you should be able to prevent the cycles of booms and busts. Because, without that, you will not be able to maintain sustainability in economic growth either.

Another point here is that even though it is difficult to intergrate the objective of financial stability into the monetary policy mandate, but I would like to say that there are simple microprudential tools that can be very useful and they work well, especially, I think, in most, if not all, countries in Asia.

The next question is: are we doing the right thing in crisis response, in preventing the next crisis? I think the answer is, yes. Putting additional focus on financial stability and strengthening supervision and regulation are the right things to do. Perhaps we should focus a bit more on supervision rather than regulation.

The next important point that I would like to make is that although these reform efforts are in the right direction, they are necessary, but not sufficient conditions to prevent the next crisis. We all know that risks or vulnerabilities tend to shift, sometimes very rapidly, and the next crisis would be here, perhaps, in a very different form and from very different causes with different impacts.

So, I think the first thing that we need to do is to focus and have more corrective efforts in three more areas. The first is in the area of risk awareness and risk management. In fact, everyone played a part in the last crisis, but at the moment, there is a lot of finger-pointing towards the central banks, towards the financial sector and financial institutions. But I think John Lipsky said yesterday that the crisis was a failure in market assessment, in risk management, and also governance. To that, I would also like to add consumers who spent beyond their means. So the first lesson to draw from here is that we need to create risk awareness. We need to praise the importance of doing risk management and we have to say that the excess is bad and not sustainable. How do we do that? We just have to keep on pressing and pressing and also to demonstrate, when appropriate, with action.

The second area that we need to focus on a bit more is to undo the moral hazards that have been put in place in this crisis. When we had our crisis in 1997, we made shareholders of the financial institutions pay. So we see a lot of moral hazard being put in place from the way resolutions are being done. This is an area that we absolutely have to pay more attention to.

The third message—I would like to say this is very important for the policy authorities—is to put in place the right policies and the right incentives because economic agents would just respond to whatever policies and incentives we put out there. So we have to be careful about that.

Martin Wolf: Thank you very much. You raised a lot of very important questions, taking the debate on in important ways, which we will come back to in a short time. Now I would like to ask Subbarao for his perspective on the implications of this crisis for the formation of monetary policy.

Duvvuri Subbarao: I want to break up your question into two sub-questions. First, what are the implications of the crisis for inflation targeting and second, how do we, from the Indian perspective, see inflation targeting as an objective for the Reserve Bank of India (RBI).

Unlike some others, I think the lessons of the crisis are clear, which is that pure inflation targeting does not work. I must admit though, that I am looking at this issue from an Indian perspective. We do not do a very sophisticated nuancing of using monetary policy and inflation targeting instruments. So I am looking at the global issue from an Indian perspective and I believe that the lessons of the crisis are very clear—which is that price stability does not guarantee financial stability. Therefore, inflation targeting, while important and necessary, is not sufficient. You need to go beyond inflation targeting. Yesterday, I talked about why pure inflation targeting is *per se* about the Greenspan orthodoxy and the unravelling of the Greenspan orthodoxy by the crisis.

Now, I want to answer the second question. In fact, I want to spend much of my time giving an Indian perspective. The RBI is a full service central bank, unlike most other central banks. We are the monetary authority, but we are also the regulator of banks, non-banks, and a large segment of the financial markets. We are the debt manager for the central government and the state governments. We are the issuers of currency. We are regulators for payments and settlement systems. So, we are a multi-service central bank. And I believe that we cannot be focusing just on inflation for several reasons. First, in a developing country like India, we have other concerns such as growth, and financial stability. Therefore, we cannot be focusing on just price stability. In fact, if you see our policy documents, you will see that from quarter to quarter, we shift relative emphasis across these three variables—price stability, financial stability, and growth. So we cannot be focusing, given our development concerns, just on inflation.

Second, much of our inflation is supply-side driven. For example, in the consumer price indices (CPI), food has a weightage of 46 per cent to 70 per cent. And everyone has agreed, including purist monetary policy theorists such as yourselves, that monetary policy is an ineffective instrument for targeting inflation when inflation comes from the supply-side as it does in our country, except as a line of defence in an extreme situation.

Third, in India, we have one wholesale price index (WPI) and four CPIs. We are a country of one billion people of different climatic zones, different poverty levels, different economic situations. So, which inflation index do we target? Inflation in different parts of the country is different.

Fourth, our monetary transmission system is quite immature. We have a large government borrowing, and fiscal concerns influence monetary policy. I would not say fiscal concerns dominate but they certainly influence monetary policy. In the phase of large fiscal deficits, we have administered interest rates. So, that all makes monetary transmission somewhat less than efficient.

For all these reasons, first, because of our concerns with growth and price stability, second, because of inflation being largely driven most of the time by supply-side concerns for which monetary policy is not an effective instrument, third, because we do not have a single inflation index measure for the entire country, and fourth, because of monetary transmission being less than efficient, I believe that in the RBI, we cannot be targeting inflation.

Martin Wolf: Thank you very much. Presumably, the crisis has not fundamentally changed that perspective in your case but it may have strengthened it.

Duvvuri Subbarao: I would think so because one lesson of the crisis for everyone, for every country around the world, including us, is that price stability does not guarantee financial stability and, indeed, even macroeconomic stability does not guarantee financial stability. So the lesson is quite clear, which is that you have to be guarding financial stability as an explicit variable—as I argued yesterday, I think that is not very clear. It needs to be included in the mandate of the central banks.

Martin Wolf: I would like to follow up as there are many things raised by this, but one, in particular, that I would like to be clear about is your different positions. So be as precise as you can. Is there interaction between monetary policy and financial stability, which many of you raised in different ways, and which seems to be a central theme of this Conference. One view is they are essentially two different things and you do your monetary policy saying that overall macroeconomic conditions in terms of inflation targeting—some sort of Taylor-rule type world—and then you have a completely different sets of policies designed to ensure financial stability. I am very interested to know whether you think that this sort of perspective makes sense. Another view, which I must say I personally hold, is that there is a rather close relationship between the two because monetary policy sets the price of credit and, therefore, must influence supply and growth.

I will just start with you Mr. Stevens. You will all have an opportunity to comment. How do you see this relationship in the light of the crisis and the role of the central bank? Whether or not it is the regulator, though I think, there seems to be a very strong consensus on this Panel that the central bank has to, at least, have a central say in the regulatory debate.

Glenn Robert Stevens: Well, I do not think there is any doubt that monetary policy intimately overlaps with the potential to maintain financial stability. Because what we are doing, at least in the advanced country set-up, with the instrument, is that the overnight interest rate is setting the price of short-term credit. It is true that in a number of countries, it is more the long-term rates that matter for much of the credit that is extended, although in our country it is mainly the short-term rate that matters. But in the US or Europe, it is more of the long-term rate. Nonetheless, the central bank is actually setting the cost of short-term credit.

As I said before, it seems to me that when you think about the behaviour of the actors in the financial sector, it is probably stretching things a bit to think that the process of setting the cost of short-term credit has no bearing on the willingness and ability to take risk, including by getting leverage. So it seems to me that they are quite connected and I am rather wary of the idea that separate objectives are achievable only by totally separate instruments. I rather doubt that division can be maintained. That does not mean, by the way, that I am in favour of running after every asset price rise that might be a bubble and trying to smash it with interest rates—not at all. But I just do not think these things are quite so separable really as the strawman that I think you set up there. I guess, that is my answer.

Martin Wolf: But just to make clear the position, I mean, because this seems to me to have been the dilemma. Let us suppose you are in a world in which inflation expectations are well-anchored, inflation is under control, nobody is too agitated about it, but you see broad credit aggregates exploding and you agree that monetary policy has an important bearing on the latter fact. You now have two concerns and one instrument. What do you actually do?

Glenn Robert Stevens: Well, the first thing I think you do is to make sure that you are not inadvertently fuelling that build-up with unusually low rates. If rates were already high, then I think the problem is more difficult. But, if you are sitting there with very low rates observing all that, I think there is actually an argument for erring on the side of not keeping them so low even if the major macro variables are apparently on track at this point in time. And I think the logic for that simply is that if a big boom and bust happens, it will not only result in a crash in demand and a big fall in inflation over some time, probably a little longer than your normal forecast horizon, but it is probably also going to damage potential growth because there will be resource misallocation in the boom. I think there is a case for at least making sure you are doing no harm, which means not keeping rates unusually low, in that circumstance. That is not the same thing as saying that you want to actually create a recession with extremely high rates in order to try to turn off the credit, but at least, do no harm.

Martin Wolf: So the implications are different—it might mean a period in which you slightly or might somewhat undershoot the inflation target for this reason. I am just trying to pull the implications out.

Glenn Robert Stevens: This is a very hypothetical scenario. Let me be very clear. There is no advanced country right now that faces such a scenario that I can think of. But it may become more of an issue for some of the emerging countries. I think you might make that case in principle, particularly if you have an inflation target characterised by a fair bit of flexibility, which I think the better targeting systems do.

Martin Wolf: Mr. Noyer, how do you see this, what I think of now as the absolutely central debate for policymaking?

Christian Noyer: I think I would make two comments on that or give two answers to your question. One is about the ranking, the hierarchy of objectives. I would say that there must be no doubt that we have a primary objective, i.e., price stability. Price stability must be described in terms of CPI, price of goods and services and this is the key objective as it is set in our statute. The ECB having a primary objective does not mean that we have prejudice to this objective, we cannot pursue all the goals, which normally go in the same direction, I will come to that in a second. Precisely, when we look at the kind of difficulty in which we might be—I think it depends very much on the time horizon that you have—if you are in what can be described sometimes as narrow inflation targeting, i.e., you aim at reaching a precise price increase objective in, say, two years or 18 months from now, you might be caught in a certain difficulty. But if you have, as in the case of Australia for instance, this sort of so-called broad inflation targeting or what we describe in the statute of the ECB as reaching price stability over the medium to long-term—that means that you need to take into account what may happen if you do not reach financial stability. Let us say, for instance, if you have huge inflation in asset prices, asset prices means, in particular, real estate prices, it may fuel, over time, adverse developments in inflation of goods and services through the price of many goods or rents, etc.

Also, as I mentioned earlier, if you have at some point financial instability, not to speak of a crisis as the one we just went through, it means that the monetary policy transmission mechanism is impaired for a certain period of time. Then you might be confronted with a lot of difficulties during a period of time simply to achieve your price stability goal and we have seen that—I mean, the price—CPIs have gone negative in a number of countries. If you take that perspective, there is no contradiction.

Martin Wolf: Before we get to the exit strategy, very very briefly, I just wondered if Ms. Watanagase would like to comment on possible prudential tools to manage the financial system and their effectiveness, given whatever you are doing on monetary policy.

Tarisa Watanagase: We adopted inflation targeting in 2000. I would like to add that even though we are now in inflation targeting, we also monitor closely financial imbalances. We monitor the balance sheets of the corporate sector, of households and of the banking sector and when we spot some early signs of imbalances, we take immediate action. Well, there are sequencings. We do not jump to using monetary policy by hiking interest rates from day one. We start to communicate our concern that we are starting to see, for example, credit card spending increasing to the tune of 40 per cent to 50 per cent a year and we follow up with needed action. For example, in the area of credit card, we issued regulations regarding the minimum income requirement for a credit card holder. We put a credit limit. For example, a credit card holder must not have credit exceeding 5 times his/her income and that the minimum monthly payment has to be more than 10 per cent. These are very simple prudential regulations and they worked. It brought down the cost of credit card to the tune of 16 per cent to 17 per cent after a year or two. We did the same thing when we saw the high-end property market heating up. We put in a loan-to-value ratio of 70 per cent and it worked as well. These are very simple examples.

I would like to add that it is very difficult to incorporate macroprudential rules into the formulation of monetary policy. We all know that our knowledge about the transmission mechanism between interest rate and credit and other macro variables is a lot less than our understanding of the interest rate, money and investment and other macro variables. Well, of course, we have to try to improve our understanding and come up with some vigorous monetary policy formulations. But in the meantime, I would submit that it is much easier just to implement simple microprudential rules and they actually have worked quite well in our case.

Martin Wolf: Dr. Subbarao, finally on this question—how you go about maintaining financial stability relationships with monetary policy and macroprudential rules? What is your perspective from the Indian point of view?

Duvvuri Subbarao: I have in the past also encountered this question being interpreted like a linear programing problem. There you have several objectives. Do you have sufficient instruments? Again from an Indian perspective, I am unable to appreciate the problem in that sense because as I said earlier, in the RBI, we had the luxury of several instruments and the responsibility for several objectives. I believe it is easier to have several instruments and several objectives rather than having a single instrument and a single objective. So the way we have handled this problem, the way we address this problem in India, is slightly different from elsewhere.

Having said that, yes—we do look at a number of factors and a number of variables in formulating monetary policy just as Tarisa mentioned about Thailand. One of the developments we do look at is asset prices. I know there is a debate about whether you must use monetary policy instruments or regulatory policy instruments for asset price management. Again, in India, we are not so *brahmanical* because we use either way, mix them up and do not make such a distinction about what policy we use for what purpose.

In the period leading to the crisis, of course, the RBI had used regulatory prudential tools to check mispricing of risk. For example, in the years 2006 to 2008, there was deployment of risk weights, provisioning norms for banks, etc., which were instituted to check asset prices building up. But I do want to say that I do not want to rule out the use of monetary policy instruments for the purpose of financial stability. Just as you mentioned when you were asking the question, you also need to look at the credit build-up. If asset prices are building up because there is credit build-up, I think, you have to be sensitive from a monetary policy perspective, not only because asset prices can have implications for financial stability, but I believe they can have implications even for your price stability objective. If monetary transmission is choked and if your interest rate signals from the central bank are not transmitting through the commercial banks, they do not then pick up the signals, then your ability to target inflation gets impaired. Both for inflation-targeting central banks and for multi-service central banks such as ourselves, I believe that you need to use a variety of instruments.

Martin Wolf: I hope to get perhaps one or two of you to comment on the exit strategy issue very briefly at the end, but I would like, at this stage, just to give you, in the hall, the opportunity to address these distinguished people. If you would like to ask a question, stand up, say who you are and ask a very pointed question. Professor Friedman.

Benjamin Friedman: I wonder if what you are collectively identifying is a new and rather different form of the Impossible Trinity, applicable now to domestic economic policy. The aggregate of what all of you are saying seems to add up to the following: that you cannot simultaneously have: one, a monetary policy oriented either wholly or primarily towards price stability; two, a regulatory regime motivated primarily or exclusively by belief in the efficacy of free markets; and three, an effective lender-of-last-resort policy. It seems to me that what you are collectively saying is that those three together are a recipe for the kind of disaster that we have just had and we are completely likely to have again if one pursues these three. Now, from the perspective of assuming that any two elements of the trinity are in place, it then becomes almost apparent that the third one is a tremendous mistake. But, like any discussion of the so-called Impossible Trinity, one can start with any part of the triangle and by assuming any two sides of the triangle, then the third one becomes problematic.

So, I wonder whether either you, Martin, or the governors whom you are interrogating so effectively this morning, would sign on to the proposition that what you are all collectively saying is that there are these three things that many central banks around the world today hold individually to be the right way to conduct policy, but in aggregate, the three of them together are a recipe for disaster. This then puts us right back to the kind of logic that the usual Impossible Trinity presents, namely, you have to pick two and jettison the third. The differences of opinion, such as we had, primarily come down to the matter of which one is to be jettisoned among the three.

Martin Wolf: I am not sure, Ben, that I got your second point clearly. Could you just restate it—regulatory regime was based on belief in the free market?

Ben Friedman: Yes.

Martin Wolf: Okay. I think everybody has just scrapped that. Bill White wanted to ask a question. I will take four and then I will ask the panelists to reply.

Bill White: I think this is a question—may be a bit of a tricky question—directed to Governor Noyer. He was talking about the second pillar and the question that I want to raise is this. The second pillar was originally brought in with the idea that money had a low frequency association with inflation and that really was its origin. And now what I hear Governor Noyer say is that the second pillar can be used as an indicator of growing imbalances, imbalances which might in the end lead to deflation, which is very similar to the Japanese second perspective. That second way of looking at things is very different from the first way of looking at things. I guess I want to ask the tricky part of the question to Christian Noyer: at what point precisely did this transformation take place?

Martin Wolf: Very, very, very nasty. Lars Svensson. Yes.

Lars Svensson: I was thinking about the thought experiment that Martin subjected the governors to. He was assuming inflation and the real economy were on track but credit was exploding. Of course, it is not really the current inflation and the current real economy that matters; it is the forecast for future inflation and future output that matters. It will be strange to see credit exploding without having any impact on the inflation and output forecast. But suppose that is the case, would you prefer to raise interest rates and cause recession under future inflation target rather than use macroprudential tools to control credit?

Martin Wolf: I will ask that question. I just would like to point out that we did have a credit explosion and the one thing we did not have was inflation. So, it is very disturbing.

Deepak Mohanty: My question to the Panel is: are we really dialling the wrong number? Because under inflation targeting, what we are looking at is goods and services prices—not at runaway inflation in asset prices. Unless we bring in asset prices and redefine the price indicator itself, perhaps we would be dialling a wrong number. If you do not do that and we try to respond just from a macroprudential perspective and, if interest rates are low, monetary policy is loose, then maybe from the macroprudential side, we have to tighten so much so that real activity is killed. So, it is very difficult again also to communicate from that angle once the goods and services prices are low, but we are responding because of the asset prices, under inflation targeting framework.

Martin Wolf: Okay. What I am going to do is this: I have been given very tight limits, but I do not suppose three minutes will matter. I am going to give each of the governors, in turn, an opportunity to answer these questions. They have two minutes each, they can answer whatever they like, in anyway they like, but that is the time limit to keep us on track. I am sorry, from my point of view, it is just beginning to get really interesting; we would like another hour or two, but we do not have it apparently. So, I will start with you, because there was a particular question addressed to you, Governor Noyer.

Christian Noyer: Yes, thank you. I will indeed concentrate on Bill White's question. I would very much agree that, in general, the second pillar was associated with the idea of low frequency association of money with inflation. But I think there is no contradiction, it is different but it is not that different. Why? Because if you have too much money or credit showing up, then our view is that it will show up into either CPI developments over the long-term or asset price developments, depending on the circumstances. We could, for instance, plead that because of the growing importance of emerging markets, the imports from emerging markets to advanced economies put downward pressure on industrial prices and also the credibility of central banks—you may imagine what you wish. But then that can explain why, although we had strong monetary and credit developments, there was not really a strong pressure on the CPI or at least it was contained and the money fuelled asset prices.

What happens then? As I said before, there can be two consequences. First, in the long-term, asset prices, if they increase too much, measure up into inflation of goods and services through rents, through a number of developments. If we take into account the long-term objective of price stability, we might be concerned by that. Second, if the bubble bursts, then we come to deflationary pressures. I would also submit that deflation is certainly not price stability. So, if we have the risk of deflation, it is as much a concern as too high inflation and so, we have to take that into account too. All in all, I think that there is not that much of difference.

Martin Wolf: So, it was right all along for more or less the right reason. I think I will go now to Governor Stevens, stick with the high income countries for the moment. I am particularly interested if you might, with your time, but it is of course up to you, address Lars Svensson's question about possible resolution of the imagined contradiction by having a sufficiently long time-horizon into the future.

Glenn Robert Stevens: Well, as with any hypothetical scenario, it would be useful to have some thought about what the underlying shock might have been to produce the scenario in question and that might have a bearing on what one thinks interest rates ought to do. But I think it is actually a bit of a strawman, is not it, to say that the options are either to do nothing or create a recession in order to deal with the potential threat to financial stability. Is there nowhere in between you could choose—you know, you are prepared to be a bit tighter, or a little bit on that side, just in case you might inadvertently be fuelling a build-up of financial imbalances with the current policy setting. I would have thought that, at least in principle since this is hypothetical, such an intermediate position might be possible, short of creating recessions. I mean, nobody is talking about creating recessions today in order to avoid possible bigger recessions in future. I have never found that an attractive way to present an argument. If you see the scenario that we were given, I would ask myself: is there a potential problem with this credit and leverage build-up and am I fuelling it inadvertently? I would like to be sure that I am not, even if that does mean a little bit higher rate than the standard Taylor rule might give you. The idea is to do no harm.

Martin Wolf: I take that as a sort of vote for leaning.

Glenn Robert Stevens: Yes, I guess so—rather than crushing.

Martin Wolf: Yes, I was going to ask you, Governor, for your last thought.

Glenn Robert Stevens: One more thing. I am not against using so-called macroprudential tools either. Of course, one would deploy those if you have them. You do not necessarily run straight to the use of monetary policy, but I think it is kind of unnecessarily polarising in this debate to ask people to jump either into the camp of 'I will always respond to asset prices through monetary policy' or 'I never will'. I want to preserve a position of 'never say never'.

Martin Wolf: Governor.

Tarisa Watanagase: I want to supplement what Glenn just said. You do not have to wait until you run into a situation of having to create a recession if you take preventive actions early in the process. I think that is very important because if you take preventive action, you do not need to have heavy-handed measures, which can be quite painful. This is a hard-earned lesson that we got from our own crisis, that when you see early signs of imbalances, do something about it.

In the end, if you realise that you have taken the move a bit too late, I think you just have to pay the price. If you have to create a recession by hiking your interest rate, I think that that would be the way to go. There is no easy way out.

Martin Wolf: I wanted to ask you Governor Subbarao, how you would like to comment on this, particularly since you mentioned the difficulty in India's context of what is the right inflation index. How does one think about, broadly if you are concerned with inflation, what inflation index one should look at? In particular, what would be the role of asset prices in inflation indices? But there are other questions which you might also want to address and that is entirely up to you.

Duvvuri Subbarao: Identifying a unique inflation index is particularly challenging in India, as I had mentioned earlier, because we have a WPI, four CPIs. There are also concerns about asset prices and suppressed inflation because a number of commodities and goods in India are under administered pricing. This question of what single inflation index to look at, or should we target, is a particularly difficult and challenging question for India. In the RBI, we look at a host of indicators—all the indicators that I just mentioned, the WPI, the four CPIs, we look at the asset price movement. We look at a number of economic variables. So I do not think we view the problem the way other central banks do.

I also want to use the time available to me to respond to the question that Lars had raised about the granular view that I had enunciated about the role of monetary policy in checking asset prices. Perhaps the use of monetary policy instruments would be appropriate if asset price build-up is driven by credit and would not be equally appropriate if it is not driven by credit. I think you answered that question partly yourself, which is that you could very well have a situation where you have a credit build-up but whch does not show up in goods and price inflation.

I want to say again that we are not, in India, very puritanical about what instruments to use. We are concerned about inflation but we are concerned about a number of other variables as well. Finally, I want to say that I agree with Glenn that you cannot take binary positions on this—that I will use this or I will not use this. I think what we have learned from the experience in India is that you have to take the entire economic situation at that point of time or over time and you have to look at all the instruments available to you and grapple with the objectives of price stability, financial stability, and growth.

Martin Wolf: Thank you very much. I would love to continue. My sense, by the way, is that everybody agrees with Ben Friedman's Impossible Trinity and I think most people feel number 2 goes and number 1—well, that is what all the debate is about, namely, how far should monetary policy be aimed at price stability. I would not dream of summing up as I do not have the time, since I have minus 5 minutes. I detect Catholic tendencies in this Panel, if I may use that word here, in the sense that we still believe quite firmly in very, very important aspects of what I might think was the old religion but it has got rather softened, I think, in various ways.

I would not go into that any further as it is getting theologically complex. There is certainly a sense, at least on this Panel, that monetary policy has to take into account what is happening with credit and asset prices, but it is probably not enough. You have to use prudential tools. It is not completely clear how well they will work. May be, this could conceivably make the public a little nervous. And there are many questions raised by all that, which unfortunately we cannot deal with—what this sort of situation does for central bank independence—but even so, I think it has been a wonderful discussion.

27 Governors Speak—Panel II

International Monetary System

Martin Wolf: I would like to start with the following question: was the international monetary system (IMS), in some relevant aspects, a central part of the crisis story? If so, in what way was it a central part and what are the issues it raises? We need to look at this before we start looking at reform of particular institutions or regional monetary arrangements, focusing on the big picture of how the monetary system operated. I have been one of those persons who believe that the perfectly understandable desire of countries to insure themselves has led to an extraordinarily excessive demand for dollar reserves and that this did play an important part in the background to the crisis.

I would like to start with Governor Carney of the Bank of Canada (BoC) for his perspectives on the relationship between the IMS, monetary policy and this crisis that we have seen and, therefore, the issues before us.

Mark J. Carney: I guess your first question was whether the system failed. I guess I would turn it around slightly and suggest that we failed the system, in that there were many causes of this crisis, but its intensity and its scope reflected the unprecedented disequilibria that built up across a number of major economies. I think Christian Noyer and others alluded to this in your previous Panel. So I will not go over it, but I would attach myself to the group that viewed the build-up of these imbalances and the bond conundrum as part of the story—only part of the story, but an important part of the story. Why did that come about? It came about because of the classic problem that has bedeviled monetary systems over the ages, which is that there is asymmetric adjustment pressures on countries. It is easier as a surplus country to delay adjustment than it is as a deficit county to forestall adjustment. And we saw over the course of the last decade that what began as prudential self-insurance grew to proportions that, given the experience of the crisis, can be deemed excessive.

The challenge that is before us is to determine a way to go back to the conventions of the system. I am sure we will have a chance to talk about different reserve currency arrangements and longer term transition and governance issues with respect to the major institutions. But I would submit for consideration that the issue is not so much about the identification of the reserve currency or currencies but the commitment of countries to adjust over time. Those commitments are not binding. They cannot be enforced in rule of international law, regardless of what articles of agreement or other arrangements are, but they are commitments to a system that serves us well or could serve us well over the medium-term. This is part of what the G20 is trying to accomplish through its framework of discussions, which is much, much broader than issues around a few of the exchange rates. In fact, that is really the residual of those discussions as opposed to the starting point.

Martin Wolf: But the core point you are making is that, essentially, this is about the adjustment mechanism rather than, specifically, single currency dominance.

Mark J. Carney: That is right.

Martin Wolf: I will stick at the moment with the high-income country viewpoint. So I will turn to you Mr. Ordonez. How do you see the role of the IMS in the crisis and the really big, broad challenges facing it?

Miguel Angel Fernandez Ordonez: Well, I share the view that the current imbalance is part of the picture of the crisis. Of course, there are many factors that have been commented upon during this Conference but the imbalances matter a lot. However, I am more interested, not in the areas where our views have differed, as for instance on the issue of imbalances, but in the reaction of all countries. If we compare with the reaction that we had 80 years ago during the Great Depression, the difference is the increased international cooperation through the G20, the incredible and important support that we have given to the International Monetary Fund (IMF) by tripling their resources and giving it an important role and now we are discussing its mandate. I think that this is extremely important. I think most analysts would recognise that the worst of the recession of the 1930s was not the recession; it was the nationalistic reaction and everybody trying to solve their problems on their own. Even if we have differences in view on various issues, it is important that we maintain the way we discussed these. And we should not take it for granted because now—I am thinking in Europe, in Spain, United Kingdom and all other developed countries, United States—I see very hard years ahead. Fiscal consolidation is not an easy task. We should avoid any temptation to solve our problems like in the past. I could enter into a discussion of issues where there are differences but I would like to highlight the importance of the way we are doing things.

Martin Wolf: I think that is an important point about the way we deal with this thing together. In that context, I have used, not infrequently, the famous phrase about 'hanging together if we do not want to hang separately'. And I think it is fair to say that we have so far hung together. I would like to turn to you now, Mr. Rahman, for your perspective on the IMS and the way it has worked. What do you feel have been the problems and its role in the crisis and how would you like to see it work in future?

Atiur Rahman: I think for the first time, the concerns of the low-income countries are being discussed here in this forum. We have been talking about emerging markets and also about the developed countries, but there are a huge number of low-income countries—in terms of population, they are quite substantial. The dialogues going on in the IMS do not always reflect their views and we do not have an access point. And from that perspective, Bangladesh and countries like her, probably need an additional kind of access point.

Despite this crisis, countries like Bangladesh, particularly Bangladesh, have done very well. As you must have heard, Bangladesh has been consistently growing at 5 to 6 per cent. In fact, even last year, when the situation was so bad in terms of international growth scenario, Bangladesh had about 5.9 per cent growth. Exports grew at 10+ per cent, remittance grew at 23 per cent. These are all indicators that despite all the pressures—because most of our exports really cater to the needs of the developed countries—they still did so well!

But Bangladesh can hardly get any opportunity to really voice its concerns in international fora and in the dialogues that are going on. From that perspective, I think the IMS should really re-orient itself to take account of concerns of low-income countries. I have one specific suggestion. We now have new members like India in international dialogues on monetary policies. Countries like India probably should have discussions with South Asian countries or countries like Bangladesh before they go to international fora—the Asian Clearing Union (ACU) could be one forum, the South Asian Association for Regional Cooperation (SAARC)-Finance could be another forum to do so—so that we distil our views through India into the global forum or fora like Financial Stability Board (FSB). They could also have at least one member from the low-income countries, even by turn, for a year or two. That could be another option so that we could present our views to the international community.

The IMF, of course, has been changing but still has not succeeded in preventing the build-up of imbalances of its important members. The mandate for the IMF, probably in a new global monetary order, will need to have adequate safeguards against the laxities of their most important members. The IMF probably also has to be more inclusive in terms of its information or data. I will just give you one example. IMF, as of today, has not reflected its concerns or its suggestions on financial inclusion, which probably the RBI, the Bangladesh Bank are pursuing, and which helped us hold up domestic demand, and enabled us to handle the financial crisis so well. So, in terms of any discussion on issues like this where we have the strength, it probably would have helped others to understand how we did better. Even the data on liquidity, probably projected by the IMF, does not always reflect the realities of these countries. So, I think there is ample scope for reforming the international financial system, to take the concerns of developing countries, particularly low-income countries, which are doing better.

Martin Wolf: I think that is a very, very important issue and I will certainly ask Governor Subbarao about his view on your suggestion for the role of India in the G20 in reflecting some of the concerns of its neighbours. And may I also congratulate Bangladesh on its performance—the benefits, perhaps, of not having an overdeveloped financial system. May I now turn to you, Governor Tenzin, to talk about this from, I think, a very special sort of perspective. How does the IMS concern you?

Daw Tenzin: As you all know, Bhutan is a really small country. We were not hit by the recession, not because we were resilient, but because we did not have the capacity to integrate, either financially or through trade. But last October, when we went for the IMF-World Bank meeting in Istanbul, after the G20 meeting in Pittsburgh, many important changes took place, primarily with recapitalisation of the IMF. I think yesterday some of the presenters brought out the issue about resilience along with the reserve level, current account balance, low deficit, low debt level, and even capital control. And I think, for sometime, the global issue in our part of the region has been whether the US dollar as the international reserve currency remains credible because most countries hold their reserves in dollars. This includes a country like Bhutan where the reserve is so small. Yet, over 80 per cent of our reserves are in dollars. The American dollar is a reserve currency, a unit of account, a medium of exchange and a store of value. Now in most of the emerging economies, the last role has been the biggest concern because of many reasons. I think if the global concern is about the imbalances—there has been too much finger-pointing at the surplus countries and the driving of demand—if too much reserve is creating imbalances, what should those countries do? But, I think if the IMS has to change and change in a positive manner including the IMF quotas as distributed among the members, the first criteria is the size of the GDP, second is the openness and third is the size of the reserve. I think these are a few things about which many emerging economies are quite concerned.

As for Bhutan, our currency is pegged to the Indian rupee. We are in a monetary union. And I think, in certain cases, the Impossible Trinity pushes us hard as the central bank. However, given the reality of any monetary authority or central bank, monetary policy is not purely economics. I think there are different dimensions to it, but it is very, very heartening that the IMF is coming back, maybe a little more relevant, primarily because when the Article IV mission comes to our country, when they look at our reserve stock, they say, you open up!

I think South Asia survived primarily because of capital control and for a small country like Bhutan where the reserve build-up is largely through grants and soft loans, there was no way we could open up. The question was, I think, the Anglo-Saxon capitalism melted the virtue of liberalism and I think we have come to a point, where we re-inforced state capitalism in its place. And the question now is, can fiscal dominance prevail over monetary policy. I think, yes. The reality is, yes. There are too many things we have to read and I think many talks are being held, questions are being raised about which currency in our opinion could emerge as the international reserve currency apart from the American dollar at this point of time. And I think many emerging economies, in our part of the region, still do not have convertible currencies.

So what are the options left even for a small country like Bhutan? We are highly perplexed with the dynamism of the crisis. It is quite sad. I always wish that Bhutan were in a position to integrate. I regret that we did not have the capacity to integrate, but that does not mean that Bhutan should not. I do not think any kind of a regional monetary arrangement at this point of time, even talking about the Association of Southeast Asian Nations (ASEAN), can be our immediate concern. We have other matters to take care of as a small country. Many times, when the IMF mission came and even at one point of time in 2005, we were being told that we are eligible for a debt pardon because the debt to GDP ratio crossed over 75. Now, we are not even talking about 130 as a threshold level, so where do we stand? And as a very small economy we are getting perplexed and confused. But I think there are good reasons to believe that many things are coming up. I think the crisis gave us an opportunity to redefine discipline in the market, our consumption patterns, even the use of a currency as a reserve currency. I think it is flowing in a very positive direction.

Martin Wolf: We raised a lot of important questions from a very different perspective and Governor Subbarao, you are a member of the G20, of course, and also a developing country. We heard also from your neighbours. I will be very interested in your perspective on where you think the IMS has gone wrong and where it should be going.

Duvvuri Subbarao: The short answer to your direct question, which is whether the IMS was found to be inadequate as a consequence of the crisis, is yes. We had found that the IMS was inadequate to deal with the global imbalances that were building up. I agree with Mark that even though this crisis erupted as a financial crisis, there were structural root causes and one of the structural causes was the global imbalances building up. It is immaterial at this point of time whether that build-up was because of excess consumption or a savings glut, but the fact is that because these imbalances were building up and because countries with current account surpluses invested those surpluses in central banks and Treasuries in the

US and other advanced economies, there was too much liquidity in the US and the other advanced economies, which, in turn, drove the search for yield and drove this financial innovation. So I believe that there is a link between global imbalances and the developments in the financial sector and it will be wrong to see them as independent developments.

About India, of course, we traditionally had current account deficits, except for a few years when we had run marginal surpluses. So, to that extent, we had not contributed to global imbalances, but because we have been a part of the global system, we have had to bear the consequences of imbalances. The question often asked is: how come nobody saw the crisis coming. Economists get very sheepish and say that some people like Bill White and others did see the crisis coming. But yes, a majority of people did not see the crisis erupting as a financial crisis, but a large majority of people did see the crisis erupting as a hard landing for global imbalances. I believe it is just incidental that we had built up an unstable system. It was unsustainable, and it had to explode. It is incidental that it exploded in the financial sector. We could very well have had a currency crisis, but we just had a financial crisis, but it is the same dirt, it is the same accumulated dirt that erupted and led to this crisis.

Now, the other question that I want to raise and answer is: are we looking at global imbalances as part of crisis resolution? I worry that we are not giving it adequate attention, even as we are talking about some redressal of imbalances, countries making some internal adjustments. I believe that this is a problem that concerns all countries around the world and everybody has to get together and solve this; but it is not getting sufficient attention. In fact, I worry that perhaps in resolving this crisis, we are sowing the seeds of the next crisis. The next crisis could be a currency crisis, it could be a fiscal crisis, but perhaps, we are sowing the seeds of another crisis.

Last, the question about India's responsibility towards its neighbours. I believe that yes, we have a responsibility. People do talk about G20 representing 80 per cent of world GDP and 75 per cent of world population, but we must remember that there is 20 per cent of world GDP and 25 per cent of world population, which is left out. In fact, I do know that when India is left out of international forum, we worry about it. So, if India is getting a place, I believe we have an obligation towards our neighbours because, as the Governor of Bhutan said, though the economic linkages are still underdeveloped, there is scope for building on the linkages. As India gains a place at the table, I think we must redeem our responsibility to our neighbours.

Martin Wolf: I hope to come to this question of representation and the reform of the IMF as an institution towards the end, but I would like to follow up a little bit on the adjustment in the currency system, which I think is being raised in different ways now. Perhaps I can return to you, Governor Carney. You argued, if I understood it correctly, that the issue is really adjustment, that we should focus on that. Now, some people would argue that the two are really intimately related because the fundamental point was that for various reasons, predominantly emerging countries decided to pursue policies that led to enormous accumulations of foreign currency reserves. They increased about 6.5 trillion dollars in the last decade, which is a really astonishing sum, overwhelmingly in developing countries. Obviously, a very large proportion of that was in dollars and for reasons that we refer to as the 'Triffin Paradox', that is likely to be associated with a large current account deficit in the currency provided in the reserve-providing country, in this case, the US. Now, we know that it need not be the case, but the association is empirically strong and we understand why. So, is it actually possible to separate the adjustment question from the key currency question? Anyway, does not that then lead one to the sort of debate that is now emerging about the possible role of international reserve assets like the Special Drawing Rights (SDRs), which of course the Chinese government, the People's Bank of China has raised? It is a long question, but it does seem to be a central set of issues. I will be interested in your perspective on these links.

Mark J. Carney: Certainly, one of the benefits of being a reserve currency, the exorbitant privilege, if you will, is an ability to delay adjustment and arguably, that is the flip side of the conundrum that we have referred to—in the United States in this case. The point I was trying to make, and I did make, is that the countries that really can delay adjustment are quite obviously, the surplus countries. And if the system evolves to either a broader range of reserve currencies or the use of SDRs (and I will come to that in a moment) as a reserve currency, surplus countries, particularly those with relatively closed capital accounts, relatively repressed financial systems and the ability to sterilise, can delay adjustment for a very long time. It will ultimately come through wages and prices and real exchange rate adjustments, but it can be delayed for a very long time and these strains can begin anew. To go back to the previous discussion, the relative efficacy of macroprudential policies can also be used to delay adjustment or can be thought to be used to delay adjustment.

The point I am trying to make is that there needs to be a commitment from major actors to adjustment over time for a well-functioning system. That does not mean an immediate move to floating exchange rates—that is not what I am talking about—but it is an adjustment of domestic policies that are consistent. What is the potential role of the SDR? We think it is an interesting issue for discussion. It is a long-term issue for discussion. The prospects of SDRs as a meaningful reserve currency are remote on any reasonable time horizon, partly because of the governance structure of the IMF and partly because it does not solve the adjustment problem in our opinion. In fact, it just distributes exorbitant privilege to the constituent members of the SDR, the usual currencies of members in the SDR. We have said that there may be some use in exploring a substitution account as a one-off reserve diversification mechanism that would be part of a broader move towards a more flexible global system. But that is a big conversation. I would term that as a medium-term conversation, if I term SDRs as reserve assets as a long-term one.

Martin Wolf: Do any of the governors wish to comment any more on this adjustment and currency link question before I go onto the mutual assessment programme of the IMF?

Atiur Rahman: Can I comment on this reserve system?

Martin Wolf: Of course!

Atiur Rahman: Of course, the US dollar and euro are the two major currencies at the moment, but there are also imbalances creeping up in the European Union (EU) and that makes the euro equally vulnerable as a reserve currency. I think the global system should gradually move into a couple of more currencies, which are more convertible. For the stability of the global reserve system, we need a handful of, perhaps around 4 to 6, fully convertible currencies of fairly large economies or regional monetary unions in the discipline of a global order to effectively maintain imbalances at a minimum. I would think that currencies of the larger fast-growing economies like China, India, Brazil, have the potential to play the reserve currency role over the medium-term and I think we need to think in that line. Currencies of new regional monetary unions would have been preferable, given the typically stronger commitment of monetary unions to balance stability. These can only be in the longer term, but these are areas we need to focus.

As for the SDR, I thought a possible option could be a reformed IMF in a new role as with the global monetary agency annually issuing or recalling SDR allocations in line with actual or potential growth in global output and in line with liquidity issues in national or regional currencies by requiring members to be fully backed by IMF SDR allocations, a mechanism similar to the gold standard with global output growth substituting for gold. I think these are some of the ideas we may focus on.

Martin Wolf: Yes, I must say that I am very sympathetic to the last line of argument. Governor Subbarao, you wanted to speak and perhaps you would like to comment on the future role of the rupee as an international reserve asset. All these were specifically raised by the Governor from Bangladesh and, of course, implies, among other things, the abolition of exchange controls in India, a matter of some moment I think for Indian policymakers.

Duvvuri Subbarao: First, I would like to address two other questions before I come to your question. First, can the US dollar be displaced as the global reserve currency and second, more particularly, can SDRs take the dollar's place?

The US dollar did not become the global reserve currency because countries around the world got together and decided that it ought to be the reserve currency. It became the global reserve currency because it inspired the trust and confidence of countries around the world. Our staff has done some research in preparation for this. I will just give you some numbers to indicate the dollar's dominance in the global system. The US accounts for 22 per cent of world GDP, it accounts for up to 15 per cent of world trade. You had referred to the 'Triffin dilemma', which is that the US is able to provide sufficient dollar-denominated assets for the global system to run. I cannot see any other country having a large enough economy to do that. I believe 67 per cent of the global foreign exchange reserves are in dollars, 90 per cent of the global foreign exchange transactions are in dollars and over one-third of the countries in the world link their exchange rate to the dollar. So, the dollar is a dominant currency and I do not think it is possible that we decide at a conference of G20 or the IMF to have some other currency. I think if some other currency or a group of currencies have to displace the dollar, it has to happen in an organic manner.

Now, about whether the SDR can displace or play some of the functions that the dollar is discharging now, I think that is a tall order. I think the total SDR issued in the world today may be about 350-370 billion including the latest issue that they have done of 280 billion. I cannot see 380 billion of SDRs being a reserve currency for global trade. Second, the SDR is not a claim on any country. I believe it is not even a claim on the IMF, in a strict sense. What do you do with the SDRs? The SDR is just a unit of account at the moment. It is not good for anything else. Unless the SDR acquires other attributes required for a global currency, I believe it is not possible for the SDR to replace the dollar.

I also want to respond to another question that has not come up, which is about diversification of your reserves. You know all central banks, or governments, as the case may be, manage their foreign exchange portfolios and we do that too. We bought gold two months ago from the IMF and the question about what view we are taking on gold or on the dollar or other currencies came up. We bought gold because we believe that was a method for diversifying our portfolio. It is a relatively small amount. Our total gold holding after the purchase is still less than 10 per cent.

Martin Wolf: Do you want to comment on the rupee as a reserve currency?

Duvvuri Subbarao: I hope it becomes a reserve currency!

Martin Wolf: It is clearly intimately related to the size of the Indian economy, its integration in the world economy and obviously the full convertibility of the currency and I would assume that the last is not going to happen tomorrow.

Duvvuri Subbarao: No, it will not happen tomorrow, but we have a roadmap for capital account convertibility and that roadmap itself is dynamic. It is adjusted depending on the evolving developments within the country and around the world. People have asked us, 'Are you backing down from your capital account convertibility roadmap?' I believe we are not. We still traverse the roadmap, but we will rework the roadmap, depending on global developments. The supplementary question to that is: what capital controls will you use until you achieve full convertibility? I believe that we will use them flexibly as we have in the past.

Martin Wolf: I will just run over a little bit on the reform of the IMF very briefly. Some people might say that just as the world voted for the dollar through decisions, the world has taken a vote against the IMF by saying that, if you want safety, you build reserves for yourselves and that is the only way to be safe. Against that background, how relevant is the IMF? I will turn to you, Mr. Ordonez, if I may. How does it need to be restructured to be a credible institutional centre of the IMS? What are the issues in your view? Are regional monetary institutions of the type that are now being developed in East Asia a relevant alternative? Of course, the currency union in Europe is quite an exceptional thing.

Miguel Angel Fernandez Ordonez: Well, I think that it is true that the crisis has vindicated certain views that we did not have before the crisis, especially this idea of reserve accumulation as self-insurance. I think, we have to accept that. But, at the same time, this does not mean that we should not try to solve this problem by other means that could be less damaging, especially if reserve accumulation goes beyond self-insurance. In that sense, I think that we should use many ways, not just one way. For instance, I think that regional monetary cooperation is a good thing and we should not see regional cooperations as competing with, for instance, the IMF's role, in this situation. When we face this question of the IMS, sometimes we are listening to a proposal that reminds me of *Esperanto* or something like that—an incredible solution.

One of the things that I said in my first intervention is that the IMF plays a crucial role and it is crucial we strengthen the IMF. I do not see any other institution—not the G20, not the FSB—that could play a role in multilateral surveillance. It is true that attempts at multilateral surveillance made so far have not succeeded but that does not mean that we should not go in that direction because I do not see any other good alternative.

At the same time, the IMF could increase the role of insurance and support what countries are doing by themselves and what their regional cooperation is doing. I think that is not something that goes against the idea of multilateral surveillance, it could be complementary. In general, I think not only the IMF, but nations could find other ways to increase the resilience to the problems that can be created by this international monetary 'non-system', as some called it. Let me only finish with one question: what has happened in Latin America? Latin America has been very resilient in this crisis. One of the reasons has been that those countries increased their local debt markets in local currencies on the depositor base and this has improved their resilience. And I follow this very, very closely because the Spanish banks are very active there and they have helped to do that. So if we take several measures simultaneously, we could increase the resilience of the system to the problems that are created. And of course, I think that IMF is crucial in this role.

Martin Wolf: Do any of the governors want to comment specifically on the future of the IMF in the context of reform? Then, we will take two or three questions.

Atiur Rahman: I think IMF could still encourage regional monetary unions and there could be scope for countries with enough reserves to go for regional bonds. I think that the stronger regional monetary unions could be a source of stability for any kind of financial cooperation and also sustainability. I think IMF could move in that direction, encouraging initiatives like Chiang Mai Initiative (CMI) or other regional unions.

Martin Wolf: I want to take questions from the floor, but I am going to give, if he wants to, John Lipsky the opportunity to respond or answer questions relating to the role of the IMF.

John Lipsky: Hopefully, we are responding to virtually all the suggestions that were placed here. I suspect that it is well-known, first, that we have a commitment to review the voting shares in the institution by January 2011, and hopefully that will settle the issue of legitimacy. Second, I would underscore remarks made here at the Panel and those that I made yesterday, of the importance of the G20 framework process as a new and innovative way of addressing the issue of global imbalances and, more broadly, making macroeconomic policy coherent. It is an important initiative, a difficult one and one that I hope receives the appropriate support and cooperation of the key G20 countries.

I would also like to say that the Fund sees the emergence and strengthening of regional arrangements, as long as they are consistent with the global system, as both natural and desirable. We look forward to continuing to deepen our cooperation, for example, with the CMI or Chiang Mai initiative that we see as a positive and not as a problem.

Moreover, as mentioned by Governor Fernandez, we are actively pursuing the review of our mandate and with that, seeking to review our facilities to be able to provide better insurance-like facilities that would represent a real alternative to individual build-up of reserves. If the lesson learned from this latest crisis is everybody needs to self-insure, it does not require a lot of ingenuity to understand that if everybody tries to build reserves simultaneously, it is going to be deleterious for the global community. Hence, on the one hand, the framework will attempt to address that and, secondly, improve insurance facilities as an alternative to individual reserve build-up through the IMF. We hope that is going to be a useful and successful initiative.

Martin Wolf: It was an extremely important additional point. Mr. Bill Poole?

William Poole: I would like to comment about the international financial system (IFS). I am going to focus on two aspects of the system. There are a number of dimensions to what we mean by the IFS. Let me talk about the exchange rate regime and about the system, if you want to call it that, of international capital flows.

I want to confine my remarks to the period of the crisis, which is, let us say, two years following the outbreak of the crisis in August 2007. When we went into the crisis, we had a system of exchange rates with floating rates among the major currencies. I would include in those the US dollar, the euro, the yen, and the pound sterling. A number of other currencies floated freely against those major currencies, some other currencies were pegged rigidly and there were other intermediate arrangements of managed floats.

International capital flows among the major countries were market-determined and were not subject to capital controls. Now, during the crisis, those arrangements did not change and the crisis was not marked by exchange rate crises. Countries did not intervene to control or affect international capital and so I would regard the IFS in those two dimensions as having worked very effectively during the crisis, largely based on market principles and not a huge amount of government intervention in the IFS.

Martin Wolf: I think it is a very important point that the crisis we did not have was the crisis many of us did expect, which was a currency crisis. Thank you very much for making it, Mr. Poole. Yes, Professor Prasad, I think.

Prof. Eswar S. Prasad: The link between this Panel and the previous discussion seems to be basically that central bankers such as yourself are being buffeted by four factors: you have an international financial system that has a variety of weaknesses—institutional and otherwise; you have listed institutional weaknesses and financial markets that are just waiting to cause mayhem and you are operating in the midst of this very difficult environment. Now, it seems to me that much of the bifurcation of views that we saw yesterday can actually be traced back—rather than views about whether inflation targeting is right or whether one should look at asset price bubbles—to a more fundamental philosophical view about how or what monetary policy can achieve. I characterise it as a modest vision of monetary policy, which would be that essentially monetary policy can do one thing, which is maintain price stability, however defined, and that leads to good things like macro and financial stability.

Now, Governor Subbarao has articulated a very different view that price stability may not necessarily be consistent with either of those and in fact, once in a while, could be in conflict with those. But then the question arises, what is the right framework to do monetary policy in? And this, what I would characterise as the omnipotent policy, is where essentially one wants to do a lot and it is led so much by choices, by compulsions that forces you into this set-up where essentially you are not working within a framework and I think this was what would make people like Lars and Bill

Poole somewhat concerned that there is an attempt to deal with a lot. They would probably agree it needs to be dealt with, but not without a clear framework in mind.

So, the question I would like to pose to this Panel is: if you are in an environment where you have to deal with deficiencies in the international financial system, deal with supply shocks, deal with counteracting the effects of fiscal dominance and so on, and you know you have to do it, is it the right approach still to take inflation targeting or some framework related to that and improve it? In other words, do we just need better models that take into account things you should care about or do we need to move to something completely different, where essentially the old vision of monetary policy, as one being limited in its objectives and what it can achieve, has to be thrown away and you have to become omnipotent central bankers?

Martin Wolf: I think we are getting additional panelists, but a very important point. I will take one more question.

Sabapathy: Taking a cue from what the Bangladesh Governor said, if we encourage regional monetary arrangements, it need not necessarily be treated as an alternative to the IMF. Can international monetary cooperation and international monetary stability be achieved through a decentralised arrangement? For instance, regional trade blocs are not treated as a contradiction to multilateral trade cooperation; similarly in the area of development, we have the World Bank, other UN organisations and we have regional arrangements in Latin America, Africa, etc. Similarly, if we have regional monetary blocs, can we have a federation type of arrangement with the IMF heading it?

Martin Wolf: I think that the question from Prof. Eswar Prasad, which is really directed to you, Governor Subbarao, though others may wish to comment on it, is a variant of the old discretion *versus* rules issue. You have put forward a very broad view of what a central bank has to do. And in the context of a very complicated and messy world, as he pointed out, does that mean abandoning rules-governed or target-governed policymaking for such a wide range of discretion as to make it almost impossible for the outsider to understand?

Duvvuri Subbarao: I wish I had a direct answer to that question, but I do want to say that we grapple with that all the time. But again, I cannot agree to everything that Prof. Prasad has said, which is that we must be targeting inflation because that way we will be transparent and we will hold ourselves accountable to a defined outcome. The world is not so simple and especially in a country like India, you have to look at not just inflation, but worry about growth, development and financial stability concerns.

It is true, perhaps, that because we shift our emphasis from one variable to another from time to time and because we are less than completely transparent or clear about what specific objectives we are driving at a point of time, it is difficult for people outside, our interlocutors as it were, to evaluate our performance or hold it accountable. I know that those are deficiencies of the system but I believe that to shift towards inflation targeting in order to correct those deficiencies would be impractical and serve our system less than well.

Martin Wolf: Governor Carney, I think you wanted to comment.

Mark J. Carney: Yes. I will make two points on this very interesting question. First, I do not think things are beyond our control. I would not ascribe it to omnipotence, but we will influence all that is within the openness of the system, the effectiveness of the G20 framework. That is the first point. The second question is on the specifics of what the objectives of a central bank are. At least in our view, we found having an inflation target during the crisis enormously useful. We must say that sentiments swung from deflation to inflation and back and just being able to have the clarity of objective was enormously useful. That said, I would subscribe to the point that Glenn Stevens made most directly, which is that in setting the price of short-term credit, there is a link by the financial sector to financial stability. And I will take advantage of Lars' tendency here, to just link that to flexible inflation targeting. And I think one of the debates or discussions we need to have is how do we square the circle without being *ad hoc*, if we are leaning for asset price reasons. And one of the things we are thinking about is whether by using price level targeting, you can retain the credibility and clarity of targeting a path where you would potentially, purposely deviate from that path for reasons of financial stability. In our final point, we are not blessed with the range of tools that

Governor Subbarao and his institution are blessed with. So it partly reflects on the institutional structure in Canada.

Martin Wolf: Does anybody else want to comment on that? It might be particularly interesting actually from the Bangladesh point of view on the regional monetary arrangement issues.

Atiur Rahman: I just want to add here, in support to Governor Subbarao, that flexible targeting of inflation should be our main course, but we should also have salads and desserts. In that, we need to have all the other objectives—the growth concerns and other concerns could be additional items on the menu.

Martin Wolf: I should bring this very enlightening Panel discussion to a conclusion and I believe I have now left myself five minutes for summing up. So, I am going to make just a few points about this very interesting discussion.

I felt that, maybe, central banks are a little less complacent than I thought they were yesterday. I think, one of the issues that arises is: when does flexible inflation targeting get so flexible that it ceases to be inflation targeting in any sense? 'Flexible' is a very flexible word and it can cover a large number of things. My sense, for instance, to comments earlier of Governor Stevens is that, it is perfectly possible within a well-anchored inflation-targeting framework, to allow for the possible longer term effects of serious deviations in credit growth and other things that might, in your view, affect credit growth and then, ultimately either inflation or deflation. Governor Noyer talked about that. And it is probably reasonable to do so without doing anything as crazy as trying to create serious recessions in order to knock on the head possible bubbles.

I take this to be a degree of flexibility, which is not inconsistent with flexible inflation targeting, but others might not. But clearly the general view remains that—I do not think any Governor disagrees with this—while it might well be reasonable to allow for other things particularly financial stability in monetary policy (it is important to allow for this link between monetary policy and financial stability), nonetheless, anchoring inflation expectations remains a very, very important objective. I do not think I heard anyone, even from any of the emerging countries, suggest otherwise. I do not know whether that is an adequate compromise position for the moment, but the dicussion more or less ended at this point with which I am reasonably comfortable.

There was a very interesting discussion on prudential tools, both micro and macro, but not as detailed as one might have liked. My sense from this is that these are very important things. We have learnt that the financial system is not automatically self-stabilising, and therefore, competent authorities should be concerned about micro-stability and also possibly the use of macroprudential type of instruments. My sense of the discussion is that there is some scepticism about the effectiveness of these, but they have to be tried. I do not think there is anybody on these Panels who disagrees with the view that if such instruments are to be used, the central bank should have them in its control. But then, given the composition of the Panel, one would be very surprised if any other conclusion were reached. I happen to agree with the view, by the way. It seems to me intellectually defensible as well.

An issue that did not really get discussed but should have been is what many people refer to as fiscal dominance. The concern is of how we get out of the extraordinary fiscal positions we have, particularly in the developed countries and that, of course, raises really a fundamental issue about whether the independence of central banks, which has been a sort of dominant theme of recent years, will be maintained and I think that is one of the bigger worries.

Finally, on the discussion of domestic policy—I think, Governors from emerging countries, quite naturally, and inevitably, emphasised the range of responsibilities they have. That was particularly true of Governor Subbarao and also Governor Tenzin from Bhutan. I think, it is very important to remember that central banks have functions, which are very special in the context of the emerging countries.

Now, finally on the IMS. I think sort of two cheers for the dollar and certainly nobody doubted that it would remain the dominant reserve asset for the foreseeable future and that we have to manage adjustments within that context. There was a general perception that cooperation and coordination among countries have been exceptional and exceptionally successful. We have got through this crisis not only, as Bill Poole points out, without a serious currency crisis or serious introduction of capital controls, but also, it has to be said, we got through this crisis with, I believe, a remarkably small increase in protection. There has been some protests about it, but if you actually look at it, I think the amount of increase in protection we have seen so far is astonishingly small given the severity of the recession, particularly in major developed countries. That may not last, but it is, I think, a massive achievement of international coordination and this is a vindication for the decision to treat this as a shared problem.

When I think of the 'winners' of this crisis, apart from emerging countries like India, which have done so remarkably well and China, of course, I have to say that there is no doubt at all that the IMF is the great institutional winner. Its resources have been greatly increased. It has been extraordinaly flexible in the way it is responding to this crisis, arranging new facilities in a way that I certainly have not been able to keep up with. It has been given responsibility for this fascinating Mutual Assessment Programme among G20 members countries, I do not know what will come out of this, but the IMF is a winner and, of course, nobody on the Panel denied its central role—whatever the regional monetary cooperation might do, nobody denied its central role. And, of course, one of the price of being a winner, John, is that more is expected of you. So you are expected to fix many problems!

I think that is, at least, a reasonable summary of some of the main points of these fascinating Panel discussions. So at the end of this, chastened in some regard, but at the same time the sense I got out of this is, the world did not collapse, the system is together to some degree, cooperation is still functioning. We seem to have got through this. Let us hope we manage to do as well with the very difficult challenges of exit over the years ahead and with that I conclude the Panel sessions.

Summing-up of the Proceedings

K.U.B. RAO*

As stated by elders, whatever begins will have to end. Time is now approaching for us to end this one and a half days' meeting of intellectuals. During this brief congregation of very fertile minds, we have learnt from each other, and have agreed with each other on certain issues. We also agreed to disagree with others on some other issues. Therefore, at the end, it is probably appropriate to make a very brief review of the broad outcome of this one and a half days' Conference. I will make a brief effort to sum up the proceedings and highlight salient points that emerged from the four technical sessions and the two panel discussions.

Our Governor, Dr. Duvvuri Subbarao, at the outset, indicated why central banking could change in important ways after the crisis and how seeking solutions to the many challenges would be important for enhancing the contribution of central banks to society at large in more effective ways and, thereby, gain greater credibility. Setting the tone for the Conference proceedings, reflecting in essence the expectations from the deliberations to follow, Governor Subbarao outlined five key challenges of significance to all central banks in the current context. The first one was managing national monetary policy decisions in a globalised environment, given the growing complexity in the interactions between external developments and domestic variables. The second challenge was redefining the mandate of central banks, given the pre-crisis attraction of inflation targeting and the post-crisis debate on the role of central banks in relation to asset prices. The third challenge, he highlighted, was the responsibility of central banks towards financial stability, particularly beyond the conventional lender-of-last-resort (LOLR) function. The fourth challenge was the ability to manage

* K.U.B. Rao is the Officer-In-charge of Department of Economic and Policy Research in the Reserve Bank of India.

the cost and benefits of regulation in view of the difficulty in drawing a fine balance between regulation and financial innovations. And the final challenge Dr. Subbarao highlighted was the need for autonomy and accountability of central banks, particularly in the context of fiscal exit plans of countries as well as possible alternatives to the mandates of central banks.

Ladies and gentlemen, it was indeed an honour and privilege for the Reserve Bank of India to have Nobel Laureate Professor Andrew Michael Spence to grace this Conference and deliver the keynote address. In his remarks, Prof. Spence outlined four clear rules for central banks, which are more or less established—the first one was managing inflation; second, managing crises, both external and internal; third, managing volatility with skill and judgement; and the fourth, achieving a level of autonomy while acquiring credibility. Prof. Spence supported a further extension of the role to cover financial stability, particularly given the challenges from asset prices, leverage, and regulatory gaps. He suggested the extension of the role because he felt that central banks have a comparative advantage and have information advantage and there is also a general concentration of analytical talent in central banks. He wondered whether national governments would delegate much extra power to central banks or not.

The first technical session thereafter started with the paper by William Poole, which questioned the role of 'discretion' in the conduct of policies. His aversion to policy discretion was evident from his concluding remark that we should not be dependent on the expertise of policymakers and the timeliness of congressional action to stabilise the economy.

The next paper by Benjamin M. Friedman highlighted the fact that self-regulation and vigilance by creditors do not represent effective substitutes for regulation; it has to be the responsibility of public policy to provide regulatory systems. Prof. Friedman underscored the point that in a financial crisis, the distinction between liquidity and insolvency generally disappears, creating testing conditions for real-life use of the LOLR function by a central bank.

The third paper by Lars Svensson stressed the relevance of flexible inflation targeting even after the global crisis, which is particularly important in the context of apprehensions expressed in some quarters about inflation-focussing monetary policy involving the possible neglect of asset price bubbles and the financial stability objective. Svensson also spoke on why asset prices and financial stability should not be explicit objectives of monetary policy, but how both are important from the standpoint of the constraints they could pose for the monetary policy transmission process.

The second session that aimed at unravelling the challenges posed by increasing globalisation to central banks started with a paper by Irma Rosenberg on a topic of immense, direct policy relevance to most emerging market economies (EMEs), i.e., the Impossible Trinity. Rosenberg explained the unpleasant trade-off associated with the Impossible Trinity and noted that the choice of monetary policy and exchange-rate regime is neither simple nor clear-cut.

The cost of delayed fiscal exit has been a general concern the world over and in this context, the paper by Stephen G. Cecchetti, Madhusudan Mohanty, and Fabrizio Zampolli cautioned that the fiscal problems of industrial countries could be much larger than the official debt figures seem to suggest now. This could be on account of two factors—namely, pressure on revenues associated with the possible permanent loss of potential output and rapidly ageing population and the large and growing unfunded liabilities. The market assessment of sovereign debt seems to be changing unlike the pre-crisis perception that sovereign papers carry no risk.

Since the global crisis had generally been viewed as the result of weaknesses in the regulatory and supervisory systems, the focus of the third session was on options and challenges to fix these weaknesses. In the third technical session titled 'Disruptions in Financial Systems and Challenges to Regulation and Supervision', the paper by Stephen S. Roach highlighted the need for both a new approach to regulatory oversight that incorporates macroprudential regulations and a major reworking of the mandate of monetary policy to include financial stability. Roach rejected the idea that the post-crisis search for a remedy should include only regulatory measures. To quote him, 'regulatory action can send an important message to market participants, but the funds rate is a far more powerful enforcement mechanism. Moreover, a financial stability mandate could also help in adding clarity and direction to the current *ad hoc* approach to evaluating the hows and whens of an exit strategy.'

Financial innovations clearly contributed to the crisis and the excesses in an interconnected financial system generally went unnoticed. The risk of excessive regulatory response to the crisis, stifling innovation, has been a general concern. The paper in this context, by John Lipsky, provided valuable insights and direction to the current debate on the subject. Lipsky cautioned that without a renewed effort to foster financial innovation in the global economy, all countries, including EMEs, will perform below potential.

The fourth technical session was devoted to examining whether financial stability should be an explicit objective of monetary policy and whether the absence of such a mandate contributed to the crisis. John C. Williams explained how the Bagehot principle in the 21st century looked like in the US when the Fed responded to the subprime crisis. There are, however, limits to the Bagehot prescription, i.e., LOLR cannot address the insolvency problem. Williams then emphasised that issues of insolvency cannot be solved by central bank liquidity policies. These are properly in the domain of the fiscal authority.

Another dimension of central banking activities which gained prominence after the crisis is the size and composition of the balance sheets of central banks. The paper by Krishna Srinivasan outlined the key policy actions that central banks had to adopt nimbly, decisively, and creatively to alleviate the financial crisis and examined their effectiveness in designing the exit strategy. Srinivasan stressed that three aspects may have to be given particular attention, i.e., careful and consistent communication; unwinding should not compromise central bank's independence; and international spillovers of differentiated exit should not be ignored. After the technical sessions, which deliberated extensively on the key challenges for central banks and options to deal with them, it was time to elicit the views of central bank governors who face the real challenge on a day-to-day basis and often deliver without the benefit of hindsight.

In the two panel discussions for which Martin Wolf was the Moderator, Governors of eight central banks offered their candid views on ten important issues with the flavour of country-specific positions nicely interspersed with their own global perspectives.

The theme for the first Panel, as we are aware, was domestic monetary policy. In this context, Governor Christian Noyer of the Bank of France advocated that financial stability should be the second pillar of strategy. Financial imbalances are better addressed by macroprudential policy, and there is need to better understand the interaction between monetary and macroprudential policy.

Governor Glenn Robert Stevens of the Reserve Bank of Australia put forward the argument that notwithstanding the questions raised about the utility of inflation targeting in the current crisis, it would be wrong to abandon it completely. Instead, it would be useful to develop a more realistic model, explaining the interaction between financial sector and monetary policy.

Governor Tarisa Watanagase of the Bank of Thailand outlined the need for focussing more on supervision rather than on regulation. Financial stability should be part of a central bank's mandate so as to maintain sustainable growth and prevent boom-bust cycles. More corrective efforts are required in areas such as risk awareness, risk management, moral hazards associated with the policy response to a crisis and the right kind of policies for creating the right incentives.

Governor Subbarao, Reserve Bank of India, was emphatic when he said that a lesson from the crisis is that pure inflation targeting does not work because price stability, though necessary, is not a guarantee against financial instability. He also explained why India has not adopted explicit inflation targeting even though price stability is clearly one of the overriding objectives of the RBI.

The theme for the second Panel was the issues related to international monetary system, which also covered five very critical issues. Governor Mark J. Carney of Bank of Canada emphasised that the important issue right now is the adjustment mechanism between surplus and deficit countries rather than a single currency dominance or the issue of reserve currency. Governor Fernandez Ordonez of the Spanish central bank highlighted that we must recognise the significance of unprecedented, coordinated action led by G20 in avoiding another Great Depression and in view of the difficult years expected ahead, we must sustain the global approach despite domestic differences in policies.

Governor Atiur Rahman of Bangladesh Bank underscored the point that the international system should re-orient itself to take into account the concerns of low-income countries. In this regard, he emphasised the role of discussions between India and other Asian countries in fora like the ACU, SAARC-Finance, etc.

Managing Director Daw Tenzin of the Royal Monetary Authority of Bhutan emphasised the importance of reserves in the case of small economies like Bhutan. He felt that the crisis gives an opportunity to redefine market discipline and consumption patterns. He noted that the IMF should focus on issues relevant to EMEs.

Dr. Subbarao, Governor, RBI was categorical in his remarks that the international monetary system was inadequate to tackle global imbalances, which had to manifest in the form of some crisis or the other at some stage. He noted that even though India did not contribute to global imbalances, it has to face the consequences of global imbalances.

Ladies and gentlemen, the critical question we need to pose now is, where do we stand at the end of this Conference and what are the key messages or findings that could shape the future policy actions in central banks.

In the first session, there was no consensus on the role of monetary policy in directly doing something about asset prices and no single view was expressed on whether financial stability could be an explicit mandate of monetary policy. LOLR and regulations were, however, generally seen as prudential instruments to safeguard financial stability though they were not enough.

The second session did not offer a clear direction to resolve the Impossible Trinity, implying that countries have to adopt their own individual approaches. In the third session, the need for macro-prudential regulation as an important, if not sufficient, next step was recognised. How financial innovations with appropriate precautions could contribute to high global growth, more particularly in emerging markets and developing countries, was explained. That LOLR cannot solve the insolvency problems was the key message from the fourth session. The debate on what could be an appropriate Bagehot rule for the 21st century will continue. It was also felt in this particular session that different dimensions of central bank independence may come under threat if high government debt levels persist over protracted periods of time.

Let me express a very special and specific thanks to Martin Wolf, who has been with us for the last two days and made the panel discussions an extremely lively event.

During the course of these deliberations, there were a few specific issues highlighted by our Deputy Governors and Executive Directors. Deputy Governor, Shyamala Gopinath, felt that besides monitoring capital flows and exchange rate, the impact of capital flows on asset prices should not be ignored. Deputy Governor, Usha Thorat, raised the issue of the relevance of capital controls for EMEs and whether stricter capital requirements post the crisis could limit the role of credit in promoting growth and development in EMEs. Deputy Governor, K.C. Chakrabarty, made two critical points of general relevance to all central banks: first, it is difficult to know whether LOLR provides liquidity support or solvency support and there is no clear framework on that and second, despite the debates on exit, it is difficult to predict what the actual exit path could be in any country. This suggests that it will be an evolutionary process, which has no precedence. Deputy Governor, Dr. Subir Gokarn noted that for growing and globalising EMEs, challenges for central banks will be there even without the crisis. The expansion of mandate has to be seen in relation to both accountability and capability. India has not adopted inflation targeting as yet, despite the pre-crisis trend. Executive Director, Deepak Mohanty, raised the issue of whether flexible inflation targeting could lack credibility. Executive Director, H.R. Khan, wondered whether India's SLR requirement implicitly lowers pressures on the LOLR function.

Finally, a key message from the entire Conference possibly is that given known challenges and despite the lack of consensus on many critical issues, every central bank has to take whatever steps it deems right and appropriate without waiting for the global system to make a move. It would be possibly wrong, however, as noted by Stephen Roach, to presume that best global practices are the sum of best national policies in a globalised world. National policies cannot prevent a crisis alone even if these are the most appropriate unless some of the global challenges are addressed collectively at the global level.

Let me now convey our sincere thanks and gratitude to our Governor, Dr. Duvvuri Subbarao, who has been intimately associated with the planning of this Conference for the past six months. Amidst his preoccupation with both crisis management and recovery management efforts, he was associated with every minute detail of planning this particular major and memorable event. All of us in the Reserve Bank's research department team owe him a debt of gratitude.

Our senior Deputy Governors, Shyamala Gopinath, Usha Thorat and Dr. K.C. Chakrabarty have been with us from the conception phase guiding us in the planning and execution process at various stages during the Conference. We are grateful to all the three senior deputy governors. Our own Deputy Governor, Dr. Subir Gokarn, has been the source of strength behind the organisation of this Conference. He closely monitored the tying up of all arrangements and meticulously planned virtually every detail.

It is my pleasant task to thank and express our gratefulness to our Executive Director, Deepak Mohanty for very ably supervising the whole process. We thank him for his guidance and encouragement.

I would also like to thank all the contributors for the rich collection and high quality of the papers presented. Notwithstanding my unreasonable demands, most of them have given the papers within the stiff deadlines imposed. I apologise to all of them for insisting on timely submission. I will also fail in my duty, if I do not put on record our deep appreciation for the invaluable contribution of the four chairmen—Charlie Bean, Lars Svensson, Jaime Caruana and Michael Foot, the co-chairpersons and the discussants for various sessions. It is this intellectual treasure left with us by the chairpersons, lead speakers, and all other participants that will keep the memories of this Conference alive for a very long time.

Several departments of the RBI collaborated and assisted at various stages of this event. In particular, Regional Director of Mumbai office, Secretary and Chief General Manager, Secretary's Department, Chief General Manager, Department of Communications and Bank's medical officers have been of great help to us. I want to place on record our sincere gratitude to all of them.

Getting to this point in the programme and to this stage of the Conference has involved the commitment, collaboration, cooperation and goodwill of numerous individuals within and outside the RBI. We have been fortunate enough to be backed by a team of highly motivated and dedicated colleagues from the research department and other departments, who worked day and night and did their job exceedingly well. I am sincerely grateful for their help to me and the top management in organising this Conference with reasonable success. I must thank 10 young bubbling students from a local business school who helped us at various stages.

Coming to others who made the Conference possible, we owe special gratitude to the officials of Ministry of Home Affairs, Government of India, Government of Maharashtra and Mumbai Police Department for providing us mandatory clearances and providing us an invaluable and impregnable security cover. I must thank the anchor, Ms. Lobo and the major service provider Neil Bank for arrangements at various stages. The Hotel Trident management and staff deserves our gratitude. I would like to thank the members of the media for evincing interest in the event and enthusiastically covering the same. We are indebted to several individuals who may not be here but who have made significant contribution through the provision of various services.

As some learned men have said that, 'great is the art of beginning, but greater is the art of ending'. Let us make this end a new beginning. Let us agree to disperse today with the understanding that we will all meet again in some other forum to discuss possibly new concerns and to find new solutions. In any case, we will possibly host our next International Research Conference in 2012. Till we meet again, goodbye to all of you and wish you all a pleasant and safe journey back home.

List of Contributors

Charles R. Bean
Deputy Governor,
Bank of England,
United Kingdom.

Carlos A. Primo Braga
Director, Economic Policy and Debt, Poverty Reduction and Economic Management Network (PREM), The World Bank.

Mark J. Carney
Governor,
Bank of Canada,
Ottawa,
Canada.

Jaime Caruana
General Manager,
Bank for International Settlements,
Basel, Switzerland.

Stephen G. Cecchetti
Economic Adviser and Head of the Monetary and Economic Dept., Bank for International Settlements (BIS), Basel, Switzerland.

K.C. Chakrabarty
Deputy Governor,
Reserve Bank of India,
India.

Jørgen Elmeskov
Chief Economist (Acting),
OECD,
Paris.

Michael Foot
Chairman,
Promontory Financial Group (UK) Limited,
United Kingdom.

Benjamin M. Friedman

Professor,
Harvard University,
Massachusetts, USA.

Subir Gokarn

Deputy Governor,
Reserve Bank of India,
India.

Shyamala Gopinath

Deputy Governor,
Reserve Bank of India,
India.

Gill Hammond

Director,
Centre for Central
Banking Studies,
Bank of England,
United Kingdom.

Ravi Kanbur

T.H. Lee Prof. of
World Affairs,
International
Prof. of Applied
Economics and
Management,
Prof. of Economics,
Cornell University,
New York, USA.

John Lipsky

First Deputy
Managing Director,
IMF, Washington, D.C.,
USA.

Makoto Minegishi

Economist,
Macroeconomic
Policy Division,
Economics Dept.,
OECD, France.

Deepak Mohanty

Executive Director,
Reserve Bank of India,
India.

M.S. Mohanty

Head of
Macroeconomic
Analysis Unit,
Monetary and
Economic Department,
Bank for International
Settlements,
Basel, Switzerland.

Christian Noyer

Governor,
Bank of France,
Paris, France.

Miguel Fernandez Ordonez
Governor,
Bank of Spain,
Spain.

William Poole
Formerly Chief Executive of the Federal Reserve Bank of St. Louis; Senior Fellow, Cato Institute.
Washington, D.C., USA.

Eswar S. Prasad
Nandlal P. Tolani Senior Prof. of Trade Policy, Dept. of Applied Economics and Management,
Cornell University,
New York, USA.

Atiur Rahman
Governor,
Bangladesh Bank,
Bangladesh.

K.U.B. Rao
Officer-in-Charge,
Dept. of Economic and Policy Research,
Reserve Bank of India,
India.

Stephen S. Roach
Chairman,
Morgan Stanley Asia,
Hong Kong.

Irma Rosenberg
Member of the Board of the Swedish National Debt Office,
Stockholm, Sweden.

Andrew Michael Spence
Phillip H. Knight Professor Emeritus,
Graduate School of Business,
Stanford University,
California, USA.

Krishna Srinivasan
Division Chief,
Research Department,
IMF,
Washington, D.C.,
USA.

Glenn Robert Stevens
Governor,
Reserve Bank of Australia,
Australia.

Duvvuri Subbarao

Governor,
Reserve Bank of India,
India.

Lars E.O. Svensson

Deputy Governor,
Sveriges Riksbank,
Stockholm, Sweden.

Daw Tenzin

Managing
Director,
Royal Monetary
Authority of
Bhutan, Bhutan.

Usha Thorat

Deputy Governor,
Reserve Bank of India,
India.

Tarisa Watanagase

Governor,
Bank of Thailand,
Bangkok, Thailand.

William R. White

Chairman of the
Economic and
Development Review
Committee of the
OECD, Paris, France;
and Former Economic
Adviser and Head of
the Monetary and
Economic Department
(MED) of the Bank for
International
Settlements (BIS).

John C. Williams

Executive Vice-President
and Director of Research,
Federal Reserve Bank of
San Francisco,
California, USA.

Martin Wolf

Associate Editor and
Chief Economics
Commentator,
Financial Times,
Head Office,
London, England.

Fabrizio Zampolli

Senior Economist,
Bank for International
Settlements,
Basel, Switzerland.